Mr. Lincoln's Washington

Selections from the Writings of Noah Brooks
Civil War Correspondent

Mr. Lincoln's Washington

Selections from the Writings of
Noah Brooks
Civil War Correspondent

Edited by

P. J. Staudenraus

South Brunswick
New York • Thomas Yoseloff • London

© 1967 by A. S. Barnes and Co. Inc.
Library of Congress Catalogue Card Number: 67–10591

Thomas Yoseloff, *Publisher*
South Brunswick, N.J.

Thomas Yoseloff Ltd.
18 Charing Cross Road
London W.C.2, England

To the memory of
WILLIAM BEST HESSELTINE

6592
Printed in United States of America

Editor's Introduction

Early in December, 1862, a short dark, powerfully-built man of thirty-two arrived in Washington, D.C., to serve as special correspondent of the Sacramento *Daily Union*. In the next 30 months, Noah Brooks wrote more than 250 dispatches over the pen name "Castine." He covered congressional debates, Supreme Court decisions, military reviews, courts-martial, General Hooker's preparations for the great Battle of Chancellorsville, General Meade's cautious pursuit of the Army of Northern Virginia after the Battle of Gettysburg, the Presidential conventions, campaign, and election of 1864, the inaugural ceremonies of 1865, President Abraham Lincoln's funeral, and, finally, the Grand Review marking the war's end and the dispersion of the armies of the republic.

Noah Brooks made all Washington his "beat." He saw wounded soldiers, both rebel and federal, being brought to Washington hospitals. He mingled with the cheering crowd as workmen hoisted the giant Statue of Freedom to the top of the newly completed Capitol dome. He witnessed the burning of the Smithsonian Institution and its treasures, suffered in the Potomac summer heat, and shiv-

7

ered in the Washington winter damp and cold. He attended receptions, levees, dinner parties, society weddings, funerals, hearings, torchlight processions, and, near the end of the war, the brilliant public illuminations greeting each Union victory. He stood beside President Lincoln when he spoke from his White House window to Negro residents of the District of Columbia who cheered emancipation. He interviewed General Grant in his headquarters tent near City Point, Virginia, and he looked down from the reporters' gallery in the United States Senate to watch Andrew Johnson, "in a state of manifest intoxication," take the oath as Vice-President.

Brooks took his pen name from his native place, Castine, Maine, where he was born October 24, 1830. His parents, Barker Brooks and Margaret Perkins Brooks, were both descendants of old Massachusetts families. Though he left Castine when seventeen years old, he regarded Castine as his home—"a picturesque, old-fashioned, quiet town, situated on a lovely peninsula which slopes gently to the waters of Penobscot Bay." His mind's eye readily recalled the outstanding features of the neighborhood, especially the "broad, bright bay, studded with innumerable islands; a sweeping river, which flows past the town on the one side and a hilly and woody shore on the other; a bare eminence, crowned with the ruins of an ancient fort, overlooking the town, bay, river, forest and a wide panorama." Here Brooks had "learned his a b c's, made mud pies, stole his juvenile apples and did his first courting." In later years, the wanderer returned to Castine as an old man and spent his last years there, an honored and respected native son living in a fine home he humorously dubbed "The Ark."

The years between Noah Brooks' departure from his boyhood home and his return as an elderly man were busy and sometimes exciting. He left Castine to learn to be a painter and landscape artist in Boston, but by the time he reached his majority he had already tried his hand at writing. He worked part time as an ornamental painter and spent spare moments writing for the Boston *Atlas,* a Whig newspaper, the *Yankee Blade,* the Chelsea *Pioneer,* and for a weekly literary and humor magazine, the *Carpet-Bag,* first to publish Samuel Clemens (Mark Twain) and Charles F. Browne (Artemus Ward), both to become good friends of Brooks. For the next 45 years, Brooks pursued—and sometimes tried to evade—the ubiquitous smell of printer's ink. In 1854, he migrated to Dixon, Illinois, working as a house, sign, and carriage painter and retailing paints, brushes, putty, and glass. In his spare time he wrote for the Dixon *Telegraph.* In 1856, he married Caroline Augusta Fellows of Salem, Massachusetts, but they were briefly separated while Brooks migrated to the tumult-ridden Kansas Territory where he homesteaded a farm near Fort Riley. A year convinced him that farming was not his métier, and he returned to Illinois and the Dixon *Telegraph.*

During two terms with the Dixon weekly, Brooks had an opportunity to meet a future president of the United States, Abraham Lincoln, a leading Springfield lawyer and prairie politician already famous as the "Henry Clay of Illinois." Brooks met Lincoln in September, 1856, in Dixon, and several times again when Lincoln was stumping the state for John Charles Frémont, the Republican party's first Presidential nominee. Brooks described Lincoln as "tall, spare, sallow in complexion, square-shouldered, with long arms hanging awkwardly by his side, his small head covered with short dark hair brushed carelessly back from his high square forehead." During a lull in an Oregon, Illinois, mass meeting, Lincoln and Brooks sprawled beneath a shade tree and discussed the Republican party's prospects.

Lincoln astonished the younger man by saying that he had no hope that Frémont would be elected, but that by 1860 "every free State would go for the Republican nominee, provided he were an exponent of the principles of the party, and not committed to any extreme or radical measures." The candidate of 1860, Lincoln told Brooks, had to be a "national, conservative man, unhackneyed by political tergiversations, and untrammeled by party obligations," and, above all, a "man fresh from the people, who should be able to embody in himself the expression of the popular will."

The two men met again in the Illinois senatorial campaign of 1858 in which Lincoln ran without hope of victory against the popular and powerful Senator Stephen A. Douglas. Brooks, an admirer of both Lincoln and the Republican party, heard portions of the famous Lincoln-Douglas debates. He especially admired Lincoln's "plain, straightforward and sledge-hammer logic," his "clinching power of argument, and a manly disregard of everything like sophistry or claptrap."

Early in 1859, Brooks and a small party of Dixon men joined an ox team emigrant train and followed the long, tiresome, and sometimes hazardous overland trail to California. Finally, in October, 1859, exhausted and penniless, he reached the new and fast-growing city of Marysville, Yuba County, 42 miles north of Sacramento. In the next several months he worked to raise enough money to bring his wife to California. During an illness he returned to writing. He wrote descriptive accounts and newsletters over the pen name "John Riverside" for the short-lived San Francisco *Daily Evening Mirror* and occasional pieces for the Marysville *Daily Appeal*. In October, 1860, Brooks became a part-owner of the *Daily Appeal*. The newspaper proudly proclaimed the Republican party to be the "party of conservatism and security" and the only party that "maintains the dignity of labor, and defends it against the despotism of capital." Election day, 1860, was as "bright as the hopes of the Republicans, but as windy as a Democratic harangue," Brooks recorded. "Clouds of dust flew high in air, and the electioneering vehicles, decked with banners and tickets, dashed around, loaded with shouting voters, filled with enthusiasm and fighting whisky." To Brooks' delight Lincoln carried Marysville, previously a Democratic stronghold, with a plurality of 19 votes over Breckinridge and 153 votes over Douglas.

In the fall of 1862, Brooks quit the *Daily Appeal*. His wife Caroline had suddenly died, and Brooks gratefully accepted an assignment from the Sacramento *Daily Union* as Washington correspondent. On November 1, 1862, Brooks sailed from San Francisco on *The Golden Age*. Brooks' new employer was the largest California newspaper outside San Francisco. In 1860, the newspaper had supported the Douglas wing of the Democratic party, but after the outbreak of the war it gave full support to President Lincoln.

Brooks arrived in Washington early in December, 1862, a winter filled with anxiety for the friends of the Union and war-weary Washington residents. The war was already 20 months old. Victory was still beyond Union grasp, and it seemed to be slipping still further away. From the Battle of Bull Run in July, 1861, to George B. McClellan's inconclusive encounter with Robert E. Lee at Antietam Creek in September, 1862, there had been few Union victories and many disasters in the eastern war zone. When Brooks reached the national capital, General Ambrose E. Burnside had replaced the flashy, self-confident "gravedigger of the Chickahominy," as Brooks called McClellan, and he was preparing a massive assault on the armed heights behind Fredericksburg as a preliminary step to a bold, overland march to Richmond. For Brooks and other anxious Washington inhabitants the winter gloom grew heavier when news came of the bloody repulse of Burnside's splendid army before the battlements of Fredericksburg. The defeat, at first incredible, stunned the capital. Rumors, wild improbabilities, hearsay, and unsuppressed fears swept over the city. Washington, Brooks commented in disgust, was the "veriest nursery of faithlessness and unbelief." With shock he reported that some Washington residents imprudently sympathized with the rebel cause and were preparing to welcome General Lee's soldiers.

To Brooks' dismay, military reverses and disappointments were working against Lincoln's party and the popular support of the administration. In the fall elections of 1862, the Democrats had added 31 congressional seats and overturned seemingly secure Republican governorships in New York and Pennsylvania. Within the administration there was concern over the mounting national debt, scarcity of specie, inflation of prices, and long, demoralizing delays in paying Union soldiers and sailors. Casualty lists grew dismally long and discouraged voluntary enlistments. The prospect of compulsory service through a national conscription—certain to be unpopular in many northern states —did not comfort the Unionists. With Burnside's defeat, peace advocates in the Congress, led by Clement L. Vallandigham, boldly pressed for a negotiated settlement and, if necessary, the division of the Union.

Brooks was one of a small army of "Bohemians," as Civil War correspondents called themselves, stationed in Washington during the agonizing years of the War of the Rebellion. Reporters representing newspapers in New York, Philadelphia, Boston, Cincinnati, and the national capital vied with one another for news. Among the outstanding correspondents were Whitelaw Reid who represented the Cincinnati *Gazette*, Benjamin Perley Poore of the Boston *Journal*, Lewis A. Gobright of the Associated Press, and John Russell Young of the Philadelphia *Press*. To Brooks' disgust, some of the correspondents for New York papers used private information gathered in the course of their work to speculate on the stock market. To Brooks' greater disgust, many correspondents recorded only routine information "to an utter exclusion of the spirit and grand characteristics of the conflicts which they witness." Brooks attempted to understand the epochal qualities of the struggle he watched, and in his writings he tried to encompass the grand proportions of civil war, but always from the point of view of a "sensitive loyalist" and an uncompromising foe of rebellion, appeasement, and Democrats.

The *Daily Union's* special correspondent followed no method or system of reporting, but whenever the Congress was in session he gave priority to congressional affairs. For the stirring debates he sat in the reporters' gallery of either house, just above the head of the presiding officer, and, during the more tedious portions of ordinary business, he lingered in the lobbies and chatted with members, visitors, and other newsmen. For a time, he held a clerkship in the House of Representatives. In reporting debates he made no effort at non-partisanship, for both he and his newspaper were strong supporters of Lincoln's Union party and the war policy. He rarely referred to opposition members as Democrats except with a sneer, and more frequently he labeled them "Copperheads," "semisecesh," "secesh," and "disloyalists." Union party members, regardless of internal bickerings and sharp disputes over administration policies, generally received kind treatment. Their opponents sneered, gibed, displayed "querulous egotism," and stomped in anger when thwarted or outmaneuvered. Union men, in contrast, were apt at repartee, superior in debate, and always sincere and straightforward.

When the Congress recessed or adjourned, Brooks idled in the Supreme Court chamber, visited the battlefields in Virginia or Maryland, wandered into government bureaus, and surveyed—sometimes churlishly—the still vigorous social routine of the national capital. He spent spare hours in the White House, chatting with the President and listening to the President's anecdotes. Sometimes he was present for conversations between the President and senators, congressmen, military officers, and cabinet members who hurried to and from the executive mansion.

Despite the disparate nature of the episodes and topics covered by Brooks, the energetic reporter preserved a sense of simultaneity and immediacy of the incidents as they unfolded into grand events, and he skillfully interwove congressional matters, battles and battle preparations, cabinet activities, weather changes, and social diversions. Because of his deep commitment to the Union cause, he absorbed and conveyed the anxieties and apprehensions felt in wartime Washington when victory seemed to be a frayed hope, and correspondingly he reflected the exuberance and joy that came with eventual triumph.

In general, Brooks' letters tended to be more commentary than a summary of the daily news, for news stories flew across the continent in a few flashes of the electric telegraph, but lengthy dispatches going by overland mail did not reach the Pacific coast until nearly a month had passed. The long time gap encouraged Brooks to concentrate on the men and measures behind the news, to comment on events as they unfolded, and to attempt to place episodes in their larger perspective.

Brooks' descriptions of people and situations are superior

to his frankly partisan and sometimes shortsighted analyses of war politics, military policy, and economic problems. With a keen eye for details of clothing, posture, gestures, and facial expressions, and with an ability to state his impressions trenchantly if not brutally, Brooks permitted the reader to dwell on the faces and forms of famous jurists, generals, congressmen, senators, and bureau chieftains. Congressman Reverdy Johnson of Maryland had "a very repellent, dishonest face," and Henry L. Dawes of Massachusetts was "youthful, hirsute, and pimple-faced." Taking a careful look at Salmon P. Chase, Brooks noted that the Secretary of the Treasury was "very nearsighted and never pretends to know anybody without a very close examination. Consequently, his style is frosty even with his best friends." To Congressman James C. Allen of Illinois he gave the distinction of having "a high, sharp voice which is just suited to startle people with a midnight cry of 'Fire!'" Daniel W. Voorhees, Indiana Democrat, gave the appearance of "a fastidious dry goods clerk." At a White House reception, Brooks observed foreign ministers who were "gorgeously arrayed, being covered with stars, garters, and medals of honor," but he noted mischievously that "in such illustrious company" Secretary of State William Henry Seward "looked like a molting barnyard fowl among peacocks."

A passing interest in phrenology, the study of size and shape of cranial contours as indications of mental faculties, prompted Brooks to remark that Senator William Sprague of Rhode Island had "a small, light head, showing shrewdness and calculation but not much mental power" and that General Ambrose E. Burnside, the discredited ex-commander of the Army of the Potomac, had "a massive head which is more statesmanlike than military and showing great mental power rather than executive force."

Brooks' descriptions of parties in wartime Washington were rarely sympathetic. At one party the wife of a Kentucky congressman came under the reporter's harsh examination. "She was a huge lady and wore an ample skirt of some sort of gray silk, and over her brawny shoulders she wore a three-cornered cape of white lace, while at the top of her huge, fat arms hung big white lace bows, and a triangular lace napkin laid on top of her head." At another party Brooks saw both the high-born and the "sovereigns" jostle, push, fight, and elbow their way through reception lines and around food tables. "White glasses of champagne, fragments of cake, and empty plates flew to and fro in air like seaweed tossed up from the yeasty ocean which broke in foamy whirls around the loaded tables." At the White House reception honoring General Grant, Brooks saw bold curiosity-seekers mount damask sofas to get a glimpse of the hero.

The men who fell in battle evoked poetic tributes. Brooks wept to see the maimed and wounded brought to the crowded Washington hospitals, and he shuddered at the sight of the dead lying on the field of battle. Riding over the ground just after a skirmish between Confederate and Union troops, he quietly noted that the dead "lie among the wheat sheaves which the fight overturned, their faces toward the sky—graybacks and bluebacks—sleeping the gory sleep that knows no waking."

Unlike other newspaper correspondents assigned to Washington, Brooks became an intimate friend of President Lincoln and enjoyed ready access to the Presidential study. Soon after reaching Washington, Brooks renewed his acquaintance with Lincoln, and by the time of Lincoln's death two and a half years later, they were close friends. Brooks visited the President and his family almost daily. Brooks later claimed that Lincoln invited him to be his private secretary in place of John G. Nicolay but died before making the change. The President's appearance, altered since 1856, surprised and dismayed the younger man. "His hair is grizzled, his gait more stooping, his countenance sallow, and there is a sunken deathly look about the large, cavernous eyes," Brooks sadly remarked soon after he arrived in the capital.

The President appeared often in Brooks' dispatches, the friendship of the two men being only hinted at. Brooks' wartime letters recorded several Lincoln anecdotes and stories, but only those that would neither embarrass nor belittle the President in the eyes of the reading and voting public. The reporter scrupulously preserved the President's confidence, and he did not flaunt his special access to the White House before his readers, but his close association with the chief executive provided him with insights, points of view, and unique experiences that newspapermen in any Presidential administration would envy. For example, at Lincoln's invitation, Brooks accompanied a small Presidential party on a five-day tour of Hooker's army in Virginia. On several occasions, the younger man stood beside the President as well-wishers massed before the White House to celebrate battle victories or political triumphs. One night Brooks held the candle as Lincoln read a prepared speech from his White House window. On election night, 1864, Brooks was one of the small party that sat up with the anxious President to watch election returns trickle in by telegraph. On the fateful evening of April 14, 1865, Brooks stood at the White House door to watch the Lincoln party wheel away to Ford's Theater. No man felt the tragedy of Lincoln's assassination more keenly than Noah Brooks.

When the war ended, Brooks' work in Washington also ended. He accepted an appointment from President Johnson as naval officer in the San Francisco customs house. A year later, following a dispute with Johnson, he resigned and joined the editorial staff, headed by James McClatchy, of the San Francisco *Daily Times*. He rose to managing editor and then moved to the *Alta California*, where he remained as managing editor for four years. In later years he prided himself as the man who encouraged Henry George, a young compositor, to pursue his talent as a writer. During his stay in San Francisco, Brooks helped Bret Harte in editing and writing for the newly founded *Overland Monthly*. In 1871, Brooks moved to New York City to become night editor of the *Tribune* and then to *The New York Times* as an editorial writer. In 1884, he accepted the editorship of the Newark *Daily Advertiser* and remained there until his retirement nine years later.

In middle life, Brooks weighed 180 pounds. A genial, charming man, he enjoyed good food, good company, and sparkling conversation. An extrovert, he had a store of anecdotes of his earlier life. He was an organizer of the Author's Club and member of the Lotus Club and the Century Association of New York City. Though never prosperous, he wore expensive clothes of the latest fashion, wore pince-nez glasses on a cord, and smoked good cigars.

Before quitting the newspaper business, Brooks found time to write scores of newspaper articles, juvenile books, and minor historical works. In his early sixties, Brooks returned to Castine, Maine, to write and fish and reflect on his career. A tour of the Mediterranean gave him fresh material for travel books describing his visits to Egypt, Turkey, and Palestine. In the last decade of his life, several articles in *Harper's*, *Scribner's*, and *The Century Magazine*, in addition to ten books, measured the success of his retirement. Book titles included *Tales of the Maine Coast* (1894), *Abraham Lincoln and the Downfall of American*

Slavery (1894), *Washington in Lincoln's Time* (1895), *Short Studies in American Party Politics* (1896), *The Mediterranean Trip* (1896), *Henry Knox, A Soldier of the Revolution* (1900), *Abraham Lincoln, His Youth and Early Manhood* (1901).

The kindly story teller and amateur historian amused his neighbors and delighted his friends with books and anecdotes until poor health struck. Once more Noah Brooks journeyed to California, this time to recover his health and perhaps to recapture his youth. He died in Pasadena, August 16, 1903.

In print, Brooks' wartime dispatches would equal 2,000 pages. Some criteria of selection were necessary in reducing the whole to book size. The criteria used in selecting portions of letters began with the requirement that Brooks was a witness to the events he described or that he personally interviewed eyewitnesses. Paragraphs containing color, human interest, and amusing anecdotes are included, such as descriptions of life in the White House, parades, or an occasional angry debate in the Congress. In editing portions selected for publication, I have corrected misspellings, punctuation, and typographical errors, omitted repetitious sentences, and broken continuous sections into smaller paragraphs.

I have incurred debts of gratitude to helpful scholars, librarians, typists, and friends. I wish to thank Dr. John Denton Carter of Headquarters, United States Air Force, Professor James H. Shideler, Mrs. Linda Somerton Hesse, Mrs. Lee Barker, Mrs. Marlene Frade, Mrs. Paul Anne Snyder, Mrs. Carol Ladd, Miss Betty DeAlmeida, Mrs. Anne Altieri, and Mrs. Margaret Brush. Others who helped in various stages were Wayne Kint, Diana McConkey, Don Ranstead, and Don K. Greelis. The California State Library, the University of California libraries, the Library of Congress, and the National Archives also deserve my thanks.

My wife Nancy gave encouragement and aid.

P. J. Staudenraus

State University of New York
at Stony Brook

Mr. Lincoln's Washington

Selections from the Writings of Noah Brooks
Civil War Correspondent

Washington, December 2, 1862

WARTIME WASHINGTON

Washington is plethoric with strangers. They overrun every boardinghouse, hotel, and restaurant. They burden the horsecars and omnibi, inundate the departments, fill the galleries of the House of Representatives and Senate Chambers, and swarm through all the labyrinthine halls and passages of the national Capitol. Conspicuous among all these tides of humanity gleam the buttons and shoulder straps of the military officers, and there is a plentiful streaking of the light blue of the rank and file. This new and large infusion of the military element and the universality of shinplasters and postal currency for small change are the two most noticeable changes from the old times which a stranger from the Pacific coast notes. Both features are congruous and pertain to the exigency of the present. Both are necessary though undesirable, and, let us add, they both disappear right speedily.

The inflation of paper currency, added to the great demand, has stimulated the price of everything here to an enormous degree. The prices of living are exorbitant, and the Californian who has dulcet recollections of the good

23

old days when he paid three or four dollars per week for "genteel board" in Boston or New York may dismiss all such notions now and make up his mind to increase those figures threefold if he visits the national capital, where $75 per month will barely suffice for the necessaries of life. *Everything* costs money here, though it is hard for one used to metal currency to realize it. It is not much to give a hotel porter a bit of green paper for merely looking at your trunks, but your green paper is current funds, redeemable in postage stamps at the rate of five ten-cent stamps per square of paper. Funny, isn't it?

THE LAST SESSION OF THE THIRTY-SEVENTH CONGRESS

Of course public attention is now turned toward the third and last session of the present Congress. It meets under such momentous circumstances and with such important questions before it that every thoughtful person will regard its proceedings with deep interest. And when the members assembled yesterday at the Capitol there was an air of unusual gravity and even solemnity pervading the somber-hued gathering, which augurs well for the character of the doings of the next three months.

The shifting light of the cloudy and dark December day was stained and further sobered as it fell through the ground glass of the Senate Chamber, but dimly filling the gorgeous and ornate recesses of the room. On the tapestried floor were slowly circulating the grave Senators, exchanging hearty and even affectionate greetings as they met after their vacation. There was burly Ben Wade of Ohio, always leaving a ripple of smiles behind him; [Henry] Wilson of Massachusetts, rosy, portly, and with a dash of military on his waistcoat; [Solomon] Foot of Vermont, President pro tem. of the Senate, a man of magnificent figure and presence; [Charles] Sumner of Massachusetts, his hair prema-

turely grizzled, eyeglass on nose, and drawing a knot of
senators around him wherever he goes. There is the dapper
form of [James A.] McDougall of California, his head
whiter than ever and his legs hidden in long military boots.
He is joking with [Milton S.] Latham of California, who
is stroking his smoothly curling whiskers and smiling out
of his cold steel blue eyes. At the right of the President's
stand is [Benjamin F.] Harding, the new Senator from
Oregon, who has just been introduced to some of the older
Senators by his good-looking colleague, [James W.]
Nesmith. The new Oregonian will have more polish on
him when he vacates his seat, March, 1865. There is the
tall and elegant form of Jim Lane of Kansas. He is earnestly talking with [John W.] Forney, the good-looking,
dark-haired, and well-dressed Clerk of the Senate. Lane
looks careworn and nervous, and somewhat repellent withal.

   All these and more dot in groups over the soberly glowing floor of the chamber, and above them rise the galleries
with their crowded slips, every seat being filled except
where the crimson benches of the gallery reserved for the
diplomatic corps gleam out, exclusive and untenanted,
among the crowds of men and brightly dressed women.
Over all the paneled ceiling, rich in gold and color, gleams
with subdued light a single ray of sunlight irradiating the
chaste gloom, as the single rap of Senator Foot's hammer
on the desk of the President of the Senate called the Senate
to order at twelve o'clock noon, and the last session of the
present Congress had begun.

   In the House of Representatives the scene was much the
same, differing only in the large number present and the
more mercurial temper of the members. . . . At his desk
was [Clement L.] Vallandigham of Ohio, the mischievous,
with his youthful, rosy, and pleasant face. Behind him a
few desks was [Charles A.] Wickliffe of Kentucky, an old,
decrepit, querulous man, his crutches by his side and his

sour face rising over an abundance of shirt ruffle. Further
to his right is [Daniel W.] Voorhees of Indiana, a trim
built, shopkeeper-looking man. At the left of the Speaker
is [Owen] Lovejoy of Illinois, the raw head and bloody
bones of the Secesh Democracy, a portly, full-fed, dark-
hued, and clean-shaven man with a good-humored face
rippling with kindly feeling and belying the radicalism
which he shows in some of his printed speeches, for he
looks too lymphatic for a nervous radical. We must not
stop to photograph Schuyler Colfax of Indiana, [John A.]
Gurley of Ohio, Alfred Ely of New York, ... [Justin S.]
Morrill of Vermont, of tariff notoriety, and the host of
notables, congressmen, and otherwise who attract our attention, for the clock points at twelve and the hammer of
Speaker [Galusha A.] Grow raps to order, and the Chaplain,
the Reverend Thomas H. Stockton, implores the Divine
blessing upon the national Congress, its army, navy, mag-
istrates, and government.

At fifteen minutes past one o'clock, John G. Nicolay
appeared at the door of the hall with "a message from his
Excellency, the President of the United States," which
document was received and read amid the most profound
attention, every ear being strained to catch for the first
time the sentences of this most remarkable document.
Upon the conclusion of the reading there was a long breath
of released attention, and the House adjourned after the
usual action on printing was taken, though hindered by
the pettifogging Vallandigham, who embraced the chance
to hinder the business by attempting to discuss the motion
to print the documents. The blessed previous question cut
him off, and the House was adjourned at three o'clock.

In the Senate the conclusion of the reading of the message was greeted with a muffled throb of feet in the galleries, which broke into a burst of loud applause in spite

of the hammer of the President of the Senate. At what did
the people applaud? Emancipation—the burden of the
message—or the name of Abraham Lincoln? . . . Of course,
it is too early to say how the message is received here, but
the first impression is one of surprise—surprise that the
President leaves all allusion to the war to the Secretaries
of War and Navy, and that every other branch of our
national affairs has received such close and intelligent attention. The geographical argument for Union is heartily
approved by all, and nobody questions his honesty and
singleness of heart in urging his pet scheme of emancipation through eight of his twenty page message. One thing
is certain—the present policy of this administration will be
carried out *in toto* so long as it remains in power. President
Lincoln will not abandon a carefully formed and intelli-
gently conceived theory of government and administration
of affairs against his own convictions, and that his convictions are settled is perfectly apparent. Whether the original
conception of "compensated emancipation" belongs to the
President or to Secretary of State William H. Seward is
not so clear.

THE MILITARY SITUATION

Our army, of numbers unknown, now lies opposite Fredericksburg, separated from that city by the Rappahannock,
a stream too shallow and narrow for transports and too
deep for fording artillery. Opposite, and beyond the plain
in which is built Fredericksburg, rises a low line of hills
indented with ravines and gullies at all angles. Succeeding
these is the narrow, irregular valley of Massaponax, succeeded by another range of wooded hills. Here the enemy
has entrenched himself, covering both ranges with his
fortifications and leaving his railroad to Richmond, two

turnpikes, and a plank road in his rear for a line of retreat. To cross this river and carry these positions appears to be the greatest work yet attempted in this war. And to do this devolves upon [General Ambrose E.] Burnside, upon whom all eyes are now turned. . . .

The work has been delayed unaccountably from lack of supplies which should have been on the ground as promised to Burnside when he changed his base of operations to that point. The delay in furnishing him with pontoons has been almost fatal, and who is responsible therefor is now a vexed question. Public opinion sets against [Montgomery C.] Meigs, Quartermaster General, who casts blame upon the Engineer Corps. This morning it is rumored that Meigs is removed for this culpable dereliction of duty. This retardation of the army is unfortunate, as it affects Burnside who, though he has the confidence of all right-thinking men, has the unreasonable partisans (now but a corporal's guard) of [General George B.] McClellan, whose removal provoked so much discussion, opposed to him. The public feeling on this question has well-nigh subsided, and should Burnside achieve a victory before the month is out, everybody will applaud the firmness of the administration in sacrificing a personally popular general to the more popular demand for an infusion of vigor into the prosecution of war.

Washington, December 4, 1862

HOW THE PRESIDENT LOOKS

Last Sunday I saw the President and his wife at church at Dr. [Phineas D.] Gurley's (Presbyterian), where they habitually attend. The building was crowded, as usual, with dignitaries of various grades, besides sinners of lesser note and rank. Conspicuous among them all, as the crowd poured out of the aisles, was the tall form of the Father of the Faithful, who is instantly recognized by his likeness to his published likenesses. The President and his wife are both in deep mourning for their son, [Willie,] who died last spring, and his Excellency has grievously altered from the happy-faced Springfield lawyer of 1856, whom I then met on the stump in Illinois for Frémont. His hair is grizzled, his gait more stooping, his countenance sallow, and there is a sunken, deathly look about the large, cavernous eyes, which is saddening to those who see there the marks of care and anxiety such as no President of the United States has ever before known. It is a lesson for human ambition to look upon that anxious and careworn face, prematurely aged by public labors and private griefs, and to remember that with the fleeting glory of his term of office have come responsibilities which make his life one long series of harassing cares and, while compelling him to save himself and his country from disgrace and reprobation, mark him with the daily scars of mental anxiety and struggle. Whatever may be said of Abraham Lincoln by friend or foe, no one can ever question the pure patriotism and the unblenching honesty of the man. He inspires that feeling by his personal presence as much as by his acts, and as he moves down the church aisle, recognizing with a cheerful nod his friends on either side, his homely face lighted with a smile, there is an involuntary expression of respect on every face, and men who would scorn to "toady" to any President look with commiserating admiration on that tall, mourning figure which embodies Abraham Lincoln, whom may God bless.

Washington, December 9, 1862

HOW THE FITZ-JOHN PORTER COURT-MARTIAL LOOKS

For the sake of sketching...a court-martial, with its military bigwigs, we will suppose that we are in the room over Butler's Restaurant, opposite Willard's Hotel, yesterday morning, where the trial is held. It is eleven o'clock, but in this city of late hours it is yet breakfast time with many, and the room is pervaded with the odor of buckwheat cakes and fried sausages from the restaurant below. The room is not overly large, low and poorly furnished— a few cheap prints of Perry's doings in Japan gracing the papered walls, and the bare windows looking out on the noisy street below. In the center of the room is a long table covered with maps and documents, at the end of which next [to] the door is Major General [David] Hunter of independent proclamation fame. He is president of the court, says but little, speaks in a low voice with a slight impediment, and sits leaning forward on his arms, with his eyes on the table and his thumbs twiddling. He is a heavy, dark man about fifty years old, has no whiskers or beard, but a jet black mustache which is suspiciously suggestive of hair dye. His straight black hair looks wiggy, and his whole person is, somehow, not attractive.

Next [to] him on the right is Major General [Ethan Allen] Hitchcock, a fine-looking old man though still in the prime of life. His nearly bald head is fringed with a fuzz of white hair, which makes his rubicund countenance look "like a rose in the snow." He, too, is a large man and wears a fine uniform—all being dressed in full uniform, with swords, etc. His fine figure sets off his brilliant garb admirably. Next [to] him is Brigadier General [Benjamin M.] Prentiss of Shiloh fame. He is a little pale but otherwise looks none the worse for his long imprisonment in Secessia. He is smaller than the other generals, has a pleasant face, mild gray eyes, and his dark hair and full whiskers are streaked with gray. He is slightly lame, holds a gold-headed cane in his hand, remains motionless, and seldom speaks.

Next to him on the right is Brigadier General [Silas] Casey, a comical-looking old fellow with a small, bald head fringed with white hair, generally silently fussing with small bits of paper and tearing up scraps of manuscript. He wears his spectacles on the top of his head in the identical place where the wool ought to grow, and he has his sash hitched almost up to his armpits and wears an uncomfortable air generally. He is a brave officer and a good general, for all that. That fine, erect figure, full and robust, next above Casey, is Brigadier General [Napoleon B.] Buford, and he is marked as the best-looking general in the room. He has gray and white whiskers and mustache, which, for some reason, reminds me of a certain knowing terrier I once knew in a California printing office. He is flanked by the Honorable Joseph Holt, the Judge Advocate, who appears in behalf of the United States. Next [to] him is General [John P.] Slough, burly, bald, light in complexion, famous for his exploits on the New Mexican frontier when a colonel, and is about thirty-five years of age.

On his right, opposite the odd-looking Casey, is [James A.] Garfield, who has distinguished himself at sundry times and in divers places. He is young and awkward, has a redundant head of unkept, frowsy light hair which might be shared with some of his unthatched brother officers. Brig-

adier General [James B.] Ricketts, dark, medium in height,
scar on forehead, hook-nosed, farmer-looking, is next, and
[Rufus] King, also a Brigadier, with a shabby and tarnished
uniform and leather sword gear, sits below, thus complet-
ing this list. . . .

General Porter is in full dress, except his sword, is tall,
well-built, bullet-headed, has closely cut black hair and
face hair. He is quite at ease and occasionally puts in a
legal point himself in very good style. In the opposite
corner Major General [John] Pope, the witness under examination, is knocking about in a rocking chair with his
usual nonchalance. He is in undress uniform, and though
he tries to sit erect, he will get his legs over the chair arm
and slip down to the small of his back. Pope is never dis-
concerted by any of the leading questions of the accused
or counsel. He states with perfect coolness and offhand
freedom such things as, "It is my firm belief that if the
accused had obeyed orders the whole rebel army would
have been cut to pieces." His black eyes twinkle with fun
sometimes, and he occasionally gives his words a bit of
satire, which enlivens the tedium of business and puts
the waiting crowd around the room in good humor.

The impression one gets of Pope from frequently seeing
him on the witness stand is that he is a jolly, careless good
liver; prompt, sanguine, offhand, not particularly careful
as to what he says, but impulsive and decided. He is unquestionably brave, and his skillful arrangement of plans
in the short campaign in which he was made the victim of
Fitz-John Porter's intended or unavoidable failure to cooperate with him showed that he has considerable military
ability. But while his honesty may not be doubted, his
personal appearance and manner would not inspire a close
observer with implicit confidence in his generalship.

Washington, December 12, 1862

GENERAL MC CLELLAN ON THE STAND

During the past few days there has been a grand rush to
the McDowell Court of Inquiry, commonly called McDowell's Whitewashing Shop, to see General [George B.]
McClellan, who has been under examination. The little,
mean room in which the court is held is crowded long
before the hour of trial comes and overflows into the
narrow hall and stairway with an expectant, eager, jostling
but good-natured crowd, which wants to see "Little Mac,"
to hear his voice, and feel the magnetism of that awful
presence which has loomed in the newspapers for the last
twelve months.

The perspiring orderly, probably one of those who
"fights mit Sigel," was in despair at the pressure on him,
and, as he savagely elbowed his way through the crowd on
his errands, his "Mein Gott, genlemens! Vot you want
to schqueeze for?" was truly comical to hear, and if he had
not been a little man it is likely that the crowd, good-
natured as it was, would have revenged his elbow thrusts
right and left by punching his head. As it was, his size—
or want of size—was his protection. And so it was, perhaps,
with the redoubtable ex-Commander-in-Chief of the Army
of the Potomac who was dodged through the crowd before
anyone could notice the opera-cloaked, dapper little fellow
who had slipped through the disappointed jam squeezing
around the doorway.

"That's him!" "What, that little fellow with the yellow
mustache?" "Certainly." "What! He McClellan? Oh

Lordy! Come, Bill; let's go." Such was the brief comment
and conclusion of some few in the crowd, though the majority waited to see and hear more as the General seated
himself at the table to hear the testimony of the previous
day read over by the clerk. [General Irvin] McDowell
writes the question on a piece of paper, the clerk writes
that down and wafers both answer and question to a paged
sheet. So you see there is not much to be read, for the
session is only four hours long each day.

The feeling of disappointment of those who went downstairs when they had seen McClellan is usual to all who
have only seen his photographed portraits. The General
is small, quite small—rather dapper and trimly built, not
slight, but with round, full outlines, the face being smooth
and almost boyish, though not fair but indicative of good
living. McDowell, who sits opposite, is, with his square,
full face and commanding figure, twice the general in looks
that McClellan is.

The hair and mustache of the late Commander of the
Potomac Army is light, and—I regret to say—verging on
what is known among the vulgar as carroty. It is closely
cropped and well-brushed, and everything about him is as
neat as possible. He is in citizen's dress, wearing a fatigue
cap, and only a splash of bright buttons on his vest invest-
ing him with any military prestige. He throws off his opera
cloak, hangs his arm carelessly over the back of his low
chair, and answers the questions propounded to him with
a quick, clear, low voice, keeping his light gray eyes quietly
fixed upon the questioner, who reads to him the inquiries.
His manner is modest, almost to diffidence, and his mouth
constantly wears a pleasant and winning smile. I thought
that there I could see much of his power over men; that
playing smile, I am sure, is the most lively expression ever
seen on a man's countenance. Once seen it can never be

forgotten. All in the crowded, uncomfortable room feel the magnetism of that face, and it is curious to note the admiring, half-loving, half-pitying expression which moves over the unconscious faces of the steadfastly gazing spectators as they all bend forward, intent upon the slightest look and intonation of the commander.

THE BUREAU OF INTERNAL REVENUE

The creation of this new and important branch of the Treasury Department has called into being a novel exercise of federal resources, and demands a new set of national energies to meet the constantly recurring emergencies. In putting in motion so vast a system of complicated machinery for the first time, there must be some friction, but from Commissioner George S. Boutwell I learn that the general result far surpasses expectations. . . . It all grows out of the war, and that seems to have come home to the minds of all, and it is indicative of the spirit and temper of our people, as well as their plastic adaptability to circumstances, that the voluminous correspondence of the collectors and assessors proves that the people everywhere are more ready to comply with the far-reaching requirements of the law than the most sanguine had supposed would be the case. Our people talk a great deal, but they usually do about right.

The headquarters of the Internal Revenue Service is in the second story of the Treasury building, and in a long but not very large room are crowded fifty or sixty clerks all sitting at single desks which are arranged in double rows through the center of the room and on each side, giving the department the appearance of a day school for boys of larger growth (some being bald-headed), or, better still, looking like a sewing machine factory, the noise of the

swift-running machines being that of the smooth scratch
of the goose quill (Uncle Sam ignores steel pens) gliding
over multitudinous sheets of paper. The clerical force is
divided into classes or specialties, [such] as Licenses, Ad
Valorem Duties, Correspondence, etc., having a chief clerk
to each division, and at the upper end of the room are the
crowded desks of Commissioner Boutwell and his chief
clerk, Estee.

It is here that are made those multifarious and wise decisions which are now piled upon the desk in a voluminous
heap. That sallow, short-faced, and bright-eyed man at the
desk was formerly a country storekeeper in the village of
Groton, Massachusetts. His administrative abilities attracted attention, and about ten years ago the same coali-
tion of Free-Soil Democrats which beat the Whigs, sent
Sumner to the Senate, and put N[athaniel] P. Banks, another self-made man, in the Speaker's chair of the Massachusetts House of Representatives also placed Boutwell
in the gubernatorial chair of that state. He is now at the
head of the new revenue service, commonly reputed to be
the best managed branch of the civil service.

FIGHTING AT LAST

It is sad to think that our people are better satisfied today
because a battle is raging on the Rappahannock, but so it
is. Last night we began to receive the particulars of the
opening engagement of yesterday, . . . and the town is on
the *qui vive* to know how goes the fight. The importance
of the struggle and the anticipated severity of the battle,
and the long delay and preparation all serve to invest the
fight with peculiar and sad interest. Yet our citizens are
now so familiarized with the sights and sounds of war that
its terrors are inconsiderable. We have become adapted to

this change as we do to all other mutations, and the results of a fight are now as succinctly stated and as thoroughly understood as the commercial bulletins or statements of marine arrival and clearances. At dinner last night at Willard's, a brisk lieutenant, who wears the scars of Antietam, said to my neighbor, "Somebody getting hurt down there today, isn't there?" (with a nod southwardly). "Yes, more or less damage done by this time. Lively there at noon, they say." "By tomorrow night these newspaper chaps (expressive nod at the writer hereof) and the hospital men will be as busy as the devil in a gale of wind. Palmer, the artificial leg man, is around rubbing his hands." And that was all that was said then and there about the battle of Fredericksburg.

Washington, December 16, 1862

FREDERICKSBURG—THE KILLED AND WOUNDED

The first report of killed and wounded which reached Washington was that we had lost 5,000. Another and later dispatch put the number at 10,000. But on Sunday night General Burnside telegraphed to the President that the number would not exceed that at first stated, including both killed and wounded. The first wave of suffering from the field of blood reached us here on Sunday night, when 500 wounded were brought up from Aquia Creek on the steamer, having been taken to that place on the cars from Falmouth. The regiments which suffered most were the Twentieth Massachusetts, Fifty-ninth New York, Nineteenth Massachusetts, Sixty-ninth New York, Eighty-ninth New Jersey, First New York, Seventh Michigan, and Fifty-seventh New York. . . . The Seventh Michigan will always

be renowned for the bravery with which a small detachment of their number dashed across the river and dislodged
the rebels, who were firing upon our bridge builders, before
the fight began. The casualties among our officers were,
as usual, very large. . . .

Here in Washington the public heart throbs heavily,
and fears of a defeat cause an anxiety too deep for words,
but we all have confidence in the commanding generals and
hope for a result which shall be favorable. All day Saturday
the dwellers on the heights across the Potomac heard the
sullen boom of the vast batteries of artillery which belched
their thunders against Fredericksburg, fifty-five miles away,
and you can imagine the suspense of the friends of the
Union who knew that those peals betokened the opening
of a fight which shall seal the fate of our winter campaign.

ACCOUNTABILITY WANTED

The extraordinary exigencies of war try all the weak
points of our republican form of government, and in none
is it found lacking more fatally than in that deference to
the popular will which an English writer calls "lawless
law." . . . The real strength of the South has been in the
autocratic rule of its single head, for its central power is
recognized in a single individual, while we are cautiously
dividing the power among all the people and have no cen-
tralization anywhere. Just now this spirit of insubordination, or rather reckless disregard of authority, is the curse
of our army to an extent you cannot conceive of. . . . From
the major generals down to the lowest private they all set
up individual opinion, will, and inclination against imperative authority and command.

I recollect, many years ago, a militia muster in New

England, where a dapper captain of a company issued the order of "present arms" to his corps, when one contumacious six-footer, who longed to pick a quarrel with his captain, blurted out, "Shan't do it!" "Wal," meekly responded his gallant commander, "Tain't no matter." Not quite so bad as that but precisely the same feeling too much animates our soldiers of the great volunteer army in the field. They fight like men and behave well, but when they do take a notion to go home, they wander off or coolly leave the ranks by hundreds. The officers set the example. Last week a Californian met an old acquaintance who belongs to the army before Fredericksburg, who had left his regiment, in which he was a lieutenant colonel, in the face of the enemy and, without leave, had come up to Washington to amuse himself. He went to the circus with his friend, concealing his uniform with his overcoat. Soon the provost patrol came in and asked if he was not an army officer—*he denied the fact.* Such a man should be broken (yes, have his neck broken) on the spot for such outrageous conduct.

The rules are held down with great strictness in regard to arresting officers absent without leave from their commands, yet the number of violations of the rule is very considerable, notwithstanding. Last Saturday night a captain of a New York regiment and a lieutenant of a Pennsylvania regiment were arrested in a house of ill-fame in this city, having no leave of absence from their commands. On the same night a lieutenant and a sergeant of a Massachusetts regiment were arrested at the Simpson House where they were having "a lark," charged with the same offense. A party of commissioned officers were with them, but they ignominiously skedaddled out of windows and back doors at the sight of the patrol guard. The recital of these things is not comfortable, but they afford a clue to many things which our amiable newspapers are in the frequent habit of charging to the wrong account altogether.

SEEKING A HOUSE OF REFUGE

Coming down the main approach to the Hall of Representatives the other day, I met an honest-looking squad of the 177th Pennsylvania, raw recruits who were out sight-seeing. The spokesman of the party stopped me with, "Can you tell me, sir, where the House of Refuge is?" "The House of What?" was the involuntary but not very mannerly response. He repeated that he wanted to find the "House of Refuge." "Perhaps you mean the House of Representatives," explained my companion. "Oh, yes, that's it —the House of Representatives!" and the poor fellow went off, blushing all the way to the roots of his hair at his queer slip of the tongue. Our honest friend knew better than to call the lower branch of our national Congress a House of Refuge, but it is undeniable that it has proved an asylum and house of refuge to more than one worthless do-nothing who warms a leather-cushioned chair and draws his mileage and per diem for lack of better employment.

COSTLY FASHIONS

In former times ten dollars or even less was a fair allowance for a female headpiece, but now three times that amount is absolutely *needful* for the same variety of gear. Feathers are in now, and they are in for the neat sum of six and eight dollars each, while ribbons are a dollar a yard, velvets at ten, flowers at two and a half, and a rep silk and marvelous laces, all at marvelous prices, go to make up a "love of a bonnet" which cannot be beheld without emotion. . . . One bonnet would leave scarcely a Post Office shinplaster out of a fifty dollar "greenback." Silk velvet cloaks lined with silks of the hues of an auroral dawn and rich as the plumage of a butterfly are the *ton,* and the graceful folds are frosted over with guipure (the ladies know what that is) at ten dollars per yard. Then the rattling moire antiques—they wear lavender now, my dear —and point lace and its five dollar a yard imitations are the go. The pearl-and-jet headdresses together with sensational four-story bonnets aforesaid do make a sight wonderful to behold. Truly, Solomon in all his glory was not arrayed like one of these. It is fortunate that ladies ride in carriages here, for the trains of costly material which they drag around now are preposterous. I saw a lady come into the dining room the other night with so long a train that her following papa (poor old man) could not get nearer than fifteen feet behind her. Her dry goods might very properly have been *retailed.*

Washington, December 19, 1862

IS IT DEFEAT?

Nobody supposed last Friday, when we were still in suspense as to the future movements of our army at Fredericksburg, that a retreat was impending. But . . . the public, expectant, hopeful, yet fearful, was astounded by the news that the magnificent Army of the Potomac, vast and well-appointed, yet torn and bleeding, had been returned to the north bank of the Rappahannock where it had lain for so many weeks preparing for a victorious onslaught upon the enemy's works. As the news flew and the excited crowds gathered around the bulletin boards, "Are we defeated?" was the question on every lip. We *were* defeated, if we admit that the Federal army moved across the Rappahannock with an intention to carry the position of the rebels beyond Fredericksburg. Whatever may be said of the wisdom of attempting to carry a strongly forti- fied position by a force of infantry in the face of a pro- digious fire of artillery, it is evident that our men and officers did all that could be done and, after the awful slaughter, retired only when it was evident that further endeavors and struggles were in vain. We must make the best of this defeat and must acknowledge that it *was* a defeat.

THE EFFECT UPON THE PUBLIC

Indignation was the prominent manifestation of public feeling upon the receipt of the news from Fredericksburg— indignation that our brave boys should have been sent to slaughter so uselessly and that with abundance of men, means, and military appliances we should have been de- feated and forced to retreat ingloriously. The prestige which this unfortunate movement gives to the cause of the Union cannot be easily estimated, but it is certain that nothing like it in the whole war has before occurred. Bull Run, Ball's Bluff, and other earlier reverses pale their in- effectual fires before this later defeat. The effect upon the country will be disastrous, but we must hope that before any general depression can result to the nation, another and more successful movement will be made upon Rich- mond and its approaches and that complaint and mur- muring will be effectually stopped.

Everywhere people are asking, "What next?" and here the rumors of another advance are snatched at with hope-

ful eagerness. It is idle for your correspondent, constantly
anticipated by the telegraph, to indulge in any detailed
recital of the various rumors which are floating around the
capital, but the most plausible theory of future operations
is that Burnside will detach a great part of his army from
its present position and cross the river at a fording point
far above Falmouth, leaving enough of his force at the
point now occupied to beguile the enemy and make a
defense from this side of the rebel works necessary. Should
he be able to effect this movement and fall upon the flank
and rear of the enemy, a brilliant success might yet attend
our banners. . . .

WHO IS RESPONSIBLE?

It is impossible that so much public feeling should become patent and not seek or attempt to seek to fasten the
responsibility for the failure upon somebody. Against
[Henry W.] Halleck, General-in-Chief, [Edwin M.] Stanton, Secretary of War, and [Montgomery C.] Meigs, Quartermaster General, the popular current sets so strongly that
it is very possible that their resignations will take place.
The Quartermaster's Department comes in for a larger
share than the other branches of the military service. Upon
that department, it would appear, is justly fastened more of
the responsibility of this and other failures than is comfortable for the officers of the department. Had Burnside
been able to cross the Rappahannock when he first arrived
there, as he expected to have done, he would have occupied
the heights beyond Fredericksburg which were taken by
the rebels and fortified impregnably while our forces were
waiting on the opposite side of the river for the means to
cross the Rappahannock. Why were not the pontoons sent
in time? Requisitions were made upon the Quartermaster's

Department in ample time to have received them, and the time consumed in their transportation was *not* extravagantly long, all stories to the contrary notwithstanding. Plainly, then, the habitual dilatoriness of the Quartermaster's Department was the cause of the failure to cross the river earlier; and if upon that hinged the whole disaster, it is easy to fix the responsibility in the right place.

... The defeat at Fredericksburg has not only created a profound public sensation, it has also caused a commotion in the governmental departments which is bound to result in some upsetting somewhere. In Congress the undercurrent of feeling has not yet manifested itself, but it is likely to at any time, and in a day or two some strong resolutions bearing upon the conduct of the war will be offered. The Joint Congressional Committee on the Conduct of the War is now at the army front, and when it returns we may expect something definitive in the way of public action. In the meantime the friends of General McClellan are discreetly silent, but they are industriously working for his reinstatement. The pressure brought to bear upon members of Congress is very great, the partisans of the deposed general seizing upon this favorable opportunity to urge his replacement as Commander of the Army of Virginia. A simultaneous movement is being made to induce Congress to adopt a resolution recommending that General McClellan be recalled to the command of the army. It is, however, not probable that any such foolish proposition will be seriously entertained, and however a majority of the members of the House may feel upon the question, none but such disorganizers as [Clement L.] Vallandigham, [Samuel S.] Cox, and [Charles A.] Wickliffe, who delight to worry the administration, would consent to such a measure which would be so foreign to all of the functions and purposes of the national Congress.

THE COMING OF THE WOUNDED

Right upon the heels of the excitement of the battle of Fredericksburg comes the long waves of the wounded, streaming and surging back from the bloody slaughter. The Washington hospitals were not empty before; now they are crowded with the hapless maimed and wounded who constantly arrive in hundreds by every boat from Aquia Creek. Yesterday I met on one of the principal streets a long and grim procession of the slightly wounded who were coming up on foot from the steamboat landing. Here they come in squads of a hundred or more, wounded in the face, with fingers gone, armless perhaps, with cruel furrows plowed along the arm by grape or musket ball, with faces grimed and blackened with smoke and powder, ragged, dishevelled, and dropping with fatigue and weakness. Here they come creeping, shuffling, limping, and hobbling along, full 1,500 strong, so faint and longing for rest; so weary, oh, so weary, that the heart bleeds at the pitiful sight. Yet they are but a small squad and are able to walk to the hospital, though slowly, and when they all stop for a rest on the sidewalk and lean wearily upon the iron railings or sit on the steps or edgestones, they can answer the questions of the pitying passersby and speak kindly of their commanders who led them to the field and manfully acknowledged that we are beaten because the rebel position was more than equal to federal bravery.

A sadder sight is the unlading at a hospital of the long train of ambulances which bring up the more severely wounded from the landing place. Some recline on litters which are placed two and two in each vehicle, and as each ambulance in turn drives up to discharge its fearful freight, there are pitiful faces and moist eyes in the compassionate crowd which offers willing hands to help the wounded, and parts with respectful alacrity before the bearers of the maimed soldiers. Here is a little drummer boy with his right hand gone. The rattle of his drum at the head of a Massachusetts regiment was stopped by a storm of iron hail which beat down its thousands; and his mother among the Berkshire hills is waiting to know whether he is alive or dead. There comes a line of stretchers with men who have left arms, legs, hands, feet, and much blood upon the fatal field of Fredericksburg. Rebel guns have maimed these men for life, and those who went forth full of vigor, hope, and ambition, their hearts beating high with visions of glory and prowess, have returned again—broken, decrepit, useless, and disfigured by the enginery of war against which they manfully surged in solid columns again and again.

Now and then as a litter is lifted carefully out, an attendant lifts the corner of the covering of the pale, suffering face and directs the burden to a lower room, for the man whom they carry is dead. The passage from the steamer to the hospital is his last, and sisters, mother, and maid will weep tomorrow when they see his name in the fatal list of "Since Dead." These legless, armless, maimed, and suffering men are such as we, for they all have loving friends somewhere who grieve to hear of their suffering; and there are also others who are lying stark and stiff upon the battlefield or are hastily and indecently buried hard by the spot where their lifeblood ebbed away. Mothers sent them to the war with blessing and prayer, and now they are daily thinking and dreaming of those who today are swept away into undistinguished and unknown graves. My peace-blessed California reader, this is war. God help its victims!

THE WASHINGTON HOSPITALS

There are now in this city a little more than twenty hospitals located in various buildings; some in churches, public halls, the Patent Office, and other public buildings, and many in temporary wooden structures which have been put up for this special purpose. It is one of the new and hitherto unknown features of our military experience, which has been developed in this war, that we should suddenly be obliged to provide for thousands of sick and wounded men, to arrange for a partial assuaging of their pains upon the field, to remove them to a place of security and rest, to make provision for medical and surgical treatment, and to surround them with such means and appliances of comfort as shall ameliorate their unfortunate condition. Whatever may be said about the mismanagement of the medical staff upon some of the battlefields, I am glad to be able to say that, thanks to the persistent and thorough inspections of the Sanitary Commission and the public visitations to hospitals in this vicinity, no just foundation for complaint exists in any of the general hospitals. At Alexandria, however, is a rendezvous known as Camp Convalescent where patients discharged from the hospitals are sent until such time as they are fit for duty. This camp has become overburdened and crowded by being also made the receptacle of vast numbers of those who are taken up as stragglers from the army. Consequently the occupants of Camp Convalescent now number nearly 10,000 and are in a condition which I can characterize only as *infamous*.

Here are thousands of men, sleeping on the cold ground without fire, with no order or system of arrangement, with insufficient medical assistance, and exposed to the rigors of winter in their canvas tents or rude board huts. Some of these men are just convalescing from severe illness or wounds received in battle, while others—thousands of them—are idle but physically sound, reprobates, deserters, and stragglers, the veriest riffraff of the federal and rebel armies. Imagine this motley, heterogeneous crew of half-sick and well men without any occupation but to eat and sleep, crowded into the miserable camp which I have partially described, playing cards, telling stories, and idling away their time, and you can approximate the real situation of things at this camp and the mate to it, Camp Straggle. The attention of Congress, I am glad to say, has been turned toward this insufferable nuisance, and the Committee on the Conduct of the War is at work diligently reforming its abuses.

One of the representative hospitals in this city is that of Harewood erected by the government on the private grounds of the ex-banker of this city, W[illiam] W. Corcoran, who has turned his back upon the city where his wealth was amassed and, converting his funds into millions of gold, has departed out of the coasts of the nation whose peaceful and liberal rule was the guardian and security of his gains. His spacious private grounds, just on the edge of the city, are beautifully situated and are as well adapted for the purposes of barracks and hospitals for the wounded defenders of our country as for the recreant subject of national liberality. There is a highly ornamented barn full of hospital stores and other goods. Nearby is a long row of cattle sheds boarded in and transformed into a hospital bakery, while below us, in a sweep of gentle slopes, is a piece of ornamented water where a host of attendants are washing the garments and bedding of the hospital patients.

The temporary buildings erected by the government are only a story high, are of wood, whitewashed inside and outside, well-ventilated but tight and warm. These buildings are arranged in the form of a hollow square, row within row, the kitchens being arranged so that food is taken to each ward dining room without being carried into the open air, and the wards are connected with the dining rooms in like manner. All of the accessories of water closets, baths, etc., are complete, neat, and faultlessly clean, and the comfort of 1,000 patients here assembled seems to be carefully studied. The diet for those who get to the hospital table is generous and full, yet wholesome; while the fare of those who are unable to leave their wards is nutritious and simple. Regular rations are served to the men, and from the regulations established there are no departures, except in extreme cases where the nurses are allowed discretionary powers.

At most of the hospitals in this vicinity the female nurses supplied by the Sisters of Charity (Roman Catholic) and Sisters of Mercy (Protestant) are employed, the two different faiths working together harmoniously in the same hospitals, side by side. Formerly, the Sanitary Commission at the request of the War Department examined all nurses, male or female, before they were permitted to enter the service. But lately, Miss [Dorothea] Dix has had charge of that duty when it is done at all, and, as a natural consequence, where there are so many applications to be attended to and so many situations to fill, suddenly at times, there will be persons pressed into employment who are unfit for their position and who seek such employment for merely mercenary motives or with worse designs. Think of the thousands of irresponsible and unknown individuals who are daily employed in the hospitals as attendants and nurses and you will not be surprised that in this, as

in all other professions, worthless and dishonest persons
are occasionally found. I am told, however, that in many
of the hospitals are found benevolent men and women,
some of high moral and intellectual culture, who have
sought the position of hospital nurse through the Sanitary
Commission for their own desire to do good and are now
unobtrusively and humbly employed in these scenes of
suffering in camp, field, or hospital, silently ministering to
the wants and woes of the dying or the suffering
wounded. . . .

Washington, December 22, 1862

RUMORS

The past week has been one of harvest to the newsmongers. It has not only rained rumors, but a complete and
utter deluge has swept over the city, so that we have at
last, under the fearful influence of the quidnuncs, fallen
into a state of incredulity delightful to behold. If we were
to be told upon "the highest official authority" that the
sun rose this morning, it is quite uncertain whether the in-
formant would be believed at first. The grand "movement"
at Fredericksburg and its nonsuccess, the row among the
war managers, the commotion in the cabinet, the resignations of Chase and Seward and the high probability that
all except Welles would follow, together with the conse-
quent cabinet-making involved—all these have followed
in quick succession and afford our ingenious friends, the
New York reporters and the Washington quidnuncs, with
an abundant field of operation, the only difficulties being
that *everything* was not compatible with coherent truth
and that Secretary Stanton inexorably forbade that mere

rumors of cabinet changes should go over the [telegraph] lines. Consequently, our Bohemian gentry were bursting with intelligence but could not get out of Washington with it. . . .

NOT SO BADLY HURT

. . . Our loss in the late battle near Fredericksburg is not so serious as was at first apprehended. For several days the figures have stood at 13,000, but they are now reduced by actual count to a point near 8,000, and if stragglers come in next week at the same rate which obtained during last week, the number will yet be reduced greatly. Stragglers to the number of *over two thousand* came in during two days last week, strange as it may seem. There are excellent hospital accommodations at Falmouth, where the more seriously wounded are provided for, only a small number of that class having been brought to Washington. The fact that an unusually large number of wounded was immediately sent to this city created an impression that the slaughter was much greater than subsequent reports warrant us in believing.

Great praise is awarded to the Sanitary Commission for the efficiency with which it met the wants of the suffering wounded at Fredericksburg. [It] has distributed 1,350 suits of hospital clothing, 200 cans of condensed milk, 600 blankets and quilts, 200 bottles of spirits and wines, 200 cans of beef soup stock, 600 pounds of dried fruits, 400 towels, quantities of chloroform, bandages, lint, and other articles. Many a wounded soldier on the bloody field of Fredericksburg has occasion to bless with gratitude the almost unknown and unnoticed labors of the Sanitary Commission, whose operations upon the bloody verge of battle are like the imperceptible dew—noiseless but invaluably refreshing.

Washington, December 26, 1862

CHRISTMAS

The Washington Christmas passed off quite as pleasantly as might have been expected, considering that the day was one of those damp, dull gray ones peculiar to this latitude. The churches were decorated with evergreens, and religious services [were] held in many, and Christmas Eve was a busy one all over the city. Christmas trees and gifts were carried home through the streets all night, and bonfires and [fire]crackers startled the air as though the anniversary of the advent of the Prince of Peace were to be celebrated during these warlike times by the jubilant and explosive sounds of Independence Day.

The streets were not as lively as they usually are during the day, as so many congressmen and the vast train of hangers-on had temporarily gone home. But the darkies, male and female, were out in all their glory. Those who but last Christmas were in bonds and celebrated their festal day within the magic circles of their iron servitude were yesterday able to add a new element of joy to their favorite holiday, and in the various camps of the contrabands in and around the city the Great Deliverance was the burden of the thankful theme of the poor yet happy crowds. Never tell me that these poor creatures are better off in slavery, after what I have seen here. Naked, poor, despised, forsaken, they yet lift their ragged arms to Heaven in thankfulness that their Christmas day is to them their new birth to freedom and liberty. "Free! Free! Free!" shouted one aged Negro at the contraband camp yesterday, with an exultant and joyful burst of passion which moved the

most unsympathetic. "Oh how good it is to be free and
to know that what I earn is mine, mine, mine, and dat
no man can eber say he owns my body or my soul." Poor
creatures, their joys and triumphs are greatly animal and
sensuous, but whose fault is it?

Under the energetic and kindly supervision of Mrs.
[Caleb B.] Smith, wife of the retiring Secretary of the
Interior, a generous and ample dinner was provided for
all inmates of the military hospitals of the District. When
one remembers that there are over twenty hospitals in
this city alone, it will be seen that the work proposed by
this thoughtful and benevolent lady was one of some
magnitude. But the people far and wide responded to the
call, and day before yesterday the basement rooms of the
Interior building presented the appearance of a huge provision store, rather than the gloomy affair which it usually
is. Huge piles of dressed poultry, game, and meats, stacks
of vegetables, long rows of barrels of fruit, cases of pies,
and hampers of delicacies were crowded on every hand,
while the almoners of all this bounty were busy as bees,
distributing the rich stores to the messengers of each hospital. The tables were spread yesterday at all the hospitals
with ample Christmas dinners of turkey, pudding, and
pies, with jellies, fruit, and other delicacies; those who
were not able to come to the table were served at their
bedside by the ladies with such refreshments as the surgeons in charge designated as proper for them. The whole
was carried out and executed under the supervision of Mrs.
Smith [and] by the ladies of Washington and vicinity,
among the waiters at one hospital being Mrs. Lincoln,
and at another, presiding at the head of tables largely indebted to her own private bounty was Mrs. [Stephen A.]
Douglas, widow of the late-lamented Senator from Illinois.

SUNDRY

It is commonly believed and reported in Washington circles that Secretary [Salmon P.] Chase will soon wed Mrs. Stephen A. Douglas.

The entire staffs of several Michigan cavalry regiments, encamped near here, made a series of calls upon the President, Secretary Stanton, and General Halleck on the day before Christmas. Their brilliant cavalcade created so much stir on the street that it was commonly believed to be *Frémont's staff* by the uninitiated. General Frémont is again placed by rumor at the head of an army. It is the Mississippi River expedition this time. A very doubtful rumor that.

The Old Captol Prison in this city is full of prisoners of war, many of them being rebels who have been paroled by the Federal forces, some of them *five or six times,* and have been again caught in the rebel ranks. There are also three spies sent from the rebel redoubts who were arrested in the Federal camp near Fredericksburg and are now confined in the above-named prison.

Washington, December 31, 1862

THE LAST OF AN OLD FRIEND

...1862 has come and gone, and we have not yet reached our coveted goal, and the immediate prospects for the speedy consummation of our wishes do not appear brilliant. It is true that we have reclaimed much rebel territory from the hands of the usurpers and that many points are now gladdened and illuminated with the light of the flag whose stars and stripes were strangers a year ago to the regions where they now wave. But, in the popular mind, the feeling of disappointment at the general result of the war is too apparent and too deep to bear contradiction or ignoring. *We have not taken Richmond*—that eyesore to all loyal men and the coveted prize to which all loyal hearts have ever pressed; and victories or advances, however cheering, ... have failed and will fail to satisfy the public, which—like a spoiled child—will have Richmond or nothing.

AN AMERICAN FLORENCE NIGHTINGALE

When the Massachusetts volunteers were shot down in the streets of "the murder-haunted" town of Baltimore on April 27, 1861, Mrs. [Joseph T.] Fales was the first to reach them with such kind offices as a thoughtful woman alone can give; and from that time she devoted all her spare time to the increasing wants of the sick and wounded soldiers. Whenever there has been a battle in this vicinity she has been on hand early in its cessation with restoratives, comforting draughts, and food; and when the wounded are poured into the hospitals, she is there to speak a kind word to the neglected or weary ones, to cheer the desperate, and to make note of those for whom she has been asked by distant parents to take special messages to. When the battle of Fredericksburg was subsiding into night, an acquaintance told me that he saw, to his astonishment, Mrs. Fales not far off, making tea, chocolate, and simple nourishment for a knot of wounded, and with heroic hands she staunched the gaping wounds of more than one soldier on that bloody field. All of the city hospitals know her constant care and visitation, and the sick soldiers have found out her multifarious gifts of letter writing to their distant friends, of reading when they are sick and weary, of healing ailments with a touch, and of directing their thoughts to wholesome channels when they are in that desperate mood which none but strong men, away from those who love them, shot down in cruel battle *ever* know.

So general and widening has become her field of unobtrusive usefulness that the Secretary of War has recognized her value to the hospital service, and has placed at her command an ambulance and driver and a pass to all of the camps and posts of the army. Furnished by more wealthy persons with delicacies and needful articles, she is thus enabled to reach a great number of people in the ranks of the suffering with her swift and ready aid; and should her biography and experiences ever be written, it would be a glorious example of what one true woman, clad like Lady Godiva in her own chastity, can do to alleviate the woes of others....

Washington, January 3, 1863

THE NEW ERA

... The chief topic of conversation hereabouts, in the absence of anything sensational, is the freedom proclamation of the President. None doubted its promulgation, yet it did take everybody by surprise, for notwithstanding all of the pooh-poohing of the opposition, this long looked for document comes fraught with momentous consequences. In this age of marvels and mighty events nothing seems greatly marvelous, and we rush on to the next sensation heedless of the last. But the proclamation has proclaimed liberty and freedom, broad and unconditional, to all of that dark dominion of rebeldom which our arms are now to bring back to the sway of the sovereign rule. This is the new era, and is but the beginning of the end. Whatever may be the consequences, the act and the theory of the proclamation are sublime.

... The proclamation was received with great sensation, and when it made its first appearance in the last edition of the *Evening Star* there was a grand rush for it. The popular verdict is that the document is a dignified, able, and statesmanlike paper. That it is a considerable improvement in tone and composition upon the proclamation of September 22 is generally remarked, and even those who doubt the value or the expediency of the measure cannot but admire the calm, judicious phraseology of the paper. What nobler and more touching words than those concluding this extraordinary and important proclamation:

"And upon this act, sincerely believed to be an act of justice, warranted by the Constitution upon military necessity, I invoke the considerate judgment of mankind and the gracious favor of Almighty God."

HOW WE WENT A-CALLING ON NEW YEAR'S DAY

... A small party of us, chiefly Californians, went the rounds of the dignitaries who "received" on New Year's Day. The good old custom is still kept up here—the cabinet ministers and other public functionaries being obliged to follow the custom or be thought exclusive, which would be bad for the cabinet ministers and such, you know, and people who bore the President with a perpetual flood of audiences because he was made President for the people's use would think it very hard of Seward, Chase and Co. if they should retire from their workaday world to a closed house on the day for universal calling. So they keep open house, and anybody who behaves himself can go and see them at home.

Secretary [Gideon] Welles and Postmaster General [Montgomery] Blair did not receive their friends, on account of recent deaths in their families. Secretary [Caleb B.] Smith had handed in his resignation of the portfolio of the Department of the Interior and had departed for the interior to assume his new duties as United States Judge for the district of Indiana, and so he was also exempt. But the "Pres.," as he is familiarly termed by the unwashed, had no excuse, and at eleven he commenced his labors by receiving the foreign diplomats and their attachés. These dignitaries made a truly gorgeous appearance, arrayed in gold lace, feathers, and other trappings, not to mention very good clothes. After they had paid their respects to the President and his wife and departed, the naval and military officers in town went in a shining body to wish the Commander-in-Chief of the Army and Navy "A Happy New Year," which, we must suppose, was gratefully received by "Old Abe," with a sincere hope that it might be happier than his last two years have been.

Precisely at twelve o'clock the great gates of the Executive Mansion were thrown open, and the crowd rushed in. Our delegation from California, being vehicularly equipped, was obliged to fall into a line of coaches and march up the drive at a truly funeral pace. The press was tremendous and the jam excessive. All persons, high or low, civil, uncivil, or otherwise, were obliged to fall into an immense line of surging, crowding sovereigns who were all forcing their way along the stately portico of the White House to the main entrance. There were a detachment of police and a small detail of a Pennsylvania regiment on hand to preserve order. But bless your soul! there was precious little order in that crowd. Here was a member of Congress, [William] Kellogg of Illinois, with his coattail half torn off, there was a young lady in tears at the wreck of a "love of a bonnet" with which she must enter the presence as there is no retreat when one has once committed oneself to the resistless torrent of that mighty sea which surged against the doors of the White House and around the noble columns thereof. Anon, a shoulder-strapped brigadier general, too late for the military *entree*, entered the crowd with a manifest intention of going in directly, but he found his match in the sovereign crowd, which revenged its civil subordination by very uncivil hustling of the unfortunate officer.

"If I could get my hand up, I would make you remember me," was the angry remark of a burly Michiganer to a small Bostonian who had punched him in the victual basket. Bostonian knew that such a thing was impossible in that jam and smiled his contempt. But the doors, closed for a few moments, open for a fresh dose of the "peops," and all, combatants and non-combatants, changed their base about five feet, with the same brilliant results which McClellan announced of his Peninsular fight. The valves of the entrance close until the monster within has digested his new mouthful, and we fetch up this time against a fresh-faced soldier created in "this hour of our country's peril" to mount guard at the White House with a piece of deer skin, meant to typify a bucktail, on his cap. Says this military Cerberus, "My gosh! gentlemen, *will* you stan' back? You can't get in no faster by crowdin'! Oh, I say, *will* you stan' back?" To which adjuration the gay and festive crowd responded by flattening him against a pilaster, never letting him loose until his fresh country face was dark with an alarming symptom of suffocation, he the while holding his useless musket helplessly in the air by his folded arms.

Inside at last, we pour along the hall and enter a suite of rooms, straightening bonnets, coats, and other gear, with a sigh of relief. . . . A single line, such as we see at the post office sometimes, reaches to the President who is flanked on the left by Marshal Ward H. Lamon who receives the names of each and gives it to the President as each advances to shake hands. Thus Lamon: "Mr. Snifkins of California." To whom the President, his heavy eyes brightening says: "I am glad to see you, Mr. Snifkins— you come from a noble state—God bless her." Snifkins mumbles his thanks, is warmly pressed by the hand as though the President had just begun his day's work on the pump handle, and he is replaced by Mr. Biffkins of New York who is reminded by the Father of the Faithful that the Empire State has some noble men in the Army of the Union.

And so we go on, leaving behind us the poor besieged and weary President with his blessed old pump handle working steadily as we disappear into the famous East Room, a magnificent and richly furnished apartment. . . . A long window in an adjacent passage has been removed and a wooden bridge temporarily thrown across the sunken passage around the basement of the house. By this egress the fortunate ones depart, smiling in commiseration at the struggling unfortunates who are yet among the "outs." A primly dressed corps of cavalry officers, glorious in lace and jingling spurs, dash up to the portico and are disgusted to find that they must be swallowed up in the omniverous crowd. But they must, for this is pre-eminently the People's Levee, and there is no distinction of person or dress shown here.

AMONG LESSER LIGHTS

At the residence of the venerable [John J.] Crittenden we found a touch of Kentucky hospitality, which was quite refreshing after the formal jam at the White House. The distinguished ex-Senator, now Representative in Congress, yet retains all of the sprightliness of earlier years, though his lower face shows unmistakable evidences of old age. He is slight in figure and rather under the medium height of men. Mrs. Crittenden, a portly matron, is just in the full, rich bloom of maturity, and did the honors of the reception with great dignity of manner. At this house were spread refreshments in liberal but not ostentatious profusion, and the guests were hospitably entertained by the urbane Kentuckian.

At Secretary Chase's we were received by a likely young gentleman of color who had a double row of silver plated buttons from his throat to his toes, and handing this doorkeeper, efflorescent in buttons, our "pasteboards," we were ushered into the presence of the Secretary of the Treasury, a tall, good-looking man, slightly bald and guiltless of whiskers; also nearby, Miss [Katharine] Chase, the belle of Washington *par excellence*, arrayed in white muslin and natural flowers. Mr. Chase is easy and gentlemanly in his manners, though he has a painful way of holding his head straight, which leads one to fancy that his shirt collar cuts his ears. His daughter is certainly very beautiful—slight, graceful, and the wavy, willowy order of figure. The family appears to be popular, as the parlors were crowded, and the Secretary and his daughter had their hands full. Being a financier who recommends economy, Chase did not have any "spread" at his house, and the same evidence of good taste was evident at Secretary Seward's where we next called.

The Secretary of State does not keep great state at his residence, though his upstairs parlors were quite tastefully furnished—marble busts, engravings, flowers, and paintings being the most noticeable objects in the room, unless it was the prodigious nose of Seward. He advanced from the rear of the parlors as a batch of names was called, shaking hands with all of his matchless *suaviter in modo* as each caller was presented. With a few kind words the visitor was passed over to Fred W. Seward, Assistant Secretary of State, a nice young man with black hair and whiskers and unexceptionable pantaloons. He, in turn, introduced the party to Mrs. Seward, Jr., who made the remark that it was a beautiful day, to which we cordially assented with the addendum that is was an auspicious opening of a new year, which original observation, I am happy to say, met with her approbation and that of a young lady in flounced silk whose name we did not learn. Seward, who has a great deal of very white or light hair and what we used to call a "cowlick," had subsided into the depths from whence he had emerged at our coming, and so we departed, meeting Adjutant General [Lorenzo] Thomas, with all his glory and epaulets on, coming upstairs.

At Secretary Stanton's we were met by the wife of that warlike gentleman, and we found her a ladylike-looking woman of Pittsburgh extraction and a pleasant demeanor. ... However, she wounded the feelings of our cicerone by remarking, in connection with original meteorological observations, that it must be quite warm *walking*—as though the likes of us were willing to soil shining boots on such an occasion. Secretary Stanton, a shortish, full-fed man with spectacles, black hair, and full, grizzled beard, greeted us in the dining room where was laid out an extensive spread of provender. Oysters, salads, game pastries, fruits, cake, wines, and various other fixings were arranged with a most gorgeous display of china, glass, and silver, two silent and attentive colored men serving the guests, who were numerous. Passing out we met a couple of dignitaries, very portly and "nobby," with *chapeaux bras*, gold lace, feathers, medals, and other toggery. As they were extremely rotund and rubicund and said "pon honor" and "demme" continually, we agreed that they were English officers and secretly maligned them for their country's sake.

... We called on Speaker [Galusha A.] Grow who received his friends in his own hired house, as is said of Paul, and dispensed excellent coffee in his dimly lit parlor. ... We must mention the mayor's reception where were the "sovereign people" again and a spread of edibles commensurate to their tastes and wants. Some of the guests must have dieted for the occasion, for their inroads upon the ham, beef, and mutton were fearful. I mind me now of a tall young man, with one of those peculiar "slab" frames which are never full, gorging himself on great hunks of bread and meat and gagging desperately over the profuse array of bounties before him. He may be gormandizing at that free lunch yet, for aught I know. Mayor [Richard] Wallach's finished up our round of visits, and we drove home, more than ever convinced that "this world is all a frog pond" and that the best of us are only medium swimmers in the same.

Washington, January 9, 1863

A LIVELY SCRIMMAGE IN THE HOUSE

The most exciting and lively debate of the present session of Congress came off in the House yesterday while that body was in Committee of the Whole. [George W.] Dunlap of Kentucky, in reply to some remarks of [Thaddeus] Stevens of Pennsylvania impugning the loyalty of Kentucky, made an excited speech in defense of that somewhat fishy state. He acknowledged that fully one-third of her able-bodied citizens were in the rebel ranks and that thousands of her citizens were silent sympathizers with rebellion, but also rejoiced to know that other thousands were in the ranks of the Union army. He was for the Union first, last, and all the time, and he would thank gentlemen on the opposite side of the House to exclude Kentucky in their aspersions upon southern or border states.

Stevens replied that he was glad to hear the statements of the gentleman from Kentucky, and he added that he based his remarks of a former occasion on the statement made by the adjutant general of Kentucky that three-fourths of the able-bodied men of that state were in the rebel army. This brought up [William H.] Wadsworth of Kentucky, who, jumping to his feet, excitedly vociferated that it was a lie. Stevens said he was glad to hear it, and Wadsworth again repeated that it was a lie. Stevens then went on in his cool, slow, ponderous style to show that Kentucky had refused to take part for the Union though she had professed to hold herself aloof from the rebellion also, and that her delegation on the floor of Congress had always been found voting and working against all measures for the actual support of the government and against the administration in every particular. He would leave the inference to the country, but he thought that when Kentucky, with one exception, always strove to embarrass the administration and balk the war, such professions of loyalty as theirs were worth little more than rank secession.

Upon this up jumped little Jimmy Kerrigan of New York, who has been lately liberated from Fort Lafayette by the too lenient government and who had been "spilin' for a fight." He charged Stevens and his party with being the rankest secessionists in the country, and he continued to foam and gesticulate with all the energy of a mad monkey—the Speaker, meanwhile, rapping so that no one could be heard. When he subsided and the noise and confusion which had reigned in the hall were quieted, the imperturable "Thad," who had stood quiet as an iceberg

all the while, said that the gentleman from New York
(Kerrigan) was perfectly in order—that he had only lately
had an opportunity to speak here and that he ought to
have some liberty now to indemnify himself for the restraints which he had lately been under. This silenced
Kerrigan who soon after slunk out of sight.

Then ensued a long and highly interesting debate, the
whole Kentucky delegation making a raid upon Thaddeus
Stevens who met them singlehanded, enunciating his peculiar views with great clearness and force. The debate was
chiefly upon the exact status of the seceded states, a question upon which Stevens is known to have widely different
views from his associates; and in reply to a question from
Dunlap of Kentucky, Stevens said that he did not consider the seceded states in the Union, the ordinance of
secession, backed up by an armed power, having taken
them out of the Union; and in reply to a question as to
how he proposed to collect taxes in these states, he said
that he proposed to levy and collect taxes as a war measure,
but, if necessary, he would take every inch of territory of
every disloyal man and his real and personal estate and sell
them for the benefit of the nation carrying the war. We
are to treat them as provinces until we conquer them. It is
absurd to say a man in arms is entitled to the same constitutional provisions as a loyal man when he does not
obey the laws and repudiates their binding obligations.

Washington, January 13, 1863

THE RETURNING CLOUDS

For a few days we were jubilant over the fall of Mur-
freesboro and the prospects of capturing Vicksburg, but
now, hard upon our blooming hopes, comes the nipping

frost of the loss of Galveston and a repulse of the Vicksburg expedition of Sherman and McClernand. Today, we are all gloomy. In the Senate chamber there were "grave and reverend seigniors," friends of the Union and of the administration, who are willing to croak loudly and to say "when the end of this nation shall have come, if it be not already come." The congressmen are lachrymose and despondent and talk savagely of our mischiefs and mishaps as though the country were gone to the "demnition bowwows" and it were time to pack up our few articles of dunnage and prepare to migrate.

The air is heavy with the dolor of the hour. Though God's own sky above us is clear and fair and the glorious sun rains down his brightest rays with equal largess upon rebel and upon patriot, a cloud hangs over our mercurial people and they are unmistakably "deeply, darkly, and beautifully blue." They need the sudden notes of a great victory to stir their sad souls as with a clarion blast. Some ringing bugle of a glorious military success must peal on the air and fall welcomely upon the waiting ear before this despondent mood can pass. Oh, how we long for it, and how like a glad evangel would come the tidings of a decisive, triumphant, undoubted achievement of the federal arms.

Let us not be deluded by the lulling song of Hope—the life of the republic is ebbing fast, and unless we shall shortly pluck a military success from the troubles which now environ us, we are lost. Not that rebel armies are nearer than ever before to the great heart of the nation, or that defeat in the field is more imminent, but the non-success of our armies, the supineness of our arms, and the slow progress of the war—gigantic in its machinery and organization—all these fed the monster which threatens our ruin. And now draws nearer, huger, more definable, the dreadful specter—Debt. Stronger than rebel arms and more inexorable than death grows day by day the ogre of our prosperity, and every failure in the field, every repulse of beleaguring forces of the Union arms, every dreadful rout of destroying battle sap public confidence in our strength, impair national credit, and add millions to the growing burdens of a steadily accumulating debt. Here is a greater terror than an insurgent army. Here is the true peril of the republic. . . .

Washington, January 14, 1863

THE ARMY OF THE POTOMAC

Public attention, for a while diverted by the extensive operations in the West, is turned again to the favorite and ever popular army raised to defend Washington and to take Richmond but now lying supinely upon the banks of the Rappahannock and wasting like a snowball in the sun. Whatever successes may be achieved elsewhere and however brilliant the operations by sea or river, the people of the more populous Atlantic and middle states must have action in the Army of the Potomac or they are dissatisfied. Just now the position and condition of their favorite legion of the Union are humiliating and disheartening to itself and to the country. Repulsed at the rebel lines of defense on the road to Richmond from the Rappahannock, forced to fall back with severe losses, deprived of a favorite commander—it is not surprising that the spirit of the army is weakened, that demoralization and disintegration are imminent, and that the people are clamoring loudly for an advance or change of position. It is difficult . . . to realize the feeling of bitterness which is made to prevail here in consequence of this long delay of the promised activity of the Army of the Potomac, whose repulse was said to be only temporary and whose rest was only to be long enough to allow recuperation and reorganization.

There is no use in concealing or denying the fact that public confidence in Generals Halleck and Burnside is fast ebbing away, and before long the cry for their removal will be just as vigorous and determined as was that for the removal of McClellan. And, speaking of McClellan, it would be no surprise if he should be reinstated in command of the Army of the Potomac. The soldiers love not Burnside less, but McClellan more. It is, I believe, a sort of infatuation and an almost unreasoning devotion, but it is true, and we may as well look the facts in the face. The rank and file, many of the commissioned officers, and most of the non-commissioned officers talk longingly of the return of McClellan. Mixed in with these are many intelligent men who do not hesitate to say that they believe McClellan to be a traitor, a K[night] [of the] G[olden] C[ircle], and aider and abettor of the enemy, and a general who fights for the rebels and against his country. This, however, is the spirit of a minority of the army, and the greater portion entertains quite different views.

Now, then, is a propitious hour for the partisans of McClellan. The army fails to advance, though it is notorious that the rebel force beyond Fredericksburg has been almost wholly withdrawn. Our men, burning to advance, are held in check and are wasting in numbers and being soured and made malcontent by inactivity and idleness. So the impression prevails that a demoralization of the once noble Army of the Potomac has begun, and people say, "Well, McClellan may as well ruin them in the swamps of the Chickahominy as to leave them melt away on the banks of the Rappahannock." They will not do anything without McClellan, but will they do anything with him?

And if Burnside and McClellan are not sufficient for these things, who is? There is a California general in the field who hates the former commander of the Army of the Potomac, whom he denounces as unfaithful to his country. He has no confidence in the present general in command, whose first fight was at Bull Run. He shares the popular belief in the talents of Major General Joseph Hooker. But it is useless to speculate. If "Fighting Joe" Hooker is to be in command nobody here knows it.. . .

VALLANDIGHAM DEFINES HIS POSITION

Today Vallandigham, the archtraitor of the Democratic Assistant Rebels, made a set speech in the House of Representatives. He defined his position in his usual, venomous, bitter, and snappish manner. He started out with the proposition that he was opposed, at the beginning of the war, to coercion, for the reason that he believed it would lead to civil war and disunion—as though disunion had not been already declared by act of the South. This opinion, he said, he had seen no reason to change, and his early conviction that the South could not be conquered had been deepened by subsequent events. He believed then and now that the war, nominally undertaken for the defense of the Union, had become a war for the abolition of slavery, as it was originally intended that it should. He admitted that this war existed by consent and with the endorsement of the united North, people, Congress, and administration, but he denied that the war could ever result in the preservation of a union founded on good will and mutual amity, and hence he had steadfastly opposed the war and all measures for its support and prosecution. He reviewed the conduct of the war, spoke of its great cost, and argued that it could not and should not be continued.

Chancing to use the term "rebel," Vallandigham apotheosized the shade of Washington who, he said, was also a rebel—a rebel against an oppressive and tyrannical government. "So," said he, "we have all descended from rebels." He said separation was not to be desired, but that we should cease our fraternal strife and *compromise*. This specter of compromise he kept in the background, continually referring to it but never defining its shape, so that his audience was unable to say whether it was "a spirit of health or goblin damned," it came in such questionable shape.

He went on with an elaborate argument in support of the proposition for reunion, adducing many historical instances to prove that reunion, after long alienation, was possible. He denied that there was any irrepressible conflict between free and slave labor, but he said, nevertheless, that this war was one of the Yankee against the Southron, the Cavalier against the Roundhead. In passing he gave a dab at New England, which, he said, had been overslaughed by its Puritan sentiment and had been misrepresented in Congress by men who, a few years ago, could not be elected as selectmen under the old Whig domination. He said that if New England did not want to stay in the Union as it was—with slavery—she might stay out. He was willing to stay in any Union, but if this war was prolonged and the South should establish its independence, the great Northwest would go with the South, wherever interest led her, and not be a mere appendage to the Atlantic states. He dilated this proposition at great length and with considerable "vim."

This speech, important as being the utterance of the Northwestern Democrats, was long and able. When finished, it was replied to with great force and with cauterizing logic by [John A.] Bingham of Ohio, in an offhand, impromptu speech.... [Hendrick B.] Wright of Pennsylvania, a War Democrat, also made a set speech, replying to Vallandigham, and successfully controverted his sophistical arguments one by one, making his chief point on the proposition that the South will not compromise and that all the specious offers of compromise from Peace Democrats are only to serve as bridges by which the South shall pass over to independence and final disunion. This long and exciting debate made an exciting day in the House.

Washington, January 17, 1863

A FORWARD MOVEMENT—PERHAPS

We are hopeful, once more, of a forward movement, and for the fiftieth time since the repulse at Fredericksburg we are treated to important rumors from the front indicating activity, stir, and, in fact, a forward movement. We have been fooled so many times, however, that incredulity is the order of the day until assurance is rendered doubly sure. All rumors of five day rations being ordered and a base of supplies being pushed up the Rappahannock, indicating a crossing above Falmouth—all of these and other authentic reports pass for nothing with these unbelieving Thomases whose business it is to gather the news of the day for the edification of the body politic.

One thing is certain, however. The Army of the Potomac is so impatient for an advance that serious consequences are apprehended from the insubordination of the rank and file. An officer from the front told me the other day that if a mutiny were to occur among the troops, it would not be for the reason that the soldiers had not their pay, but because they *would* go on to Richmond. People here want to see Burnside make one more essay to victory, and they hope that he will have a chance to prove himself the soldier that all have hoped him to be. If he fails this time the instant cry will be, "Off with his head; so much for Bu—rnside."

A SINGULAR AND BEAUTIFUL INCIDENT

Day before yesterday, just after the House of Representatives had assembled, a tall, fine-looking woman dressed in deep mourning entered one of the doors of the east gallery and, advancing to the front of the balustrade, looked benignantly down upon the members for a moment, then drew from under her mantle a small silk flag, and, unrolling it from its staff, she waved the Stars and Stripes over the heads of the astonished members once or twice, and then rolled it up and departed as she came. Who she is and where she came from are unknown. Possibly she is the Goddess of Liberty in flesh and blood or America in mourning for her children and she is admonishing Congress to be about its business.

Washington, January 21, 1863

PRESIDENT LINCOLN UPSETS A BEEHIVE

Monday morning, bright and early, Congress was greeted with a message informing that honorable body that the President had signed the joint resolution authorizing the issuance of $100,000,000 of legal tender notes for the payment of the army and navy, and at the same time he gave his views on the financial question at some length. It must be confessed that the message partook somewhat of the character of a lecture, but the turmoil, buzzing, and fretting of Congress was unnecessary and undignified. To the astonishment of the congressmen, who have been wrangling and spouting for weeks over the Revenue bill, the President is actually found to have an opinion and a mind of his own. Remarkable impudence and unparalleled boldness! The President has dared to disturb the windy lucubrations of Congress and tell them what he thinks is right and fit in such a deplorable fix as the present.

Instantly the House was up in arms, and a motion to refer to a special committee was lost, the House adjourning without making any disposition of it. Representatives grumbled and swore, and senators were indignant and being so lectured would not even print the message. Senator Wilson [of Massachusetts] fumed and said that the President took occasion to ring in a speech every time he sent the most trivial message to the Senate. But the people are pleased, for they are in the main (except the bank interest) in favor of the views of Secretary Chase, which the President endorses. Public confidence is accordingly reassured, and the popular mind is pleased with the independence of the President, who has brought up Congress with a round turn to a sense of its duty.

It is now seven weeks that Congress has been in session, and nothing yet has been done to determine the financial policy of the country for the next two years. Each member of the Ways and Means Committee has had his own peculiar views and hobby to advance, and Congress has frittered away its limited time in long speeches and in the consideration of impracticable schemes, leaving the credit of the country to go steadily down to ruin, the soldiers unpaid, the war debt accumulating, and the financial world unable to predicate any action whatever upon the action of Congress and the Treasury department. The President's message, notwithstanding the turmoil which it has created, will be likely to bring about a compromise of financial views and thus insure the speedy action of Congress upon some sound measure. In the meantime, however, the soldiers are being paid, and it will not be long before every one of them will be in full receipt of all his dues from the government. . . .

THE DEBT OF THE UNITED STATES

Recent debates in this Congress upon the bills providing ways and means for raising the revenue for the current and coming fiscal years show the present indebtedness of the United States to be as follows:

Old debt falling due within a few years
    from time, at different periods, about $ 70,000,000
Loans under acts of the Congress. 250,000,000
Certificates of indebtedness, about. . . . 100,000,000
Loans on ten days deposit, about. 100,000,000
The unliquidated debts due the army,
    contractors, and others, estimated at
    (besides postal currency). 200,000,000
                    Total. . . . $720,000,000

The bills now before Congress contemplate an increase of indebtedness of $900,000,000 and will leave with the Secretary of the Treasury the authority to issue $500,000,-000 of five-twenty bonds authorized by the last session, which will make when all issued a debt of $2,120,000,000—rather a startling calculation if it were not that we are past being startled at anything. But is it worthwhile, after all, to look at figures as compared with the consequence of ending this rebellion by submission to the rebels? Those who worry about the big debt which grows upon our hands and point with dolorous dread to the taxation which already looms upon the horizon of the future, a legacy for generations to come, should not forget that the alternative lies between debt and death. We are daily having this lesson pressed upon us, and must not forget it: comfort and luxury are worth less than a government, a nationality, and a place among the powers of the earth. All of these depend upon the successful issue of this war, and if we cannot afford to give *all* if necessary, we cannot afford to live.

Washington, January 23, 1863

SUSPENSE

We are still hoping and fearing, still in a state of suspense concerning the movements of our army, and though we have had a week of rumors, positive and authoritative as usual, nothing has happened yet. The stirring address of General Burnside to the Army of the Potomac, published in last night's papers, is evidence that the military authorities do not pretend any secrecy as to the fact of a forward movement but only conceal the nature of it. So we are all waiting and watching once more for an offensive movement, the necessity for which grows upon us daily. It will be but three months before the time will come when 75,000 of our soldiers will be at liberty to leave the ranks of the army and return to the peace of their homes, their term of enlistment being expired, and it is useless to suppose that any considerable portion of them will re-enlist. This is a pity, but it is so and cannot be disguised.

The imbecile conduct of many high officials in command, the jealous bickerings of the generals, and the wanton waste of life by wrongheaded commanders—all these things have had the effect to weaken the confidence of the rank and file in the military authority and to inspire the feeling that their patriotism avails nothing when led into the fight by incompetent commanders.... No movement has been made for the purpose of calling out more volunteer troops, except a resolution of inquiry which was offered in the House of Representatives and at once smothered. It is patent that with the present condition of affairs in the army so well known, and in the present character of public sentiment, enlistments are impossible, and a call for troops would be worse than useless, for it would be unheeded, and the effect of such a disregard of the call would be most unfortunate. The draft has been virtually abandoned all over the United States, and we have come to the conclusion that there is too much popular sovereignty in our people to attempt to coerce any of them into a service which they do not voluntarily seek. They manage the "sovereigns" better in Secessia.

Is patriotism extinct? By no means. Let us have a few great decisive victories, such as will show that the war is nearing a triumphant close—such victories as will show that we have generals in command and that the government itself is dreadfully in earnest—and we shall see just such another outpouring of men and money as we have witnessed once and again in this country. Up to this date we have had no generalship, no policy, and no consummate management anywhere. We have had all the money, men, means, and moral aid that were needed and more than were asked for, and where are we? ... I have run over this recapitulation of the situation just to show why we have come to the pass in which we find ourselves today, when it is palpable and confessed that we can have no more volunteers until we have more military successes. It is not pleasant to be obliged to admit such truths, but it is useless to attempt to disguise them, and it is mischievous to shut our eyes willfully to the real state of the case. We will not believe that the God of justice and liberty can have deserted us, but will hope that, though for a season we are humiliated and tribulated, we shall be eventually triumphant, and, despite mismanagement, inexperience, and treason within and without, we will achieve success and victory. If we do not, the cause of civil liberty the world over is put in extreme jeopardy. Hope may again bid the world farewell for a season.

"A HIT—A PALPABLE HIT"

During the debate upon the Revenue bill in the House yesterday, [George] Pendleton of Ohio (Democrat) made a good point on the Republicans by saying that the anti-administration members were in awkward position, for the opposite side of the House appeared to be divided against the administration on the question of finance. The recommendations of the Secretary of the Treasury appeared to be treated with utter contempt by the Committee on Ways and Means, the chairman of which (Thad Stevens) is one of the chief lights of Republicanism, and the President's finance message had been incontinently smothered in the house of his friends while the House committees were persistently urging a financial policy directly in opposition to the recommendations of both President and Secretary. Now, continued Pendleton, as loyalty to the government is at present considered to be loyalty to the administration, we, who are suspected of disloyalty, do not know whether we must follow the lead of the administration members or the recommendations of the administration itself.

The rebuke to the Republicans who have been so high-handed in their willful and dogmatic opposition to the plainly expressed and reasonable policy and wishes of those who have the management of the financial business of the nation was deserved, though it was not given out of any good will to the administration. When [Charles J.] Biddle of Pennsylvania, a little irrepressible, . . . said that Congress ought to be thankful that the President had not compelled the nation into his financial policy by a proclamation, Owen Lovejoy [of Illinois] retorted that the President was the last man in the world to be charged with an attempt to exercise arbitrary power. The gentleman must know it, and he thanked God that the great mass of the people believed it. He warned gentlemen who are in high favor now at recent successes obtained under false pretenses that the triumph of the wicked is short. He desired in reply to Pendleton to read from the Constitution the duties of the President, whereupon Thad Stevens, temporarily in Vallandigham's seat, asked with mock sternness how he dared to read the Constitution here.

Washington, January 26, 1863

THE FINANCE QUESTION

Congress is still laboring with the bills to provide ways and means for the support of the government. . . . The running debate of the last week has been exceedingly interesting and it developed some important facts, among which is that the western states are almost unanimously in favor of a national currency to the exclusion of corporate banking institutions. The West has suffered too much from wildcat banks not to be predisposed to favor such a reliable and safe currency as that of the United States is proved to be. Consequently, ever since it made its appearance greenback money has been the favorite medium of circulation in the West, and those who know best say that the hoarded money in that part of the country is in greenbacks, rather than in gold.

In debate the other day in the House of Representatives, while the proposition to tax the banks was under consideration, [Elihu B.] Washburne of Illinois ... adjured the House, for the sake of the Republicans of the West, to give them an opportunity to vote for a proposition to tax the banks, and he addressed the Democratic members of the House from the Northwest to come up to the rack and redeem the pledges they had made on the stump in the last canvass, when they charged upon the Republicans a desire and intention to flood the country with paper money and to encourage the banks in a similar course. The opposition members who were charging such a course upon the Republicans during the late congressional canvass are not noteworthy champions of an antibank movement now but will vote on any measure which may come up just as they believe will be for the injury of the administration.

While the finance bill was under discussion last week, one of the irrepressible Negro Democrats—[Samuel S.] Cox of Ohio, I believe—presented an amendment, similar to the scores which these fellows are continually presenting, providing that none of the funds accruing to the United States by the passage of the bill should be used for the purpose of feeding contrabands. [Clifton A.] White of Ohio supported the amendment in a hot speech in which he asserted that 60,000 Negroes were now fed and clothed at the expense of the government and that the providing of rations to these persons was unconstitutional as was the appropriation of public money to liberate the slaves of states by any system of emancipation.

[Abram B.] Olin of New York replied that the assertion of the member from Ohio was baseless and false, and that so far from the Negroes having been an expense to the government it will be proved, when the department reports are all in, they have been a source of actual revenue, and he was willing to stake his character upon the assertion. [William McKee] Dunn of Indiana further showed how these contrabands had been used for military purposes, quoting from the act of Congress which authorized such employment. [Charles A.] Wickliffe, the venomous old man of Kentucky, wanted to know if the old women, young women, and children living in Washington and being fed by the government were used for military purposes. To which Dunn replied that he was not aware of any such class of persons now in Washington, not being so familiar with the colored population of the class alluded to as was the honorable gentleman from Kentucky. Whereupon the ruffled Confederacy incontinently subsided and was heard no more upon the Negro question so dear to him.

Does it not look strange for Missouri and Maryland to be asking aid and assistance in emancipating their slaves, and Ohio, Indiana, and Pennsylvania objecting? Yet so it is, and today the opposition to emancipation comes from the Democrats of free states who are unwilling that slavery should be abolished even by those who own slaves, practically saying "You shall not abolish your slaves if we can help it, but we shall keep for our future political use the human chattels now so burdensome to you." Truly, the ways of the "Democracy" are past finding out. All of this long and exasperating debate on "niggers" was lugged into the finance debate by these proslavery Democrats only for the purpose of retarding legitimate legislation and disorganizing the public sentiment; yet these are they who are so fast to charge "nigger" legislation and agitation upon the friends of the administration.

THE NO-POLICY POLICY

... More than once an honest Douglas Democrat sent to the Senate by Union votes has asked, "What *is* the policy of the administration? Has it any?" The reply is not easy. Though we can answer in general terms that it is to put down rebellion, we are met by another query as to how the government proposes to meet the question of the status of the rebel states. ... Other issues are arising also, but no settled policy is pursued in regard to the various vexed questions which are blundered over, but not met, by army officers in the field and by members of the cabinet. Much of this is owing to the no-policy of the government. And the lukewarm who might be attached to the moral support of the administration are without any tangible incentive to induce them to the ranks of what might, under other conditions, be a great national Union party.

The Republicans will not forget that they have a party which must be saved out of this long struggle, and do not propose, it would appear, to allow the errors of the administration and the weak ratiocinations of Seward ruin their future prospects and vitiate their own policy. The recent secret caucuses of the Republican congressmen may have something to do with this; and it is generally believed that ... the real object of the caucus was to make a platform and define a policy which the cabinet must shape to its policy or lose the support of Congress. Certain it is that the Republican congressmen are awake to the fact that they have no test of fealty to their party or to the President

except in so far as the uncertain standard of votes upon
appropriation bills may be deemed to divide the sheep
from the goats. Upon other more radical measures Republicans themselves are divided and have failed to make
a record.

THE GROWL AGAINST SECRETARY SEWARD

Meanwhile, the feeling against Seward is considerably
augmented by his gentle dalliance with the Franco-Mex-
ican question and his known opposition to the emancipation policy. In such times as these it is reasonably believed
that unless the cabinet can be a unit upon the great questions of the day, the administration will be weak indeed.
It is well-known that Seward yields a tardy and reluctant
concurrence in the emancipation measures proposed by the
President and that he is responsible for the one hundred
days of grace granted before the final issue of the proclamation, by which means the measure was made to enter into
the political canvass in several of the states, to the utter
discomfiture of the President who saw a rebuke to the
proclamation and of the conduct of the war in the double
verdict of the November elections.

The public dissatisfaction with Seward was shown in the
half-concealed gratulation of the newspapers when his resignation was announced and the ardent expressions of
relief and satisfaction which I heard from Republican
congressmen when that event was announced here. Horace
Greeley has broadly intimated that the removal of Seward
has become necessary. Wendell Phillips has fulminated
against the Premier. And more latterly George Wilkes has
made his sporting paper [*Wilkes' Spirit of the Times* of
New York] an anti-Seward organ. All of this is indicative
of a combination of the "radicals" against the Secretary of

State. ... The "radicals" are in a majority, immense and growing. I greatly fear the "conservatives" are essentially used up, and Mr. Seward's roseate dreams of the future and his tender dealings with the past are not calculated to gain him or his partisans anything more valuable than the "distinguished consideration" which he so lavishly tenders to his foreign diplomatic correspondents.

THE LATEST MILITARY EMEUTE

Early this morning the public was astonished to learn that Burnside had at last tendered his resignation as Commander of the Army of the Potomac. I say they were astonished, for that expresses the sensation made by the sudden divulging of an item of news which had been daily expected by those who are on the inside. Last week ... a feeling of dissatisfaction and lack of confidence in the plans of the commander took tangible shape by the strenuous opposition made to the War Department and the President against the plans of Burnside by some of the generals under his command. Brigadier General John Cochrane acted as spokesman for these malcontents, and came to Washington with the extraordinary statement that if Burnside's plan of a movement then under contemplation was carried out that, in the judgment of said subordinates, the issue would be fatal, and that they could not go into the movement with confidence. The President did not order General Cochrane under arrest but listened to his arguments, and the result was that the whole scheme of Burnside was withdrawn and he at once tendered his resignation of a command which had been thrust upon him and of which he had long been very sick.

Burnside and Hooker were sent for, and this morning we learned that the resignation of the Commander-in-

Chief of the Army of the Potomac had been accepted and that "Fighting Joe" Hooker was in the place successively occupied by McClellan and Burnside. Coinstanteously with this change came the applications of [General William B.] Franklin and [General Edwin V.] Sumner for relief from their commands in the Army of the Potomac. This was expected, as the dignity of these division generals was not supposed equal to the pressure which would be brought upon them if they were to serve under a commander who had been their equal and coadjutor. What will be the result of this general pulling up and weeding out of the Army of the Potomac is now difficult to say. . . .

The promotion of Hooker is a matter of congratulation to those who believe that fighting qualities are of the foremost importance just now. But it is a pity that any change reveals such a deplorable state of things in the army. We can only wait and hope for better things. The Potomac Army is so demoralized that not much can be hoped for it now, and it is no longer so important a matter as to who is in command as it once was. In the meantime, Hooker is a popular officer and can carry the enthusiasm of his own corps with him. Should he succeed in infusing the same spirit into all the corps under him he will achieve a great victory and redeem the waning reputation of the Army of the Potomac.

Washington, January 27, 1863

PAYING FOR THE DARKIES

This morning the Treasury department commenced paying off the claims allowed by the award of the commissioners appointed under the act to emancipate the slaves in the District of Columbia. At an early hour a large crowd gathered at the department in and about room number 18 in the second story where W. R. Woodward, clerk to the commissioners, and L. E. Middleton, cashier of the Sub-Treasury, were seated. The routine is this: as the claimants come in and give their names, Woodward looks up the number of the claim, and Middleton gives a check which bears the same number, the claimant signing a receipt on the list of claims, and endorsing the check, and Woodward countersigning with his initials. The check is then taken to General [Francis E.] Spinner, United States Treasurer, where the claimant signs another receipt and the check is signed by that officer. The claimant then can receive his money at the Sub-Treasury. . . . At noon today there were at least 300 persons present awaiting their turn, and it will probably be several days before all can be paid.

CONFEDERACY WICKLIFFE RISES TO A QUESTION OF PRIVILEGE

A few days ago, one Lieutenant Garnett, a paroled rebel, sent in his card to a member of the House . . . and was introduced to some of the Peace Democratic members by [Charles A.] Wickliffe of Kentucky. The rascal wore his secesh butternut garb, and was so noticeable on the floor of the House that he was requested by the doorkeeper to leave, as it was contrary to the rules of the House for him to be present. A correspondent of the Cincinnati *Gazette* . . . [wrote] that Wickliffe acted as the chaperone of the secesh lieutenant. Today, the venerable Confederate rose in his seat and read the spicy item to the great amusement of the House. Wickliffe then explained with great acerbity of manner that the rebel lieutenant was no acquaintance or relation of his and came to borrow money of him which he did not lend him for the reason that he hadn't any. Vallandigham denied that he was in the arrangement at all, except by accident, and so the affair blew over, though

Wickliffe called for the expulsion of the reporter who had so maligned him. The House, however, did not see it in that light, particularly as the statement was true, and the ruffled Confederacy admitted that the rebel officer was familiar enough with him to apply for the loan of cash. [Daniel W.] Voorhees of Indiana, that pure patriot and Union defender, showed the paroled secesh around the Capitol—another instance of the old adage that "birds of a feather flock together."

A RADICAL ON THE RAMPAGE

[Martin F.] Conway of Kansas, a sanguine tempered little radical, made an insane speech in the House today, in which he made a fierce attack upon the administration for its proslavery character, asserting that the President was attempting to build up a *proslavery Republican* paper, and that he had filled the departments and the army with pro-slavery sympathizers with the rebellion. He took the radical, antislavery ground that the war was not prosecuted sufficiently for abolition purposes and that a Union restored with slavery was the worst evil which could possibly happen. When his hour was out, [Owen] Lovejoy [of Illinois] objected to his going on, which stopped his speech with, "And you, too, Brutus!" The whole scene was quite exciting.

Washington, January 28, 1863

A RAID ON THE PRESIDENT

... At the same time that Conway was making his speech, the House bill to indemnify the President and other officers of the government for their responsibility in suspending the privilege of the writ of habeas corpus came up in the Senate, and [Lazarus W.] Powell [of Kentucky], [Garrett] Davis [of Kentucky], and [Willard] Saulsbury [of Delaware] made their usual points against the bill. Davis was as radical as ever, and stated that the President had promulgated three of the most startling edicts that had ever originated from the chief magistrate of any people. The chief of these was the proclamation which took effect on the first of January, 1863, which proposes to emancipate all the slaves of the United States and to aid them in their efforts for freedom. The Constitution gives the right of suspending the privilege of the writ of habeas corpus to the Congress. He stated, also, that the clause in the Constitution itself should be respected at all times, which states that the Constitution of the United States and the laws which shall be made in pursuance thereof shall be the supreme law of the land and that the judges in every state shall be governed by that—anything in the constitution or laws of any state to the contrary notwithstanding. He said the President had frequently violated the principle and thus done great injury to the rights of the people. The Constitution is the arm of American liberty and should be regarded as the lawful rights of the people of every state. Upon this principle, he stated the President had no right to confiscate $1,500,000,000 worth of property, and that the President had given three millions of slaves the privilege of rising to massacre their owners to make their freedom good, and this notwithstanding the President took the oath . . . to preserve, protect, and defend the Constitution of the United States, which makes it his duty to do all things in his power to put down insurrection and domestic violence in all the states.

Saulsbury of Delaware attempted to talk against time to prevent a vote being taken upon the hill, but was so drunk that he could not stand without holding by his desk. It was now past nine o'clock in the evening and still these borderers talked on, interrupted occasionally by some of the administration senators—[James R.] Doolittle of Wisconsin giving a dressing down to the class of rebels represented by the drunken Saulsbury, who obtained the floor and poured out a torrent of the most foul abuse of the President, concluding by saying that Abraham Lincoln was the weakest man ever placed in a high office; that he had conversed with the President and knew him to be an imbecile. Saulsbury was called to order, but he did not notice the order and proceeded to denounce the President in language fit only for a drunken fishwife or dirty drab.

When the Vice President called him to order and said that if he persisted in his conduct he would consign him to the custody of the sergeant-at-arms, the drunken senator, with a chivalric flourish, said, "The voice of freedom is not allowed in the American Senate." He was then ordered into the custody of the sergeant-at-arms, who approached Saulsbury, who drew a revolver and kept it pointed at [the sergeant-at-arms], saying, "D - - n you, Bassett, if you touch me I'll shoot you dead." The excitement in the Senate chamber was great. Some of Saulsbury's friends tried to coax him out, but he refused all counsel but finally left the chamber only to return again, and when he took his seat, [Charles] Sumner called the attention of the presiding officer to the fact that when he called the sergeant-at-arms to take Saulsbury into custody, Saulsbury said that he would like to see the man who could do it. Taking his seat, he swore at Sumner, calling him a thief, a dirty abolitionist, a liar, and indulging in all the "high-toned" vulgarity which is so ready on the tongues of these chivalry representatives. He was finally coaxed away, his pistol taken from him, and the conservative exponent of

modern Democracy was snaked from the Senate chamber
by the sergeant-at-arms and two assistants, affording the
first instance of an American senator being forcibly removed from that place.

This morning [Senator Daniel] Clark of New Hampshire offered a resolution setting forth the fact that Saulsbury had brought into the Senate chamber a loaded pistol
which he had exhibited and had resisted the sergeant-at-
arms of the Senate and that he be, in consequence of that
act, expelled from the Senate of the United States. The
resolution lies over, under the rule, and Saulsbury objected,
saying that he neither avowed or disavowed the conduct
charged to him, but he wanted to know the man who
dared to offer such a resolution. He was drunk again this
morning, being on a regular "tear" evidently.

Washington, January 31, 1863

MILITARY GOSSIP

Once more we have a reorganization of the Army of the
Potomac, and all of the heartburning misunderstandings
connected therewith. General Hooker—"Fighting Joe"—is
in command. . . . And now we have only to wait a short
time for Hooker to be in fighting trim before we shall see
"the fur fly" from somebody. He says he will fight the enemy wherever he finds him, and we all know what that
means and do not look for any very profound strategy to
amuse the enemy withal from the new commander of the
army.

It is unquestionable that the appointment of Hooker
is a much more popular one than that of Burnside, both in
and out of the army, [the soldiers] giving evidence of their

enthusiasm by cheers the whole length of the lines when the news of his appointment was received. For once even the McClellan partisans ... dare not say aught against a general of such known popularity and fighting qualities as Hooker, though unquestionably it will not be long before they will open on the new commander as they did upon Burnside, and it must be acknowledged that there are some habits of Hooker's which may render him open to animadversion, though it is to be hoped that his present responsibilities will teach him sobriety and temperance. The malignant enemies of the government are watching him and will be ready to open their howls and call again for McClellan if they can discover a failing in him.

The resignations of ... Generals Franklin and Sumner have been severely commented on here, but as it is true Hooker made their relief from command a condition of his accepting the position of commander, it is not quite just to blame the generals. Between Franklin and Hooker there is no love lost, the former being, in Hooker's opinion, little better than a traitor and responsible for the loss of the battle of Fredericksburg by failing to bring up his command in mass against the weak place on the enemy's left as he was ordered to do. The popular feeling just now runs as strongly against Franklin as it did against Fitz-John Porter, and Franklin will probably ask for a court of inquiry to determine whether he failed to cooperate at Fredericksburg as Porter did at Centreville and that, too, from the same cause—jealousy at the commander over him.

It is discouraging and saddening to see this spirit of jealousy and insubordination in the army creeping from the ranks up to the generals, but ... it is an indubitable fact, and it is useless to shut our eyes to it. Insubordination is and has been the original evil of the American army, and so long as subordinate generals are allowed to interfere with the plans of the generals in command and allow themselves to hinder the execution of those plans by a tardy and reluctant obedience, so long will the rank and file criticize tactics, military changes, and movements, and leave the ranks when they think that fighting is no longer useful or necessary. . . .

SITTING UP ALL NIGHT WITH KENTUCKY

On Wednesday last the bill of Thad Stevens authorizing the President to raise, arm, and equip Negro regiments came up as a special order in the House. . . . It was predicted the Opposition would filibuster all day and night to prevent the passage of the bill. The previous question on its passage was moved by Stevens, and, as all debate was thus cut off, there was no other recourse for those who opposed it but to impede legislation by the usual system of parliamentary tactics. Accordingly, they organized their forces, and, though the friends of the bill outnumbered them by two to one, they were able by moving an adjournment, calling the ayes and noes, introducing all sorts of resolutions touching adjournment, and calling the ayes and noes on them to prolong the session and stave off all action upon the bill. The friends of the bill were equally determined not to yield, and it was simply a test of physical endurance.

Both parties were very good-natured, and when they occasionally came to a block when absolutely nothing could be done there were all sorts of ridiculous motions and quizzical remarks. . . . There was no drunkenness as there would have been under the old proslavery regime and no special excitement, except once about half-past nine o'clock at night when Vallandigham appealed from the decision of the Chair and was told that the Chair could not receive his appeal under the rules. "But the Chair *will* hear my appeal. We have rights on this floor and will have them," said Vallandigham with great vehemence. The Opposition members had hidden themselves in the cloak-rooms to destroy a quorum and make a call of the House necessary. They came pouring out into the aisles pell-mell, filling up the space in front of the Speaker's desk. Order was finally restored, however, and the Speaker pro tem.— the indomitable Schuyler Colfax—sent the members back to their seats and established his point.

Colfax carried the House through the long and tedious night and was apparently just as fresh and vigorous in the morning as when he commenced. He is certainly a most remarkable man and will make an excellent Speaker should he ever be placed in the chair. For instance, an Opposition member moved that when the House adjourn, it adjourn to March 3. Another moved to amend by making it March 4. The previous question was called upon each motion and amendment and the ayes and noes upon each motion, and the tellers were demanded on each call for ayes and noes, and motions to lay each motion on the table were made, and several members made motions to excuse other members from voting, and demanded the ayes and noes each time, and tellers were demanded upon the ayes and noes. Yet Colfax never faltered once nor had the least difficulty in unraveling the snarl.

And so the night wore on. Members were snoozing on the sofas around the hall. Others were writing letters. Others were visiting their wives and female friends in the galleries which were deserted after midnight, and a few were sauntering up and down the aisles, wishing for a release, for early in the campaign a call of the House was made and the doors were closed and absentees sent for by the sergeant-at-arms. A few who had gone home were lugged

forth in the night air by the officer and were brought up
to the bar of the House and fined, much to their disgust.
All absentees who are not sufficiently excused lose their
per diem when a call of the House is made, so that it was
an expensive piece of business to some of them. About
daylight symptoms of compromise began to appear, and
the hints of an amicable arrangement which had been
scouted down earlier in the night were listened to. Finally,
after much coquetting, it was agreed that if the previous
question were withdrawn and a chance for free debate
given, no more filibustering should be allowed by the Opposition. So the House adjourned at half-past five o'clock
in the morning. This disgraceful scene will not likely be
repeated, as both parties were well tired out and heartily
ashamed of themselves. The House met as usual, however,
on the day following the all night campaign and went on
with the debate.

... The only real argument which the Opposition has
made is that of the objection by white soldiers to associate
with blacks in the ranks and of associating black and white
officers together is really an insuperable obstacle to the
success of the measure. This is proposed to be obviated by
the following amendment offered by Congressman Albert
G. Porter of Indiana:

"But no person of African descent shall be admitted
as a private or officer of any regiment in which white
men are in the ranks, nor shall any person of African
descent, in any case, be placed in command of white
soldiers."

OMNIUM GATHERUM

A beautiful full-length, life-size statue of Washington
has been placed in the rotunda of the Capitol. It was ex-

ecuted by [Hiram] Powers for the state of Louisiana and sent here from Baton Rouge by General [Benjamin F.] Butler when that place was captured. It is said to be the best marble likeness of Washington extant, and it has been fortunately saved from the destruction which would have overtaken it at the burning of the Louisiana capitol.

Washington, February 3, 1863

PASSAGE OF THE NEGRO REGIMENT BILL

After four days debate and one night and day of filibustering, the bill authorizing the formation and organization of Negro regiments passed the House of Representatives. ... The debate on the last day (Monday) was exciting and able. [James F.] Wilson of Iowa made a good speech in favor of the bill, in which he showed that the government had more right to those who had been held to service or labor than anyone else, and that when the life of the nation was in danger it may call into its employment all persons capable of bearing arms and not owing allegiance to any foreign government. He made copious citations from American history to prove that the precedent of arming Negroes had been established long since. He animadverted very severely upon the course of the Opposition and said that if they had expended half of their labors upon the attempt to present an undivided front to the rebels the war would be ended before the Fourth of July. . . .

[William] Allen of Ohio and Chilton A. White of the same state made speeches against the bill, the latter saying, among other things, that the people of Ohio would repudiate the taxes levied for the purchase of slaves as provided by the emancipation acts. The only limitation to this bill, he said, was the color of the soldier. The number could be indefinitely increased. [Henry] May of Maryland, a Baltimore secessionist, made a flaming speech against the bill which, he said, he should oppose because he opposed the war. He was not in favor of raising soldiers of any color for the reason that he thought our army ought to be called home and peace made. This remark was not in keeping with the argument of his more subtle comrades who have all along declared that the arming of the Negroes would end the war by driving home the white soldiers. [Thaddeus] Stevens of Pennsylvania closed up the debate with a characteristic speech full of sarcasm and sharp irony of which he is so complete a master. . . .

. . . Several Republicans voted against the bill. . . . They believed that such a measure as that contemplated in the bill was calculated to divide the Union sentiment of the North and afford new capital to the secession sympathizers in our own section of the republic. This view of the case appears to be a correct one, and though the abstract justice of the measure cannot be doubted and though the free discussion of its merits has been of immense benefit to the cause of freedom, the proposition is inexpedient in the present state of public sentiment, which is largely against the measure. . . . In the army I am well aware that there exists a very strong prejudice against arming the Negroes, and, unless the bill fails in the Senate, as is probable, the dissatisfaction already existing there will be greatly increased. It is all very well to talk of the cowardice of refusing to carry out a measure which is sanctioned by the laws of humanity and self-preservation, but we must deal with facts as we find them, and, as it is morally certain that the public mind is not prepared for a specific and authoritative sanction by Congress of the proposition to arm the

Negroes, it would be just as well to postpone it for the present. . . .

Washington, February 4, 1863

THE POLITICAL SITUATION

. . . I have hinted heretofore at the want of harmony which exists between the Executive and the Republican party, but I have not spoken so plainly as is now necessary; and it may as well be understood first at least that the President does not have the cordial and uniform support of his political friends. It is true that upon all great questions, such as emancipation, confiscation, suspension of the writ of habeas corpus act, and other kindred measures, the administration party, *per se,* is a solid column. But beneath all of this there is an undercurrent of dissatisfaction and an open manifestation of the spirit of captious criticism which is painful and calculated to shake the confidence of every true patriot.

It is a common thing to hear Republicans abuse the President and the cabinet as they would not allow a political opponent to do, and to see Republicans who would vote for sustaining the President in any of his more important acts deliberately squelch out a message from the White House or treat it with undisguised contempt.

The heads of the departments, the Congress, and the President are not in harmony with each other. The common danger is all that appears to force them to act in common unity of purpose. This comes, say the party, of choosing a fourth-rate man for President. When Lincoln took the executive chair it was thought that as he did not know much of statesmanship he would be ready to be managed by those of his own party who did know a great deal. Consequently, many a prominent Republican came to Washington with the idea that he was to have the management of the President. They found their error and were chagrined that Honest Old Abe would have none of their counsel or reproof. There the first breach was made. Next, he thought that the border states must be conciliated and kept in the Union by pleasant promises. The hyena was fed with sugar plums, and it snapped at the hand which caressed it. Buchanan's appointees from states in rebellion were retained in office, and while treason still rioted upon the fat pickings of government patronage it served its base ends better by secret espionage and correspondence than though it were in the rebel army. What wonder that loyal friends of the President who in vain remonstrated against a state of things were embittered against an executive who through a mistaken sense of duty to the country tolerated in office those whom he confidently believed to be Union men but who were sympathizers with rebellion and despisers of himself?

The President found that he must hunt up his own friends. His political associates supported him only as the man who had been placed in power by their success and only for the sake of the country to which they look for future support. The border state conservatives, including the Vallandigham Democracy, looked upon the President's policy of conciliation as an evidence of weakness and treated his concessions not as grateful acts of mercy and condescension but as surrenders to their just demands, and, consequently, deputations of borderers, impudent in their exactions, have visited the White House, presuming upon the conciliatory policy of the President, to secure their growing demands. The "border state policy" has proved a failure, and those states which it was designed to conserve to the Union are, possibly, more dangerous and more difficult to deal with for the reason that they are out of the Union while they profess to be in it. Were the "actual cautery" applied to Kentucky, Tennessee, Maryland, Delaware, and Missouri in the beginning we should not have had the perils with them which have already overtaken us by their sending disguised secessionists to engineer for them in Congress and spy for them in the departments. Between these half-confessed traitors and the loyal Republicans the President has failed to ride easily, and it is no wonder if our honest, patriotic, and singlehearted Chief Magistrate today looks over the heads of mere politicians to find his best friends most distant in the mass of the people who love and revere Abraham Lincoln for his noble and manly qualities of mind and heart.

Just now, however, the people can do the President no good, except in so far as he has an assurance of their sympathy. And as the fate of the Union is soon to be decided by arms, it is some consolation to feel assured that the political parties of the republic must inevitably be reconstructed. In point of fact, the Republican party ceased to exist when the rebellion broke out and war commenced. The necessity for its existence was merged in the greater need for a Union party ... for the principles for which it had contended had been established and the need of their further practice had departed.

The party which has since come into power, triumphing by the misfortunes of its country, has no permanent basis of action, and in the event of a defeat of the federal arms it must fall with the country, or in the event of a success it must fall into line and be an ardent supporter of the war. Already the Democrats see the danger of their position, and since the speeches of Vallandigham and Cox they manifest a disposition to disavow the sentiments of these extremists. Terrified at being the victims of another reaction in favor of war which would be certain to follow great military successes, they deprecate any "dishonorable peace" or "weakening of the federal arm." It is easy to

see how a succession of federal victories would destroy the
prestige and bankrupt the capital of these artful men. . . .
If our next decisive struggles shall place us in a position to
dictate terms of peace, these lamblike disciples of submis-
sion and surrender would sink into a signal and deserved
infamy.

In this light again looms before us the importance of a
victory and success which shall again fill the channels of
public credit, paralyze the rebels in arms, and set the final
seal of silence and infamy upon the demagogues of our
own kith and kin who have achieved success on the reverses of their country.

Washington, February 6, 1863

"RELIABLE" WASHINGTON RUMORS

That you may see how difficult is the task of the unfortunate newsmongers whose business it is to select the
genuine from the flood of bogus news which inundates
this metropolis, I will give you a brief catalogue of the
leading rumors of the morning. . . . First—That General
Butler is to be the Secretary of War, *vice* Stanton, removed
by the President and public opinion. Second—That General Butler is going back to New Orleans *vice* General
Banks, sent to Texas. Third—That General Butler is to be
sent to the new department of the city of Charleston, *vice*
Beauregard, *to be* skedaddled. Fourth—That the President
has said that if he were to name his successor he would
designate General Banks as a man who had cost the country less anxiety and had given it more substantial glory
than any other man with his limited powers and support.
Fifth—That General Butler has said that he will not go
back to New Orleans if Banks is to carry all of the troops

off to Texas. Sixth—That Seward is going to resign. Seventh—That the Republicans are glad of it. Eighth—That if Seward does not resign, the Republicans in the House of Representatives will make him. Ninth—That the leading Republicans of the Northwest are ready to come out and ask the President to resign if Seward does not. These are all "reliable" and have been derived from the usual "authentic" sources, and if the New York papers do not publish all of them it will only be because they do consider them too re-*lie*-able.

THE ARMY OF THE POTOMAC

The condition of the Army of the Potomac is now such as would be encouraging were it not for the wretched weather we have had for the past week, in which we have rain, snow, freezing cold, thawing soft, and now we have had a steady, warm, steamy rain of two days in length. Nothing could be more undesirable and nothing more unfortunate at this juncture. The mud is truly terrific all around here, and at the camps on the Rappahannock it is said to be beyond description. The policy of not going into winter quarters is now evident. We have made haste slowly. The people would not hear of winter quarters. Consequently the army has struggled against the elements as well as against the enemy, and today it is demoralized, degenerated, and degeneraled thereby. But we have avoided winter quarters, expensive as the avoidance has proved, and the people ought to be satisfied.

THE CLIMATE OF WASHINGTON

. . . It is never cold but it is very cold, and never warm but it is very warm, and those two conditions of the weather are alternated upon with surprising rapidity a dozen times in a week. Today it rains warmly, tomorrow it will freeze, and the day after it will thaw, and the young ladies on "the Avenue" will put forth their tender leaves of fashionable attire, and Spring will seem to have come again as the sidewalks flush with sudden bloom. But the next day comes a frost, a killing frost, and the streets are black with ice.

The wretched streets of Washington, a sea of mud by yestreen, are now rough as the rhyme of Alexander Smith, and the falling rain is frozen in the air. Sleek congressmen are corrugated with the cold, and the blue-coated soldiers, pinched with cold, stand wearily and homeless at the street corners, thinking of home and home comforts, poor fellows! which they may never see again. No wonder that with all of these changes and rapid transitions in the weather, Washington is the very paradise and manufactory of coughs, colds, and influenza. In most well regulated and Christian communities only one pocket handkerchief a day is needed, but here four a day is the minimum allowance, and people with moist heads and big noses usually manage to blow up a half dozen, which is good for the clothes-washing contraband. 'Tis an ill wind which *blows* no good.

Washington, February 11, 1863

THE CONSCRIPTION BILL

Senator [Henry] Wilson's bill, more commonly called "The Conscription Bill," causes considerable sensation and fluttering, as it is exceedingly stringent in its provisions and makes but few exemptions. The most remarkable feature of the bill is that it virtually places the whole country under martial law, as it authorizes the appointment of a provost marshal for each congressional district in the United States with deputy marshals under these. The provost marshal and two others, to be appointed by the President, are to be the enrolling and drafting commission, and under their direction such a quota of those enrolled between the ages of 18 and 45 years, not exempt, as may be deemed needful, are liable to be called out by order of the President to serve for three years or during the war.

The bounty to be paid for re-enlistments is too small for any practical value, being only $50, much less than the sums usually paid for substitutes. It would appear to have been a wiser plan to have made provision for accepting from the drafted a fixed sum—say $250—which could be used by the government for the purpose of providing substitutes. This would have obviated the necessity of the substitute agencies which are generally the veriest sharking institutions known and are a curse to the country. Such a provision was originally inserted in the bill but was left out before it was presented to the Senate, as the author of the bill thought it was susceptible of being construed into special legislation in favor of the rich. A shallow objection, certainly.

It is not likely that the draft will be enforced should the bill pass, as it will, until we have enough of victory to make it more popular. In the present condition of affairs in the Northwest, resistance and trouble are certain to follow any attempt to enforce the draft in that region unless a great victory should operate like a thunderstorm to break the "doldrums" of the Northwestern atmosphere.

Washington, February 15, 1863

A VISIT TO THE HOUSE OF REPRESENTATIVES

... The galleries are usually full of silent, attentive lis-
teners, some of them so silent and attentive that they are
possibly asleep, resting very comfortably in the cushioned
seats. Scattered plentifully through the thronged galleries
are the stars and straps and the blue overcoats of Uncle
Samuel's soldiers, many of whom come here because it
is more pleasant than idly lounging out-of-doors in the rain.
The galleries where the ladies sit bloom with the winter
"bonnet trimmings" and other bright-hued gear, and a
few, *very few*, pretty faces appear in the long lines of feminine countenances. The seats of the members rise in
carved oaken arcs of a circle, of which the chord is the
wall behind the Speaker's dais, and the outer segment is
the imaginary line outside of which the Chair will not
recognize a member, and known as the bar of the House.
The members are circulating about the House while various business is going on, and dotted here and there, we
recognize the Dahlgrens, the rifled guns, the Minié rifles,
and the smooth bores (many of the latter) of the
House. . . .

THAD STEVENS

This redoubtable Republican leader is undoubtedly the
foremost man in the House. Whatever he opposes is well-
nigh predestined to die, and whatever he supports is almost

certain to go through. The secret of this lies in his indomitable will, his energy of purpose, and the dominant character of his mind. He is never tender, winning, or conciliatory, but always argumentative, harsh, ironical, grim, and resolute. He sits at the left of the Speaker in the center of the Republican side of the House, and when he rises to make a speech all of the members of that side cluster around to hear, hanging on the desks like boys listening to the instructions of a father, while the Opposition, as if half-ashamed to concede so much, hover on the outside, filling up the area in front of the Speaker's desk, to listen to the irony, the gall, the polished wit, and the rough denunciation of the master of satire. . . .

Stevens is about sixty-five years old, wears a dark brown, wavy-haired wig, is thick-set, has a high and massive forehead and deep set, dull, gray blue eyes almost hidden under his enormous brows. When he rises to speak he locks his hands loosely before him, and never makes a gesture, but calmly, slowly, and ponderously drops his sentences as though each one weighed a ton. His voice is low, and he only moves his head slowly in the direction of the Opposition desks when he makes such points as the classic comparison of Cox and Vallandigham to the co-conspirators of Catiline, who sat in the Roman Senate while brethren in arms were thundering around the gates of the Imperial City. . . . Stevens has a deformed or "club" foot which detracts some from his dignity of appearance when moving about the House, but standing at his seat and calmly thundering his anathemas upon the Copperheads he wears the very front of Jove himself. Nothing can terrify him, and nothing can turn him from his purpose. He is elected to the next congress where he will shine brighter should he be in a minority.

THE LEADER OF THE COPPERHEADS

Clement L. Vallandigham of Ohio is the leading spirit in the mischievous faction of peace Democrats in the House. As I write I look down upon him seated just in front of the reporters' gallery, to the right of the Speaker, and in the center of the Opposition side of the House. The man is a study as he sits quietly there, smoothly smiling and leaning his pleasant, rosy face upon his hand as he softly strokes his face and watching cat-like for a chance to spring. The smaller tactics of demanding previous questions, ayes and noes, and so on, he leaves to the smaller fry, such as [William S.] Holman of Indiana, [Samuel S.] Cox of Ohio, [Charles J.] Biddle of Pennsylvania, and the degenerate Kentuckians. But when the opportune moment arrives, he is on his feet instantly, makes his point, persists in its being considered, and then sits down, watchful, attentive, and smiling as a spring morning, for "a man may smile and smile and be a villain," as Vallandigham is.

He is of medium size, well-formed, about forty years of age, with a small head, regular and small features, nose slightly Romanesque, and dark-haired but growing gray. His complexion is fresh and fair, though a nearer view shows innumerable wrinkles about his eyes and mouth. He dresses with great neatness and care, and as he sits at his desk turning over his *Globe*, smiling ever at the petty discussions of Holman or the small jokes of Cox or the uncouth ascerbity of old Wickliffe, he is altogether a personable man. He is what is popularly called a pretty talker, smooth, plausible, and polished. But when he makes a set speech and becomes excited, the expression of his face is fearfully changed—his mouth becomes wide and

his thin lips are drawn tightly over his teeth, while a vin-
dictive, ghastly grin replaces the pleasant smile which is
his wont. Then the real man speaks out, and as he waves
his arms in the air, fluttering his open hands convulsively
and constantly, his voice rising higher and higher as he
shrieks—"Can you tax any more? Can you draft any more?
Will the people bear it?"—then the devil within breaks
through his fair disguise, and Vallandigham the disorgan-
izer, the mischief-maker, the ally of Jeff Davis and the
devil speaks. His power over his comrades is omnipotent.
A word from him or a wave of the hand will send them all
into the lobbies and cloakrooms when the "filibustering"
tactics are going on or bring them back when they are
called for. He will not return to the next Congress, but
Fernando Wood [of New York] will wear the mantle of
his leadership.

THE ILLINOIS WASHBURNE

The Maine family of Washburnes have made themselves famous in public life for years past, but only one of
them, Elihu B. Washburne of Illinois, is a member of the
present House of Representatives. He is called one of the
best working men now in Congress. Something like Stevens
in harshness, he has a dominant, leading mind and can
lead men sometimes where Stevens cannot drive them.
He is in the prime of life, is stout built, gray, and unpol-
ished in appearance. His forte is not in speech making,
and nothing but a desperate case, like that of the Illinois
Ship Canal bill, can drive him into a speech. And on that
memorable occasion he failed ignominiously; and it was an
instructive spectacle to younger members to see one of
the more influential men in the House damage his own

cause by his own ineffectual fight and by his display of bad temper. Provoked by his own slowness of speech and unreadiness, he revenged himself for his defeat on the bill by making a singlehanded and factious opposition to every measure, even the most trivial, which came up thereafter, and he moved an adjournment right in the midst of the session as a mark of his querulous displeasure. But for all that, E. B. Washburne is a sound man, a good legislator, and an honest patriot, having his failing, like most of us "poor critters."

THE ORATOR OF THE COPPERHEADS

... Daniel W. Voorhees of Indiana [is] one of the more able debaters and naturally eloquent men in Congress. He is tall, well-made, trim and spruce in appearance, more of a fastidious dry goods clerk than the able lawyer which he is. He has a high head, low, wide forehead, long hair which we will charitably call auburn—not red. The lower part of his face is covered with a full smooth mass of hair which conceals all expression. He is a polished speaker, a good parliamentarian, and the most subtle logician in the House. He dresses in olive green cloth, lounges outside of the bar a great deal, and does not often make much of an appearance in the House. When he does speak, however, he is sure to command attention, and has a way of assuming things which is perfectly astonishing to the candid mind, as he states his premises and draws his rapid conclusions therefrom before one has fairly had time to see how utterly false and baseless are his forcibly put assumptions. If he possesses one great desideratum of a successful politician it is impudence which in him is almost sublime at times.

SCHUYLER COLFAX

The favorite of the House is Colfax of Indiana. He is young, almost boyish-looking, under medium size, versatile, indefatigably industrious, quick as lightning, and the readiest and most rapid debater in the Republican ranks. He is light-haired, blue-eyed, has a light complexion, has a wide mouth which is almost always laughing, thereby showing a very poor display of teeth, and is quick in all his motions almost to nervousness. He is good-humored, lively, and full of his jokes and pleasantries in private, though in debate he is straightforward and plain, never jesting except in repartee when interrupted and then he is always readier than the readiest. Colfax is said to be the best parliamentarian in the House and is "smart as lightning." He is more agreeable and affable than [Galusha] Grow, the present Speaker, but equally decided and clear. He is likely to be a prominent candidate for the next Speakership, for which he has the best wishes of all the reporters, for he has served his apprenticeship in the newspaper business and is "of us."

He is the most rapid talker in Congress, being faultily fast in his utterance. Such a thing as a falter in a speech or debate by Schuyler Colfax was never known, and the stenographers say that he puts more words into an hour than any man in Congress. He is a working legislator, great on engineering, and seldom makes a set speech but is sharp and formidable in debate. Schuyler Colfax will "do to tie to" in these squally times when the eccentricities of Stevens and Washburne may lead to an uncertain and doubtful goal, for Colfax is an earnest and thoughtful man and is sincere and open as the day in all he says and does. His devotion to the Union and to the government shines

out in all that he performs or says, and no man is more
unostentatious or free from attempt at parade of principle
than this same noble Indianan. He is dreaded by the Opposition. They fear his cutting, convincing logic, while they
are yet often cajoled by his good-natured persuasive-
ness....

TWO OHIO REPRESENTATIVES

The Buckeye State sends several representative men to
this Congress, among whom [Samuel S.] Cox on the Democratic side and [John A.] Bingham on the Republican
side are prominent. Cox is a little, dark-skinned, black-
haired, bewhiskered man with a bulging forehead, keen,
dark eyes, and a thin and somewhat querulous voice. He
is, *par excellence*, the wit of the Opposition side of the
House, and he never fails to raise a laugh among his own
retainers when he ventures on a joke. His farcical account
of the retreat from Bull Run of his colleague, the Reverend
Phineas D. Gurley, holding on the bull's tail, his epitaph
on [Owen] Lovejoy, and other witticisms, have given him
a cheap reputation for wit which he keeps by virtue of
gibes and jokes innumerable. He is not equal to Vallandigham in anything but desire to do mischief, and he is perpetually bobbing up to a point of order or calling for some
foolish thing or other, so that it is a relief to see him take
hold sensibly and manfully of any proposition whatever.

Bingham is the reverse of Cox in most respects. He
says some sharp and fierce things often but never jokes.
He is a nervous, spare, pale man with long thin, light hair,
blue and sharp eyes, a wrinkled half-scowl on his forehead
always, as he turns his head to one side inquiringly of the
Opposition when he makes a point. He is the most useful
man in the House in debate, for he can take up a set

speech and offhand answer it, point by point, from the rough memoranda which he nervously scratches down as he hears the speech he has resolved to demolish. He is at his best when he is interrupted and contradicted. Then he rises in his might and, seizing the very argument cast against him, turns it into a weapon of offense against his opponents. Again and again does he overwhelm them with his plain, practical logic and convincing argument in which common sense is more than the warp and woof than is common in political debate. He is justly feared by the Opposition who let him alone usually, for he never engaged in a fight out of which he did not come victorious, and that, too, without resorting to any of the shallow arts or special pleading of demagogues and pettifoggers. It is a pity that he has been gerrymandered out of an election to the next congress.

A RADICAL REPUBLICAN AND A REBEL REPRESENTATIVE

I take a secret pleasure in placing side by side the portraits of Owen Lovejoy of Illinois and [Charles A.] Wickliffe of Kentucky. Two sharper antagonisms probably never met in Congress than these two men—one with his sympathy with rebellion and hatred of the Union but half-concealed and the other outspoken in his hatred of slavery, its wrongs, its vices, its fundamental crime, its defenders and apologists everywhere, and all alive with jealousy for the Union and fervid in his appeals for an unbroken unity of purpose for its restoration. They are cordial haters of each other, too, and never allow an opportunity to pass when a good hit can be made by one upon the other.

Wickliffe is crippled with a chronic rheumatism and goes hobbling about with a crutch and cane, his natural ascerbity of temper doubtless exasperated by his infirmi-

ties of body. He is over sixty years of age, white-haired,
and large-framed. He sits in his desk, scowling at the rest
during the greater portion of the time, but, like his ampli-
fied shirt bosom, he is always ruffled, and is perpetually
rising painfully to a point of order, a personal explanation,
or a privileged question. When he bawls out, "Mr.
Speaker!" and pauses with a grim scowl of servile rage at
not being at once recognized, everyone knows that he has
a personal grief to be redressed. The newspapers have
called him a secessionist, or the *Globe* has failed to report
him correctly, or somebody has misquoted him, and so he
goes on with his "thar" and "whar" and "pint of order,"
until he is called to order. Then he subsides in a rage,
growling his complaints so that he can be heard all over
the House. The aspect of the impotent rage and querulous egotism of the hoary old traitor is disgusting indeed,
and his own Democratic allies will probably be well satisfied if he is never sent back to Congress. His coarse impudence is complete. Yesterday he strove to introduce a bill
in Committee of the Whole which had been ruled out of
order by the chairman who had presided the day before.
When he presented his resolution he was reminded by
the member in the chair that he had been decided against
by another chairman. "I know that," snarled the old Confederacy, "so I thought that I would try *you* to see if you
knew anything."

Lovejoy is a large, powerfully built man, erect, handsome, with a dark face, curly gray hair, and blue eyes. He
speaks with his hands in his pockets, pressing forward
against his desk, and has a queer way of turning his tongue
in his mouth at the end of a sentence as though he were
licking his chops. He is full of humor and runs over with
as many Scripture quotations as ever had "Scripture Dick"
of elder days. He is apt at repartee, and when he becomes

warmed up in a speech he is fervent, impassioned, and even eloquent. He has a great deal of faith in "the great American heart," the love of man for man, a universal brotherhood of nations and of humanity, all of which are postponed to a millennial season by less sanguine politicians. Lovejoy has toned down of late and is really radical only in past reputation. Some of the old-time Democratic conservatives are far ahead of him in antislavery and pro-liberal sentiments, so he delights to twit them for their excessive radicalism.

THE TWO SPEAKERS

Galusha A. Grow of Pennsylvania is the presiding officer of the House, and is a tall, slightly built man with a bilious temperament and a somewhat querulous voice and manner. His health is imperfect, and he has not always had that command of temper which was the great charm of the matchless [Nathanial P.] Banks when in the chair, but sings out for order with more petulance than dignity. Grow is not a favorite with the members, but he is a good parliamentarian and useful in his place. He is dressed with scrupulous neatness, and his gray and black locks are always arranged with a tonsorial skill suggestive of the barber's shop.

When [James L.] Orr of South Carolina was Speaker of the House, he discovered in one of the pages, a German boy, extraordinary parliamentary knowledge combined with a great memory and faculty for remembering names and faces. When the boy once heard a ruling made he never forgot it, and the face and name of a member being once before him was never out of his memory. Such an aid to a new Speaker was invaluable, and young [Thaddeus] Morris was constituted the special page of the Speaker to stand by his desk, prompt him when at fault, and give him the name and state of each member who rose and addressed the chair. Morris has kept his position through all of the mutations of administrations, and now, grown to be a tall, slim, quiet, young man, he leans on one corner of the marble stand of Speaker Grow, watchfully regarding the running debate, keeping track of the maze of business, and noiselessly unraveling for the bewildered Speaker the labyrinth of parliamentary chaos just as he did in the reign of the recreant Orr. Does a knotty point arise, Morris has the ruling of some Speaker in the time of the elder Adams, it may be, to fortify the decision which he has whispered to the Speaker. While the clerk is reading that decision he has hunted up four or five others, all of which the Speaker causes to be read as the foundation of his ruling, and, gathering his argument as he proceeds, he states his point dogmatically and silences the appellant who is no match for the two Speakers.

This friendless boy, now a young man, is one of the features of Congress, and is the compass which enables the tempest-tossed presiding officer to steer clear of the eddying currents which might otherwise wreck him. But probably no casual visitor ever notices him or ever supposes that the slim young Teuton who leans at the desk watching the members with his pale eyes or glides around among the clerks in front of the Speaker with his face toward that officer is anything but an errand boy or a lounging page who ought to be set to work at something to stop his lounging on the marble steps of the Speaker's dais....

A REPRESENTATIVE MOB

... There is [Wisconsin's] John F. Potter of bowie-knife-and-pistol duel notoriety—thickset, youthful, but gray.

He speaks seldom but is an invaluable committee man. There is John Hickman [of Pennsylvania], a fluent speaker, and bold, tall, spare and jaundiced—with gray hair and whiskers; [Henry L.] Dawes of Massachusetts, famous for pecking at governmental abuses and no friend of the executive—youthful, hirshute, and pimple-faced, with a moderate, slow delivery and a good debater. [Benjamin F.] Thomas, his colleague, is sanguine, fiery, ardent, red-haired, stout, and vehement; [William S.] Holman of Indiana—tall, shapely, dark-haired, quarrelsome, officious, pettifogging, and a demagogue; [Justin S.] Morrill of Vermont—tall, elegant, affected in speech, frequently engaged in debate, and a good financier; [William H.] Wadsworth of Kentucky—small, with long, wavy, gray-streaked hair falling over the right temple in the true chivalry style, always in his seat, quick but not vigorous, and very secesh; Roscoe Conkling of New York—a handsome, showy man, frequent in debate but not especially useful as a legislator, though his dogmatic utterance and self-poised bearing impresses the casual visitor with a sense of an importance which does not belong to him. . . .

Washington, February 24, 1863

SLEIGHING THE DEARS

This city has just been visited by one of the biggest snowstorms it has known for many a long year. It commenced on Saturday, February 21, and snowed all night. It snowed all day Sunday, likewise Sunday night, and by Monday morning the ground was well covered with dry, powdery snow through which the early milk wagons and butcher carts labored painfully, their wheels miring down to the substratum. . . . The horsecars were obliged to go into temporary suspension. Mails, like other males, were very irregular. The roofs were covered with the piled up harvest of snow, and the premature spring grass in front of the Interior building became invisible green beneath the sudden fall. The air was keen and cold, bright and clear on Monday morning, and straightway everything in the shape of sleigh, sled, cutter, or pung was pressed into service, and [Pennsylvania] Avenue was alive with a motley panorama of vehicular contrivances laden with rosy, gay, and laughing people, "the tintinabulation of the bells, silvery bells" making joyous music in the air which was tinting the cheeks of other belles whose bright eyes slayed as they were being sleighed along the gay avenue.

I believe that it has been said that cold weather is favorable to the warmer affections, which flourish best in a winter's sleigh ride, when "Cupid comes up as Mercury goes down." Your correspondent cannot affirm that, but he has jolly recollections of a Washington sleigh ride on February 23 when we celebrated, after our poor fashion, the birthday of Washington (the day after, to be sure) by being as gay as could be expected under the circumstances, for it must be confessed that such street sleighing as we had is not just the best that the world ever saw. But if we did get stuck in the mud it was only one of the funnier features of the ride, for the girls, of course, must yell as the sleigh careened in the yielding mass, and the man does not live who is insensible to the comicality of a wild yell of a female who mixes a very little affectation of fright in a very wholesome terror of being upset. . . .

But hard upon these scenes of gaiety comes the sorrowful reflection that there are this day thousands of our noble soldiery in camp upon the banks of the Rappahannock [who are] deprived, in the midst of this unusual storm of snow, of the comforts of life. In the drifts they stand or lie, almost shelterless, being protected from the raging of the storm only by a low canvas kennel known as a shelter tent. Firewood is very scarce along the Rappahannock, and though many have made themselves huts and barracks there are many more who are frostbitten by exposure.... We cannot forget these men, fighting for their country and suffering her hardships. Let us hope that the time will soon come when they may be restored to their homes, to comfort, and to peace.

Washington, February 28, 1863

A MUDDY CITY

At this writing the city of Washington, the capital of the nation, is probably the dirtiest and most ill-kept borough in the United States. It is impossible to describe the truly fearful condition of the streets. They are seas or canals of liquid mud, varying in depth from one to three feet, and possessing as geographical features conglomerations of garbage, refuse, and trash, the odors whereof rival those of the city of Cologne which Coleridge declared to be "seventy separate and distinct stinks." At some points where a street has a sloping intersection with another I have seen a torrent of thick, yellow mud flowing in unruffled smoothness over the concealed crossing, bearing on its placid surface the unconsidered trifles which have been swept out of saloons, shops, and houses.

Through such masses as this labor the unfortunate animals which are condemned to drudge their miserable life in such a wretched vocation as fall to the lot of a government contract horse. Numbers of these unfortunate animals, near death, are turned out at large to wander in the bone through the scenes they knew in the flesh until they drop their frames in some soft spot and are carried off by the city carrion cart—a peculiar vehicle which has an apparatus for hoisting the carcasses into its embrace, the stiff legs of the departed equines shaking helplessly in the air as they are hauled off. Everybody has heard of the great corruption of the city of Washington, but I will venture to say that its moral corruption is far exceeded by the physical rottenness of its streets.

Washington, March 2, 1863

BRIGHTER SKIES

The enemies of the government in Congress have been defeated again and again, and have confessed themselves vanquished by the superiority which honest patriotism always has over tricky disloyalty. Nobody questions the effect of the policy of these factionists in and out of Congress, and we must rejoice to be able to say that aid and comfort to the rebellion is greatly stopped by the defeat of the measures of such men as Vallandigham, Cox, and the Woods. It is no longer a question as to the extent of the reaction against these men. It is widespread and is growing. As the knell of slavery was rung by secession, so the fatal sentence of death to the disloyalists of the North has been hastened by the action of their leaders in Congress. The people now see that the real motive of these so-called Democrats is not an honorable one, but one of the basest and most selfish character; and the record which the Copperheads have made in this closing Congress is sufficient to damn them to everlasting fame. They go back to the people with their names recorded upon votes they cannot justify, and to that record the people are holding them.

One of the more encouraging signs of the times, so far as congressional policy is concerned, is found in the triumphant passage of the Conscript bill which went through the House by the largest vote on any measure passed at this session. There was a great deal of wordy talk when it came up in the Senate for concurrence in the House amendments, but when it came to a vote the frightened Opposition broke and skedaddled. . . .

The Conscript bill, so-called, affects a great variety of interests and of individuals, but it is uncertain how they will meet its obligations, but it is most likely that opposition will pass away as the magnitude of the exigency is pressed upon the people. The fierce onslaught upon the bill in Congress has had the effect to inflame the prejudices and passions of the disloyal, and we must expect a furious opposition on the part of the state rights men when the bill goes before the people. But the moral tone of the people is better than ever before, and it really would seem that they are fully alive to a sense of the awful duty and responsibility demanded of their self-sacrificing patriotism.

Another promising indication of future prosperity is the final adjustment of the differences between the two houses upon the financial question which was narrowed down to a proposition to tax the banks. The Senate was disposed to levy a tax which would almost amount to coercing the banks into the new banking policy of the nation, but the House demurred. The crusade against [Secretary of the Treasury] Chase and his policy has been unrelenting and persistent, and the bank men in the House, headed by such men as Roscoe Conkling of New York, have been swift to avail themselves of all possible measures to scare the timid into opposition to any measure calculated to bear with any degree of weight upon the great banking interests of the country. But the Secretary has measurably triumphed, and after two weeks of painful incertitude, the House has agreed to the report of the third conference committee appointed since the disagreement began.

The bill has finally passed, and that section which was chiefly in dispute is the conclusion of the financial measures before the present Congress. The small banks having a capital from one to three hundred thousand dollars are taxed one percent semi-annually or from ten to thirty percent of their circulation, the remainder being left free. The larger institutions having a capital varying from a half million to two million are taxed upon twenty-five to sixty percent of their circulation, the remainder being free. Though this is not all that was desired, it is measurably a success and will probably bring about the looked for result to retire a great portion of the corporate banking circulation of the country and replace it with governmental currency.

Secretary Chase has departed from his usual custom in his anxiety for the fate of the financial measures of which this is the key and has come down to the Capitol very often during the sessions of the conference committees and while the matter was before the House. In his belief, and that of such men as Robert J. Walker, the financial prosperity of the country was bound up in the life of this new system of finance, and it is a matter of congratulation that it has triumphed over moneyed monopolists, timid time-savers, and anti-war politicians.

A CAPITOL WEDDING

There was an unusual spectacle in the House of Representatives yesterday (Sunday), the occasion being the marriage of a Miss Rumsey and Fowle, two members of the choir which has led the singing in the House during the Sunday services of the session. Miss Rumsey and Fowle have had charge of the Soldiers' Free Library, an excellent institution of considerable extent and usefulness. The hall was crowded to overflowing, the galleries, which ordinarily seat about 1,200, being packed and jammed full. The Reverend Dr. [Thomas H.] Stockton, the venerable Chaplain of the House of Representatives, preached his farewell sermon and indulged in some personal reminiscences which were very interesting, as he was Chaplain during the administrations of Jackson and Van Buren in the days when nullification first showed itself in Congress.

The hall presented a novel sight to one who has never seen any other exercises therein but those of the congressional "bear garden." The desks were chiefly occupied by ladies. I noticed a worthy old lady in the chair of the venerable Wickliffe, reminding me that it was as well for an old lady to occupy the seat on Sunday as on a weekday. The prevailing hues were red and black, which appear to be the only wear just now, the russet of the oaken desks being interstreaked between. "And what do you think the bride was dressed in?" asked an old song. . . . She was small and graceful and wore a neutral tinted dress of some woolen stuff and a bonnet of the same hue. Upon her bosom she wore a huge knot of stars and stripes—showing that she was for the Union—and when she threw off her cloak to stand up, I noticed that she had a red, white, and blue jacket underneath. They were married in the Episcopal form; and when the audience was streaming out after the ceremony, some well-meaning but inconsiderate friend asked the bride to sing the "Star Spangled Banner." She is a notable singer and complied, but it was rather funny under the circumstances, and, I may add, in very poor taste for the bride of the Capitol.

Washington, March 5, 1863

THE LAST DAYS OF THE THIRTY-SEVENTH CONGRESS

The three months of the third and last session of the memorable Thirty-Seventh Congress have passed away rapidly.... For better or for worse—for weal or for woe— with all its train of momentous consequences yet to follow it, the Thirty-Seventh Congress is no more, and its record is now made.

During the last days of the session there was great solicitude felt that some of the important bills necessary to the support of the government might not pass, as there seemed to be some doubt in the minds of many. But unexpectedly and fortunately, most of the difficulties were removed, and by the night of March 3 it was apparent that there would be no failure of necessary bills, and that the need for an extra session would not be left behind a departing Congress. The insidious enemies of the government in the House were all alive with their burning desire to defeat every vital measure, and they fell into filibustering as readily as though it were the most legitimate and honorable system of parliamentary tactics. This reprehensible habit of preventing the action of a majority in the House by dilatory motions has always been resorted to in extreme cases when the importance of an exigency seemed to demand it. But never until the last Congress did a minority so habitually and constantly use these doubtful tactics to delay legislation and to coerce a majority into the abandonment of any measure to which they happened to take a dislike. Whatever record may have been made by the Congress as a whole, the Copperhead representatives have gained the deserved reputation of being the first who have willfully wasted time to gain a temporary triumph.

On the night of March 2 the crowd at the Capitol was immense—everybody being anxious to see the last hours of the Congress, and many hoping, doubtless, that they might see a "right smart" bit of a free fight on the floors of either house as in the ardent days when chivalry and whisky reigned together. But there was no special excitement further than that of the members who were anxious over the fate of their pet measures.

The vast hall of the House of Representatives was flooded with the light which rained down from the stained glass ceiling where the coats-of-arms of the Carolinas and Louisiana were in gleaming companionship with the state insignia of Vermont, Massachusetts, and California. The galleries flowed out into the brilliantly lighted passages with the crowds of people who watched with interest even the most unimportant business of the members below. Pages darted to and fro. The Secretary of the Senate, Colonel J[ohn] W. Forney, handsome and business-like, came in ever and anon with an armful of bills, and every member was on the watch for his bill or bills and looking sharply for a chance to kill something against which he owed a grudge. The rules were suspended and a growing file of bills upon the Speaker's table, which had been passed upon by the Senate, were commenced upon, read (sometimes *in extenso* and sometimes only by title), a few sharp words said, then the previous question was called, put, and away went the bill either to life or death, even while the slender secondhand of the clock had scarcely marked a minute....

Occasionally a bill not desirable to the Copperhead interest came up and was quietly laid aside by its friends until a more convenient season; and once in a while some

bill which had passed the ordeal of the Senate would meet
with a slight ruffle of opposition—perhaps some member
would only "rise for information," but the little breeze
was the inevitable premonition of the swift gale of noes
which sent the measure lower than the Thirty-Seventh
Congress could ever reach again. A reference to committee or laying on the table was sufficient.... In this way
was killed the bill ... which authorized the sale of the
Mendocino Reservation in California and the extension of
the Round Valley Reserve. [Timothy G.] Phelps [of Cali-
fornia] had the bill in charge, and [Abram B.] Olin of New
York, one of the impracticables of the House who is always
finding some "mare's nest," thought that he detected a
scheme to rob Indians of their rights covered up in the
proposition, so he demanded an explanation of this "extraordinary measure" which contemplated the removal of
the Indians of Nome Lackee and Mendocino to Round
Valley. He wanted an explanation and Phelps gave it to
him, but unfortunately he alluded to the fact that it was
possible that minerals might possibly be discovered some
day on the new reservation. That was enough. The members smelt "mineral lands," and there was a perceptible
snicker all around, and the bill was killed. [Aaron A.] Sar-
gent [of California] came to the rescue, but in vain. Without calling the ayes and noes, the unfortunate measure
was unceremoniously bundled out of sight, despite the
protest of the entire delegation from California.... I mention this only as a sample of the style in which things are
done when it is necessary to put bills through upon the
high pressure, double back action plan of legislation.

At twelve o'clock the House adjourned for the night,
leaving the Senators talking against time on the bill to
indemnify the President and others for the suspension of
the privileges of the Habeas Corpus Act. The bill had come

back to the Senate with House amendments. They hung to it all night and never came to a vote until five o'clock the following morning (March 3) when, by an ingenious dodge on the part of the Unionists, the vote was called and the bill passed.

There was introduced in the House on Tuesday a bill to reorganize the courts of the District of Columbia, which, in effect, legislates out of office three judges, one of whom is incompetent from age and infirmity, and another is semi-disloyal, being, by the by, a son-in-law of old Wickliffe of Kentucky. Whenever it was called up, the Copperheads commenced to filibuster, being determined that it *should not* pass. It so happened that one appropriation bill known as the Miscellaneous and containing a clause giving the mileage for the extra session to members of the House was yet behind. Accordingly, when the rebels had filibustered for three precious hours of this last day of Congress they begged that the court bill be temporarily laid aside. "No," said the solemn and sardonic Stevens, "never, never; I cannot afford to have this bill placed out of order, and we cannot afford to lose the Miscellaneous Appropriation bill." You see where he had them. The court bill passed and so did the Miscellaneous Appropriation bill, for the members love mileage better than they love old Wickliffe's daughter. He gets his mileage, but his son-in-law, Judge [William M.] Merrick, loses his fat office. There *is* a law of compensation somewhere. After this sudden wilting the rebels behaved so well that they were surprised at themselves.

The last night of the session drew slowly on, and the rules were again suspended for the final passage of such Senate bills as were on the Speaker's table. Unfortunately, the bill to enable the Territory of Nevada to assume the dignity of name of a state did not come in from the

Senate until a short time after the rules were so suspended. It did not therefore fall into the category of privileged bills and was lost for this session. Idaho was fortunate, for the Senate amendments to the bill to create a territory of that name—changing the title from Montana to Idaho— were reached and triumphantly passed the House.

As the night wore away the excitement grew apace, though there was nothing special on the floor to warrant it. But there was an electric snap and rush to the business which instinctively drew down the sympathetic interest of the vast crowd which filled the galleries tier above tier and crowded the open doorways of the entrances thereto. The reporters were crowded into their comfortable quarters by the eager outsiders. The lobbies and outer portion of the House floor were filled with state dignitaries and persistent lobbyists. The snowy head and beard of Grandfather Welles of the Navy was conspicuous among the privileged on the floor. There, too, was the extremely ugly, baboonish form and face of F[rank] P. Blair, Senior, and the awkward, homespun Montgomery Blair of the Post Office department. Secretary Chase, comfortable-looking and well-dressed, was vibrating between the Senate and House, having been very attentive upon the sessions for the past few nights and days. He ought to feel comfortable, for the last appropriation bill has passed, and nearly every financial measure which he has asked for has become a law.

It is midnight and yet the crowd hangs on, determined to see the thing out, and their desire to see some of the usual exhibitions of temper and spirit is rewarded when the Missouri Emancipation bill comes up among the last things. The ayes and noes are called upon a motion to suspend the rules that the House may go into Committee of the Whole for the consideration of the bill, and the necessary two-thirds vote was not obtained. Many friends of emancipation consider the bill not in fit shape to pass. While the clerk is reading the list of names of those who voted, [James] Kerrigan of New York, a "rough" who was broken of his colonelcy for corresponding with the enemy and erewhile a Fort Lafayette prisoner, bounced into the area in front of the Speaker's desk, shaking his fist and bawling that he will not vote for buying Missouri Negroes while women and children are perishing for bread in the streets of New York. The Speaker pro tem., Schuyler Colfax, the indomitable, raps loudly and demands that the sergeant-at-arms take him into custody. That functionary soothes the irate scion of Bowery chivalry and gets him into his seat again, but he soon springs out again, and, full of rage and whisky, bawls, "Go to the army and ask them—." The rest is drowned in the raps of the Speaker's gavel and the cries of "Order" from all parts of the House. Vallandigham, white with anger, menaces the little Kerrigan who, cowed before the master spirit, slinks into his seat again. [Thaddeus] Stevens moved a vote of censure, but upon the appeal of [John W.] Crisfield of Maryland, who humbly apologized for his neighbor, he withdrew his motion. Voorhees and Vallandigham had been dining out and came in late, the latter being resplendent in good clothes and brilliant with champagne. He went swinging about the aisles, damning the abolitionists, and gave his vote with the addendum that he had always been opposed to the slave trade and would not vote that the United States should go into it at this late day for Missouri's sake. Save these escapades, there were no special rufflings of the swift current which ran with the night.

In the Senate the sight was more brilliant, for the galleries are seen to better advantage of an evening and were largely filled with ladies in full dress. The business is also rapid here but less disorderly. Senator [Solomon] Foot is in the chair, and the bill to admit Nevada as a state is under discussion. Garrett Davis of Kentucky, a small, thin man with a wiry voice and a manner of sawing the air in gesture, is speaking against it. Big Preston King [of New York] is dozing in his chair, and [Henry M.] Rice of Minnesota is slightly oblivious. [James A.] McDougall of California has been sick for days past and is not present. [Milton S.] Latham of California is in his seat, and most of the other Senators are in their places, not knowing what may come up.

Secretary Seward, dapper and white-haired, is chatting cosily on a sofa with [Lazarus W.] Powell of Kentucky and [former Senator] Tom Ewing [of Ohio], dwarfed between these mountainous men into a very small Premier as he sits carelessly upon the small of his back, his blue stockings and low cut shoes showing conspicuously as he crosses his thin legs on a level with his chin. He has nothing to reproach the Senate with, except that a majority would be glad to confirm a new Secretary of State tomorrow. The first and second assistants of the Postmaster General, Randall and McClellan, are on another sofa, holding converse with Major General T[homas] L. Crittenden, who is a casual visitor here. The President is in his private room in the rear of the Senate chamber, where he has been all night, signing bills as they are sent to him from the House or Senate. [John G.] Nicolay and [John] Hay, his private secretaries, are kept busy running to each chamber with the rolls of parchment acts of Congress which the signature of Abraham Lincoln has made law and announcing to the houses that such bills have been so signed. . . .

THE LAST HOURS

About four o'clock in the morning (March 4) the House took a recess until ten o'clock A.M., the Senate having done the same a few hours before. At the appointed hour there were but few of the members present, but the galleries were crowded to suffocation. The report of a conference committee upon certain disagreements between the House and Senate upon an appropriation bill was agreed to, and then sprang up a lively and somewhat acrimonious debate among [Elihu B.] Washburne of Illinois, [Henry L.] Dawes of Massachusetts, and [Charles H.] Van Wyck of New York upon a minority report made by the latter upon the investigations of a committee to which they had severally belonged, and which report was upon the result of an examination into the New York custom house frauds. Van Wyck made a severe report, while the majority were disposed to whitewash and asked that his report should not be printed. The matter occupied an hour, but Van Wyck was triumphant and his report will be given to the world.

This over, an immense shower of "little local bills" poured in, each member being half convulsed with his own anxiety to get his bill or resolution passed at this late hour; and at half-past eleven the noise and confusion were great in the hall, in the midst of which the President's secretary appeared at the bar of the House with lots of bills, the hard-working President being still hard at work in his private room. At ten minutes to twelve noon the last batch came in, and the President returned word by the House committee that he had no further communications to make to the body. Gradually the confusion subsided. The hands pointed toward twelve o'clock when Speaker Grow arose in his place and spoke his farewell. . . .

The Speaker's hammer fell, and the session was ended. Handshaking and farewells were the only subsequent business of the day. The crowd stayed lingeringly about the littered hall of the House, but it was soon vacated, and the few left behind were packing up their small movables for a flight homeward. . . .

Washington, March 6, 1863

ON THE WING

The adjournment of Congress has been followed, as might be expected, by a sudden flitting of congressmen and the vast army of attachés, lobbyists, and hangers-on who have attended patiently upon the final obsequies of the defunct Congress. A week or two ago, there were no accommodations in town for either man, beast, or member of Congress. Now none are so sad as the deserted boarding-housekeepers—none so hard up to do them reverence. Willard's is like a banquet hall deserted, and the groaning railroad trains daily carry off loads of people who have passed their winter here and are now, like the trees in Capitol park, leaving for the summer. Everybody is on the wing, and the glorious weather of the past few days lends a new sense of enjoyment to the relieved people who are delivered from the pressure and exciting suspense of congressional doings....

If financial relief is anything to be prayed for, we have an auspicious opening of a new season which has been signalized by the tumbling of the price of gold immediately upon the conclusion of the financial measures in Congress. Money interest and government interest are one and the same, and public confidence is again restored. As our congressmen go home to their constituency they carry with them the assurance that the national credit and the public good are one, and henceforth there will be in the department of the national treasury a mighty power which shall check all selfish speculations upon the needs of the government and will sustain the financial credit of the United

States against all assault with a firm and unshaken hand. Never since this tremendous struggle began has there been so healthy and promising a condition of the financial affairs of the government, and the Secretary of the Treasury has a power given him by Congress which will enable him to bring the nation safely through all of its financial difficulties.

Washington, March 12, 1863

IN THE SUPREME COURT OF THE UNITED STATES

On March 10 ... there was quite a rush to the Supreme Court to hear the delivery of the decisions of the court in several cases of importance which have been lately argued before the court by distinguished counsel. The fact that the court closed its present term that day probably had the effect, also, to increase the interest felt by the spectators present, most of whom knew from the newspapers that the great New Almaden case [Castillero v. the U.S.], involving the right of title to a California quicksilver mine of incalculable value, would be decided by the court before adjournment.

The Supreme Court commences its daily session at eleven o'clock A.M., and it opened with considerable show, pomp, and solemnity. Precisely at the hour appointed, a venerable colored gentleman opens a door on the corridor leading to the Senate chamber, and the procession of ponderous and silk gowned judges emerges therefrom, crosses the corridor, enters a pair of red baize doors held open by a pair of reverential darkies whose dignity and age comport with the awful majesty of the Supreme Law which they bow in, and shortly the respectful stillness of the courtroom is disturbed by the rustling of the robes of office of the judges who enter a side door behind the bar of the court, take their places at their desks, and while they are still standing the Chief Justice gives a very polite bow to the right and another to the left, meant for the assembled bar, who rise upon the entrance of the procession. Then the officer of the court in a sepulchral tone of voice meant to be solemn delivers himself of the announcement that the Supreme Court of the United States is now open for the consideration of such business as may come before it. This being happily achieved, the bigwigs seat themselves in their comfortable armchairs, and the lawyers and other common people follow their illustrious example.

The courtroom is what was formerly the Senate chamber before the enlargement of the Capitol, and it is admirably adapted for the uses to which it is now put. The chamber is semicircular, the bench occupying the chord of the same and separated from the bar by a massive mahogany balustrade. Behind the bench is a colonnade of beautiful Tuscan architecture of Potomac and Carrara marble supporting what was the gallery of the Senate in ancient days. Behind the colonnade is a row of red curtained windows looking out upon a park—and pages are flitting to and fro noiselessly as the business proceeds. The bar is railed off from the spectators who are comfortably provided with cushioned sofas. The floor is covered with a rich carpet. The marble pilastered walls are decorated with sculptured busts of the past Chief Justices—that of Roger B. Taney, the present Chief Justice, being at the present time waiting in the hall of the House of Representatives for that distinguished functionary to tumble down—his actual death having taken place some time since. Over all stretches the chastely decorated dome whose artistic purity is a reproach to the meretricious adornments of the modern additions of the Capitol and whose smooth curves have reverberated with the eloquence of [John Quincy] Adams, [Henry] Clay, [John C.] Calhoun, [Daniel] Webster, and other mighty minds of a past age. . . .

Washington, March 13, 1863

AN IMPORTANT SECRET SERVICE

The detective department of the military service is one of the most peculiar of the times. It is conducted with great secrecy and efficiency, having at its head Colonel L[afayette] C. Baker, formerly of California. He was in Richmond on a special mission about two years ago, was arrested and thrown into prison by the Confederates, was subsequently discharged and ingeniously urged himself into the confidence of the Confederates, and was sent north by them as their accredited agent to purchase supplies, being furnished with $69,000 in bills of sterling exchange and letters of endorsement by L[eroy] P. Walker, Robert Toombs, and others. The cash was confiscated to the United States government, and a lot of plans and drawings brought up by the skillful Baker were passed over to General Winfield Scott, then in command, to whom they proved of considerable value in subsequent operations.

Those who murmur and sneer at the facility with which our plans are carried to the rebels should be told that this is only one of similar instances where our secret service has brought useful information from rebel lines. The only difference between the rebel and the federal branches of the same service is that the fruits of the former occasionally get into the newspapers. The latter never does. Colonel Baker is the Provost Marshal of the War Department and he has his force and influence ramifying wherever the jurisdiction of that department extends. The usefulness and efficiency of the service may be inferred when it is stated that during its brief existence 350 persons have been arrested for running the blockade of the lines of the Potomac, for smuggling, or as spies. Fortunes of secesh cormorants have been ruined, and hundreds of thousands of dollars in gold, notes and merchandise confiscated to the government, as much as $20,000 in gold captured at one time. This, for the most part, has been taken from secesh traders attempting to run the blockade, who sell their goods in Secessia for Confederate rags, making a big profit, turn their receipts into southern money or treasury notes, and thence into gold, if practicable. They were formerly discharged on the "swear 'em and let 'em go" policy, but they are now sentenced to hard labor when convicted and sent to the Rip Raps or Dry Tortugas with other offenders against the law.

A GROUP OF NOTABLES

Yesterday, I saw two clusters of notable men whose names are frequently before the public. . . . The most noticeable man of these times is Major General Joe Hooker, not alone because he is commander of the Grand Army of the Potomac, but for the reason that his noble presence, his vigorous, manly action, and bright, fresh face carry wherever he goes a magnetic influence which makes a hum of admiration and a cluster of observers attend his every motion. He looks the live general that he is, and he is in striking contrast to the dapper and trig McClellan whose jaunty *insouciance* does not set well upon a commanding general. Hooker is tall, shapely, and commanding in figure and face, his bright blue eyes flashing openly as he speaks. He is always in a hurry and irresistibly carries in all his action the conviction that *his* forte is dash—preeminently dash. There is a wholesome, hearty air of frankness and freedom from diplomatic reserve about him which at once charms those who come in contact with him; while his clear-cut features, evenly balanced head, and keen eye all bespeak the iron will and the executive energy of the man. May he be prospered in his defense of the Union.

[Ambrose] Burnside has a noble presence, and there is a dignity and sincerity in his appearance which attracts the commonest observer. He is over six feet high, well-built, and full in figure, bearing above his broad shoulders a massive head which is more statesmanlike than military and showing great mental power rather than executive force, and perhaps a trifle sensuous, the full red lips reminding one of the portraits of the Bourbons. He has a frank and hearty smile, a bright black eye, and scarcely any hair on the top of his big round head. . . . He dresses in citizens' clothes, his splendid form being wrapped in a close fitting overcoat. He is immensely popular, and a dash of sympathy at his reverses is mingled with the respect and admiration which he so well deserves.

Ex-Governor [William] Sprague, now United States Senator from Rhode Island, rather disappoints one who has formed an ideal Sprague from the knightly-looking portraits published of him. He is small, spruce, wears good, very good clothes, and his smooth, beardless face is adorned with a pair of spectacles. . . . He has a small, light head, showing shrewdness and calculation but not much mental power. If there is anything in phrenology, he has "order" large, which fact may be further shown by his careful piling at his senatorial desk of his numerous letters, a proceeding which excited the telegraphic encomiums of some Washington toady of the [New York] *Tribune*. That which is of no account in a little man is a great virtue in a big man. But we will be grateful to Governor Sprague for the signal services which he has rendered to his country by his influence and his money, and we will not compare his liberality with his colossal fortune nor believe the story that he has been silent of late because the reporter who formerly wrote his speeches was killed at Fredericksburg.

Another ex-governor in range of our lorgnette is Edwin D. Morgan, United States Senator from New York. He is just twice as large as Sprague, has a high narrow head covered with brown, stiff hair, and wears a somewhat forbidding and morose expression. He too has a brand new suit of clothes, is high shouldered and sedate, and is not especially notable in appearance save in the size of his nose, which is as big and *romanesque* as Seward's.

... What shall we say of Robert J. Walker? Once an accomplished Secretary of the Treasury, a prominent member of two Democratic cabinets, a first-rate Governor of Kansas, where I first knew him, and one of the richer lawyers in Washington, he is, for all that, about as insignificant a little dried up old man as one can meet on a summer's day. His old-fashioned clothes are seedy and faded. His ragged neckcloth is tied under his ear, and the shockingly bad hat, which he has carefully placed on the table as he sits uncomfortably down, would be disgustfully rejected by the ancient colored gentleman who sweeps the crosswalk at the corner of the Avenue. His little bald head is carefully polished with a venerable "wipe," his face wears a comfortable smile, and his bleared eyes gleam with hu-

mor as his thin voice pipes out some story of the old regime. Walker is fussy and nervous, but for all that he is
one of the very shrewd men in this capital city, a firm
friend of the government, an able financier, and an elegant and forcible writer. He has earned a good reputation,
and, despite his oddities, he has the respect of the leading
men of the nation.

... Attorney General [Edward] Bates [is] a small, white
haired man, not noticeable in appearance, with a good
head, sharp features, and pleasant face well-fringed with
gray whiskers. He is not meddlesome in public affairs, lives
retired, and, next to Montgomery Blair, is the least influential man in the cabinet. Blair, by the way, has the name
of being the "meanest man in the cabinet." Can't say
as to that.

Beyond Bates, as we sit, is Reverdy Johnson, lately
elected Senator from Maryland, and a very repellent, dishonest face he has, though it may be slander to say so. He
is short, stout, round-shouldered, has white hair, a long
head, pursed out lips, and a "cockeye," as the vulgar have
it, *a la* Buchanan, only more so. He is a good lawyer, a
dignified, sententious speaker, and, in the opinion of people other than General Ben[jamin] F. Butler, very much
of an old rat.

His colleague, ex-Governor Thomas H. Hicks, is a handsome, frank old gentleman of polished and courtly manners, stout and English-looking, and respected for his
manly loyalty in the stormy days of the incipient rebellion
of "My Maryland," but not so acceptable here as would
have been the return to the Senate of Henry Winter Davis;
but a hearty, honest gentleman, no doubt, who leaves a
pleasant impression behind him as the door closes upon
the exit of himself and our group of notables.

Washington, March 18, 1863

THE DAWNING OF THE DAY

... The political aspect just now is particularly bright and cheerful. A month ago one would hardly know where to look for a gleam of light, but now it reaches us from all directions, North and South. Not that there has been any great military victory or political success, but the tone of the times is cheerful, hopeful, and reasonably encouraging, and men who were but a few weeks ago desponding and gloomy are now lifted out of the state of sadness in which they were erewhile plunged. The rebellion is now hemmed into a smaller space than ever before, and from its confined boundaries come dismal stories of destitution, distress, and famine. It is yet six months to harvest and meanwhile the rebels suffer for the want of the food which their mad rebellion has driven from their doors. Their hope for foreign intervention is gone, for the piracies of the *Alabama* and *Florida*, the French reverses in Mexico, the Polish rebellion, and the manifestation of antislavery feeling in England have all served to bind over the great European powers to keep the peace.

The blockade of the southern ports is more than ever effective, and we have captured during the past twelve months nearly every cargo which has attempted to enter a southern harbor. We are apt to make a great outcry over the capture of a single gunboat by the rebels, for we do not want them to capture even one, but we ought to remember that our captures of Anglo-rebel prizes more than compensate for all our losses by rebels or by pirates. During the past three weeks there have been condemned to the government naval prizes whose aggregate value will amount to nearly three million dollars, to say nothing of the operations of our force upon the Yazoo and Mississippi or of the destruction of the dreaded *Nashville* at Fort McAllister. Richmond and Charleston are closely blockaded or invested, and their fall seems to be not far distant. Vicksburg, if not ours already, is useless to the rebels, and is surrounded by fire and water and must soon be ours, when, with the speedy fall of Port Hudson, the Mississippi will once more be open to commerce and the great West will have her natural outlet to the Gulf restored to her. Everywhere success and victory appear to await us.

Our moral triumphs in the midst of our deepest adversity have been greater, and today the cause of the Union is better, brighter, and more beloved than ever before. The glamour which the insidious enemies of the Union had for a while cast over the minds of the people of the North is disappearing, and that faction which was securing power by the misfortunes of the nation is everywhere suffering defeat and mortification. The Vallandighams, Woods, and Walls find that they have gone too fast and too far in their insidious attempts to prepare the people for a compromise with rebels in arms, and they have brought upon themselves the denunciations of such of their party associates as John Van Buren and James T. Brady [of New York], who think that the Democratic vehicle is so imperiled that it is safest for them to "get out and walk." It has been suddenly discovered that the people are not ready to commit themselves to a dishonorable peace, such as these demirebels contemplate. . . . Blatant demagogues cease their appeals to the lowest passions of the mob, and, under the healthy, invigorating breeze of returning confidence in our cause and its certain triumph,

men look in each other's eyes with hope and cheeriness.
Material prosperity has much to do with all this, and
the fact that the financial condition of the government
is relatively in the best possible condition is, no doubt, a
powerful cloud dispeller with many minds. The government is no longer at the mercy of loan sharks and usurers,
but its finance minister can today go into Wall Street and
secure the means necessary for the support of the government on the most favorable terms. There has not been
for many months so great confidence in the immediate
crushing of the rebellion, the termination of the war, and
the ability of the government to maintain itself as now.
In Washington—the veriest nursery of faithlessness and
unbelief—even here, the public sentiment is wonderfully
changed, and men who have croaked dolefully through
the long fogs of winter are coming out of the clouds with
a cheerful chirp which sounds strangely coming from such
unaccustomed lips. Let us rejoice and be glad, for if the
proper signs are in the sky the day is at hand when peace
shall end this troubled night.

WHERE THE SOLDIERS' BREAD IS MADE

At the upper end of G Street, near Georgetown, the eye
of the stranger is attracted by what appears to be a re-
doubt or fortification of cordwood piled up in a bristling
escarpment some twenty feet high and forming a large
hollow square of several acres in extent, in the center of
which floats from a tall flagstaff the Stars and Stripes. On
the eastern side of this singular fortification is a wide
entrance, looking through which you perceive the low,
whitewashed, and numerous buildings where the bread
for all the hospitals, camps, and barracks in and around
Washington is made. The barricade, more compact and

impregnable than any of those ever thrown up by the Parisian revolutionists, is of the fuel which supplies the numerous ovens of the bakeries, and is repaired with fresh installments as often as the occasion requires. Here are storehouses for flour, containing several thousands of barrels, rows of buildings with brick ovens therein, and warehouses where huge stacks of the staff of life, piping hot, are piled up for delivery to the fast going and coming army wagons.

The bakery proper contains twenty ovens, each having sufficient capacity to bake 150 twenty-two ounce loaves of bread at one time. Opposite each oven is the apparatus for raising and molding the dough, which is managed by neatly dressed and tidy men to whom tobacco in any form is a forbidden article so long as they are in the bakery. Each two of these ovens constitute "a shop," which has its gang of men and a "boss"—their pay varying from $30 to $45 per month, according to their position. They are provided with comfortable quarters on the premises, and they have regular military rations of meat, coffee, sugar, rice, bread, etc., issued to them daily, and they live well and wholesomely, luxuries being added from their own savings. There are now 280 men employed at this mammoth bakery, including laborers, firemen, watchmen, etc., and the bakers are divided into two gangs, one working by night and the other by day.

There two gangs manage to turn out in twenty-four hours the very respectable baking of 210 barrels of flour, which, as may be guessed, makes a formidable pile of bread when aggregated in the warehouse, whence it is delivered at all times of the day. The big, covered army wagons cart it off as they would so much fencing or flagstone, the fifteen loaves of each panful being stuck together like a sheet of buns. Each loaf is a soldier's daily ration of bread, being twenty-two ounces, which is ample for camp life but not enough for marching rations, when some of the other articles are left out. The bread is sweet, wholesome, and always fresh, comparing favorably with that of the best private bakeries. No fancy fixings are baked in this military institution, the nearest approach to that being some "French twist" loaves of bread, as the Bostonians call it, for the use of the officers in camp....

Uncle Samuel has the best of everything that is going for his boys, and thousands of barrels of flour piled in the warehouses were all "super" and cost him $8.87 per barrel, while he has bids out now for 30,000 barrels to be delivered at the bakery and will probably have to pay more for it. Connected with the institution is a yeast manufactory. ... "The sweet German accent" was the prevailing lingo in that part of the concern, as might be expected. The discipline upon the premises is very strict, the whole being under military law and superintended by a gallant captain from Illinois who, having spent three months in loafing with General Halleck's army before Corinth, Mississippi, thinks himself well-bred to the business in which he is now engaged. Uncle Sam's bakery is one of the sights of Washington, and many a soldier has reason to thank his lucky stars that its proximity has delivered him from the poor fare of "hardtack" of doubtful age.

Washington, March 24, 1863

THE LOYAL UNION LEAGUES

Simultaneously with the new uprising of the loyal people of the North comes the natural result of such a spontaneous and decisive action—the formation of Union Leagues by those who pledge themselves and all they have to the sacred purpose of sustaining the Union and the government which is protecting and defending that Union by all of the means which can be used to suppress the rebellion, punish treason, and secure the perpetuity of our national existence.

In most of the principal cities of the Atlantic states these leagues have been formed, and the loyal people of the North have rushed in masses to enroll themselves upon the lists of those who are desirous of affirming anew their allegiance to their country, and pledging their lives, their fortunes, and their sacred honor in defense of her integrity and existence as one nation. The sovereign people is out in all its might, and the boundless enthusiasm which has marked the formation of the leagues in Philadelphia, New York, Baltimore, and Washington has struck terror to the hearts of those designing politicians who fear to see any union of the people which will ignore party for the sake of the Union. The [New York] *World* scents afar off a dodge on the part of the Unionists to influence the presidential campaign of 1864, and it soundly berates "that feeble and valitudinarian patriotism which requires too frequent reaffirmation" as that contemplated in the formation of the Union Leagues. . . .

REPUBLICANISM OR UNIONISM?

The Copperheads are swift to brand all of these evidences of the returning spirit of the people as Republicanism. They have never greatly affected the word Union, and now they condemn it more than ever and stigmatize it as a mere catchword to conceal some hidden plot, which has an undefinable, dreadful meaning to somebody. It is an ancient and truthful saying that the thief fancies each bush an officer. We are very sure that honest men do not, and so these perturbations of the openly disloyal and secretly traitorous are only indications of that injured conscience which does make cowards of us all, and they are glad to affix to all of the demonstrations of a loyal public sentiment the stigma of "abolitionism," etc. Said the Washington correspondent of a New York Copperhead newspaper to me yesterday, despondingly: "I don't see but what the Republicans have got it all their own way now, however it may be in the field." I objected to the use of the title "Republican" as being incorrect as to fact. He responded: "Oh, it's all the same—Unionist where it is politic; Republican where that is popular, and abolitionist where you dare." Copperhead's acumen is rare. But if Republicanism or abolitionism means an unrelenting determination to sustain and stand by the government in its effort to crush out the rebellion by the armed hand of power, why, then, we are all becoming dreadfully abolitionized, and some illustrious converts to those long proscribed tenets have lately kept even step with the masses of the people, who have showed that they stand shoulder to shoulder in defense of that which may be called Unionism, Republicanism, or abolitionism—it matters not which, so that it is right, logical, and truly conservative.

WIDOWS, ORPHANS, AND INVALID SOLDIERS

One of the features of the strange times upon which we have fallen is the augmentation of the pension service of the United States which, from being an unimportant and inconsiderable bureau, had risen to a large department employing over 100 clerks and daily receiving and examining hundreds of applications for pensions for disabled soldiers or the widows or heirs of those slain in battle. By the Pension Act of 1862 provision is made for disabled soldiers who, for wounds received or disease contracted while in service, receive a yearly pension varying in amount with their rank and the character of their disability, the pension being graduated to total disability, or one-eighth, one-fourth, or one-half, as the case may be.

Widows of those who die or are killed in the military or naval service receive an annual pension during their widowhood, which ceases upon remarriage. The widows of those who rank from major general to lieutenant colonel receive a monthly pension of $30. A major's widow receives $25 a month, a captain's widow, $20, a first lieutenant's widow, $17, and a second lieutenant's widow, $15. The widows of surgeons receive pay according to the rank of their husband, whose station is either that of major or captain. Privates' widows are entitled to a monthly pension of $8. Pensions are issued in certain specified but limited and restricted cases to the heirs of those who die or are killed in the service of their country. The amount is equal to that due a widow of the person killed and is apportioned among the claimants.

An inspection of the pension system is interesting and full of food for thought, for here we see some of the first practical results of this wasting and cruel war; and here, too, we meet the names of many who have been famous in the record of this rebellion and learn new facts which seldom reach the public eye. Here is the name of the widow of the gallant [Jesse L.] Reno, slain in battle. She was left penniless and applies to the government for the small pension—$30 per month—to which she is entitled by law. Even among the widows of the major generals killed during the war there has been no exception to the general rule but all apply for the pensions due them. There are now on file ... 15,000 applications for pensions to widows of soldiers and officers, of which only 1,200 have been issued, the rest being under examination or having been rejected.

16,000 applications for pensions for sick and disabled persons in the army service have been made, of which 1,052 have been issued. 202 applications for naval pensions to widows have been made, and 52 have been granted. . . . The applications for pensions for heirs is smaller in proportion in the naval than in the military service, showing that the killed in the Navy are for the most part unmarried men.

No one who has not inspected the working of the United States pension system can form a very comprehensive idea of the amount of labor which is involved in receiving, examining, and passing upon the claims presented for adjudication. Each mail brings several hundred applications, the papers in each make a formidable-looking package. It is gratifying to know that great care and indefatigable attention is given to a pursuit of all of the knowledge bearing upon the justice of the claims. And . . . the instances are rare indeed where any neglect which it is possible for the government to remedy is shown to the wounded or disabled soldiers or the surviving friends of those who have given their lives in the defense of their grateful country.

RETURNED PRISONERS FROM RICHMOND

At the meeting of the Union League in this city last night there was present a band of returned federal prisoners from Richmond, whose accounts of matters and things at the Confederate capital and of their own experience was very interesting. The party is four in number, the remnant of a small detachment of picked men sent from Shelbyville, Tennessee, on April 7, 1862, into the rebel lines for the purpose of seizing an engine on the Nashville and Chattanooga Railroad, to run down into Georgia, and to cut off an important rebel line of communication. The expedition failed for the reason that telegraphic communication south was not cut off soon enough to prevent a knowledge of the expedition being sent to the rebels. The party was seized, and a portion of their number were hanged summarily without a moment's warning to terrify their comrades into betrayal of their plans and purposes. After the most terrible sufferings in prison, repeated and dreadful floggings, incarceration in loathsome underground prisons and in Castle Thunder and in Parson Brownlow's former iron cage, they were exchanged at last and are alive to tell the story of their perils and sufferings.

These soldiers say that want and famine at Richmond are very severe and that the rations of the soldiers is about one-half what it was when the war began. One of them [Jacob] Parrott, bears on his back the scars of 100 lashes inflicted by these scions of chivalry, and his denunciations of those in the North who are apologists and friends of a system and a cause which has such a savage and brutal spirit as he saw in Secessia were truly forcible and eloquent. He has good reason to have a *feeling* recollection of the hospitalities of the amiable rebels.

"LO! THE POOR INDIAN" IN COUNCIL

The rooms of [William P.] Dole, Commissioner of Indian Affairs, were crowded yesterday afternoon by the curious public, which wanted to look in security upon the deputation of red rascals who were but a short time ago plundering and robbing every white man upon whom they could lay hands but who were now amicably hobnobbing with the veteran commissioner preparatory to a full and fair understanding as to the future. These "plumed riders of the desert" appeared at the levee with all their glory on, being gay in paint, feathers, and beadwork, albeit some of the party had been coaxed into hiding their nakedness in dingy garments of civilization in which they looked about as comfortable as bears in moccasins. The majority of the party, fine-looking fellows, wore blankets embroidered with colored quills and made of the skins of animals. Their legs were encased in buckskin leggings gaudily decorated with beadwork. They squatted on the floor of the room in a semicircle in the midst of which a spokesman for each tribe—six in all—seated himself uncomfortably and had his say, which was interpreted by their "guide, philosopher, and friend" who accompanies them, and the reply of the commissioner was then translated to the crowd who manifested their approbation by a unanimous howling grunt of applause or "You bet." The chief spokesman of the deputation is "Ten Bears," a splendid-looking and intelligent Comanche who can speak a very tolerable Mexican patois. He informed the commissioner that he considered himself a highly respectable Indian and the commissioner a nice old man, that the party had a big disgust at the noise, confusion, and crowd of the city, that they looked for their prairies and dog soup, that they were much obliged for their fare at the hotel, and that they preferred, like sensible Indians, to settle up affairs, promise to be "heap good Indian," and go back to their hunting ground. All of which the commissioner promised in the most approved style of white man's Indian, highfalutin lingo should be done. They are to see the President before they go and have a small palaver with their Great White Father.

Washington, April 12, 1863

A PRESIDENTIAL VISIT TO THE ARMY

As it is not every day that one can get an invitation to accompany the Commander-in-Chief of the Army and Navy of the United States on an excursion to the vastest

army now on the face of the earth, you may be sure that
your correspondent promptly availed himself of a request
to make one of the small suite of the President on a visit
to the Army of the Potomac. The thoughtful wife of the
President, an able and noble woman, ought to have the
credit for originating the plan of a tour through the army
by the President, as she saw what an excellent effect would
be given to the troops, now in good condition and ready
to march, by coming in contact with their Commander-
in-Chief and his family. The party was small, consisting
only of the President, Mrs. Lincoln, "Tommy" Lincoln,
the President's ten-year-old boy, Attorney General [Ed-
ward] Bates, Dr. A[nson] G. Henry, Surveyor General of
Washington Territory, Captain [Medorem] Crawford of
the Overland Service, and your humble servant. Though
the trip had been postponed several days on account of
unfavorable weather, it was snowing furiously soon after
the special steamer left Washington Navy Yard, and before night the wind blew a gale, so that we were obliged
to come to anchor in a little cove on the Potomac, opposite
Indian Head, where we remained quietly until the morning
of April 5.

It was a rare chance for a daring rebel raid upon our
little steamer had the enemy only known that the President of the United States, unattended by any escort and
unarmed, was on board the *Carrie Martin*, which rode
peacefully at anchor all night in the lonely roadstead. And
it was a scene which was peculiarly characteristic of American simplicity in the somewhat dingy but comfortable
cabin of the steamer on that stormy night, where the chief
magistrate of this mighty nation was seated familiarly chatting with his undistinguished party, telling stories, or discussing matters military and political, in just such a free
and easy way as might be expected of a President who was

out on a trip of relaxation from care and toil. There was no insignia of royalty or pomp, not even a liveried servant at the door, but just such plain republican manners and style as become a president of a republic.... And though the rebels might have gobbled up the entire party without firing a shot, nobody seemed to think that it was worthwhile to mount guard to prevent so dire a calamity, and nothing of the kind occurring, we arrived safely at Aquia Creek next morning, the snow still falling.

"The Creek" is now a point of considerable importance, as a vast amount of supplies pass through the little entrepôt daily for the use of the army. Huge warehouses have sprung up since the construction of the railroad to Falmouth—a large fleet of transports and government steamers lie at the wharf or in the stream, and enormous freight trains are constantly moving toward the Grand Army which is encamped among the rolling hills of Virginia lying between the Rappahannock and the Potomac. You can form some idea of the amount of freight transported when it is stated that *one million pounds* of forage are daily transported from Aquia Creek to feed 60,000 horses and mules now in the Army of the Potomac. The railroad is a temporary affair but well-built and in good running order. When our party started for the special train in waiting, there was a tremendous cheer from the assembled crowd who gave another parting peal as the rude freight car, decorated with flags, moved off with the President and suite.

The day was disagreeable and chilly, though the snowing had ceased, and the face of the country, denuded of trees, hilly, and white with snow, was uninviting and cheerless. All along the road are camps more or less distant from the track, and the inmates appeared to be comfortably housed from the weather by embankments about their log huts covered with canvass shelter tents. We stopped at Falmouth Station, which is the terminus of the railroad, and is five miles below or east of the old town of Falmouth. The station is an important one and, of course, is now doing a big business in the way of receiving and distributing supplies for the Grand Army. Several carriages and an escort of lancers awaited the President and his party, the honors being done by General Hooker's Chief of Staff, Major General [Daniel] Butterfield. We reached headquarters after a long drive over a fearfully muddy road, the "sacred soil" is red and clayey, almost fathomless in depth, and made more moist by the newly fallen snow.

HEADQUARTERS OF THE ARMY OF THE POTOMAC

General Hooker's headquarters are quite as simple and unpretending as those of any of his men, as he abhors houses and prefers tent life, being unwilling, he says, to live in better quarters than his humblest soldier. The headquarters are about three miles from the Rappahannock in a direct line, situated upon a high, rolling ridge, and not very extensive, as the staff is not large or extravagant. The various staff officers and aides have their tents on either side of what forms a street, at the head of which is the wall tent of General Hooker, which at the time of our visit was flanked by a couple of similar tents put up for the President and his party, who were provided with the luxury of a rough board floor, stoves, camp made bedsteads, and real sheets. The quarters were comfortable and the President and Mrs. Lincoln enjoyed the sharp contrast with the White House hugely, while "Tad," the juvenile Lincoln, had made the acquaintance of nearly every tent before the first day was done.

The headquarters has every convenience for army use, as there are here a printing office, telegraph office, topographer, stenographer, artists, bakery, not to mention various mechanical shops and their appurtenances. The printing establishment is a wall tent and has as much work as it can do printing blanks, army orders, etc. There were nine hands employed in the establishment, detached from various regiments and representing New York, Pennsylvania, Massachusetts, and Minnesota. They had two small army presses, each taking a "form" of half-sheet letter paper size and being very simple in construction, the ink being rolled upon the form by a small hand roller. The work done was very neat.... The printers have brevier, burgeoise, long primer, and nonpareil for body type and several varieties of fancy or "display" type besides, all of which is securely packed in cabinets and packed up when the army is on the march. The whole establishment can be packed up in a compass of an ordinary dray load and can be set up in working order within one hour from the time of a halt. The printers shoulder "shooting sticks" in a general engagement, and though they have not "fat takes" in their office, they manage to give the enemy a fair share of "leaded matter" whenever they get at him with a good "leader."

A CAVALRY REVIEW

April 5 was so unpleasant that nothing was done further than to receive the officers of Hooker's staff by the President, who shook hands and had a pleasant word with each one. But on April 6 there was a grand cavalry review by the President and General Hooker. The entire cavalry corps of the Army of the Potomac is now massed as a whole, instead of being distributed among each of the corps as formerly. It is commanded by Major General [George] Stoneman, the best cavalry officer in the service, Brigadier General [William W.] Averell, the hero of Kelly's Ford, being the second in command. The cavalry force is probably the largest ever known to warfare, being now about 17,000, larger than the famous force of Murat, who is esteemed the pattern of all cavalry officers. This arm of our service has been of little account heretofore, owing to the mismanagement and imbecility of General McClellan, but now, educated by experience and allowed a latitude of operations by the present commander of the Army of the Potomac, it promises to make a brilliant record for itself when the time comes, and already the gallant Averell, one of the more modest and quiet officers in the army, has inspirited the whole cavalry corps with a feeling of emulation which will tell when it is called into action.

The day for the review was not very propitious, the sky being overcast and the air very raw and cold. The roads were in a dreadful state, and on our way to the spot selected for the review we had a taste of the quality of the country over which General Burnside, last January, conducted what is known in the army as "the Mud Campaign." The cavalcade was a brilliant one, the President and General Hooker heading it. Several major generals, a host of brigadiers, staff officers, colonels, and smaller fry followed, the rear of this long tail being tipped out with the showy accouterments of the Philadelphia Lancers who act as an escort of honor and who are an effective and brilliant corps.

Arrived on the ground, the President was greeted with the usual salute of twenty-one guns, which was the first intimation, by the way, that most of the army had of his presence among them. The troops were drawn up in squadrons on the long swells of the rough country where we were, and the cavalcade rode through all of the splendid lines at race horse speed, colors dipping, drums rolling, and trumpets blaring wherever the President appeared. It was very muddy and also windy, and the sacred soil flew in all directions, making the gala clothes of the military bigwigs and their train appear as though they had been bombarded with mud shells. Occasionally a luckless wight got thrown and ran a narrow chance of life among the rushing feet of the cavalcade.

In the midst of all rode little "Tad," the President's boy, clinging to the saddle of his pony as tenaciously as the best man among them, his gray cloak flying at the head like the famous plume of Henry of Navarre. The President had the glorious privilege of riding bareheaded, while common folks could cover their nobs from the raw and gusty weather. It is a nice thing to be distinguished.

The tour of the cavalry in line being finished, the party took position and the columns were set in motion, marching past the post of the President and party. It was a grand sight to look upon this immense mass of cavalry in motion with banners waving, music crashing, and horses prancing, as the vast columns came on and on, winding like a huge serpent over hills and dales, stretching far away out of sight. Never before upon this continent was there such a sight witnessed, and probably never again will there be in our country so great a number—17,000, assembled together, men and horses, and all looking in excellent condition and admirably fit for service.

It was a saddening thought that so much of this gorgeous and imposing display is only for the purpose of killing as many men as possible, and that so many of the gallant men whose hearts beat high as they rode past must, in the course of events, be numbered with the slain before many days shall pass. But these are all the necessary concomitants of any war, and it is more melancholy that the necessity for war exists than that the war itself does exist. Nobody seemed to forget that a battle was not far off, but all enjoyed the present after a certain grim fashion and deferred any anxiety for the morrow until that period should arrive.

The artists of the New York papers were on hand, and I suppose the scene and those which followed will be given the cheap immortality of wood engraving after the veracious custom of those irrepressible gentlemen. I ought to say, however, that these artists do really sketch from life most of the pictures of the scenes through which the Army of the Potomac passes. [Alfred R.] Waud of *Harper's Weekly* and [Arthur] Lumley of the *New York Illustrated News* have quarters with the army and accompany it on its marches.

The President today used a saddle which had lately been received by General Hooker from Main and Winchester, saddlers in San Francisco, as a present from that firm. It is a very handsome affair, and, as Hooker well said, could only have been made in California, as its style and thoroughness of workmanship are just what a military Californian can best appreciate. . . . So excellent a horseman as the President was the first man to sit astride the magnificent gift. General Hooker has also lately been presented with a fine horse by George Wilkes, formerly of California, and he rode him for the first time in some of the reviews which we witnessed during our stay with the army. The general prefers to ride his old war horse, a light gray, which has been with him during all of his fights. The gift of Wilkes is a splendid animal, a dark chestnut in color, of great power and graceful action, costing a fabulous price, I am told.

A PEEP OVER THE REBEL LINES

The day after the cavalry review, a small party of us went down to our pickets opposite Fredericksburg to take a look at the rebels. The Phillips House, General Burnside's headquarters during the battle [of Fredericksburg], stands in ruins on an eminence about two miles from the river, having been lately burned down by accident. It was an elegant mansion of olden time and was built in seventeen hundred and something of English-made brick, and commanded an extensive view of the surrounding country, though it was rather distant from the "slaughter pen" for a commanding general's headquarters during a great battle, it struck me. The Lacy House is another of the aristocratic mansions of old Virginia which yet stands, a monument of the past, in the midst of the desolation and waste which the progress and occupation of a vast army has made.

The banks of the Rappahannock descend in abrupt terraces and steeply to the river in front of the Lacy House, and for a considerable distance up and down the stream, where the pontoon bridges were thrown across the narrow current, the banks were cut down in deep roads, and the batteries where the enormous siege guns were mounted bear upon the ruined city opposite and upon the plain below the town. The painfully famous plain, which was a slaughter pen for so many men, lies beyond and below Fredericksburg, and with a good glass we could see the ridges where their unnamed graves are made. Beyond rise the two ridges of woody hills which our forces so vainly attempted to scale upon that dreadful day and where thousands fell a useless sacrifice. The smoke from rebel camps rises peacefully from behind the ridge, and a flag of stars and bars is floating over a handsome mansion among the heights just above that stone wall where the rebels slew our men by hecatombs. Almost all else bears no sign of the enemy supposed to be lying in force on and behind the wooded ridge of hills beyond Fredericksburg. But while we look a small squadron of infantry wheel over the hill, as if on review, and then disappears again, its traitorous arms gleaming distantly in the broken sunshine as it sinks behind the hill.

The town of Fredericksburg is well-built and ancient in appearance, but scarcely no building in sight from where we stood was free from battle scars. Bomb, shot, shell, and cannon ball have made many hideous holes in the walls of the doomed city, and even from the tall and graceful spire of one of the churches were flying the torn sheets of tin which flying shot had ripped off, and huge rents and fissures gaped from every wall. Near the river bank, which is low and sloping, a tall chimney stood solitary and alone, the house to which it once belonged having been burnt or torn down, and at its lonely fireplace two secesh pickets were toasting their shins by a cheerful fire. Presently, attracted by our little party's appearance, they got up, when I was galled to notice that while one wore the "grayback" garb of Secessia, the other was comfortably clad in a United States blue military overcoat. Federal clothes on rebel backs is no novelty, but it is never a comfortable sight to a sensitive loyalist. They yelled at us and made menacing gestures, but we could not understand what they were at. Later in the day the wind went down and they bawled to our sentries that we had been beaten at Charleston. A rebel officer, dressed in dark clothes, with his badges on his coat collar, attended by an orderly, came down to the water's edge, doubtless to see if Uncle Abraham was of our party. Failing to see him, he bowed politely and retired.

A train of rebel army wagons passing into town; a passing dray with two little sacks of flour; a crowd of graybacks at some officer's headquarters; a crowd of noisy darkies at play; an idle grist mill near the dam above; the white marble monument of Washington's mother in the midst of the plain beyond—all of these things and more that were novel to our stranger eyes were noted, and then we turned our backs upon Fredericksburg, a city which will ever be memorable as the scene of one of the bloodiest repulses this war has ever known.

THP PRESIDENT IN THE HOSPITALS

During the day the President and several of the commanders reviewed the Fifth Corps, Major General [George G.] Meade's, and afterwards went through several military hospitals. These are all in tents, and the sick appear to be comfortable and well taken care of, the tents being large enough to contain six beds each and are well-ventilated, neat, and clean and are arranged in rows or streets apart from the rest of the camp. One would suppose that it would be better for the sick to be sent to the hospitals in Washington, but experience shows that treatment in the camp hospitals is the most successful, and the good health of the Army of the Potomac speaks well for the sanitary regulations of General Hooker and for the medical treatment of those who have the health of the army in charge. The percentage of sickness in the Army of the Potomac is now only six, being much less than was ever known in any Union army and probably quite as small as it would be were the same men all in the ordinary habits and avocations of life.

The President, with his usual kindliness of heart, insisted upon going through all of the hospital tents of General Meade's corps and shaking hands with everyone, asking a question or two of many of them and leaving a kind word here and there. It was a touching scene, and one to be long remembered, as the largehearted and noble President moved softly between the beds, his face shining with sympathy and his voice often low with emotion. No wonder that these long lines of weary sufferers, far from home and friends, often shed a tear of sad pleasure as they returned the kind salutation of the President and gazed after him with a new glow upon their faces. And no wonder that when he left the camps after his long tour a thundering cheer burst from the long lines of men as he rode away to the chief headquarters.

A GREAT INFANTRY REVIEW

April 8 was a great gala day in camp, as on that day there was a grand review of the infantry and artillery of four corps of the Army of the Potomac, namely: the Fifth, under Major General [George G.] Meade; the Second, under Major General [Darius N.] Couch; the Third, under Major General [John] Sedgwick; and the Sixth, under Major General [Daniel E.] Sickles.... The day was brightening, and the weather a bit more emollient than heretofore, and the ground was drier. After the usual Presidential salute and cavalcade through the lines, the troops were set in motion and commenced passing by the usual headquarters in solid columns by regiments and brigades. It was a splendid sight to witness these 60,000 men all in martial array, with colors flying, drums beating, and bayonets gleaming in the struggling sunlight, as they wound over hills and rolling ground, coming from miles away, their arms shining in the distance and their bayonets bristling like a forest on the horizon as they disappeared far away.

The review was commenced by a parade of the reserve artillery force, eighty guns, commanded by Captain [Gustavus A.] De Russy, a gallant and efficient artillery officer. These guns are of several patterns—Parrott's rifled 14 and 32-pounders, Napoleon smooth bores, and a three-and-one-half inch rifled gun which sends a 42 pound ball about three miles. The favorite artillery, however, is the Napoleon gun—a brass piece which sends 32 pounds of grape or canister with terrible effect. It was this gun which did such deadly work in that historic cornfield at Antietam where the rebels were mowed down at the rate of a man to each hill of corn.

It was a touching picture of the vast show to note the many stands of regimental colors which had been riddled by shot and shell in the various sanguinary fights where they had been so bravely upheld by the noble soldiers of the Union. The tattered fragments of colors which were presented to the regiments in their peaceful homes in the North or West are held exceeding dear to the proud survivors of the gallant braves who have died by hecatombs beneath the starry folds which they loved so well and fought for so gallantly. Among the flying splendors of banners I noticed many a green flag bearing the crownless harp of Erin and carried by the side of the Stars and Stripes of the Union. Many of the regiments have the names of battles won by them inscribed upon their stripes, conspicuous among which was the Fourteenth New York which had not less than eight famous names upon its flag, the last being Cedar Mountain and Antietam.

The Zouave regiments were very picturesque in appearance, with their unique uniform and masterly drill. The impression has somehow obtained that this arm of the infantry service is of little account, as the vagabondage of some of the earlier Zouave regiments brought them into disrepute. But General Hooker has great confidence in the Zouave corps, and says that as skirmishers they are invaluable, while their rapid movements and accurate fire makes them a terror to the rebels. Their dress forms a lively contrast to the uniform appearance of the rest of the infantry, who wear the regulation uniform, the only other exception being a few regiments who wear cutaway jackets, efflorescent with buttons and red vests, making a gay appearance in the ranks. The most experienced generals say that fancy uniforms are desirable in inculcating a spirit of pride and neatness among the men.

The review lasted five and a half hours, during which time there was not the slightest interruption, but all moved on like clockwork, the solid and soldierly columns moving by in perfect order and retiring from the field in double-quick time. The general appearance of the men was first-rate, being admirable for drill, discipline, and neatness, and each man bearing a cheerful and confident look which was encouraging to note. If these brave fellows do not fight well under their beloved commander, General Hooker, it will be for occult reasons beyond the ken of man.

The President was highly gratified at the appearance of the men, and many a serried rank turned eyes involuntarily as it passed by their chief commander and magistrate, who sat bareheaded in the wind in reverence in the presence of the tattered flags of the army and the gallant men who bore them. I noticed that the President touched his hat in a return salute to the officers but uncovered to the men in the ranks. Of all the corps reviewed during our stay, that of Sickles's, in which are Kearney's and Hooker's old divisions, is undoubtedly the best. Their drill and discipline are perfect, and there is a hardy, brave look about the gallant fellows who have been so often led to battle by the two most popular men in the army, which is most peculiar and inspiriting.

MORE REVIEW OF TROOPS

The original intention of the President had been to stop with the army only one day, but he found that the visit was pleasant to the men and an agreeable respite from labor to him, and he prolonged his stay until he should be able to see all of the different corps of the army. When we first went down he began to receive the first intelligence of our operations before Charleston by the Richmond papers brought from the rebel pickets across the Rappahannock, and the President appeared anxious and, if possible, more careworn than ever, though he has never had any faith in an attack upon Charleston by sea forces alone. But after a few days the weather grew bright and warm, and the news appeared no worse, and he rallied his spirits somewhat, and the jaunting about appeared to rest him physically, though he said quaintly that nothing could touch the tired spot within, which was all tired. He always speaks, by the way, of this war as "this great trouble," just as a father might speak of a great domestic calamity, and he never says "the Confederates" or "Confederate States" but always "the rebels" and "the rebel states."

April 9, the day after the grand review of four corps, the First Corps, Major General [John F.] Reynolds, was reviewed by the President. This corps numbers about 17,000 men and is encamped upon a beautiful plain at the mouth of Potomac creek where it puts into the Potomac river. The day was beautiful and bright, and the scene was one of the finest which we met in our brief campaign. The camp is eight miles from Camp Hooker, and the road thither was over one of the roughest Virginia roads which can be anywhere found. But when reached, the parade ground was a choice spot, opening to the broad Potomac river on one side and encircled by half-wooded hills on all the others. The evolutions of the men were excellent, and the whole spectacle was most inspiriting and superb.

One prominent feature of this corps is its splendid drum music. The regulations allow one band to each brigade, but many regiments furnish their own bands, and, in some cases, the states pay for the extra bands furnished. In the First and Eleventh Corps drums and trumpets or fifes are the only martial music, and it is preferred by the men for marching as being firmer and more accurate. In some of these drum corps I counted eight snare drums and thirty trumpets, and in others there were seventy-five or eighty drums and half that number of fifes or piccolos. One who has not heard such a band can scarcely imagine the glorious and inspiring effect of the roll and beat of so large a number of drums intermingled with the martial blare of the trumpet and the shriek of the ear-piercing fife. Men who are weary with a hard day's march will prick up enough freshness to march many more hours at the striking up of a band of music, even though it be but a drum and fife.

On one occasion during the peninsular campaign it is related that [General Samuel P.] Heintzelman ordered a forlorn host to march against a murderous fire of the rebels to reach whom they must pass waist-deep through mud and water. They replied that they had no ammunition. He ordered the band to play but found that they had nothing left but a drum and fife. "Never mind," said he, "blow us something, if it is only a penny whistle." The little band struck up "The Girl I Left Behind Me." The men charged with empty guns and the fight was with them. When their thin ranks returned past Heintzelman, the warworn veteran uncovered his head with reverence as they filed by and sat silently upon his horse, the big tears dropping upon his gray beard as he bowed to the heroes who never can forget the fight nor the involuntary homage paid to their bravery by their beloved commander.

... The last review was held on April 10, when the Eleventh Corps, Major General [Oliver O.] Howard, and the Twelfth Corps, Major General [Henry W.] Slocum, were inspected in due form. The first of these bodies of troops were formerly commanded by Franz Sigel who, like most of his Teutonic brethren, is a gallant man but cannot be persuaded to live in harmony with his brother commanders who are not German. The President expressed the gist of the Sigel difficulty when he said that Sigel would never forget that he and his Germans are stepsons. The corps is now commanded by Howard, a gallant son of Maine who lost his right arm upon the Peninsula. Carl Schurz has a division in this corps, and his brave Dutchmen are splendid soldiers, some of the best drilled, probably, in the whole army. Schurz abolished brass bands and has several very large drum and trumpet corps of great efficiency. He is no great general himself, and he is ambitious of a better place.

Slocum's corps was the last reviewed, and then the presidential cavalcade took up a line of march for the Brooke's Station where we were to take the cars for Aquia. The march was a triumphal one, the troops of several corps being drawn up without arms along the line of travel. For miles there was an intolerable yell of cheers for "the President," "Josey Hooker," "Mrs. Lincoln," "the boy" (meaning "Tad"), and occasionally there was a jocose cheer for "a fight, shure" or "the bully boy of Williamsburg" and once a good-humored call of "and send along the greenbacks." I am glad to say that the last installment of funds due the Army of the Potomac is now in the hands of the disbursing agents, and no man will march without first receiving every dollar of his pay.

Amid shouts and cheers, a novel salute of multitudinous steam whistles, and dipping of flags, the presidential party, accompanied by Major Generals Sickles and Schurz, with several staff officers, left Aquia at sunset and arrived safely at Washington at night, well-satisfied with the ever memorable visit to the Army of the Potomac.

Washington, April 17, 1863

THE SUBLIMATION OF MEANNESS

It would really seem that as this war has stirred society to its very bottom, it has brought to the surface some of the more wicked meannesses which have ever disgraced poor human nature. We have, it is true, some shining examples of noble self-denial, of heroic fortitude, of immortal heroism, and of disinterested patriotism, but the black catalogue on the other side of the page is enough to show that the human heart is still depraved in spots, and that the millennium is not at all imminent. The latest case of wickedness which has come to light in this city is that one Joliffe, a shyster of the police courts, has been in the habit of counterfeiting the mortality returns of the different military hospitals in the city and vicinity, the names of the deceased soldiers being furnished to him by the hospital clerks who receive one dollar per name thus furnished. These blanks, containing the name, age, address, and cause of death of the deceased, he would enclose to the friends of the dead soldier with a few condoling and appropriately sympathetic remarks and offering, for a consideration, to forward the body to the bereaved. These letters generally brought back money enclosures to his assumed address, and he either omitted to send the body as agreed or procured, by other false pretenses, the body of some deceased soldier which passed for the expected body, except in such instances as an inspection showed the deceit. In one instance a red-haired man was sent in place of a dead soldier who had black hair, and this led to an investigation, and Colonel [Lafayette C.] Baker, the Detective Provost Marshal of the War Department, unearthed the villain. I have heard of the height of meanness being that of stealing the coppers from the dead mother's eyes, but an offender guilty of that crime would be a worthy member of society compared with this speculator in sacred affections and dead men's bones—the maw worm, Joliffe.

Washington, April 20, 1863

A NEW PORTRAIT OF THE PRESIDENT

Some of the public-spirited gentlemen of Philadelphia have commissioned D[alton] E[dward] Marchant, an artist of that city, to paint a portrait of President Lincoln for Independence Hall. The picture is about finished and is quite successful as a likeness though nothing wonderful as a work of art. The figure is life-size, a half-length, the sub-

ject being in a sitting posture, pen in hand, and with a
warmly tinted background. The President says he had no
idea that a painter could make so good a picture of such
excessively poor materials.

WEDDING CAKE TIED WITH RED TAPE

... The Prince of Wales, in the exuberance of his bridal
joys, did not forget his American cousins but sent to the
amiable wife of President Lincoln the conventional slice
of bride cake. Of course it had to go through the usual
diplomatic channels and was transmitted, at the request
of the happy bridegroom, by his chamberlain to the
minister of foreign affairs. He duly forwarded it to Lord
[Richard B. P.] Lyons, British Minister Resident at Washington, which functionary, temporarily oblivious to ...
semi-belligerent diplomatic affairs, passed it over to our
silken Secretary of State, as it is not *en règle* for any foreign minister to recognize any channel of communication
with the President but that of the Department of State.
So, in due season, but rather dry, the wedding cake reached
the White House from the State Department, the Secretary, it is slanderously asserted, whipping off a good bite
as his share, and Mrs. Lincoln cut the somewhat meager
modicum of cake into a large number of small bits and
sent the precious relics to her friends, selecting All Fool's
Day as the most appropriate time to perform such a kind
action for her friends, some of whom were greatly perturbed in spirit as they were at a loss to know if they were
really the happy owners of a simon-pure piece of cake
from the Prince's table or whether they had been sold at a
low price. But red tape says that the thing was genuine
and is vouched for by His Royal Highness's chamberlain

in waiting, Her Majesty's minister of foreign affairs, and the minister resident at Washington, to say nothing of our American Premier's "most distinguished consideration."

THE ARMY OF THE POTOMAC

Public expectation is feverish with anxiety as to the movements of this army, and public curiosity, lately so uniformly patient, is greatly taxed to know what is to be done and what has already been done. We are not permitted to know anything, except that a movement of some sort has actually taken place. What it is none can tell. A correspondent of the [New York] *Tribune*, determined to relieve the bursting ignorance of the waiting public even at the expense of the truth, actually invented the outrageous roorback that a large federal force of cavalry and infantry had crossed the Rappahannock and occupied Gordonsville, thereby severing the connection of the Virginia Central Railroad, flanking the rebel position at Fredericksburg, and doing other very nice things—all of which was a pleasant fiction which amused the public for a brief space and helped the unreliability of army correspondents in general. The fact is known, however, that a portion of the cavalry did cross the Rappahannock when a forward movement was begun last week. What they did and how they got off when the order for "Column forward!" was recalled we do not yet know. . . . The President and General Halleck went down to the army very privately yesterday, leaving here before daylight and returning the same night. What they did, said and saw are matters which agitate the minds of the few who know of the sudden visit. Perhaps it means a change of plan. The day is dark and rainy. Plans are held in abeyance, and the army cannot move. . . .

Washington, April 24, 1863

THE NATIONAL OBSERVATORY

A visit to this institution is always an interesting one, and the visitor to Washington who had *done* all the rest of the sights and neglected this makes an error. The view from the building, on high land over the city on the banks of the Potomac, is the finest one of the city of Washington and surrounding scenery which can anywhere be had. All of the localities around Washington are classic, and the visitor to the observatory will always find occasion to put up his knowledge of history as he scans the landscape about him. The National Observatory is in the charge of the Navy department and is now superintended by Captain J[ames] M. Gilliss, who has succeeded to the office since the flight of the recreant [Matthew F.] Maury, the scientific Esau who sold a reputable position for life for a very indifferent mess of secession pottage and is now a refugee in Europe. . . .

During a time of peace there are usually about thirty persons employed in the institution, but now so many are drawn into more active service that only half that number are employed. The country is tolerably familiar with the system of astronomical and other observations which are made at the National Observatory, for which purpose some of the finest instruments in the world are in use here. The most notable instrument, of course, is the great equatorial telescope in the dome, a huge affair, with an unlimited power but used with a power of 800 most effectively. This splendid instrument was made for the United States government at Munich, [Germany,] where most of the other apparatus about the observatory was manufactured, and it is the most famous of its kind, except that at Cambridge University, which is its companion or pattern. The apparatus connected with the great equatorial is very complete and effective, the whole great machinery being as easily moved upon its axis as an ordinary parlor stereoscope. It is so connected with clockwork and has its axis with the axis of the earth that its motion and that of the observer keeps with the apparent motion of the object, so that the planet or star is kept continually in the center of the field of vision. As the telescope reveals stars of the fifteenth magnitude and the naked eye discerns with difficulty those of the fifth magnitude, it will be seen that an object would soon pass out of the focus without some such contrivance.

The system of electric telegraphing has proved of great use to these observers of the night sky, as they now hold an apparatus in their hands while looking at the passage of the heavenly body by which every motion is communicated to a telegraphic machine and accurately dotted down upon a revolving cylinder of paper, which makes a diagram of all the motions of the object during the survey. In one of the rooms, too, is a clock corrected daily by solar observations, the pendulum of which has a point which touches a globule of quicksilver at every swing, and so establishes an electric circuit which can be communicated by means of the electric wire with every telegraph station in the country. Thus the regular pulsations of the clock in the observatory at Washington can be heard in every town and city in California which has any connection however circuitous with the overland wire.

The observatory is also a depot for the charts and nautical instruments used by the Navy, and the demand for these has greatly increased since the war, the supply of charts—chiefly of our own coasts—being fivefold greater than ordinarily. These charts are mainly the result of our own surveys, though many of the English Admiralty charts are used by our Navy, an international exchange being kept up with Great Britain, France, the United States, and other nations. A foreign war would compel us to duplicate these charts at home instead of obtaining our supply from abroad. Here also are many splendid chronometers, sextants, quadrants, and other nautical instruments. Before the war most of these were imported, but as the demand for them is very great and the new tariff protects their manufacture in the United States, it is proven that it was only necessary for the government to foster our own manufactures of instruments to procure the best at home, for the American-made apparatus is now conceded to be excelled by none of the work of artisans of the old world where centuries have brought perfection in mechanical skill. From all our pains and dangers we are plucking a sheaf of benefits, and this is one of them.

Washington, April 28, 1863

COMING HOME

... Between April 20 and June 26 the term of enlistment for thirty-eight New York regiments expires, and already we have had four or five of these returning regiments in Washington on their way home. The subtraction of their number from Hooker's army will be an undesirable item, it is true, especially as active operations by the Army of the Potomac are now so imminent. But the loss is not so great as might at first thought be supposed, for the reason that the ranks of none of these regiments are full, death-dealing war having so decimated their lines that only about 12,500 men are actually returning from the army. A great proportion of these men will re-enlist, though they are all to be returned to their homes and given sixty days' furlough before they can have an opportunity to do so. But prior to their leaving camp many of the regiments assembled informally and agreed to re-enlist under their old regimental officers. . . .

During the past day or two this city has been all alive with soldiers, some of them getting out of the ranks here in spite of the cavalry escort which accompanies them to the railroad from the point of debarkation. They appear to enjoy their freedom from restraint and their flush pockets hugely, and explore the town in pursuit of whatever money will buy. Among the disbanded volunteers are one or two regiments of Zouaves, Hawkins's and Duryea's being of the number, and Pennsylvania Avenue is suffering with an eruptive disorder of "Zoo-Zoo" uniforms, the picturesque and unique gear of these *insouciant* soldier boys breaking out in every group on the leave. Just emancipated from restraint and rigid camp duty, it is not surprising that some of them should burst over the bounds of decorum, but for the most part our "brave defenders" are well-behaved, and the Metropolitan Police do not have many flagrant cases of excesses to look after. God bless "the boys," and may we soon receive all of their companion-in-arms to peaceful homes.

WAITING FOR THE NEWS

We are all up to fever heat in Washington just now, as it is well known that active operations are being resumed by the Army of the Potomac. Yesterday large masses of troops were in action, and the faint rumors of their advance set Washington all agog. Everybody expects great things of Hooker and his gallant command. But we have been so frequently disappointed of late by untimely and inopportune rains that the popular fever is always dashed with the proviso "if it doesn't rain," and, sure enough, as I write, the pleasant summer sky has become overcast with clouds, and our three days of dry and sunny weather are succeeded by a pouring rain. How long this new impediment will last none can tell, but it rains today as though it were a new thing. This is discouraging and intolerable but must be endured. . . . From the President down to the newsboys, all watch the signs of the sky with as much anxiety as that which possesses a Wall Street broker during the rise and fall of the gold barometer. Last night, with a cloudless and moonlit sky, the President prophesied rain, and the falling flood of today proclaimed Abraham a veritable prophet.

TREASON IN WASHINGTON

. . . It is provoking to think that so much treason exists here and that it is so beyond the reach of the law. There are scores of former citizens of Washington now in rebel ranks, and it is notorious that many of them receive constant revenue from property which they have left here and which has been conveyed to fictitious owners by the recreant and legitimate possessors. A gentleman who has looked into this matter very closely estimates the amount of real estate owned in this city by persons now engaged in war against the Union, which protects their property, at seven million dollars, and it is not likely that the estimate is at all exaggerated.

. . . It is stated that Robert Ould, formerly United States District Attorney under [President] Buchanan, but at present rebel Assistant Secretary of War, still owns $15,000 worth of property here. [Raphael] Semmes, the pirate, owns a couple of brick dwellings, some telegraph stock, and other property. Jacob Thompson, another of Buchanan's pets, owns valuable real estate in Washington, and many furnished houses are occupied and used by people who pay nothing to any person here for their rental, so far as can be ascertained, and it is fair to presume that their former owners, now in Dixie, receive the rents by underground express as per agreement made when they took their flight. Indeed, the very telegraph company which transmitted the important government messages has still its shareholders in the rebel states, our own government being less rigid and hardhearted than Jeff Davis, who has confiscated every share in the lines of the same company in the South which was owned by a Northern or a Union man.

It is a shame that such things are permitted, and that men who have voluntarily enlisted in the rebel cause should own property and draw income therefrom in the national capital, while thousands of Union families, natives of the South, have been persecuted like wild beasts, driven from home, and stripped of all they called their own. If I am asked why such things are permitted in Washington, I can only answer that I suppose that somebody is afraid that we shall "inflame the feelings of the South."

Washington, May 2, 1863

IN SUSPENSE

We are still hungering and thirsting after news from the Army of the Potomac and find but a precious little of it. Nobody knows anything "for certain," not even the

Secretary of War himself, for Hooker cut the wires at Aquia Creek when he got ready to leave, just as he said he would, saying that he had no more requisitions to make upon the War Department, and he did not know that there was any special need for that bureau to know what he was to be about for the next few days. The mails from Aquia Creek are also temporarily suspended. The newspaper men are in despair, and the military censor rigidly forbids anything concerning army movements going over the wires, even the reason for silence being suppressed. This may be necessary, but we don't see it. Hooker's whole force crossed the Rappahannock on April 29, and this is all we know. But all of the rumors, unfounded and confounded, with which the town is full today are in the main very favorable and the President is in good spirits—two good signs on which we pin great hopes in these uncertain days.

THE NATIONAL DAY OF FASTING

was very generally observed in the national capital. Every store in the city was closed so far as any observation could show the fact, and, to make the thing more certain, a couple of squads of the provost guard moved up each of the principal business streets, one on each side, summarily closing the stores of those who were inclined to break in upon the general custom, thereby compelling them to make their doors fast if they did not fast themselves. The churches were all full during the day, there being large and well-attended prayer meetings held at each. In the evening the large edifice of the First Presbyterian Church was filled to overflowing by those crowds who were anxious to hear the sermon of the Reverend Byron Sunderland, the eloquent pastor of the church and Chaplain of the United

States Senate. His text was the first part of the 58th chapter of Isaiah, and the sermon was a powerful résumé of our dark catalogue of national sins, among which human bondage and secession were made prominent. The preacher has been obliged to see many of his flock depart, angry at his denunciations of treason as a crying sin. Some of them have gone to Seceshdom and some to less outspoken preachers of the Gospel. It was refreshing to hear in this proslavery, treason-ridden city such noble and free utterances as those of Dr. Sunderland's Fast Day sermon, and it was another evidence of the great change of public opinion which has taken place that every one of his vast audience seemed to be ready to re-echo the sentiments of the freedom-loving preacher.

THE CABINET SKETCHED

... [Secretary William H.] Seward is small in stature, big as to nose, light as to hair and eyes, averse to all attempts upon his portrait, and very republican in dress and manner of living. He is affable and pleasant, accessible—from a newspaperman's point of view—smoking cigars always, ruffled or excited never, astute, keen to perceive a joke, appreciative of a good thing, and fond of "good victuals," if not of luxurious furniture. He has a desire for the presidency, and all of the protests to the contrary cannot shake my humble belief in that fact or his consummate tact and ability. He is an advocate of conservatism and McClellan, not generally popular here, and sits on the small of his back, twirling his watch guard and telling pleasant stories of the past and present. He is unpopular with Mrs. Lincoln who would like to see [Senator] Sumner in his place.

[Edwin M.] Stanton is what is popularly known as a

"bull-head," that is to say, he is opinionated, implacable, intent, and not easily turned from any purpose. He is stout, bespectacled, black as to hair and eyes, and Hebraic as to nose and complexion. He has a little, aristocratic wife, lives in handsome style, consuming much of his large fortune, probably, in his ample and somewhat gorgeous way of living. Stanton is exceedingly industrious, mindful of the interests of his bureau, never off from his post, works like a trooper, and spends day and night at his office when under a strong pressure. He does not appear to have the maggot of the next presidency in his brain, but plugs right on, unmindful of what anybody says or thinks concerning him. In cabinet councils he is always for fight, and he hopes to have a lick at England before he vacates his place. He is very arbitrary and shuts and no man openeth, or opens and no man shutteth, with much vim and decision. The newspapermen, with the exception of the [Washington] *Chronicle*, hate him as they do Original Sin, for he is as inexorable as death and as reticent as the grave. He wears good clothes, goes to an Episcopal church —if at all—and would be much more popular if he were not so domineering and so in love with the beauties of military law.

Secretary [Salmon P.] Chase is dignified, able, and ambitious.... He is the special antipathy of the New York *Herald* and the mirror of perfection for the [New York] *Times* whose Washington staff of correspondents are the favorites of Mr. Chase and his first assistant flunky, Mr. [George] Harrington, whose humble origin makes him no better but much worse in his present influential position. Mr. Chase is large, fine-looking, and his well-flattered picture may be found on the left-hand end of any one-dollar greenback, looking ten years handsomer than the light-haired secretary. He is reserved, unappreciative as to jokes, and has a low opinion of presidential humor and fun generally. He gained a transient reputation for fairness by refusing to give positions to Ohio people when he first took his seat in the cabinet, but afterward he revenged himself and his fellow citizens by filling his immediate office and many subordinate ones with Ohioans. He has a long head. He lives in a moderate style, is a widower, has a beautiful and somewhat airy daughter as the head of his household, and is a regular churchgoer. If he should be the next president of these United States the executive chair would be filled with more dignity than it has known since the days of Washington. As to his ability, it is only a trifle below the dignity, or the Secretary is greatly deceived.

Father Welles, as the populace terms our venerable Secretary of the Navy, is not so old as he is painted, although his white beard and snowy hair—wig, I mean—give him an apostolic mien which, in these degenerate days, is novel and unusual. He is a kindhearted, affable, and accessible man. Unlike his compeer in the Treasury, he does not hedge his dignity about him as a king but is very simple and unaffected in his manners. He is tall, shapely, precise, sensitive to ridicule, and accommodating to the members of the press, from which standpoint I am making all of these sketches. That he is slightly fossilized is undeniable, but it is a slander that he pleaded, when asked to impersonate the grandmother of a dying sailor, that he was busy examining a model of Noah's ark, albeit the President himself tells the story with great unction. Welles is a genial gentleman, and he has, in the management of his department, all of the industry of Stanton with all of the pride of Chase, which is saying a great deal. He will not lose his place in a hurry.

The rest of the members of the cabinet can be "run in" in a single paragraph: [John P.] Usher, of the Interior department, is fair, fat, fifty, and florid, well-fed, unctuous, a good worker, as good a liver, an able lawyer, an accidental member of the cabinet by the law of succession, socially dignified and reservedly get-at-able. [Attorney General Edward] Bates is a nice old gentleman, short as to stature, gray-headed, modest, quiet, conservative, and painfully reserved. He is somewhat of a patriarch—having a large family—is a profound student of human nature, and is one of those close, quiet observers of people who see through a man at first glance. [Postmaster General] Montgomery Blair is the best scholar in the cabinet, but beyond that he is of but little account. Awkward, shy, homely, and repellent, he makes but few friends. . . . If I have been flippant, forgive me, but here you have the cabinet, such as it is.

A PAIR OF LINCOLN ANECDOTES

No colored persons are employed about the Executive Mansion, but the President has succeeded in getting about him a corps of attachés of Hibernian descent whose manners and style are about as disagreeable as can be, barring one "Charlie," a valet whose services during our late visit to the Army of the Potomac I hold in grateful remembrance. One morning the President happened to meet his Irish coachman at the door, and he asked him to go out and get the morning newspaper. The Jehu departed, but, like the unfilial party of whom we read in Scripture, he said "I go" but went not, and the anxious President went out himself and invested five cents in a *Morning Chronicle*. It afterwards transpired that the coachman did not consider it his business to run errands, which coming to the President's ears he ordered up the carriage the next morning at six o'clock and sent a member of his household in the equipage to the Avenue where he bought a paper and rode back with the mortified coachman on the box.

That plan of punishing the hauteur of an exclusive servant was not original with the President, but this is: A gentleman who has been waiting around Washington for three months past in vain pursuit of a pass to Richmond applied last week, as a *dernier ressort*, to the President for aid. "My dear sir," said the President, "I would be most happy to oblige you if my passes were respected, but the fact is I have within the last two years given passes to more than 250,000 men to go to Richmond, and not one of them has got there yet in any legitimate way." The applicant withdrew with a rush of blood to the head.

Washington, May 8, 1863

CHANCELLORSVILLE—THE EFFECT

The first intimation of defeat was known here at three o'clock on Wednesday afternoon, May 6, when the War Department received a dispatch from General [Daniel] Butterfield, Hooker's Chief of Staff, informing that bureau that for prudential reasons the army had been withdrawn from the south side of the Rappahannock and was safely encamped in its former position. Had a thunderbolt fallen upon the President he could not have been more overwhelmed. One newly risen from the dead could not have looked more ghostlike. It actually seemed that we had been overwhelmed and forced to abandon the campaign and had been driven back, torn and bleeding, to our starting point, where the heart-sickening delay, the long and tedious work of reorganizing a decimated and demoralized army would again commence. Despair seemed to dwell in every word of that curt and fatal dispatch, which was the first to pass over the wires after an interruption of a whole day in consequence of breakages made by the swollen streams.

Before an hour had passed the President accompanied by General Halleck was on his way in a pouring rain to the army, having taken a special steamer at the Navy Yard for that purpose at four o'clock in the afternoon. In the course of a few hours the tidings got out through Washington and the effect was indescribable. Nothing was known of the movements of the army, past or prospective, except that it had recrossed the river and was at its old position. The panic spread, and by night the town was well-nigh demented with excitement. All of the most notable sources of information were at once in a state of siege, and all public places were crowded with eager and anxious inquirers after knowledge from the army. The wildest conceivable rumors were at once set on foot, and if one believed half that he heard he would go to bed that night with the full consciousness that Hooker was under arrest, that the President had gone down to put Halleck in command, that Stanton had resigned, that Lee had cut Hooker to pieces and was approaching Washington via Dumfries, that McClellan was coming on a special train from New York, also Sigel, likewise Butler, ditto Frémont and several other shelved generals. The crowd at Willard's was so great that the astounded passengers on the evening train from New York found it difficult to get admission to that caravansary. The McClellanites and secessionists (they are about the same thing) who had prophesied defeat and disaster sprang to new life and animation and with smiling faces and ill-suppressed joy were dotted through the gloomily excited crowds. The blood of every honest man boils within him to know that there are in Washington, drawing pay from this government, men who found in this unfounded and baseless panic more consolation than a victory by the Army of the Potomac could have given to the most desponding patriot. These bloodsuckers are the open or covert friends of Jeff Davis or of George B. McClellan—may their memory rot!

OUR LOSSES IN BATTLE

Of course it is now impossible to state accurately our loss in the late battle, but the highest authority—that which the President obtained at headquarters—puts it at 10,000 killed, wounded, and unaccounted for, and 1,700 made prisoners. During the past few days we have been constantly receiving rebel prisoners and rebel wounded together with Union wounded at Washington. While the number of prisoners brought in far exceeds that of any previous battle, the number and severity of cases of our own wounded is much less than at the December battle of Fredericksburg. We have brought to Washington, up to this date, 2,450 prisoners of whom 1,500 were captured upon the Fredericksburg heights by [General John] Sedgwick. We are now receiving stragglers at Falmouth, which lessens our losses materially.

NARROW ESCAPE OF HOOKER

The brave and gallant Hooker set a new example of courage to his officers. Unlike some commanders who retire to the rear in a fight, he was in the advance always and ran the same narrow chances of life which he demanded of his men. Once he was knocked down by the falling upon him of a pillar from the portico of the Chancellor House which was demolished by a rebel solid shot over his head. He was senseless for a moment but soon rallied and mounted his horse to show himself to his men, but, feeling faint, he lay down in his tent soon after to rest. The situation demanding his presence, he soon got up again, and five minutes after he left his pallet a rebel shell entered the side of his tent and raked his bed from end to end, tearing it into a mass of rags. May we not hope that the providence which saved our commander from instant death will spare him to a glorious victory?

Washington, May 12, 1863

THE CENSORSHIP OF THE TELEGRAPH

The Secretary of War may not deserve the harsh criticism which he is obliged to bear as being responsible for our military nonsuccess, but he well deserves the very general reprobation of the public for his unwarrantable and blundering supervision of the telegraph. During the late campaign upon the Rappahannock the censorship of the telegraph was so rigid that absolutely *nothing* relating to the affair in the most remote way was allowed to pass over the wires. The people of cities north and west of Washington only knew that a great battle was progressing. But not a single word as to its results or how the tide of battle ebbed and flowed was allowed to pass out. The people who poured out their treasure and gave their husbands, sons, fathers, and brothers a willing sacrifice to their country were not vouchsafed a single word from the government to enlighten the darkness of their fearful doubts, but, aching in tearful suspense, they were compelled to wait for days before the slow process of mails unfolded the facts from the ponderous and voluminous accounts of army correspondents.

A few brief words from the War Department would have quieted all of the natural excitement of the people and could have been of no use to the enemy nor harm to the people, which is big enough and strong enough to bear any of the worst news with patient equanimity. But the War Department was dumb, and the inexorable Secretary forbade the most trivial allusion to the fight going over the wires. A soldier wanted to send to his mother that he was alive and unharmed. A wife wanted to telegraph her mother that her son was slightly wounded. The acquaintances of the late Major General [Hiram G.] Berry applied for leave to telegraph to his friends in Maine that he had fallen while gallantly fighting for his country and that his remains were in process of embalming in this city. All were treated alike and were refused. This would be infamous if it were not simply absurd, for by going over to Philadelphia one could get at an un-Stantonized telegraph wire and send as much of rumor as he pleased. Secretary Stanton triumphed in the Washington telegraph office, but the newspapermen beat him at Baltimore, and though the Washington censor would not allow correspondents to transmit over the wires matter which had already been printed in our city newspapers, the mails were free to carry all of the vaticinations, complaints, and sensations of the bothered Bohemians. The result is that a general onslaught has been made upon the Secretary of War, and the press may yet compel our willful chief of the War Department to make friends with his adversary quickly, lest it drag him before that fearful magistrate—public opinion —which bears no love to Secretary Stanton and would rejoice to see him dismissed today by a chief magistrate who profoundly disapproves of this last despotic measure of the War Office. . . .

VARIOUS AND SUNDRY

The hospitals of this city contain over 1,000 rebel wounded, which accounts for the fact that many women of secesh proclivities who have never before visited such places now frequent the hospitals with unremitting pertinacity. It is ordered that delicacies sent to rebel wounded shall be shared with their Union companions in the war.

A Massachusetts soldier wounded at Chancellorsville had his life saved by a rifle ball being stopped in his pocket Bible which lay just over his heart and in which the ball was found imbedded. The President has sent the boy another Bible with an appropriate inscription written therein.

Washington, May 20, 1863

NEGRO TROOPS

Yesterday I went to see the drill of some of the colored troops being mustered into service in the District of Columbia. The drill was in an enclosed field back of the Capitol, and the men numbered about 200, of whom more than two-thirds are contrabands who have come into our lines from central and eastern Virginia, while a few have worked their way up from the Carolinas and Georgia. The appearance of these men is indescribable: motley, variegated, ragged or well-clad, full of all their tropical luxuriance of style, odorous, unkept, and shambling, yet resolute and ambitious. It defies all my power of description to convey to the reader an idea of this grotesque array of darkies straggling about the enclosure in sinuous columns, preparatory to being mustered into service. There they go crookedly over the turf, clad in blue, black, white, or secesh gray, some with caps, some with hats, and some with their native wool uncovered entirely, and all of them covering more real estate with their enormous plantation feet than they will ever again cultivate for their rebel masters.

While the ranks are standing at rest for a moment, a few of the nascent soldiers divert themselves by executing an involuntary double-shuffle of the genuine "old Virginny" style. Another is stuffing a portion of his ration of bread into his enormous mouth, and another is standing on his head, while, seated on a log in the rear, an incipient fifer is endeavoring to torture "Dixie" from a new fife. The fence around the enclosure is the roost for a crowd of colored folks, most of whom being of the Washington sable aristocracy regard the proceedings with greater disfavor and are profuse of their satirical remarks upon "the niggers." Nevertheless, there is real spirit in these black men. They are docile and will soon learn the drill, and when they are uniformed and armed they will look as much better as white soldiers look when transformed from a rabble into an armed and uniformed body of men. In sooth to say, it cannot be denied that with all their roughness and ungainly ways the colored men whom I saw in their first drill looked every whit as well as the ill-clad and dirty secesh who are gobbled up by our cavalry in Virginia and brought here every few days.

There will be two regiments of colored soldiers formed in the District, of whom 800 have already been enlisted. A great deal of opposition which has been arrayed against the movement has neither dismayed nor effectually hindered the friends of the cause. The colored population of this city are only opposed to it because contrabands are chiefly the composition of the colored brigade, but that foolish opposition will soon disappear. It is intended to arm and uniform these men and, as soon as they become well-drilled, to place them in the fortifications around this city, with a view to sending them farther south by-and-by, the white soldiers whom they replace being sent into the field.

MISCELLANEOUS

The property of W[illiam] W. Corcoran, ex-banker of Washington, is likely to be confiscated, as District Attorney [Lucius E.] Carrington, acting under instructions from the Attorney General, has commenced legal proceedings in the case. Corcoran is now in Europe, engineering the Confederate loan, and his handsome private property in and around this city—amounting to some $250,000 in value—should be but a slight penalty for him to pay to the government which helped him to his wealth and whose existence he is plotting to destroy.

Washington, May 27, 1863

A PESTILENCE DREADED

An enemy more insidious and deadly than a rebel army threatens alike Washington and the Army of the Potomac. This ill-drained, badly governed, ill-kept, and dirty city, built upon a marsh and bordered by a stinking canal which is but an open sewer, will certainly be the scene of a deathly pestilence during the coming summer unless some immediate and active steps are taken to prevent it. The report of a military sanitary commission just made shows a state of things which, though every observing man knew before, ought to stir up our slothful people to some attempt to cleanse Washington. There are no regulations concerning the disposal of garbage, offal, and filth, heaps of which accumulate in back streets, lanes, door yards, and vacant lots, while the imperfect sewerage of the city is discharged into an open canal which skirts the city on the southwest, running from East Branch around what is known as "the Island," upon which stands the Smithsonian Institution, into the Potomac. This canal is filled to high water mark with surface soil, debris, and offal which is swept into and through the sewers. It is, accordingly, the prolific source of all the foul smells and malaria which such a duct can be imagined to have.

The rolling hills where the Army of the Potomac is now encamped are interlaced with gullies and are broken with level, moist tracts of country in and over which are now scattered all of the refuse, garbage, and debris which a large and wasteful army would naturally create in an occupation of the same ground during a period of seven months. The carcasses of dead animals, the graveyards of soldiers who have died in camp, the cloacae and sinks of the camps, decaying trash from camp kitchens, and the standing pools which abound—all of these, acted upon and aggravated by a fervent Virginia climate, conspire to make the present camping place of the army one of the most undesirable, and it is not surprising that the former good health of the army is beginning to give way to low fevers, malarious complaints, and disorders of various sorts. It is likely that a change of position will be made imperative from sanitary considerations if from no other. The summer heats of June cannot be met upon the Rappahannock with impunity.

Washington, May 28, 1863

CONCERNING NEWSPAPERS

There is probably no city in the Union where the daily newspaper pabulum of the people is so varied as in Washington. From dusky morn till dusky eve we have a fresh relay of printer's ink, and a continuous and strident cry from the newsboys salutes each waking ear. The first upon the field are two Washington morning papers, which are yelled, "Ere's the daily *Chronikill* 'n' *Telligencer*." The latter is seldom sold by the boys, however. The early train brings the "Baltimore *Sun, Clipper*, 'n' *American*" about seven o'clock, and a couple hours afterward the Philadelphia *Inquirer* and *Press* make their appearance upon the street. The former is a small quarto sheet, closely printed, and is largely read here. Then there is a rest for the space of four hours, except where a few persistent newsboys who have got "stuck" with a surplus stock still hold out and yell. But at two o'clock in the afternoon come the "*Republican* and *Star*, fust 'dishion," having the latest sensation dished up in one column with yesterday's stale news in another column. This runs until four o'clock when the tatterdemalions flutter their flags of truce behind them and the second editions of the same papers before them as they rush down the Avenue, hardly stopping for a customer. Their calls die feebly away as the sun sets, when they mingle sadly "*Star* for a cent" into the savage whoop of "New York *Erald, Times, Tribune*, and *Wurruld!*" These sheets arrive here twelve hours fom New York.

Occasionally we have an "extra," but the editions of our city papers follow so hard upon each other that there is not much room, and with the boys, who lie fearfully, everything is an "extra."

While upon the subject I may as well say a word as to the character of some of our newspapers.... The big stories of the sensation papers are not always contradicted, and it is well enough to know who is reliable here and who is not. The [Washington] *Chronicle* has the favorable side of the War Office and is mainly reliable as to news, but its editorials have no special character, except in their persistent praise of everybody connected with the government. A manly support of the government is handsome and desirable, but the *Chronicle's* chief duty is to act as the Greek chorus upon all possible occasions, wait for the announcement of intentions or opinions, and then applaud the act as the height of wisdom, skill, and ability. Not so with the [Washington] *Intelligencer,* an ancient fossil whose faultfinding has become a chronic malady and whose high-toned conservatism is so very high-toned as to be above the intelligent comprehension of simple-minded loyalists. It is published by W[illiam] W. Seaton, the surviving partner of an ancient house. It is slow but reliable, circulates but little, and will be the organ of the conservative Unionists in the next campaign. The [Washington] *Star* is a sensational guerrilla, loyal enough to keep on passable terms with the War and Navy Departments, where it must have news, and is edited by Douglas Wallach, a Virginian, brother of the mayor of Washington. Its news and that of the *National Republican* are mainly reliable though somewhat expanded. The *Star's* evening contemporary, the *National Republican,* is Republican only in name, has no special politics, is thoroughly loyal, liberal, and gossipy, but not very reliable. Its editor is S[imon] P.

Hanscom, formerly of the [New York] *Tribune*. The Philadelphia *Inquirer* is a lively sheet but utterly unreliable and possessing not one particle of reputation for truthfulness. The [Philadelphia] *Press*, owned by John W. Forney, with the Washington *Chronicle*, is a respectable newspaper of very handsome typographical appearance, famous for its "occasional" letters, but having an unreliable telegraphic correspondent in Washington who has fabricated some outrageous roorbacks.

Of the New York papers the *Tribune* has the most accurate Washington news, and the *Times* the least accurate. The *Herald* is sensational and distorted in its Washington telegraphic correspondence, and the *World*, though quite accurate in the main, shows all of its proclivities in its Washington news sent from here by a clever and loyal gentleman, strange as it may appear. The New York *Evening Post's* Washington reporter is great on meteorological items, is a little sensational, and is perhaps too radically radical for an impartial purveyor of news, for such men are apt to be frightened at reverses and popular agitations. These candid criticisms of my brother Bohemians will be a tolerably accurate guide for such as care to inquire into the truthfulness of these who furnish the whole country with "reliable news from Washington." Of course, the whole tribe of army correspondents differ as to accuracy, agreeing only in giving "items" to an utter exclusion of the spirit and grand characteristics of the conflicts which they witness.

STOCKJOBBING IN NEWS

Many of the New York and Philadelphia newspaper reporters in Washington turn an honest penny by availing themselves of their knowledge of events not made public, telegraphing to their Wall Street agents or partners how to buy or sell, thereby operating in stocks at an advantage over those who wait for the publication of news in the legitimate course of business. Some of these men have made a great deal of money by their early acquaintance with results of battles, buying and selling upon the successes or reverses of our arms in the field. Treasury decisions, rulings in the Internal Revenue Bureau, and other such matters coming to the knowledge of the long-headed reporters have enabled them to operate by telegraph against the sharps and flats of New York. A great deal of money was made by knowing ones upon the early knowledge of the New Almaden decision in the Supreme Court, of the Treasury decision in the coasting trade question as applied to the Pacific Mail Company, and during the pending of the Ways and Means bill during the last Congress. The New York brokers, of course, are smart enough to see the advantage thus gained, and they also have their agents here, some of whom act in the double capacity of reporter and brokers' spy, telegraphing the indications of Vicksburg for the money market some hours before the newspaper gets its daily items.

The censorship bothers these *chevaliers d'industrie,* and accordingly an innocent dispatch as "There is every appearance of rain" conceals the information that it is desirable to "hedge" in Wall Street. "The wheat crop in the West is reported here to be improving" gives the operator a hint of the favorable news from Vicksburg which comes out in the evening papers. It is sad to think that the loss of thousands of brave men in defense of the Union, breathing their last sigh upon the bloody turf, is watched in Wall Street and has the same effect there as a sudden failure of a crop or the loss of a million in treasure upon the ocean. We cannot hope for success until there is a nobler, purer conviction of our national position than we have now, and, though the mass of the people may be in earnest, we cannot expect to prosper while the war interest is looked upon by so many in the same light as the wheat or cotton or stockraising interests of the country.

OMNIUM GATHERUM

650 contrabands of all ages and shades of color, male and female, were brought up from Aquia Creek last night, having come to our lines during Stoneman's raid and our brief occupation of Chancellorsville. Their appearance was unique and variegated in the extreme, and they attracted a great deal of attention as they marched up the Avenue to the contraband camps.

Washington, June 2, 1863

REBEL DESERTERS AND SPIES

Rebel prisoners and rebel deserters have been very plentiful in Washington during the past few days. [Brigadier] General [Julius] Stahl, in the vicinity of Fairfax Court House, has been very busy gobbling up guerrillas, and he usually sends in a detachment of graybacks every day. These fellows are for the most part a sorry-looking set of vagabonds—ragged, dirty, ununiformed, a red rag on the sleeve or a turkey feather stuck in the hat being the only badge of position. But they are just as plucky and full of brag as though they had a better cause and better clothes. They hurrah for Jeff Davis and the Confederacy whenever they get a chance, and they have all the vigor and *esprit de corps* of veteran patriots. But we have crowds of rebel deserters to counterbalance the hardihood and braggadocio of these self-confident tatterdemalions. Just now deserting appears to be fashionable in the rebel ranks, and our government has been much bothered as to what disposition to make of these doubtful characters. It has been finally decided, however, to let them take the oath of allegiance, which they all desire to do, and send them north to shift for themselves. None of them are allowed to come south of Philadelphia on pain of being shot as spies, so they will be likely to fall into peaceful pursuits at the North and remain there quietly. Most of these men tell doleful stories of suffering from rebel despotism and conscription, but they unite in their belief that the Confederates cannot be starved out. There is too much corn there, but they believe that they cannot get military supplies much longer, and that *all* of the men who can fight are now in the ranks of the rebel army. Where can this depleted and fading rebel army be replenished?

GENERAL MATTERS

Another military feature of this city is the large number of "disbanded volunteers" who are daily seen in the streets. These newly made civilians evidently do not enjoy their emancipation from the restraints of camp life as much as they expected. One meets them in the saloons and places of amusement, and one always knows them by their air of conscious freedom which your soldier in the ranks never has. Many of these men wear citizen's garb now that they have been mustered out of service, and their slipshod "sheep clodings" sit uncomfortably upon them. The "fighting out" of the hair and the browned face proclaim them to be just out of the ranks. There seems to be a very general desire among the men to re-enlist, but many, perhaps most of them, "rather calculate" that they will wait until the draft comes and then secure the $300 bonus for substitutes. Practical pecuniary patriotism is evidently "played out" with them.

Washington, July 4, 1863

INDEPENDENCE DAY

Notwithstanding war's alarms and the agitated state of the public mind, the citizens of the national capital are celebrating the anniversary of our independence in a becomingly spirited manner. No expense has been incurred for the celebration of the day, but the "old-fashioned Fourth of July" appears to be the order of the day with our people here who believe that the dawning of a national existence should always be commemorated although the national life may be threatened....

The procession this morning was very fine, being under the auspices of the Washington Union Leagues. It was led off by the United States Marine Band, followed by diverse civic and national functionaries, next the Masons and Knights Templar in full fig, then Odd Fellows, temperance societies, more functionaries, and numerous bands. There were four regiments—splendid-looking fellows—of the Washington defenses doing duty as escort, and the entire turnout was highly creditable. The usual exercises of the day are to take place in the park of the Executive Mansion, the Declaration of Independence being read by L[ucius] E. Chittenden, Register of the Treasury, and the oration pronounced by Hiram Walbridge [of New York]. The streets are all alive with people, and the air resounds with the clangor of bells, the boom of cannon, and the crash of martial music.

GETTYSBURG

But while we are celebrating the Fourth of July in Washington, our gallant army is arduously struggling with an invading foe upon the soil of Pennsylvania. There is no holiday there, but thousands are being laid low in battle as they strike once more for liberty and union. The first battle in a free state has been fought, and it had well-nigh proved a defeat for the Union forces, but providential circumstances turned the tide of battle against the rebels, and the result was, if at all decisive, in our favor. . . .

Numerous rebel officers were killed and wounded, and the prisoners number by the thousands, the total number up to the morning of July 3 being over 3,000. Among the rebel dead is General [Lewis A.] Armistead, who, during the Kansas war, was a major commanding at Fort Riley, having succeeded P[hilip] St. George Cooke. The result of these fights appears to have been highly favorable to the national arms, and it may be safely claimed as a signal victory and as one of the greatest battles of the war. Our loss is estimated now at 10,000 but it will probably exceed this number. Mingled with our national jubilee comes the bitter and poignant grief which every patriot must feel that so many of our noble sons of America are laid low in death, over whom the Angel of Destruction walks hand-in-hand with Victory. Speed the day when cruel war shall be over and the star of peace return. We hold the field where the fight occurred. The rebel dead and wounded are within our lines, and the enemy is so crippled that at last advices it was probable that he would attempt to recross the Potomac. [General] Meade threw out an armed reconnoissance on his left, it seems, to see if such were the fact, but found him yet in force.

THE REMOVAL OF HOOKER

Right here I may be excused for interleaving a few words as to the removal of Hooker from command of the Army of the Potomac.... Public and official confidence in him was shaken when he made the Chancellorsville failure, but... the President felt that the ineffectual end of that campaign was capable of being attributed to the inexperience of General Hooker in handling so large an army as that of the Army of the Potomac, and he felt that justice to Hooker and to the country demanded that he should have one more trial before he was removed. The trial was had when appearances indicated a rebel raid across the Potomac and Hooker failed to prevent it, as it is now apparent.

Allow me to put in a bit of personal gossip: on the night of June 2 I had a conversation with the President in which I expressed some natural anxiety that a rebel raid might occur soon. The President said that all indications were that there would be nothing of the sort and that an advance by the rebels could not possibly take place so as to put them on this side of the Rappahannock, *unless Hooker was very much mistaken and was to be again outgeneraled.* Hooker was mistaken and was outgeneraled. In the course of his somewhat blundering program after the army of Lee was across the Potomac, Hooker ordered the evacuation of Harpers Ferry, as that point was of no special importance to us so long as the rebels had other channels of retreat and communication, and Major General William H. French's force was needed in the field. Halleck protested against this action and notified French that he

was not subject to Hooker's orders, at which Hooker asked
to be relieved. As one of Meade's first orders was the
evacuation of Harpers Ferry and no interference was made
with him, it is a fair supposition that the objection of
Halleck was only a subterfuge to get rid of Hooker. General Hooker has the popular sympathy in his misfortunes,
for he is unquestionably brave, high-spirited, and gallant,
but the public also believes that he was not the man for
the emergency. Meade assumes his difficult role in the face
of the enemy with a great sigh of relief from the people.

THE DEFENSES OF WASHINGTON

The fortifications around the city consist of lines of forts
each within the other, making a complete circle around
the city, the guns of which sweep every road leading to
Washington, and rifle pits are cut across every approach,
thus connecting the forts with a continuous line of defense. These forts are now garrisoned by detachments of
regiments, no one of them having a full regiment in it,
and the whole number of troops now in the fortifications
around Washington cannot exceed 15,000. There are forty
forts in the District of Columbia, and it can thus be seen
that the garrison in each must be quite small. But there
are eight regiments of militia in the District, and of these
four, at least, have seen active service. This morning they
were notified on dress parade that they had been called
out for sixty days' service but were not to leave the District
of Columbia. The presumption naturally is that they are
to go into the fortifications.

The clerks and employees in the different departments
have for a long time been under arms, and they have their
regular drill three times a week. These men number about
3,000 of whom many have seen actual service, the gov-

ernment having lately given preference in the appointment of clerks and employees to such persons. In this large force there is, for instance, one battalion of infantry known as the Provost Marshal's Guard. It is made up of clerks in the office of the Provost Marshal, Paymaster's Department, and War Office, of which every officer is a West Pointer and the majority of them have seen actual service.

Another efficient arm of defense and offense is Baker's regiment of Mounted Rangers. These men are all picked and choice, and are commanded by Colonel L[afayette] C. Baker, an old Californian, and for a long time the Provost Marshal of the War Department. These men have made nightly excursions to the circuit of twenty miles around the city, bringing in important information of the movements of the enemy, capturing spies, skirmishing with rebel pickets, and playing mischief generally. They are armed with the usual saber, with a sixteen-shooter volcanic rifle known as Henry's patent, and with Colt's navy revolvers with Remington's improvement. They are terrible fellows and have already proved themselves a great pest to the enemy.

Our citizens have recovered from the fright of last week and appear to have settled down into the comfortable belief that Washington is safe and that the national army, stretched along the Maryland line, is sufficient to protect the city and beat back the advancing horde from rebeldom. It is noteworthy that the crowds of rebels who suddenly appeared in all ranks of Washington society have as suddenly subsided, evidently believing that Lee will not be able to bring their day of deliverance just yet. The government also rests secure and has declined the offer of service made by the veterans of 1812, and has notified the regiments of the departments that they may continue their drill but that they are not likely to be called out unless some new and unforeseen exigency shall arise.

THE CONSCRIPTION

People captiously wonder why the conscription is not made, and some of the newspapers are grimly sarcastic over the announcement in the midst of the rebel invasion that the progress of the arrangements for the enforcement of the act is highly satisfactory. These cavilers forget that the enrollment has long since been ordered, and the final action of the War Department is only now retarded by the fact that the enrollment officers have not yet sent in their returns. When that is done the conscription will come. Secretary Stanton has formally receded from his position that the act of Congress left it optional for him to fix a sum the payment of which would exempt a drafted man from service, and has designated the Collectors of Internal Revenue as the receivers for the the funds so raised, which sums are to be paid over by the drafting officers as fast as collected. It is now proposed that an enlistment bounty of $300 be offered to such men as have already been in the military service, the fund accruing from the payment of exemption money by those who avail themselves of the $300 clause being used for that purpose. It is true there are 100,000 returned soldiers who would re-enlist under such an inducement. Suppose that out of a draft for 300,-000 men (the probable number) there are 150,000 who avail themselves of the $300 clause. We should then have a fund of forty-five or fifty million dollars to be distributed among the re-enlisted soldiers. With 100,000 returned soldiers, an equal number of conscripts, and a large force of colored troops all added to the men already in the field, we should have an army for the fall campaign which might be justly considered as sufficient for all future purposes.

The evil of short enlistments is strikingly seen in the fact that three Maine regiments actually passed through Baltimore while your correspondent was there, day before yesterday, on their way home, their term of service having expired. This was being done while the free North was being invaded and Washington was threatened with isolation, and yet not one of those three Maine regiments had been in any engagement or upon or near any battlefield. This is not their fault, of course, but how many regiments in the rebel army have thus escaped active service...? To its honor, one regiment, the Twenty-Seventh Maine, has offered its services to the government until the present crisis shall have been passed.

THE SOLDIERS' HOME

... The institution bearing the above name is a large, fine building of stone in castellated style about two and a half miles due north from Washington. The grounds are extensive and beautiful and belong to the government, which erected the large center building for disabled, homeless soldiers of the regular service, of whom a large number here rest from the services in the field. Near the central building are several two-story cottages built of stone in the Gothic style and occupied by the surgeon in charge, the adjutant general, and other functionaries. One is occupied during the summer by the President and his family. Mr. Lincoln comes in early in the morning and returns about sunset, unless he has a press of business—which is often— when he sleeps at the White House and his "prog" sent up from Willard's. He goes and comes attended by an escort of a cavalry company which was raised in this city for the purpose, and the escort also stands guard at the premises during the night. But to my unsophisticated judgment nothing seems easier than a sudden cavalry raid from the Maryland side of the fortifications, past the few small forts, to seize the President of the United States, lug him from his "chased couch," and carry him off as a hostage worth having.

Washington, July 8, 1863

THE NATIONAL CAPITAL JUBILANT

The official dispatch of Admiral [David D.] Porter announcing the surrender of Vicksburg was received at the Navy Department at five minutes before one o'clock yesterday noon. Secretary Welles immediately went over to the Executive Mansion with the joyful news, nearly upsetting Father Abraham in his excess of enthusiasm. The tidings soon got out and caused the wildest excitement throughout the city. The newspaper officers bulletined the brief, pungent dispatch of Porter, whereat great crowds assembled to read it over and over again and went off cheering. In the department buildings the announcement of the news was received with cheer upon cheer from the crowds of officers and clerks, and I do not believe that there was much work done in private or public offices during the rest of the day. The peace-at-any-price men and rebel sympathizers generally were *non est inventus*, having retired to their holes like evil beasts at sunrise, while Union men were shaking hands wherever they met, like friends after a long absence. Joyful faces were to be seen everywhere—many of them *smiling* joyfully at the multitude of bars in the city and their spirited enthusiasm deriving new pabulum from juleps, cocktails, and sherry cobblers.

MAJOR GENERAL ABNER DOUBLEDAY

This officer was wounded [at Gettysburg] on Thursday by a fragment of a shell which inflicted a severe contusion on the back of his neck. When [Major General John F.] Reynolds was killed, Doubleday, who was in his corps and the ranking officer upon the field, succeeded to the command and led the corps gallantly, but he was subsequently superseded by Major General [John] Newton who outranked him but had not been on the field at first. Out of this supersedure and some previous disagreement arose a request from General Doubleday to be relieved from his command in the Army of the Potomac, which request was granted, and the general, having stayed through the fight, is now in this city. He reports the fighting as being the most desperate which ever took place in the world. He says that our men fought splendidly and that the rebels fought with a desperation that was savage. They fought with the plan of massing all their force upon all points of our line at different times, making it impossible to say where they would strike or to form a line of battle with any sort of reliance upon its strength. The rebel loss he estimates at 30,000 in killed, wounded, and prisoners, and he thinks that our loss will slightly exceed 15,000, of which a portion is a large lot of prisoners whom the rebels could not keep and paroled on the spot, in defiance of the usages of war. These paroles will not be recognized by General Meade, as, according to the terms of a joint cartel, paroled prisoners are to be delivered only at such times and places as are agreed upon by the general commanding each army.

General Doubleday says that nothing can picture the horrors of the battlefield around the ruined city of Gettysburg. Each house, church, hovel, and barn is filled with the wounded of both armies. The ground is covered with the dead, to bury whom we have not help enough, while the air is poisoned with odors from the festering corpses which lie on the green earth or are but imperfectly buried beneath. The national wounded are cared for as soon as may be, but many of them and more of the rebel wounded die for the want of instant attention. The imagination revolts at the fearful picture thus drawn, but it is one of the inevitable concomitants of this horrid war.

NOTABLES IN WASHINGTON

Among the recent arrivals in town are General Hooker, who is here without leave, Vice President [Hannibal] Hamlin, Senators [William P.] Fessenden and [Lot M.] Morrill of Maine, [Charles] Sumner and [Henry] Wilson of Massachusetts, [Zachariah] Chandler of Michigan, [Morton S.] Wilkinson of Minnesota, [James] Lane and [Samuel C.] Pomeroy of Kansas, and many others. Major General [Daniel E.] Sickles was brought here last Sunday, and he is stopping with a friend on F Street. He bears his wound with great fortitude, having experienced no reaction since the amputation of his leg. He was worse today than he has been since his wound was received but he will undoubtedly recover. The President visited him on Sunday, and General Hooker called upon him yesterday. The latter officer was arrested yesterday for being in the city without leave, under an order of the War Department issued some time since forbidding general officers to remain in this city without special orders. General Hooker's

orders to report at Baltimore have not yet been changed
or modified.

Near Boonsborough, Maryland, July 12, 1863

TO THE FRONT

It was not until after the battle of Gettysburg that railroad communication was resumed between the Relay
House and Frederick on the Baltimore and Ohio Road.
As soon as the line of communication was restored, the
town of Frederick became our base of supplies, as West-
minster had been before, and, as a battle seemed imminent, a large amount of ammunition was at once forwarded
from Washington, and supplies of every sort began to flow
Frederickward. Your correspondent was sucked into the
stream of travel which set toward the front and found
himself, a day or two since, in the cars for Frederick from
the Relay House. The train was chiefly filled with soldiers,
the fag ends of reinforcements which had gone on before,
with sutlers, officers returning to their commands after a
short leave of absence, newspaper correspondents going
to see the fight, and, dotted in here and there, a few sensation seekers bound on the same errand.

Among the soldiers were a few of the famous New York
Seventh Militia, which regiment we found doing guard
duty along the road—brave, gallant fellows they are but yet
new to service, standing on cracker boxes while on guard
duty to keep out of the mud and greatly encumbered
with much baggage and impedimenta. But they are all
aching for a fight and beg to be sent to the front. They
must doff their jaunty gray uniform first, though, for

they look too much like "Johnny Rebs," as the soldiers call them, for safety in a fight.

All along the route we passed immense trains of supplies of all kinds—miles and miles of cars standing upon the track and laden with forage, contrabands, ammunition, pork, hardbread and groceries, horses, soldiers, and all of the means and appliances which an active army requires. At Frederick, a straggling, loyal town among rolling hills, we found a chaos of troops and trains of wagons. The stores were for the most part closed, three days of army occupation having been sufficient to sell them all out, but the streets were alive with all sorts of military features. Cavalry, artillery, infantry, supply trains, ambulances, and squads of staff officers were pushing through, while here and there a flag of some division commander denoted the headquarters for the time being. . . .

The road [to Middletown, eight miles distant,] was full of the immense trains of supply and the troops which we saw the tail of at Frederick. Artillery thundered and rumbled over the stony pike. Infantry marched gabbling along, and cavalry, jaded and travel-stained, still had courage enough to dash along with much vim. It was with considerable difficulty that we threaded our way through the varied mass of men, wagons, and horses, but we reached Middletown, between the Catoctin and South Mountain ranges. At the foot of the latter we passed a huge park of supply trains, a depot of commissary stores, which constitutes the base of supply between the army of the main base at Frederick. Near here we passed the scene of a military execution which had taken place the night before, when [Brigadier] General [John] Buford hanged a spy who had been in the Army of the Potomac ever since last winter, peddling maps and singing McClellan songs. His body was yet dangling from the tree, a terror to evildoers. Upon his person had been found a number of minute drawings of the fortifications around Washington, a statement of the forces in the forts, etc., and about $30,000 in greenbacks.

MY MARYLAND

Whatever may be the real sentiments of the people of western Maryland, there is scarcely any feeling apparent but that of complete loyalty. Here and there are Secesh families, but generally speaking the inhabitants are free to welcome the army of the Union and to proffer their hospitality. Every farmhouse has its besieging army of soldiers asking for bread, chickens, butter, eggs, or vegetables, offering money always, but not always finding what they want or always finding those who will accept money. The whole country has been swept clean of all supplies by the soldiers, and it is difficult to get anything to eat. At Middletown the only public house was too full for any further accession of guests, but we got very comfortable quarters at a private house where our party got bread, meat, and beds but not butter, milk, or vegetables.

While here we heard quite an oration from a well-to-do farmer from the vicinity of Hagerstown who had been well-nigh stripped of all he owned—the rebels having punished him for his unionism by devastating his place. He was a Henry Clay Whig, had never been anything else, and thanked God that the time was coming when the blasted Locofocos, who had baited the rebels across the line, would be down—down where they belonged. "We don't call them Copperheads up here," said he, "but we call them Locofocos, and they are jest the meanest, dirtiest snakes that ever crawled. D——n them for a pack of traitors to the best government that the sun ever shone

upon." He went on with the heartiest abuse of the "Locofocos" which he could lay his tongue to, swearing that he
would live to see the day when every northern rebel should
be driven across the lines, so sure as his name was Dick
Schackles. Good for him. His loyalty needed not his own
advertisement, for it is patent all over western Maryland.

The loyal Marylanders, however, have in many instances
had their patience and constancy severely tried, for the
rebel army has been generally scrupulously careful of the
property of all except those who made their unionism offensively prominent. But the national army which succeeded
it has not been so considerate and has had in its ranks
some rapscallions who have carried off whatever they
could lay their hands upon. At the farm where I am now
quartered two valuable horses have been carried off by
force of arms—not even a scrap of paper given as a receipt
—while some sixty bushels of grain have been taken in
the same lawless way. There are very stringent regulations
concerning such matters, and it is a hanging offense for a
soldier to take private property without a fair equivalent.
But in the hurry and confusion of a march it is impossible
for the guilty party to be followed up and identified, and
he usually escapes unpunished. Besides this, there is much
damage done to farms which cannot well be avoided.
Fences are torn down; grain, ready for the reaper, trampled
down; and ruin and desolation trace the footsteps of the
army.

THE ADVANCE

Day before yesterday, July 10, we passed on to Boonsborough, eight miles from Middletown, the road being
lined, as usual, with troops and wagons, most of them
being of the Sixth Corps, [Major] General [John] Sedg-

wick's, which was just ahead of us. The country is rolling
and almost mountainous, highly picturesque and rich in
cultivated farms, and the sight of the advancing column
was very grand and stirring. The troops were somewhat
worn and jaded, having been now some thirty days on the
march since leaving their position on the Rappahannock.
Many of the horses were lame, and it was painful to see
how many of the men were footsore and lame. All along
the roadside were stragglers, some shoeless and some without guns, asleep or resting their tired frames, poor fellows,
against the fences, or stretched at length under the shade
of the trees in the fields. But, for the most part, the men
were in good spirits and especially anxious as to the
whereabouts of "the Johnnies," as they call the rebels
affectionately. Occasionally, a guard would come down
from the front with a handful of rebels just taken prisoners
where the skirmishing was going on, and the salutations
were comical. "How are you, Johnny?" "How is Uncle
Jeff?" and "Are you going to fight for Uncle Abe at last?"
These rebels were generally good-looking, well-clad men
and by no means the scarecrows which have usually been
sent up to Washington when our army was in Virginia.

While at Boonsborough the Eleventh Army Corps, General [Oliver O.] Howard's, passed up the turnpike, occupying six or seven hours in going through the town. These
poor fellows have a sorry reputation in the army, and
though they fought well at Gettysburg there are some regiments in the corps who never will fight and oblige the whole
corps to bear the stigma of their mean spirit and cowardice.
These are the riffraff and the sweepings of one of our
large cities, and they will disgrace the army again if not
properly supported.

We found that nobody seemed to know the exact position of the enemy. The Potomac is still up, and fording

is out of the question. But it is possible for the rebel engineers to construct bridges for crossing, although Lee is too good a general to allow a portion of his troops to get over the river unless it was certain that all could cross before an attack from the national army. At present we know that a large rebel force is on this side of the Potomac, and it seems to be massed between Hagerstown and Williamsport, the right resting on the Potomac at the latter place. Our advance was made on Friday up Boonsborough pike, and the rebels who were occupying this region about three miles from Boonsborough were compelled to fall back to Hagerstown, being shelled from a ridge just back of this farmhouse. Near Hagerstown they made a stand and a brisk cavalry fight occurred during which we lost about twenty-five men in killed and wounded. It was afterwards discovered that the rebels held us at bay for the purpose of destroying a large train which they were moving from Funkstown, four miles from here, to Hagerstown three miles beyond. Our infantry came up to the rescue, but the rebels soon fell back to their main force and our force returned. It was sad to look at the lead horses which came back with the cavalry, their saddles having been emptied by the enemy. In this fight Colonel (late acting Brigadier) [Edwin H.] Stoughton, who was captured at Fairfax last spring, was wounded by a fragment of shell. He is lying at a hospital near this farmhouse where our quarters are.

CLOSING IN THE LINES

Yesterday we visited General Meade's headquarters about a mile south of here near Antietam Creek which flows just past this locality. The headquarters are in a magnificent grove of tall oaks free from undergrowth, and the tents and equipage of camp, disposed picturesquely about, give it the appearance of a picnic or *fête champêtre* rather than actual war. The officers lounge in groups in their respective quarters or lay flat on the ground pouring over huge maps which are stretched on the greensward. General Meade is in consultation with his officers or with scouts or couriers who are constantly arriving. His Chief of Staff is [Brigadier] General [Gouverneur K.] Warren, and his Chief Quartermaster is [Brigadier] General Rufus Ingalls who, with [Brigadier] General Seth Williams, Adjutant General, has been with the Army of the Potomac ever since it was formed, and they hold the same positions now which they held under McClellan. How much their love for their old commander affects their bearing and moral support to their successive commanders I would not like to say.

Meade is tall, a little past his prime, but straight and wiry; wears spectacles usually; has a sallow face and large eyes, and his hair is quite gray. He is affable but not genial, and he dresses very plainly and puts on no airs. Here, too, is Major General [Alfred] Pleasonton, a splendid cavalry officer, at the head of the cavalry corps ever since Stoneman fell out of Hooker's esteem on account of his non-success in his famous raid. Pleasonton is small, nervous, and full of dash, dark-haired and finely featured with gray-streaked hair. He is immensely popular with his men and with the whole army, which Stoneman never was.

... Last night, Saturday, July 11, our right was upon the Boonsborough and Hagerstown pike, about halfway between the two places, and during the night a connection was established with the Eleventh Corps at that point and Couch's 25,000 militia, which bends around Hagerstown on the north and stretches toward the Potomac on the west. Next to the Eleventh Corps comes the Sixth, next the Fifth (formerly Sickle's, now Sykes's), then the Third Corps under French. The last two crossed the Antietam last night and are now on the long range of hills just west of the creek, and our line crosses Antietam near the old battleground where the left curves toward the Potomac by a formation of the First, Second, and Twelfth Corps, the first named being on the extreme left. Reinforcements are now coming up, and a battle seems inevitable.

At the present writing the two opposing armies appear to be in the position of two very angry dogs who stand glowering at each other, waiting for the other to begin a fight. The attacking party usually has the worst of it, and Meade hesitates about giving battle, hoping that Lee may attempt again to break our lines toward Washington. Couch has delayed unaccountably and has effectually lost what reputation he had as a soldier by dawdling along with his militia in Pennsylvania. Had he been prompt to form a junction with Meade the rebels would have been attacked several days ago before they had any opportunity to reorganize and recover from the defeat at Gettysburg. But now they are in better condition for a defense, and they appear to rely upon their lines and entrenchments against our advance. Today our forces are all in line of battle. Last night the thousands of camp fires gleaming in the darkness from the rolling hills across Antietam showed splendidly. But today the quiet of the Sabbath rests undisturbed over the whole country, and no one could tell, if it were not for the occasional boom of distant skirmishing artillery, that we are in the vicinity of two great armies and that before the night closes a terrific battle may be fought in the fields of waving grain which cover the slopes of Washington county, Maryland.

Boonsborough, Maryland, July 14, 1863

MY SPECIAL RECONNOISSANCE IN FORCE

About noon today a solitary horseman might have been seen slowly wending his muddy way across the fields which lie between Antietam Creek above Boonsborough and the Sharpsburg and Hagerstown pike. All the morning, which was to have been the morning of a great battle, there had been rumors of a retreat of the rebel enemy across the Potomac, and headquarters were rife with injurious reports concerning the fooling of the astute commander of the Army of the Potomac, and it was slanderously asserted that the successor of "Fighting Joe" had been ignominiously sold. Therefore the solitary horseman was your correspondent who had resolved to see for himself and to make a reconnoissance in force.

About twelve o'clock noon a heavy cannonading was heard from the front in the direction of Williamsport on the Potomac, eight miles distant, but we could not tell whether it was the opening of the ball or the firing by the cavalry reconnoissance of [Brigadier General Hugh J.] Kilpatrick and [Major General John] Buford. The rebels had been drawing in their lines during the past few days and throwing up entrenchments to defend their narrow position now only six miles wide and nine miles long. About two miles from Antietam Creek I came upon a line of entrenchments which our forces had thrown up, and here found the Third Corps drawn up in line of battle. The Second and Fifth Corps had been here all the day before in the line of battle but had gone out on a reconnoissance. Beyond the breastworks I met the immense columns pushing forward without much order but formidable enough if a fight were to be precipitated upon them. They marched on in three columns over fields of grain, through orchards, clover fields, and garden spots. The last few days have been rainy, and the ground is yet soft, and the country roads are in a dreadful condition, the mud being knee-deep, soft, but not miry.

About a mile and a half beyond the Union entrenchments we came upon the rebel lines. Here were rifle pits, redoubts, and other hastily constructed earthworks, but not a picket or sentry was to be seen. All had skedaddled incontinently, leaving behind them all of the debris and refuse of their camp. Here were half-gnawed bones, fragments of harness, clothing, blankets, old letters, and all of the trash which a moving army leaves behind it—no more. I picked up a few relics in the deserted camps, shied an empty canteen at a poor horse frame branded "C. S.," and pushed on ahead of the columns of infantry. The roads to Williamsport and vicinity now began to show the traces of flight of the rebel army. All along were broken caissons abandoned in haste, ambulances, guns, knapsacks, and an occasional country wagon smashed all to flinders and left in the road by the rebel thieves who had failed to get off all of their plunder.

The cannonading had ceased, but a few volleys of musketry were yet heard in the vicinity of Falling Waters, four miles below Williamsport. Striking into the woods near Falling Waters, I came upon squads of rebel prisoners in hundreds or more, squatted upon the grass and guarded by a few Union cavalry. These poor fellows were ragged and jaded-looking, wet and muddy, many of them having been caught in the river as they attempted to ford the stream. The roads were crowded now with cavalry, and here and there were parks of artillery brought out on

a bootless errand, the drivers snoozing under the caissons
and forges.

THE LAST FIGHT ON MARYLAND SOIL

Falling Waters is a small settlement on the Potomac
about four miles below Williamsport, and here Lee had
gradually drawn in his lines while preparing to cross and
while crossing. About four miles from here I questioned
some of the inhabitants who said that the last of the rebels
came in from their lines about six o'clock in the morning,
a few stragglers only being seen after that time. A large
force of our cavalry had been the first to follow upon their
retreating footsteps, and early in the forenoon Kilpatrick
and Buford's men had dashed across the country from the
right and left and found the last division of Lee's army
entrenched upon a sharp rise of ground about three-
quarters of a mile from the crossing.

The position was well-taken. The hill rises sharply from
the fields in front, and the approaches to the crossing are
on the right and left. Once behind the hill the roads pass
over gentle undulations to the river where the banks are
sloping and the trees have been all cut away. Upon the
top of the hill which commands the road leading to the
crossing and parallel with the river are a series of light
earthworks which the rebels occupied with a rear guard of
4,000 men, being Jubal A. Early's division of the rebel
army. Behind them were still passing the rear of the
rebels when our forces came up at noon. Lee had finished
on Saturday last a pontoon bridge across the Potomac at
this place, having put in pontoons sent up from Winchester with scows and boats seized in the vicinity and
eked out the whole into very good engineering and trestle
work, all of which was standing when I got down there
today.

The rebels who were protecting the retreat of their army in the breastworks on the hill raised a white flag when our cavalry advanced in force, and the men went pouring pell-mell up the hill but were received with a volley which laid low about twenty of our soldiers and wounded many more. At the same time a large force of rebel infantry was deployed on their right where the hill slopes down into a wheat field, but the onslaught of the Union cavalry was so furious that they could not stand before it and began a fighting retreat. Our light artillery was brought to bear upon them, and then commenced the cannonade which had been heard about two hours before when I was on the Sharpsburg pike. The fighting was brief but keen, and in a very short time such rebels as could get to the bridge were fleeing across. The rest, fighting bravely through the lanes, finally were overpowered and surrendered, about 1,600 in all.

In the meantime another cavalry force had surrounded the small squads of rebels who were trying to ford across on the scows which were also used at Williamsport, and 350 were taken prisoner there, making the whole number of rebel prisoners caught exceeding 2,000 in number. And that is all we have of Lee's army of rebels which we were to bag while it was securely caged in the elbow formed by the bend of the Potomac at this place. All, did I say? There are a score or more lying fraternally with Union soldiers in the wheat field yonder in front of their breastworks. They lie among the wheat sheaves which the fight overturned, their faces toward the sky—graybacks and bluebacks—sleeping the gory sleep that knows no waking.

PARTING COMPLIMENTS

Up the last hill I rode, and looking across the turbid Potomac I could see, amid the rolling, woody hills on the

Virginia side, the numerous ascending columns of smoke which marked where the rebel encampments now lie. On a bare hill about a mile away are lines of earthworks hastily thrown up, and from these a few rebel sharpshooters pepper away at anything which shows its head on the clear space around the hither end of their rude bridge. Our own sharpshooters, concealed in the trees, return the compliment and endeavor to pick off the rebels as they warily show their heads above the rifle pits. It is only an annoying fire to cover the rebel retreat and prevent our crossing in pursuit. The Minié balls fly uncomfortably through the trees, and your faithful correspondent having seen the end of the campaign in Maryland, rides back across the deserted fields made barren wastes by the retreating rush of the rebel army, all of whose converging lines spreading to the outer entrenchments meet at the bridge where they crossed on the night of July 13.

Why didn't we bag them? Of course the country will ask the question, and with the present light on the subject we can only say that if General Meade had followed his own judgment the rebel army would have been attacked upon Monday, just in the nick of time, when a portion of their force was across and the main part of the army was congregating around the scow crossing at Williamsport and the bridge at Falling Waters. On Sunday night he called a council of corps commanders, and out of eight there were only three who favored the General's proposition to attack the next day. Those three were General Pleasonton of the cavalry corps, General [James S.] Wadsworth, acting Commander of the First Corps, and General [Oliver] Howard of the Eleventh Corps. General Meade, being overruled by his officers, deferred the attack, and the rebels escaped into Virginia. General Hooker, we cannot help thinking, would have asked the advice of his commanders and then have done just as he thought best —attacked the rebels.

The effect of this failure to defeat the rebel army will be unfortunate upon our army, which has accomplished wonders during its late hard month of service, marching from Virginia to Pennsylvania, then fighting a three day's battle, and then following the rebels to Maryland, and being all the time exposed to such privations as marching troops in rainy weather without full rations or shelter can only suffer. They see that their term of service "for the war" is lengthened a year at least by the escape of their old foe, and they have speedily lost the high spirits which they had but yesterday. But we must wait still and hope yet for a better end to all of these campaigns and believe that they will not all be so fruitless as the July campaign in Maryland.

Washington, July 18, 1863

GROWLING AT HALLECK

Unquestionably the worst hated man in public life at this moment is the unfortunate gentleman who bears the undesirable title of General-in-Chief of the American Armies, "Mr. Halleck," as some of the newspapers call him. During Lee's occupation of western Maryland we had over 40,000 troops on the peninsula and between Richmond and Washington, and yet not any attempt upon the rebel capital was made, though genuine intercepted dispatches from the rebel adjutant general at Richmond to Lee showed that the authorities there apprehended such an attack and were in great trepidation thereat. No attempt was made by the War Department, whoever that may be, to dispute the crossing of Lee or to prevent the small rebel force at Martinsburg, Virginia, from sending him the pontoons by which he made his escape. We had forces enough south of the Potomac either to have made an attack upon Richmond or to have checked Lee, but neither was done, though the condition of the rebel capital was known to Halleck, and in his note to Meade he had pointedly alluded to the possibility that Lee would cross just where he afterwards did. Now, these are facts, and the country will hold somebody responsible for the atrocious blunder which sent more reinforcements to Meade than he needed and failed to take advantage of the depleted and denuded condition of Virginia after the rebel invasion of Pennsylvania. It it not surprising that the whole country howls for the removal of Halleck if he is responsible for this long catalogue of errors.

REBEL MORALE

One bright feature of the otherwise resultless Maryland campaign is the undoubted fact that the rebel army went home in a very disconsolate condition. The concurrent testimony of the captured rebels and of the citizens who were dwelling within the rebel lines during their last sojourn in the vicinity of Williamsport is that the tone of both officers and men was despondent and that of disappointment. They had come over the line to make free states the scene of the war for the future and expected to have been able, if they retired, to have done so without much loss and carrying with them rich plunder. But they were going back with about one-half of the force which they brought over, and their extensive raid had only given them forage and rations while they had been in Maryland and Pennsylvania and had furnished them with a few thousand horses, mules, and cattle. In numbers of animals captured they had reason to congratulate themselves, but that was about all, for they confessed that they were cut down in their rations after they were hemmed in by the federal lines, and there was nothing left to eat in the rebel lines, in barn or storehouse, when our forces broke over the rebel entrenchments on the 15th of June.

The rebel prisoners from North Carolina and Georgia said that they did not see what they were fighting for, but they had become tired of "fighting for Virginia." Their continued cry was, "I want to go home!" The North Carolinians said that the generals would not trust them and always made them fight "with bayonets behind." The immense proportion of killed and captured from the Old North State is a sufficient confirmation of the truth of that statement. The system of deceit which the Confederates practice toward their men is shown in the fact that the fall of Vicksburg was officially denied by General Lee, and the statement in the newspapers smuggled into camp was denounced as "a Yankee lie." At Hagerstown a citizen was arrested for reading an account of the capture of Vicksburg to a cluster of rebel soldiers who had doubted the news. The rebel pickets were not trusted with the movements of Sunday and Monday and did not know of the rebel retreat until called in for the last time. . . .

Washington, July 21, 1863

THE DRAFT

As might be expected, this subject is yet the all engrossing topic of conversation, and all of the various questions growing out of it are discussed with great animation and earnestness. It has been decided that a drafted man may pay his exemption or substitute fee or furnish a substitute after he has applied for exemption on the score of physical disability and has failed to be so excused. A contrary ruling had been made by some enrolling officers, and the question was carried up to the Solicitor of the War Department. It has also been decided that a drafted man cannot furnish a black substitute. The attempt to do so has been made in Philadelphia. I suppose there would be no objection to a white substitute being furnished by a black drafted man, provided the drafted man would guarantee that the white substitute would not demoralize the Negro regiment.

From letters received here it appears that the drafting officers in New York believe that now will be the best time to enforce the draft. The mob has played itself out. From being an organized movement set on foot by rebel conspirators it has degenerated into a mere guerrilla party of plunderers, and the people who own portable or combustible property are naturally alarmed and have come to the conclusion that there are some things even worse than a draft, and though they do not love the draft, they fear the mob. Yesterday a Copperhead committee from New York came here for the purpose of inducing the President to forbear enforcing the draft on the ground that it *would create a popular disturbance.* Cool, wasn't it?

On the other hand another committee from the same city is here, asking that the draft may be rigidly enforced and that the majesty of the law and the dignity of the government may be vindicated by a refusal to allow the mobocratic dictation to suspend the operation of the National Militia Law. The suspension of the draft in New York was only temporary, and it will be resumed as soon as the hindering disturbance has subsided. But the government has at no time had any intention of allowing any state or locality to escape its share of the draft on account of the unpopularity of the measure with a portion of the people.

In the District of Columbia the enrolling has been completed and the draft will be made as soon as the necessary arrangements are perfected—the quota of the District under the demand for 300,000 men being about one in six. All sorts of dodges are resorted to by those who are liable to the draft, and as many persons so liable are only temporary residents it is very easy for them to get off. In the departments the clerks form themselves into insurance clubs of fifteen or twenty each, pledging each other to raise among themselves the amount necessary to furnish a substitute for any one or more of their number who may be drafted. Meanwhile, there is no sort of apprehension here that there will be any opposition to the draft in this District, for though there are plenty of genuine secessionists here who would delight to foment a disturbance, the sentiment of the majority of the people is overwhelmingly loyal and in favor of law and order.

CORPORAL MARY JANE

One of Averell's cavalry scouts lately captured in western Virginia a party of rebel infantry, among whom was a corporal who had the squad in charge. They were brought to Washington and, upon investigation, it was discovered that the corporal, a reckless, harum-scarum person, was a woman in man's attire. She says that she enlisted out of pure love of excitement and that she had not a single acquaintance in the rebel ranks when she joined the army, so no love tale can be made out for her. And her personal appearance and manners preclude all sentimentality on her part, for she is very ugly and is one of the most abusive and profane persons now in the Old Capitol Prison. Corporal Mary Jane is held for exchange, as she was found in arms against the government of the United States, but it is not easy to see how she can be justly exchanged until they catch a Union woman acting as a corporal in our own army. She boasts that she is equal to any three of the best Yankee soldiers whom she has ever seen. She is a native of Georgia, and she says that her father is a Methodist clergyman and that her parents are living in Georgia.

A NEW ORDER OF MERIT

A large number of promotions have lately been made in the Treasury Department, and it has been discovered that all of the promotions have been made among those clerks who are married men, the Secretary justly considering that these hard times demanded that the family men should have something more to meet expenses than the single men have. Whereat the old bachelors are indignant, and the wife market is looking up.

Washington, July 28, 1863

THE HEATED TERM

Has fairly commenced in these parts, and the weather is truly awful. For a Californian who has been baked in Marysville, fried in Shasta, and comfortably broiled for two days on the "stone dump" of Timbuctoo, Yuba County, this may seem an unreasonable complaint, but

California heat is healthy and bearable compared with the clammy, moist, sticky, and stifling atmosphere of Washington. Here we have an occasional breeze, but it brings no relief, for it seems to be laden with warm molasses, and one feels its adhesive sweetness upon everything it touches. The garments cling to the skin; shirt collars are laid low; moisture oozes from every object, standing in clammy exudation upon iron, marble, wood, and human flesh; the air is pervaded with a faint odor as of withered bouquets and dead mint juleps, and the warm steam of a home washing day is over everything. Truly the season is one of languor, lassitude, and laziness, and there is no chance for recuperation—

> For the nights are likewise fearful,
> And the heat which expands the day
> Steals through the dark like an Arab
> And melts our sleep away.

Consequently, Washington is as silent as a deserted village, and nearly everybody except the members of the unfortunate Can't-get-away Club has gone to the seaside or countryside. Secretary Chase is off on a tour of combined business and pleasure. His daughter is sojourning at Cape May; Mrs. Lincoln is about to leave Philadelphia for the White Mountains and Vermont, accompanied by her son Robert (Bob O'Lincoln, Prince of Rails); and even the hard-working President says that if all goes well he may take a northern trip himself during the next two months, traveling as nearly *incog.* as so well-known a face as his can, and leaving the machine of state to run itself for a few days. News is accordingly plentifully scarce in the capital city just now, and the reporters have nearly all followed the example of better men and have likewise skeddadled from the heat and the draft to come, leaving one overworked correspondent to get the daily column of sensation for the New York and western newspapers.

SPEAKING OF THE DRAFT

... It is, perhaps, not especially creditable to our patriotism that a decided majority of the drafted are applicants for exemption on the ground of physical disability or by paying the fee. Before the draft was made nearly everybody began to talk over the various expedients by which they were to get out of the anticipated scrape, and nobody ever talked of going to the war but, at the worst, consoled themselves with the thought that they could escape the service by paying a sum of money. The reason for this may be found—not in the unpopularity of the war—but in the unpopularity of the service. It is a notorious fact that the fighting and marching of the rank and file is very hard work. The freeborn American citizen chafes and frets under arbitrary rule of even such imperfect military discipline as we have in our army, and the well-fed, comfortable citizen cannot stomach the hard fare and *désagréments* of camp life; his gorge rises against pork and hardbread and dirty and lousy associates. Marching in the hot sun with musket on shoulder and knapsack on back appears to be a hard and indirect road to glory, and though the patriotic spirit is willing the flesh is very weak. We all want the rebellion crushed, the war brought to a victorious end, and Jeff Davis hanged on a sour apple tree, but when told to tread the duty road which leads to those probabilities we fail to see it in that light. . . .

The decision of the Provost Marshal General, [James B. Fry,] that black substitutes cannot be accepted for white drafted men has left upon the hands of diverse persons a great number of woolly-headed elephants. Having bought their black menagerie at a low figure, they must now sell out on the best terms which they can make, for Colonel Fry says that a substitute must have the same status as that of the drafted man. Negroes being paid less, organized differently, and given less bounty cannot be regarded as the equal of the white soldier after all that has been said and done.

Washington, August 1, 1863

HORSES WANTED

There is a fearful horse famine just now. The cavalry service wears out so many horses and our cavalry is so useful and so freely used that a great consumption has taken place, and it is difficult to obtain remounts. There are now over 8,000 men in the efficient cavalry corps of the Army of the Potomac destitute of horses, and the government is greatly put to it to find animals for them. Impressment, so long practiced in the rebel states, has been reluctantly resorted to, and officers are now traveling through Maryland impressing such horses as they can find fit for the service. The valuation of the animals so taken ranges from $135 to $150, the army regulations fixing $200 as the maximum sum to be paid by the government for any horse or mule. This seems hard, but it must be done, for the cavalry must be kept up, and the consumption of such animals by the corps is astonishing. For instance, during Stoneman's famous raid, which was in its solid results only a piece of "first rate circus riding," over 3,000 horses were used up or killed, and at present rates $400,000 would not pay for that item of expense for the "raid" about which we all glorified so much. . . .

Washington, August 5, 1863

HOW ARE YOU, CONSCRIPTS?

... The draft commenced day before yesterday and up to last night four of the seven wards of the city were drawn, and still the work goes on. The draft is carried on at the City Hall under the supervision of Captain Sheetz, the Provost Marshal of the District. The names of the enrolled are placed in a large box, each name being written upon a stout card. A blind man draws forth a card, the commissioner calls out the name, and then four enrolling clerks take the card one from the other and write down the name. The hall is crowded to suffocation by an anxious, sweaty herd of people, mostly of the "unwashed," and the silence is interrupted only when the name is called or some well-known person present is found to be elected. Occasionally some unconscious, unlucky one responds "Here!" to his name, or a happy Irishman exclaims, "That's me, bejabers!"

The crowd is good-natured and jolly, and it does not have any need of the military guard which has been on duty at the City Hall since the drawing began. Everybody is anxious to find out if he is drafted, and the evening newspapers are sought with eagerness as the names of the lucky drafted appear in each edition as fast as drawn. The newsboys have caught the humor of the day and call out "Here's the *Evening 'Publican!* Get the list of killed and wounded in the Third Ward!"

The conscripts all appear to be very thirsty—probably feverish, and they and their friends drink a great many juleps, cobblers, and brandy smashes, while grins and jokes (some of them of a ghastly sort) go around, and one would suppose that Uncle Sam was perpetrating a greater joke than even honest old Abe's "Pope's bull against the comet." The newspaper Bohemians—thirsty crowd—got off very well from the draft, for of the correspondents there were only two taken: Uriah H. Painter of the Philadelphia *Inquirer* and Edward H. House of the New York *Tribune*. But there were eight employees taken from the *Chronicle* office and one from the *Globe*. The employees of the former newspaper have been formed into a *"Chronicle* Home Guard,"* concerning which there has been a very acrimonious dispute between the *Chronicle* and the *Intelligencer*, the latter sheet poking much fun at the organization and charging that it was got up to evade the draft, which the other newspaper indignantly denies. . . .

THE HOTTEST YET

The past three or four days have been the very hottest of the season, the mercury going up to 104 degrees in the shade in some parts of the city, though the Smithsonian Institution, a fossiliferous retreat on "the Island," has only 94 degrees as its maximum of heat. But that has been hot enough to cause a great deal of sickness. In one day, Monday, August 3, no less than six deaths from sunstroke occurred in the city, and various diseases peculiar to excessively hot weather have begun to appear. In the opinion of many physicians the prevailing sickness is largely owing to the many dead carcasses which have been partially burned or partially buried around Washington during the past months. Hereafter a more strict system of regulation will be enforced, but much mischief has already resulted from the imperfect and hasty manner of disposing of the innumerable carcasses of dead animals which are left

around the city by teamsters and others in the employment of the government.

Washington, September 23, 1863

THE DRAFT A FAILURE

It is not a pleasant thing to write but it must be confessed that the execution of the Conscription Law has
been a failure. That is, it is a failure so far as the results
are concerned, for... it has failed to produce enough men
to swell the armies of the Union to anything like their
maximum standard. Various causes have combined to produce this result, the first of which is the too liberal
margin for exemption from service on account of physical
disability; and the second is the incompetence and weakness—to say the least—of enrolling and examining officers.
The details of the manner in which the draft has been
carried into effect in some parts of New England are discouraging and sickening in the extreme. Men who are
perfectly able-bodied and hale have been exempted on the
ground of physical disability, and it is notorious that such
exemption was the result of favoritism, political chicanery,
or downright bribery. A system of corruption, imbecility,
and mismanagement has characterized the machinery of
the draft throughout the country, which has tended to
bring the measure into disrepute and has filled the hearts
of all loyal and patriotic men with sorrow and mortification. It is a source of indignation and grief to every honest
loyalist that there are citizens of our own loyal states who
rejoice over this state of things and who but poorly conceal
their gratification at the failure of the draft. May the Lord
punish them; we cannot.

It is most likely that a new draft will be ordered shortly, and if it should be laid before the new Congress assembles the list of physical ails and aches which have been so prolific a source of reasons for exemption will be cut down by the War Department from whom they emanated; but if the draft shall not be made until Congress shall have met, it is most likely that the $300 exemption clause, which has been the stumbling block of captious Copperheads, will be stricken out of the law. Then we shall see if those who have cried out against this "discrimination in favor of the rich against the poor" will like it any better when they must go or find their own substitute.

THE NORTHERN COPPERHEAD

A careful survey of the field and a considerable acquaintance with the people of the North and West have convinced me that the most dangerous and least understood enemy of the public welfare at this time is the Copperhead. In the District of Columbia, where the military arm is always bare, and even in New York City, where policy prevails, the disloyal element is subterranean and smothered if not extinguished. But if we travel through the towns and villages of Maine, New Hampshire, Indiana, Illinois, and western New York, we find disloyalty under the guise of Copperheadism of the most malignant and rampant kind. There seems to be neither shame nor patriotism left in these mean creatures, who make no bones of openly expressing their sympathy with the rebels and avowing their belief in the ultimate triumph of the cause which they thus espouse.

It is beyond comprehension how such a feeling was born and upon what it feeds. When the rebellion first broke out the Copperhead element lay dormant, and it rose when disasters to the national arms seemed to promise hope to the rebel cause. Federal successes, continuous and frequent, served to check the torrent for awhile, but lately there seems to be a spirit of determined desperation on the part of the Copperheads in exact proportion with the growing desperation of the rebel cause. Just after such victories as Vicksburg and Port Hudson these unclean beasts fled to their holes and pulled their holes in after them for a brief space, but they soon emerged again.

During a late tour of New England I heard sentiments freely and constantly expressed by the natives in the interior, which, if uttered in this city, would consign the caitiffs to the Old Capitol Prison in a trice. Copperhead orators on the backwoods stump would stigmatize the soldiers of the Union as "Lincoln's minions, bearing the disgraceful badge of servitude," and Copperhead farmers along the road would ask if "Jeff hadn't sent Abe Lincoln to h--l yet," showing by their disappointment that their hopes pointed hellwards. In one of the farming towns in the interior of Maine, where there is but one voter to a square mile and each man believes that General Jackson is still a candidate for the Presidency, they lately elected a Copperhead board of selectmen or town trustees, and that triumph was seized upon as affording reasonable ground for believing that the volunteers from that benighted region would be called back from the army. That such a feeling also pervades the ranks of a more intelligent but no less malignant Democracy in that state may be well believed. The same is true in the West where the Copperheads are themselves for emergencies and hold midnight meetings and secret conclaves of the Golden Circle. The traitorous doings of these wretches which have come to my own personal knowledge would fill pages, but it is only necessary to add that, after all, these mean-spirited caitiffs are greatly in a minority, as the recent elections have shown; but it is enough to alarm (and sadden, too) the loyalist when such wicked and hell-born sentiments prevail in a loyal state. . . .

Washington, September 26, 1863

BROTHER AGAINST BROTHER

Another incident peculiar to this unhappy war occurred in Maryland lately where a body of about 500 cavalry crossed the Potomac into Maryland near Rockville, about fifteen miles from this city. They fed their horses in a cornfield of Alexander Kilgore whose son, William, is a lawyer in Washington, but was at home at the time. He managed to get word to some of the Union troops, Scott's Nine Hundred, in the vicinity, and the rebels were charged upon by our cavalry, and a brisk skirmish ensued. . . . The rebels fled, leaving upon the ground several dead and wounded, among whom was the body of Frank Kilgore, a captain in the rebel service and brother to the Washington attorney. . . . He had been in the Confederate army for two years and at last met his death upon the same spot where he was born and where his old father still lived to receive and bury the body of his rebel son. How pitiful and how unnatural are many of these incidents of this wicked war urged by unnatural children against a beneficent and paternal government!

THE PRESIDENT IN A FIX

Almost everybody would like to be president, and there are but few persons who realize any of the difficulties which surround a just administration of the duties of the executive office. The other day a delegation from Baltimore called upon the President by appointment to consider the case of a certain citizen of Baltimore whom it was proposed to appoint to a responsible office in that city. The delegation filed in proudly, formed a semicircle in front of the President, and the spokesman stepped out and read a neat address to the effect that while they had the most implicit faith in the honesty and patriotism of the President they were ready to affirm that the person proposed to be placed in office was a consummate rascal and notoriously in sympathy, if not in correspondence, with the rebels. The speaker concluded and stepped back, and the President replied by complimenting them on their appearance and professions of loyalty, but he said he was at a loss what to do with ———, as a delegation twice as large, just as respectable in appearance, and no less ardent in professions of loyalty had called upon him four days before ready to swear, everyone of them, that ——— was one of the most honest and loyal men in Baltimore. "Now," said the President, "we cannot afford to call a court of inquiry in this case, and so, as a lawyer I shall be obliged to decide that the weight of testimony, two to one, is in favor of the client's loyalty, and as you do not offer even any attempt to prove the truth of your suspicions, I shall be compelled to ignore them for the present." The delegation bade the President good morning and left.

Washington, October 2, 1863

PUBLISHING CONTRABAND NEWS

... When it was decided to reinforce Rosecrans at Chattanooga with the Eleventh and Twelfth Corps of the Army of the Potomac an officer from the War Department went to every newspaper correspondent in town and re-

quested each, at the special desire of the President and
Secretary of War, not to mention any movement from the
Army of the Potomac or in any way allude to it, thus
throwing themselves on the patriotism of the correspondents. The request was made in a gentlemanly manner and
was so reasonable withal that all the correspondents agreed
to it and telegraphed or wrote to their newspapers not to
allude to the event should it come to their knowledge in
any way. Everybody was astounded on the night of September 26 by information from New York that the *Evening Post*, an out-and-out administration paper, had published full particulars of the reinforcement of Rosecrans.
Some of the Sunday morning papers copied the intelligence, and the Philadelphia *Sunday Mercury*, a rabid
secesh concern, went so far as to republish the *Post's* news
with the addendum that it was contraband and that if
justice were done the editors of the *Post* should breakfast
in Fort Lafayette.

The newspapermen were in despair, Stanton raged like a
lion, and the President, I am free to say, was very mad.
The Monday morning papers discreetly held their peace
and quietly ignored the intelligence and the whole affair,
waiting for a proper opportunity to open their batteries
on the unfortunate *Post* which made haste in its next edition to explain by saying that its Washington correspondent was not responsible for the *rumors* which had appeared
in its Saturday edition concerning army movements, but
that it had been imposed upon by irresponsible parties.
The truth of the matter was that an occasional correspondent of the *Post* who dabbles in stocks was in Washington
at the time and to buoy up the market, which was droop-
ing, smuggled the news to New York by mail, and the
senior poetical editor who has usually nothing to do with
the make-up of the paper got hold of it and put it in,
greatly to the dismay of the managing editor.

I have been thus particular in the account of this latest newspaper escapade for the reason that the whole report was afterward contradicted with a great deal of virtuous indignation, but it was substantially correct as it first appeared. The affair is unfortunate for the *Post*, as it not long since published President Lincoln's Springfield letter, much to his vexation and chagrin. On the day before its delivery he had refused an advanced copy to the Washington agent of the Associated Press, saying that though solemn promises not to publish had repeatedly been given, he had found the practice of furnishing advance copies to newspapers to be a source of endless mischief. That night the *Post* published the letter, and it was telegraphed back to Washington before it was read at the Springfield convention. So much for newspaper enterprise, but where they got the letter is yet a secret known to the editors only.

MISCELLANEOUS

Mrs. Lincoln has returned from the North where she has been visiting since August 1, but the family will not take up quarters at the White House until the latter part of October. The coming season is likely to be more gay than usual at the Executive Mansion, and a series of "dress levees" are intended to be inaugurated soon after the opening of Congress.

Washington, October 6, 1863

CONCERNING THE NEXT PRESIDENTIAL CAMPAIGN

There is no longer any need of concealing or ignoring the fact that Lincoln is a candidate for renomination. Your correspondent has the highest authority for saying that he does not seek the nomination, but really desires it at the hands of the loyal people of the United States. In this desire, a natural ingredient, is his hope that he may receive the suffrages of the people as an approval of the policy with which he has conducted an administration through a long and arduous struggle. It is true that other Presidents may have asked the same on the same ground, but Lincoln has been called upon to administer the government in strange and perilous times, and, as it is conceded that a change in the administration during the present war would be, to say the least, risky, or, to use Lincoln's own phrase, would be "swapping horses in the middle of the stream;" it would be a direct rebuke to the present incumbent of the Presidential chair to rotate him out of office while affairs are in such a situation. It would be virtually voting him a failure; if he is a failure he ought to go, for the safety and welfare of the nation are of more value than any President's personal feelings or claims. But it is also reasonable to believe that Lincoln has, so far as any man can have, a symmetrical and coherent plan, compact in his own mind, for the adjudication of the great questions which will arise under the final pacification of "this great trouble," as he calls the rebellion. If the people are satisfied that Lincoln has done the best which could be done for the suppression of the rebellion, the protection of our varied interests, and for the whole country, and are willing to trust him with the pacification of the country, he will be the next President of the United States.

He is no seeker for a renewal of office, busies himself with no thought of his own future, and never bestows favors with any reference whatever to the relations of an applicant for office toward himself. But, patient, patriotic, persevering, and singlehearted, he goes right on with his duty, "pegging away" just as though, as he has said to me, his own life were to end with his official life, content to leave his earnest labors and conscientious discharge of duty to the disposal of God and his country. A nobler and purer nature than his never animated man. His chiefest errors have been that the heart overruled the head, and a kindness, which has been mistaken for weakness, has too often prevailed when sterner counsels have been heard. He is, also, so anxious to conserve and defend the interests of *the whole country* that he has disappointed and alienated some portions of it, and he has thus turned away those who would have been always his friends. Here, in Washington, we have frequent occasion to hear the beratings and scoldings of politicians who have been treated just as dispassionately and coolly by the President as though they had no power at all to bring to bear upon a future presidential canvass. Lincoln does not appear to consider for a moment that the men whom he kindly but firmly denies today will tomorrow be part and parcel of a nominating convention, but he does what he considers to be right, regardless of the consequences to himself. This is noble, but is it politic?

THE GREAT SPLIT

And right here comes into prominence the widening breach between the Conservatives and the Radicals of the Union or Republican party. Radicalism and Conservatism are now the opposing forces which besiege the President, which are entering into an adjustment of all the great issues for the settlement of the rebellion, and which will divide the combatants in the contest for the next nomination, now narrowed down as far as the Unionists are concerned to two candidates—Lincoln, standard-bearer for the Conservatives, and Chase, the champion of the Radicals. It is evident that Lincoln will have to fall back upon his own

conservative policy as laid down by his own administration
and become the candidate of a People's Union party. Not
that there will be more than one candidate against the
opposition or so-called Democratic party, but the fight
will be in the convention, and it promises to be almost
as interesting as the old Douglas and Buchanan quarrel,
without any of its bitterness.

Those disloyalists who hope to see a dismemberment
of the great loyal party of the North through a sharp feud
between new and inharmonious elements will not be able
to draw much comfort from an apparent incoherence of
the component parts. An ambition for the chair of state
is honorable, as much so in Chase as in Lincoln, but it
happens that the two men represent ideas and principles
which are different but not radically opposed or irreconcil-
able. Chase's views and sentiments are not manufactured
for the occasion; his lifelong record, his splendid public
services, his uncompromising hostility to every form of
oppression and slavery, his purity of character—all these
are too well-known to need recapitulation, and these,
added to his statesmanlike abilities, make him an eminently fit candidate for what is known as the radical wing
of the loyal party of the North. If our people are ready
now to go into an election upon Chase's avowed platform
of "Freedom for all," he will be the next president. Chase
keeps ahead of public sentiment. Lincoln prefers to be led
by it. . . .

WHAT THE CABINET WILL DO

If any of the members of the cabinet of President Lincoln
have had any aspirations for his uneasy chair—and it would
be surprising if they had not—all but Chase have resigned
such fond dreams. Seward has virtually relinquished his

claims and will support Lincoln, though his influence has been greatly shorn of late by the outrageous conduct of some of his ancient allies. Postmaster General [Montgomery] Blair, "the meanest man in the cabinet" and we may add the meanest man in Washington, will also support Lincoln, though Frank P. Blair, has gone over, body and soul, to the Democrats and will vote against the administration in the organization of the House of Representatives. Postmaster Blair is making speeches in which he is supposed to be defining the policy of the Lincoln administration in case it has the job of reconstructing the Union. Secretary Welles, who is of no great account anyway, will go for Chase. Stanton, known among those who know him best as "The Brute," will undoubtedly go for Chase. Secretary Usher, a goodish man, will support Chase also. Attorney General Bates, a respectable fossil, will go for Lincoln. I am aware that I am not speaking of these high dignitaries with all of the respect that their position would, perhaps, demand, but it is not easy to convey that loss of veneration which must be suffered by those who have learned by close proximity how weak and illusory is that divinity which doth hedge about the great. It is a comfort to believe, at least, that if Lincoln should be re-elected only two of his present cabinet would be retained as his constitutional advisers.

Washington, October 9, 1863

BUILDING AT THE CAPITAL

From present appearances it is quite likely that the "magnificent distances" of the national village will be pretty well filled up if the demand for houses continues much longer. The high prices of rents, especially of houses and lodging rooms, have stimulated building to such an extent that every street has its piles of brick, stone, marble, and iron encumbering the ground and stopping the way preparatory to the erection of dwellings, and the sound of the hammer, the ringing of the trowel, and calls for "more mort" now resound in every direction. The incentive to build is certainly very great, for, though the price of all sorts of materials is higher than ever before, the demand for room is truly unprecedented. Members of Congress must pay more than half their salary for the expenses of living this winter—to say nothing of whisky bills—if they live in any sort of style. The Haytian minister succeeded Senator Milton Shakespeare Latham of California in his occupation of a palatial residence on K Street, paying therefor $2,000 per annum, but as his colored excellency is about to remove to New York he has had his lease cancelled, or as his accomplished black secretary called it, "Vat you call broke off and stop." Accordingly, there has been a rush for the house which has been finally let to a virtuous quartermaster at $4,500, Senator Sumner offering $1,200 for three rooms in the second story.

Rooms which rented at $100 a month last winter go off like hot cakes now for $150, and no decent congressman would be willing to put up with anything for which he would pay less than $75 a month. With table board at $45 a month (Willard's prices), one can see what a "right smart chance" there is for a congressman or any other man to lay by much in the way of savings. Heretofore Washington people have not been willing to risk much money in building. Before the war dwellings and hotels were vacant half of the year, and since the war and the rush for buildings began, property in Washington has been deemed of doubtful value. Though the majestic dome of the Palace of the People has not been stayed for a day in its rising height, real estate owners have hesitated to build houses which Jeb Stuart might burn or Jeff Davis confiscate; but now that feeling has vanished before the moral certainty that the end of the rebellion and the safety of the capital are secure, and before another year shall have passed buildings for rent will be plentiful enough in Washington. Whether there will not be a great collapse in business in this now bustling city when the war shall be over is not doubtful. The trades and avocations which an expensive war has called into existence and centered here will find their occupations gone. The hosts of interests which now depend upon the army for support will vanish from Washington, and all of those who now supply with the necessaries of life the increased civil and military forces here will go with them.

But for the present Washington is a lively, busy, and corrupt city. The painted women who flutter their shame upon the streets, the gambling dens which infest the principal avenues, the bribery and corruption which spreads its nets everywhere—all of these are the legitimate results of such a war as we now carry on. It is no argument against this or any other administration to say that such things exist here in greater aggravation than ever before. It is one of the evil fruits of a wicked war brought on by wicked men that such things should exist. It has always been so since time began and war was made—ever since the day that Achan "detailed" the "goodly Babylonish garment, and two hundred shekels of silver, and a wedge of gold and fifty shekels weight" from the spoils of Jericho, down to the day when Frémont's "California gang" gobbled up mule contracts and other profitable bargains at St. Louis.

Jay Cooke & Company is building a superb edifice on Fifteenth Street near the Treasury for a banking office. The front is to be of white marble, highly decorated and elegant, and all of the floor joists, rafters, etc., are to be of cast iron and of great strength. By this arrangement there will be more height to the interior than could be obtained in any other way. Though the whole structure is fifty feet high, there are to be but two stories to it, the lower to be occupied by the banking business of the firm and the upper by the First National Bank of Washington.

Right across the street from this building the work on the Treasury extension is going on rapidly, and already one or two bureaus have been moved into their new quarters. The old system of many small rooms has been abolished, and each department or bureau is put in one great room by itself, well provided for light, ventilation, and comfort, and the whole being under the immediate supervision of the chief clerk or controller of the bureau. The private rooms and office of the Secretary of the Treasury are truly palatial in style and finish. The walls are richly decorated in gold and colors, the passages paved with tessellated marble and the floors are to be covered with rich carpets of appropriate design now being manufactured in Europe, and the furniture is now being made to order in Philadelphia. A luxurious bathroom with marble fittings and other conveniences is near at hand. It seems a pity, however, that there is not much prospect that any tenant of all these splendors can have more than a four years' lease.

WORK ON THE CAPITOL

During the present summer the interior of the Capitol has been renovated, refitted, cleansed of the dirt of the Thirty-Seventh Congress, and made ready for the dirt and wickedness of the incoming legislators. The halls of the Senate and House have been thoroughly purified, the lobbies and corridors whitened, and much of the unfinished fresco painting in the Senate wing has been completed. The Capitol exterior has advanced considerably toward completion. The great bronze doors, or valve, for the principal front on the Capitol, cast in Munich, Germany, after models by [Randolph] Rogers and costing $40,000, have arrived and will be put in place before the opening of the next session of Congress. The magnificent portico of the Senate wing is nearly completed, the sculpture for the pediment being in place, and the work above it being pushed forward so that the whole front of that wing will be done before December 1.

. . . The porticoes of the wings are supported by colonnades of white marble, fluted shafts of great beauty thirty or forty feet high, thirty in number. The main entrance to the Senate wing, enriched with carved marble, is complete, and the recumbent statues of Law and Justice have been placed over the doorway. The statuary in the pediment is by [Thomas] Crawford and is said to be illustrative of the progress of America. In the center is the Genius of America, a nice young woman stroking the head of a rampant eagle and gazing intently on the top of an immense sycamore tree which is just in front of the portico. On her left is a lusty backwoodsman chopping down a tree. Next, an Indian boy with spoils of the chase. Beyond him is a meditative Indian speculating on the future of his race or the price of firewater, while a sorrowful squaw and an infant Pah Utah sitting at the head of an Indian grave complete that side of the pedimental procession. On the right of the central figure is a militia general "a-drawin' of his sword," a Boston-looking wholesale dry goods dealer sitting on a cotton bale, a pedagogue fingering a terrestrial globe and teaching the young, two young ideas coming up to be taught to shoot, and a very clean-looking blacksmith . . . with a sheaf of wheat and an anchor (a portion of the harvest of the sea, I suppose) at his feet. Which way America is supposed to progress in this extraordinary collection of statuary does not appear.

The dome is receiving the ornaments of iron which now encumber all of the ground about the Capitol, and scrolls, volutes, flowers, and other cast-iron nondescripts are fast finding their places on the immense bulb which soars far above the massive pile of marble. It is the intention of [Thomas U.] Walter, the architect, to have the molus on the summit of the dome complete, and the statue of Liberty, which will surmount it, in its place by November 1; but as the work is an arduous one, it may not be done before the next session commences. At present the statue of Liberty, which is twenty feet high and weighs nearly 15,000 pounds, is lying dismembered on the ground, her ladyship's head, arms, legs, etc., gigantic in their way, receiving the attentive admiration of the daily throng of sight-seers at the Capitol. It will be "Make way for Liberty" when she begins to go up, however, for her breadth of beam is truly tremendous. The superintending authorities are profoundly agitated just now to decide upon the color for the dome when it shall be complete. At present it is white, but as its design precludes the idea that it might be marble, it is suggested by Walter that its metallic appearance be further decided by painting it a light bronze, and that will probably be the conclusion reached by the rest of the parties concerned.

Washington October 24, 1863

DARK AND RAINY

. . . There are days and weeks when events seem to come to a complete standstill, and this is one of them. The people in the streets are only such as have imperative business out of doors; the hotels are crowded with dripping, steamy people; the overloaded streetcars go swashing along the dripping rails, the unhappy animals who draw them covered with mud; the little crossing sweeps are out in all their strength of raggedness; the workmen who daily swarm over the unfinished apex of the Capitol dome have disappeared within; the national banner flaps heavily in the wet blast, and mud-bedraggled marketing women infest the conveyances or crowd the sterner sex off the sidewalks. Just now a full regiment of overcoated soldiers went marching through mud and rain past my window, their band chiming as cheerfully and loudly as though a bright sun were glinting on their accouterments, and the soldier laddies—God bless them!—stepping as free and firmly as though they were not splashing through mud and mire. Some days must be dark and rainy, and such is this gloomy Saturday.

A GLITTERING BAIT FOR SECRETARY CHASE

The irrepressible conflict between the Chase and Seward factions continues to grow interesting. Though not bitter or knife-like in sharpness, it is not less perceptible and marked. Seward is not so desirous of helping the prospects of Lincoln as he is of spoiling those of Chase; it is not that he loves Lincoln more but Chase less, and whatever of personal ambitions he may have in the matter, it is certain that he would be cut to the heart if Chase were nominated to the presidency. He need not worry. That event will never take place. But the latest plan for getting rid of the able and formidable Secretary of the Treasury originates with the astute Premier, and is nothing less than the proposition to make Chase the successor of Roger B. Taney, Chief Justice of the Supreme Court of the

United States. Another of those stated rumors of Taney's resignation is now prevalent, and it would seem that in ordinary course of nature the old man ought to shuffle off this mortal coil during the present Administration. According to the laws of the United States the vacancy which would be made by the resignation or death of Chief Justice Taney must be filled by appointment by the President, not by regular succession, as some have supposed, and the President would perhaps be willing to appoint the distinguished Secretary to that exalted position, believing that he can fill it honorably and fitly; but Lincoln would never lend himself to any *scheme* to disembarrass (as the French say) himself of a formidable rival. Much of this is, of course, merely speculative, but Chase would doubtlessly find the commanding place of Chief Justice more desirable, life-long, and bird-in-the-hand than the elusive bird-in-the-bush nomination for the presidency.

Washington, October 29, 1863

HORSE RAILROADS

... The Washington Horse Railroad Company has so far conciliated public opinion as to provide cars on their road which bear in big letters the concession that "colored persons may ride in this car." Heretofore the poor outcasts have been denied the luxury of a seat, though their regular five cents is just as freely taken by the fare-taker as a white man's, and it is a common sight to observe clean and respectable-looking colored people riding on the front platform, exposed to rain and snow, standing in the cold, and denied the privilege of so much as putting their heads inside the door. I once saw a handsomely dressed and ladylike woman sent out on the platform by a conductor whose practiced eye detected Ethiopian traces in her white face or straight hair, though unused faculties could not discern them. He indignantly said that it was just as likely as not that of a dark evening that woman had ridden back and forth in the cars and "nobody had known nothin' of it." He was incapable of reply when somebody said, "Well, what of it?" ...

Washington, October 30, 1863

MASS MEETING IN BALTIMORE

The great Union mass meeting held in Baltimore on the night of the 28th is one of the more significant evidences of the change in popular sentiment in the border states which we have had. . . . A little while ago Maryland was almost coaxed into open rebellion against the government, in simulated defense of slavery and southern rights; the legislature of the state conspired to carry her out of the Union; the streets of Baltimore—that "murder-haunted town"—were sprinkled with the first blood shed by the defenders of the nation, and everywhere the spirit of secession and proslavery ran mad and appeared dominant for a space. But now one of the larger and more enthusiastic assemblages ever known in Baltimore congregates in Monument Square, bearing banners and transparencies with such mottoes as: "Union," "Emancipation," "Slavery is dead—its Treason killed it," "Infamy the Reward of the Rebels," "Emancipation and Free White Labor," "Slavery is the Mother of the Rebellion."

Do we dream or do we actually hear with our own ears loyal Marylanders making speeches in favor of immediate

emancipation and a loyal crowd of Baltimoreans ap-
plauding to the echo the most radical utterances—the
"radical" Secretary of the Treasury making the most
conservative speech of them all? Is this "My Maryland"
of rebel boast now promising 20,000 majority to the Unconditional Union Emancipation ticket? Truly, wonders
will never cease; it is not strange that President Lincoln
could not find words to express his feelings when invited
to attend a Union meeting in Baltimore—that Baltimore
through which he was secretly conveyed three years ago.

But the great outpouring at Baltimore night before last
had another significance to those who watch political
events and who understand the inside working of political
cabals. The election of Henry Winter Davis to Congress
and the triumph of the emancipationists in Maryland is
the defeat of Montgomery Blair and all of his kind. It is
a matter of common notoriety that he has strained every
nerve to defeat Winter Davis and to give what official
sanction he could to an extra-conservative policy in Maryland. Assuming to speak for the President and the majority
of the cabinet, Blair delivered his Rockville speech, in
which he assailed Sumner and Chase and foreshadowed a
proslavery, states rights theory as being that of the administration. He went to Baltimore again and again to secure,
if possible, a candidate for Congress to run against Winter
Davis on some half-hearted war platform; and if he did
not succeed in getting up a milk-and-water candidate for
that purpose, it was not for the reason that he did not
try. He *was* unsuccessful; for few dare to attempt a campaign against the noble and loyal Marylander, and Winter
Davis will be triumphantly elected.

The Baltimore meeting had the countenance and support of Secretary Chase, and his simple words of sympathy
and cheer for the struggling sons of freedom in Maryland

were received with wildest enthusiasm. One could not but feel, as the eye took in the vast multitude which surged through the square, bearing upon the gusty waves of popular excitement banners, torches, and transparencies innumerable, that a great and momentous revolution had occurred and that a signal and grave repulse was then and there administered to that narrow-minded cabinet officer who had stooped so low as to try to drive popular sentiment against the policy of the administration of which he is a member.

POSTMASTER GENERAL BLAIR AND FORNEY

There is but one expression, and that of reprobation, toward Postmaster General Blair for his extraordinary course, and it now remains to be seen whether Lincoln will sacrifice his chances of renomination by retaining him in the cabinet. Although Blair was appointed to his place upon the urgent request of such Radicals as Sumner and Wilson, against whom he now turns, we cannot expect that any sense of obligation to them would induce him to modify his own private views or restrain his public utterances. Good faith is not a characteristic trait of the Blair family. But good sense, at least, might have restrained him from loading his own wrong-headed opinions upon the administration of which he is a member.

Soon after the Pennsylvania election, Judge William D. Kelley of Philadelphia and John W. Forney called upon the President with their congratulations—and Forney, with his usual candor, very plainly said to the President, Blair being present, that his conservative friend Governor Andrew G. Curtin desired the President to know that if the Rockville speech of Postmaster General Blair had been made thirty days earlier it would have lost the

Union ticket in Pennsylvania 20,000 votes. He also expressed his astonishment to Blair that he, a cabinet minister, should have the hardihood to utter such sentiments in public on the eve of important elections in other states. Blair responded that whatever Forney might think of the matter, he had only spoken at Rockville his honest sentiments. "Then," said the impetuous Forney, turning upon him, "why don't you leave the cabinet, and not load down with your individual and peculiar sentiments the administration to which you belong?"

The President sat by, a silent spectator of this singular and unexpected scene. I hope, however, that he was edified, for if he does not realize the unfortunate position in which he is being pushed by Blair, he must make up his mind to fall with Blair, for it is morally certain that no such fossil theories and narrow-minded policy as that of the Postmaster General are to be endorsed by the people of any of the loyal states. Every state election this fall has rejected such a notion, and the people are too far advanced in liberal ideas to consent that any standard bearer of theirs shall refuse to carry the banner of "Freedom for All."

It is not pleasant or edifying to be obliged, as a faithful chronicler, to allude to these bickerings among our public men, but they are a part of the history of the times, and the public must sooner or later know all about them. It was but a few days ago that the Loyal League of Philadelphia made honorary members of its Council the President and his Cabinet; but when the certificates of membership were made out, to be forwarded to the newly elected members, George H. Baker, the poet-patriot, Secretary of the League, flatly refused to sign his name to a document which should admit a pro-slavery anti-Administration Cabinet officer to the hall where loyal

Philadelphians congregate for council. The entire Executive Committee backed up the Secretary in his decision, and Blair has never received any certificate of membership from the Loyal League of Philadelphia. He never will.

Washington, November 7, 1863

HOW THEY LIVE AT THE WHITE HOUSE

The edifice itself is tolerably familiar in appearance to most people who have seen the engravings of the house; which is usually represented with the Potomac front toward the spectator, as that really fine face of the building is higher and not covered with the overgrown portico which so disfigures the Avenue front and looks as if built to conceal the house behind it. The Potomac front has sloping grounds, decorated with vases, statuary, and ornamental gardening, between it and the unoccupied public square on the river bank; but the main entrance is on the front which faces Pennsylvania Avenue, and a pair of massive gateways open from the Avenue upon the semicircular driveway which leads to the portico and thus encloses a small park in the center of which stands the bronze statue of Jefferson with the Constitution in his hand. The statue is green and moldy with time and is in seedy contrast with the smug-looking effigy of Old Hickory, cutting off the right ear of his rampant charger, in the square across the Avenue and is known as the Clark Mills statue.

Let us go into the Executive Mansion; there is nobody to bar our passage, and the multitude, washed or unwashed, always has free ingress and egress beneath the awful shadow of the immense portico whose tall columns stand thickly around us. A small vestibule opens into a wide hall, handsomely carpeted, which has a bronze and ground glass screen separating the state and family apartments from the more public part of the house. At the right is an anteroom for the servants in waiting, and beyond that is the dining room—not a very sumptuous room —only accommodating thirty-five at table. Beyond are family rooms and a large conservatory and in the basement servants' rooms, kitchens, etc.

We have no "kitchen cabinet" during this administration, but the present presiding lady of the White House has caused a terrible scattering of ancient abuses which once accumulated belowstairs. The suckers who grew rich on the pickings and stealing from the kitchen, garden, and conservatory and who had spies in every room in the house have been dispersed, and when they went they circulated innumerable, revengeful yarns concerning domestic weaknesses at the White House, and there were some credulous people who believed them.

The right or west wing of the house is occupied by the President's family, the center by the state parlors, and the east wing has belowstairs the famous East Room and upstairs the offices of the President and his secretaries. The parlors which are used for ordinary receptions are entered from a corridor behind the screen forming one side of the main hall of entrance, and are three in number, being called severally the Blue, Green, and Crimson drawing rooms from the color of the upholstery and fittings. The last named of these is the favorite sitting room of Mrs. Lincoln, where she receives private calls every evening in the week when in town and where the President usually meets his friends socially after dinner. The furniture is very rich—of crimson satin and gold damask, with heavy gilded cornices to the windows and a profusion of ormolu work, vases, etc., some of which stuff is very ancient, being bought or presented during Monroe's and Madison's administrations. There is a grand piano in this room and a full-length portrait of Washington; but generally, the walls of the White House are destitute of paintings, the want being remedied by gilded and richly colored hangings. It would be a sensible notion if some Congress, more thoughtful and public-spirited than any which we have yet had, would make a small appropriation for the purpose of hanging in the house of the Chief Magistrate of the nation a few pictures by the best American artists, which might form a nucleus for a gallery of art in the home of the President and his family. The walls of the house would be relieved of their unfurnished bareness, and a portion of the severe simplicity of the White House would be graced thereby.

The Blue Drawing Room is much admired by most people, as its fittings are quite sumptuous in style and finish. The room is formed in the graceful curves of a perfect ellipse, and the windows command a lovely view of the grounds in the rear of the house and of the Potomac. The furniture is of blue and silver satin damask; the woodwork of the chairs and sofas are solidly gilt as also are the heavy cornices of the doors and windows; broad mirrors, with massive frames, surmount the marble chimney pieces, and a blue and white velvet carpet covers the floor. The ceiling is painted in fresco, in which blue is the prevailing tint, and the walls are covered with blue and gold hangings; in short, it is all so "deeply, darkly, beautifully blue" that one feels quite cerulean therein. In this room are many of the Japanese presents to President Buchanan, which constitute a part of the furniture of the house under the law that confiscates all presents to government officials to the use of the government.

These drawing rooms all communicate with each other and with the great East Room, and upon some occasions they are all thrown open. The East Room occupies the entire principal floor of the east wing, and is well-known to most people by common engravings of it. The ceiling is frescoed in a very ordinary style, cupids, flowers, and such sprawling about overhead in a very loose manner, the unbreeched urchins looking as though a suit of Uncle Sam's uniform would not come amiss this cold weather. The lace curtains, heavy cords, tassels, and damask drapery have suffered considerably this season from the hands of relic-hunting vandals who actually clip off small bits of the precious stuff to carry home as mementoes, I suppose. I wonder how they have the "cheek" to exhibit their trophies to admiring friends at home and complacently relate how they stole them. Some of these aesthetic pilferers have even cut out small bits of the gorgeous carpet, leaving scars on the floor as large as a man's hand. Others, on larger game intent, have actually cut off a yard or two from the lower end of some of the heavy crimson satin window hangings. It is easy enough to do this here, for though there are always one or two watchmen about the house, a thief can have an accomplice to engage the attention of the watchmen elsewhere, while he commits his petty larceny within. I suppose such fellows take it that the White House property belongs to the people, and they will take their individual share now. In this East Room the Presidents usually hold their levees or public receptions, but Mrs. Lincoln does not always receive publicly here. When large delegations or deputations wait upon the President he receives them in this room, but he usually prefers that they shall wait upon him in his private office upstairs.

IN THE PRESIDENT'S PRIVATE OFFICE

If we go upstairs at any hour after Washington people are stirring we shall find the corridors and waiting rooms full of people who have business or curiosity urging them into the presence of the President. The grim Cerberus of Teutonic descent who guards the last door opening into the awful presence has a very unhappy time answering the impatient demands of the gathering, growing crowd of applicants obstructing passage, hall, and anteroom. It would not be a bad idea if an inside guardian of affable address as well as flintiness of face were placed on duty where the people come almost in actual contact with the great man within whom they learn to love or dislike according to their treatment by his underlings. The President is affable and kind, but his immediate subordinates are snobby and unpopular.

A wide corridor opens on the left into the private rooms of the secretaries and on the right to the office of the private secretary, John G. Nicolay, and to the private office of the President. The room of the secretary is a small office, very meagerly furnished and old-fashioned in appearance as, in fact, is all of the upper part of the mansion. The dark mahogany doors, old-style mantels and paneled wainscoting are more suggestive of the days of the Madisons and Van Burens than of the present. There are usually three private secretaries to the President, of which only one is contemplated by law, receiving a yearly salary of $2,500, carriage, and perquisites; but the extraordinary exigencies of the public service have obliged the President to employ two assistants who are clerks detailed from the departments and drawing their salaries therefrom. These three secretaries are all young men, and the least said of them the better, perhaps.

When the President lives in town he commences his day's work long before the city is astir, and before breakfast he consumes two hours or more in writing, reading, or studying some of the host of subjects which he has on hand. It may be the Missouri question, the Maryland im-

broglio, the Rosecrans removal question, or the best way
to manage some great conflicting interest which engrosses
his attention, but these two best hours of the fresh day are
thus given to the work. Breakfast over, by nine o'clock he
has directed that the gate which lets in the people shall be
opened upon him, and then the multitude of cards, notes,
and messages which are in the hands of his usher come
in upon him. Of course, there can be no precedence, except so far as the President makes it, and, as a majority
of the names sent in are new to him, it is very much of a
lottery as to who shall get in first. The name being given
to the usher by the President, that functionary shows in
the gratified applicant, who may have been cooling his
heels outside for five minutes or five days but is now ushered into a large square room furnished with green stuff,
hung around with maps and plans, a bad portrait of Jackson over the chimney piece, a writing table piled up with
documents and papers, and two large, draperied windows
looking out upon the broad Potomac and commanding the
Virginia heights opposite on which numberless military
camps are whitening in the sun.

The President sits at his table and kindly greets whoever
comes. To the stranger he addresses his expectant, "Well?"
and to the familiar acquaintances he says, "And how are
you today, Mr. ———?" though it must be confessed that
he likes to call those whom he likes by their first names,
and it is "Andy" (Curtin), "Dick" (Yates), and so on.
Seward he always calls "Governor," and Blair or Bates is
"Judge." The rest are plain "Mister," never "Secretary."
With admirable patience and kindness, Lincoln hears his
applicant's request and at once says what he will do,
though he usually asks several questions, generally losing
more time than most businessmen will by trying to understand completely each case, however unimportant, that

comes before him. He is not good at dispatching business but lets every person use more time than he might if the interview were strictly limited to the real necessities of the case. Consequently, Lincoln cannot see a tithe of the people who daily besiege his antechamber. In his anxiety to do equal and exact justice to all, he excludes or delays those who might see him sooner if he did not try to do so much. No man living has a kinder heart or a more honest purpose than Abraham Lincoln, and all who meet him go away thoroughly impressed with the preponderance of those two lovable and noble traits of his character.

Is the petitioner a poor widow who wants a writership in one of the departments? The President has read her credentials and asked a question or two in his quiet but shrewd way. He takes a card on which he writes a plain request to a cabinet minister to give the bearer what she craves, and the grateful woman goes out, blessing the good-natured President whose very next act may be to receive a distinguished foreign diplomat whose government is hovering on the doubtful verge of an American war; or it may be a Brigadier wanting promotion, an inventor after a contract, a curiosity hunter with an autograph book, a Major General seeking a command, a lady with a petition for a pass to Richmond, a cabinet minister after a commission for a favorite, a deputation asking an impossibility, or a committee demanding an impertinence; it may be all or any of these who come next, and the even-tempered statesman who patiently sits there, interlarding the dull details of business with a good-natured joke or anecdote, must wisely and quickly decide upon questions which vary in importance from a small favor to a humble dependent to the adjustment of one of the most momentous national interests of the times.

Is it not wonderful that so little that is open to criticism is done by him, rather than that we have anything to find fault with? When we recollect that every day, except Sunday, is occupied in the manner thus described, from nine o'clock until three o'clock in the afternoon, and that during the sessions of Congress several hours of the evening are also thus taken up, it is a matter of surprise that the President can find time to do so wisely and so well the various work which comes from his hands. Of course, during all of these interviews he is liable to interruption from his cabinet ministers who have free access to him at all business hours. Senators and Governors of states come next in precedence, and Representatives come last before "citizens generally." Usually, no foreign functionary seeks an interview with the President except through the prescribed channel of the State Department, and etiquette requires that all foreigners shall be presented to the Secretary of State by the minister of the country to whom the person seeking an interview belongs, and in this roundabout way the party follows up the clue of red tape until he arrives in the President's chamber.

THE LINCOLNS AT HOME

The President dines at six o'clock and often invites an intimate friend to take potluck with him, but he and his estimable wife are averse to dinner-giving or party-making, only deviating from their own wishes in such matters for the purpose of gratifying people who expect it of them. They much prefer the same sort of social, unrestrained intercourse with the family that most sensible people do and have a wholesome horror of state dinners which are invariably prolific of discord, ill-feeling, and big expense. Lincoln is strictly temperate and simple in his habits; to this and his faculty of throwing off the oppressive weight of care, the like of which no man ever before him bore, he owes his life and the country owes its security in these perilous times when a cool head, a firm hand, and an honest heart are needed at the head of our vast public affairs. While the most enthusiastic admirer of Lincoln would hesitate to claim for him a combination of all the endowments and acquirements of his predecessors in office, it does appear to me that it is impossible to designate any man in public life whose character and antecedents would warrant us in the belief that we have anyone now living whose talents and abilities would fit him to administer this government better than it has been conducted through the past three stormy years by the honesty, patriotism, and farsighted sagacity of Abraham Lincoln. That is merely an opinion, to be sure, but it is not an unintelligent one, and I share it in common with a great crowd of candid witnesses.

The wife of the President has been so frequently and cruelly misrepresented and slandered that, though hesitating to approach so delicate a subject, I cannot refrain from saying a word in strict justice to this distinguished and accomplished woman. When the present administration came into power, the national capital was infested as well as besieged by rebels and every conceivable means was adopted to render the members of the administration unpopular. To this end slanders innumerable were circulated concerning the habits of the President and his family. It is not many months since candid and loyal men were to be found believing that our temperate President drank to excess and that Mrs. Lincoln was a vulgar, ill-bred woman. Such stories are scandalous, and though time has done justice to the President who is seen and read by all men, Mrs. Lincoln is denied the privilege of defense and in the privacy of a household clad in mourning has not yet had justice done her by the public. The slanderous tales of those who prayed daily that "Lady Davis" might occupy the White House are still circulated and believed, and loyal people, more shame to them, without knowing the truth of what they repeat still allow themselves to become the media for the dispersion of scandals as base as they are baseless. It is not a gracious task to refute these sayings, but the tales that are told of Mrs. Lincoln's vanity, pride, vulgarity, and meanness ought to put any decent man or woman to the blush when they remember that they do not *know* one particle of that which they repeat and that they would resent as an insult to their wives, sisters, or mothers that which they so glibly repeat concerning the first lady in the land. Shame upon these he-gossips and envious retailers of small slanders. Mrs. Lincoln, I am glad to be able to say from personal knowledge, is a true American woman, and when we have said that we have said enough in praise of the best and truest lady in our beloved land.

Republican simplicity and republican virtues reign at the home of the American president; thousands of private citizens in our prosperous country are more luxuriously lodged and more daintily fed; but search the wide nation over and you will not find a more united household or a more noble and loving family than that which today dwells in all of the anxious cares of the White House.

Washington, November 11, 1863

WINTER UPON US

. . . The late fine autumnal weather has given place to bitter cold winds which raise a darkening cloud of dust and pierce one's very marrow, a few flakes of snow scurrying down from the wintry sky the while. One cannot help thinking of what the poor will suffer during the coming winter, which, we hope, may be mercifully mild; for everything which is needed to feed, clothe, and warm the body is fearfully dear, and the end of the appreciation of prices is not yet. Coal sells for $12 per ton and is still rising; flour is selling for $12.25 per barrel; meats are twice as dear as in the San Francisco market, and all sorts of groceries are constantly going up.... With all of these high prices it is a problem as to how very poor people will get on this winter, and already a movement has begun here on the part of the charitably disposed to provide for the more pressing wants of the very poor. The back slums and alleys of Washington are full of squalid misery and distress, and none but those who go to look for it know of the poverty which is silently endured here at the national capital by the hundreds of homeless and houseless ones....

Washington, November 14, 1863

GOSSIPING

... The whirl of dust of the bridal cortege which went from Secretary Chase's to the railroad depot last night has subsided—but not so the gentle flow and ebb of small talk which so grand an event as the marriage of Senator [William] Sprague and Miss Kate Chase has created. Who was there and who was not there; how the bride looked in her white velvet dress, real point lace veil, and orange flowers; how the President went in solitary state and white cravat and things; how Mrs. Lincoln did not go because she is yet in black wear and had an opportune chill betimes; how the President stayed two and half hours "to take the cuss off" the meagerness of the presidential party; how the bride wore a regal "tiara" of pearls and diamonds, the like of which was never seen in America since the days of the Aztec "barbaric pearl and gold"; how Secretary Chase was the first to kiss the newly made wife and say "Gobleshyou;" how the victuals and drink were lavish; how the newspapers were snubbed, having only curbstone tickets—except the editor of a New York horse paper—and how the Bohemians revenged themselves by refusing to puff the wedding. Lo! all of these things are good for Washington gossip, and the national village is yet agitated, but the "happy pair" go on their way rejoicing, and we will honestly wish them joy unstinted. . . .

Sitting in the office of the Superintendent of Public Printing the other day I saw a tidy-looking woman come in with a card on which was written the following:

"My Dear Defrees: The bearer, a poor girl, has a brother in our lines, as prisoner of war, who wishes to take an oath of allegiance. Be good enough to look into the facts and report to me. Yrs, A. LINCOLN." *

It appears that one Dennis Mack, a brother of the young woman, had been impressed by the rebels early in the war, being caught near Alexandria. Being unable to escape, he was found in the ranks of the rebels at one of the late Rappahannock fights, but he insists that he is a Union man and is ready to take the oath of allegiance. The girl

---

* Roy P. Basler, editor, *The Collected Works of Abraham Lincoln* (New Brunswick, N.J., 1953), VIII:12, quotes the letter as given in Charles B. Boynton, *History of the Great Western Sanitary Fair* (1864), page 183: "Mr. Defrees—Please see this girl who works in your office, and find out about her brother, and come and tell me.
November 12, 1863   A. LINCOLN"

had been turned away by the surly officials of the War Department, and she got access to the President whose kind heart was at once enlisted. He determined that justice should be done, so he sent the sister of the prisoner to the kindly John D. Defrees, who likes to do a generous act. We may hope that the sequel will prove that the President's kindness will be useful as it has been in so many thousands of instances of which the world knows nothing. . . .

Washington, November 17, 1863

THE GETTYSBURG DEDICATION CEREMONIES

Today the town is all alive with preparations for the dedication, day after tomorrow, of the Gettysburg cemetery for the remains of those who fell in defense of the national Union upon the bloody field where the sorrowing nation is to consecrate their last resting place with suitable rites and ceremonies. The affair promises to be a memorable and important one, as all of the leading dignitaries of the nation and many of the loyal states will be present and by their countenance and presence lend additional character to the great work which is to be, as far as possible, a national one. The President, for once laying aside the pressing cares of his office, will attend, his wife accompanying him, and most of the members of the cabinet and their families are also going with him, Mrs. Lincoln having set the good example of the women of America in showing sympathy in this tribute to the memory of the brave dead who sleep at Gettysburg. The President and suite and the cabinet officers will leave here in a special car tomorrow morning. The exercises and orders of the day are in the hands of Ward H. Lamon, United States

Marshal for the District of Columbia, and he will be assisted by deputy marshals from each loyal state of the Union. The oration is to be delivered by Edward Everett. . . .

THE NATIONAL CURRENCY

The Controller of the national currency, Hugh McCulloch, has contracted with the National Bank Note Company of New York for the engraving and printing of the notes for the new currency, and it will be out in the course of the present week. The specimens which I have been shown are very beautiful indeed, being probably the best engraving and printing of the sort ever executed in any country. The paper is firm, white, satin-like, but semi-transparent, and the engraving is a marvel of beauty and delicacy. The backs of all the notes are nearly covered by a fine engraving of one of the great national paintings in the rotunda of the Capitol, there being a different picture for each denomination, making seven in all. The five-dollar note has upon its reverse William H. Powell's famous picture of the discovery of the Mississippi River by De Soto, a dramatic work of art which has been always greatly admired, despite its anachronisms and meretricious coloring. Upon each end are lathe-work medallions bearing the number of the denomination, all in the well-known green which has given the popular name to the currency. On the obverse are several vignettes, one of which, America borne upward by her eagle, is a gem of art. The signatures of the treasurer and register are in the center of the note, instead of being at the bottom, and the name of the issuing bank is "mortised," as printers say, the notes being furnished by the government to all banks alike and only differing in the insertion of the name of the bank of issue.

The lathe-work or "engine work" and scroll are in green, but the rest of the printing is in black ink.

THE "CONDEMNED YANKEES"

There was today a grand review in this city of the Invalid Corps or, as the rebels call it, the "Condemned Yankees," there being over 3,000 in number. The day was perfect and the display very fine, and a great crowd was present, although no public notice of the review was given. The President and distinguished officers of the military service reviewed the corps. Their regimental uniform is of a sky blue color throughout, and each regiment has six battalions armed with muskets and four battalions armed with sabers and pistols, indicating the extent of injuries which the soldier has received. Being all veterans, the drill of the Invalids is well-nigh perfect.

Washington, December 2, 1863

FREEDOM CROWNED

The sensation of today has been the completion of the colossal statue of Freedom which surmounts the dome of the Capitol. This magnificent bronze figure is nineteen and a half feet high and represents the genius of freedom as she would appear to the poet with his eye in fine frenzy rolling. It was cast by Clark Mills at Bladensburg from a model by [Thomas] Crawford, the American sculptor, now dead, and it cost about $20,000. About twelve o'clock today a great crowd began to stream down the Avenue toward the Capitol, all with faces set heavenward and watching the tracery of scaffolding which, relieved against the December sky, surmounts the airy dome of the people's palace. Everybody hurried in fear that the last crowning act might take place before their arrival. There was a big concourse of people whose heads were all thrown back in eager expectation of the supreme moment. Precisely at noon the last section of the bronze statue, consisting of the head and shoulders of the incomplete goddess, left the mass of material at the foot of the dome, and, drawn upward by a slender wire cable and serenely smiling upon the crowd below, the majestic face rose slowly toward the scaffolding around the statue. It passed into the timbered chaos above and soon emerged therefrom, swung lightly over the gleaming torso below it, then calmly settled into its place. Three strokes of a ringing sledge hammer were given and the work was done. The flag of freedom sprang to a flagstaff above the work, and a volley of artillery in the East Park saluted the consummation of the work. Near me an unbleached son of freedom sprang out from the undecided crowd and shouted, "Three cheers for the Goddess of Liberty!" Then straightway from the assembled crowd arose a shout prolonged and loud. . . .

BURNSIDE IN JEOPARDY

We are still in great doubt here as to the safety of [General Ambrose] Burnside, who at last account was stoutly besieged in Knoxville, [Tennessee]. . . . Visitors at the White House remarked in the course of a discussion as to the fate of Burnside that heavy firing had been heard at Knoxville during a few days past. The President said, "I am glad of it. I am glad of it." Surprise being expressed at such an abrupt remark, the President said that he was in the same situation as an old lady in Sangamon County who had a great flock of children who were almost out of her keeping they were so numerous. When she heard one of them crying or bawling in some out-of-the-way place she would say, "There is one of my children who is not dead yet." Burnside is one of the lost children. . . .

A MORTIFYING EXHIBITION

Night before last the sound of music and laughter attracted many idlers into the drinking saloon of one of the principal Washington hotels, and the curious bystander could see a ring formed around a band of wandering musicians to whose lively strains a small, gray-headed man was dancing a comic jig to the amusement of all. His antics and gestures were such as might make an angel weep, for it was plain that he was intoxicated, and those whose laughs cheered him on pitied while they scoffed. As a couple of gentlemen turned away one asked the other the name of "the comical cuss in the big fur cap who was making such an exhibition of himself." The reply was, "That is the Honorable James A. McDougall, United States Senator from California."

Washington, December 7, 1863

THE THIRTY-EIGHTH CONGRESS

. . . The galleries [were] full to overflowing long before twelve o'clock, the hour of opening Congress. The floor of the House of Representatives was also full, all around outside of the bar being a dense mass of people. Among them was the disjointed shape and bald head of Horace Greeley;

[Henry Wadsworth] Longfellow, the poet, gray-haired and full bearded; several judges of the supreme bench; Major General [John H.] Martindale; and hosts of others. The galleries were gay with the winter blossoms of women's fashionable gear, and the reporters were crowded in their ample space by a flock of outside barbarians who were "members of the press" in a most oppressive sense. Below, the members were dotted about the richly carpeted floor in knots and squads, and over all the mild radiance of the unclouded December sun fell warmly through the stained glass of the skylights in the roof. We recognize many familiar faces: the indomitable Thad Stevens is in his old place, so also are Elihu B. Washburne, Justin S. Morrill, Owen Lovejoy, and others.

Precisely at twelve o'clock the gavel of the Speaker fell and the House was hushed to silence while he announced that by the provisions of the Constitution the hour had arrived when the first session of the Thirty-Eighth Congress should be organized by calling the roll provided by the Clerk of the former House of Representatives. A profound attention to the action pervaded the House while the Clerk called the roll, from which he omitted Maryland, Missouri, Oregon, Kansas, and East and West Virginia. Instantly upon the conclusion of calling the roll a discussion arose upon the validity of the exclusion of these names of the Representatives from the above-named states. The opposition members called for the reading of the Act of March 3, 1863, prescribing the duties of the Clerk in the organization of the House. During a profound silence which succeeded, [Henry L.] Dawes of Massachusetts called for the reading of the credentials of the Maryland delegation which set forth that the Representatives were duly elected but omitted to state that they were elected in pursuance of the laws of the state and of the United States, as the law of March 3 prescribes. The credentials being read, Dawes offered a resolution that the names of the Maryland members be placed upon the roll of the House. [James C.] Allen, an Illinois Copperhead, moved to lay the resolution upon the table, but his motion was lost by ninety-four noes to seventy-four ayes, whereupon a tumultuous burst of applause shook the House above and below. This decided the matter.

Henry Winter Davis called for the credentials of the members-elect from Missouri. They were read, and a resolution to put them on the roll was also put through without ayes and noes. The same course was taken with the credentials of the members from West Virginia and of [John R.] McBride of Oregon. Thad Stevens said that he had a curiosity to hear the credentials of [A. P.] Field, [Joshua] Baker, and [Thomas E. H.] Cottman, members claiming seats from Louisiana and placed upon the roll of the House by Clerk [Emerson] Etheridge. The credentials were given by one John Leonard Riddell claiming to be Governor of Louisiana but formerly a postmaster at New Orleans under Buchanan and latterly under Jeff Davis. The credentials appeared to be *en règle*, but Stevens offered a resolution excluding their names from the roll. Thereupon arose a long discussion which resulted in Stevens withdrawing his resolution. There was also a long strife over the credentials of the eastern Virginians which resulted in their being laid upon the table until the organization of the House should be effected.

E[lihu] B. Washburne of Illinois then moved that the House proceed to a *viva voce* vote for Speaker, it being agreed to nominate Schuyler Colfax of Indiana, whereat arose a gust of applause in the galleries and all over the hall of the House. [George H.] Pendleton of Ohio nominated Copperhead S[amuel] S. Cox of Ohio. [Sydenham

E.] Ancona of Pennsylvania nominated John L. Dawson, (Copperhead,) of the same state. [Henry] Grider of Kentucky nominated Robert Mallory of the same state—"a conservative Kentucky chap." [John B.] Steele of New York nominated H[enry] G. Stebbins of New York, a War Democrat, whatever that may be, and [Thomas E. H.] Cottman of Louisiana nominated F[rancis] P. Blair, of Missouri. Tellers being appointed, the vote proceeded, each member answering the call of his name by calling the name of his choice for Speaker.

During the calling of the roll the crowd in the galleries watched with deep interest how various members voted. The border state men, about whose vote there has been so much controversy, received the applause of the galleries—Henry Winter Davis being the first to lead off. There were a few in the hall, doubtless, who remembered that when this gallant Marylander stepped into the area in front of the Speaker's desk and voted for [William] Pennington during the strife in the Thirty-Sixth Congress he was hissed at vehemently by his former proslavery allies. Today he was cheered to the echo as his clear voice rang out "Schuyler Colfax." His example was followed by Brutus Clay, Green Clay Smith, and the rest of the Kentuckians. Washburne's honorable bearing also received a mark of approval as he gave his vote for his late opponent.

Breathless silence reigned as the Clerk announced the tellers who reported that 181 votes had been cast of which 92 were necessary for a choice. Colfax had 101; Cox, 42; Dawson, 12; Mallory, 10; Stebbins, 8; Austin A. King, of Missouri, 6; Blair, 2; and John D. Stiles of Pennsylvania received the vote of Fernando Wood only. The announcement of the result was received with another wild gust of applause, and the Clerk designated Dawson and Cox as a committee to conduct the Speaker-elect to the chair.

And then such another round of enthusiasm broke forth as plainly said, "Welcome to your exalted seat, Schuyler Colfax, the beloved of the people, fast friend of the Union, and the noble exponent of our free republican principles!" Upon taking his seat the newly elected Speaker made a brief, modest speech in which he expressed his gratitude for the honor conferred upon him, reminded the members that much more depended upon the legislation of this House, which would see the end of the great rebellion, than upon the action of any deliberative body which the world had ever seen. He invoked calmness, moderation, and freedom from prejudice and acerbity in debate, and he asked that he might be sustained in all proper and legal exercise of his duties as Speaker of the House of Representatives of the Thirty-Eighth Congress. The solemn oath of office was then administered by Washburne, and the House was ready for work. The crowd now began to pour out of the galleries, and the members were called up by states and sworn in by lumps by the Speaker.

Washington, December 9, 1863

This city is so overcrowded with people that it is really difficult getting about; the hotels nightly turn away strangers seeking rest and finding none; the streetcars run "loaded to the gunwales" with living freight; the sidewalks are so full of people that they look as though all of the theaters had just "let out" at once; and Capitol, departments, and other public places where public pap is distributed swarm with hungry "Northern Hessians" armed with credentials, recommendations, and certificates of services to party or state. The hotels and boardinghouses reap a rich harvest, and such fleecing caravansaries as Willard's are making fortunes, this being truly a golden (or green-back) shower to them.

Congress is at present the center of attraction to strangers, and the galleries are daily filled with well-dressed people from various portions of the loyal states eager to know who are celebrities and who are worth looking at. In the House of Representatives gallery almost the first question asked by the visitor is, "Which is Fernando Wood?" And when they are shown a tall, clean-shaved, student-looking gentleman, sharp as to nose, pale as to face, with an old-fashioned dress coat and sedate appearance, they are disappointed that he is not half so black as he is painted. He looks like a professor in some one-horse western "Literary Institute." Another Copperhead whose whereabouts is generally inquired of by the spectator in the galleries of this congressional bear garden is James Brooks of the New York *Express.* He is tall, well-made, wears light pantaloons always, also spectacles, but has large, sunken, dark eyes, a broad forehead, dark hair and whiskers, and a largish nose. . . .

Washington, December 12, 1863

WHAT PEOPLE SAY OF THE MESSAGE

The reputation of President Lincoln for originality is pretty general now, but nobody expected such an original message as that communicated to the first session of the Thirty-Eighth Congress. . . . It was expected that the President would either ignore reconstruction altogether or give an elaborate and decisive program therefor. He has done neither; but has pleased the radicals and satisfied the conservatives by plainly projecting a plan of reconstruction

which is just to popular rights, to the cause of liberty, and
to the loyal people of all sections of the Union. Nor is this
program a finality as to its detail, for it is generally understood here that the President weaves through the whole a
thread of contingency, plainly implying that while its
broad, general principles are immovable and abiding,
events yet to arise may change materially the plan and
theory laid down. It is obvious that we are at sea in this
whole matter of reconstruction, and that we must trust
to Providence, whose overruling care has thus far led us,
for a safe pilotage to the haven of security and rest.

The President has been forced by premature discussions
and ill-digested theories of others to announce what the
policy of the administration will probably be in the premises, and his message, a worthy document in itself, has
found its only significance in being the reflection of his
views upon this mooted question of reconstruction. As
such, then, it gives, probably, more general satisfaction
than any message since the days of Washington. As no
administration since Jackson has been able to preserve in
both branches of Congress a majority of its own until
now, so no president since that same period, certainly, has
succeeded so well in satisfying the various political antagonisms of the times as Abraham Lincoln in his last message. It is generally remarked that this has not been done
by skillful trimming or by a noncommittal, emasculate
policy. Bold, high, and original ground is taken, apparently
disregardful of the claims of either of the great factions
which profess to own the president and the next presidency.

Of course, everybody is not satisfied. The Copperheads
were determined not to be satisfied. The Missouri destruc-
tives expected that one-half of the annual message would
have been devoted to a résumé of their difficulties, which

they fondly deem the center of all political questions; and Senator Sumner is irate because his doctrine of state suicide finds no responsive echo in the generous amnesty and magnanimous offers of the chief magistrate of the United States of America. During the delivery of the message the distinguished Senator from Massachusetts exhibited his petulance to the admiring galleries of the Senate chamber by making eccentric motions in his chair and pitching his documents and books upon the floor in ill-tempered disgust as a vent to his half-concealed anger at so effectual extinguisher of his pet theory. Nobody expected, however, that his plan of territorializing the conquered rebel states would be accepted or endorsed either by the President or by Congress. As it is, both Chase and Blair—the two antipodes of public sentiment—are perfectly satisfied; and, after all, when that is said we have said that all who are reasonable and practicable are conciliated, pleased, and satisfied. ... When "the Blair family" and the Missouri radicals are alike agreed to accept so bold and original propositions as those contained in the last annual message of the President, we may well conclude that the political millennium has well-nigh come, or that the author of the message is one of the most sagacious men of modern times.

Washington, January 1, 1864

A HAPPY NEW YEAR

... Here in Washington, New Year's day was kept after the usual fashion of visiting and being visited. The day was fearfully cold and windy, it being a *galey* day if not a gala day, and last night was the coldest of the season, water pipes freezing up tight as the money market, while the morning newspaper and the milkman were alike snapped up by the nipping frosts. Yesterday the President received his friends and the public generally at the White House, beginning with the diplomatic corps, army officers, and naval and marine officers, at eleven o'clock in the day. These gentry made a brave show as they marched up in their gold lace and toggery, General Halleck heading the military crowd, Secretary Seward leading his pet lambs of the diplomacy, and [Rear] Admiral [Charles H.] Davis sailing in at the head of the squadron of naval officers. The foreign ministers were especially gorgeously arrayed, being covered with stars, garters, and medals of honor; the rush for a glimpse of these gay birds was very great, and Secretary Seward looked like a molting barnyard fowl among peacocks, in such illustrious company. The rush of the great multitude was as great as in former years; and the crushing and jamming of bonnets and things were fearful. One woman became separated from her family, and a tender female shriek being heard, the paterfamilias of the lost one was sure that it was the voice of his beloved which he heard; likewise, his son, a youth of tender years, was led to believe that his mother was killed; whereat he bawled exceedingly, and there was a great deal of excitement at the entrance to the great drawing room where all of this took place until every Jack got his gill and all went well again.

The President looks better since he had the varioloid. I don't mean to insinuate that the disease has added any new charms to his features, but his complexion is clearer, his eyes less lackluster, and he has a hue of health to which he has long been a stranger. He stood up manfully against the great crush and bore the handshaking like a blessed old martyr. Mrs. Lincoln wore a purple velvet dress decorated with white satin flutings (isn't that what you call it?) around the bottom; Valenciennes lace was on the sleeves, and an immense train flowed out behind. Mrs. Lincoln never looked better than in the dark, rich tones of her reception dress, by which she has, for the first time, left off her mourning garb.

The cabinet ministers were all at home, and all received calls except Secretary Welles, that ghostly, shadowy man who scarcely seems to have a local habitation and a name in Washington or anywhere else. The War Secretary was the only man who had a spread of edibles for his guests, and Secretary Chase had the only great rush of callers, except the President. The house of the Secretary of the Treasury was besieged by great and small people, among which former were Major Generals [George] Stoneman, [Christopher C.] Augur, [Samuel P.] Heintzelman, [Abner] Doubleday, and [Ethan Allen] Hitchcock, likewise several high naval officers. Mrs. Sprague, *nee* Chase, did the honors of the reception in a graceful style and a blue brocade gown with a long tail to it, while the worthy and dignified Secretary looked uncomfortable and generally bothered, no doubt wishing that the whole party was in Timbuctoo or some other warm place. He is very nearsighted and never pretends to know anybody without a very close examination. Consequently his style is frosty to his best friends even....

Washington, January 7, 1864

REASSEMBLING OF CONGRESS

The holiday recess having passed, Congress reassembled on the 5th, with but a slim attendance at its first session. The weather was cold, the roads were blocked with snow, and the feeling upon the opening day of a new year in the

House was that of excessive blueness. Some of the members who had been frozen up for twenty-four hours on board the ferry boat in the Susquehanna River were bristling all over with quarrelsomeness; for men who have been "cribbed, cabined, and confined" without fire, whisky, or food for a whole day are not likely to be very amiable. During the first hours of the morning session a bill was introduced in the House appropriating the old hall of the House of Representatives to the purpose of a national gallery of sculpture, each state sending thereto not more than two statues or busts of its own citizens who have been famous for civic, military, or naval achievements. [Elihu B.] Washburne said that he should oppose the bill as he should at some future occasion introduce a bill to remove the seat of government from this barren and isolated country! Washburne is evidently one of the frozen ones, or has no free pass on the railroads. . . .

AN ARMY OF EMPLOYEES

Few people have a correct idea of the vast army of supernumeraries in the various departments at Washington which the war has called into existence. Of course, the basis for this great growth existed before the war began; but the exigencies of the public service have made it necessary that the original force should be increased in some instances fourfold. The Treasury department has now 1,200 clerks and laborers; the Interior department has 450; the War department has 500; the Navy department has 100; the Secretary of State has 50; the Post Office department has 100; the Senate and House of Representatives have 100 clerks and employees. Added to this, the Quartermaster General's office has upon its rolls as high as 7,000 clerks, laborers, teamsters, and various employees;

the Navy Yard, Public Printing Office, and other institutions employ at least 3,000 more. And the gross sum of labor thus employed at the seat of government equals 12,000 men—a small army, truly.

A SMALLPOX SCARE

The accumulation at Washington of Negro refugees and poor whites fleeing from rebel destitution—to say nothing of congressmen, newspapermen, and other riffraff —has materially augmented the filthy and crowded condition of the city, never overly clean, and the loathsome disease of smallpox is unusually prevalent and fatal in its effects. The death of Senator [Lemuel J.] Bowden of West Virginia by this disease has stirred up considerable excitement upon the subject. The fact that so prominent a man has fallen a victim to the contagion has created a general scare in the District, people suddenly discovering that the dreaded disease is prevalent here. A resolution of inquiry, touching the expediency of establishing new sanitary regulations in the District, has been introduced in the Senate by [Solomon] Foot of Vermont.

Washington, January 12, 1864

ICE AT WASHINGTON

At this moment the city of Washington is well-nigh in a state of complete embargo from ice. The Potomac is frozen across to Alexandria, so that teams are crossing on the ice, and above this point the ice is strong enough to bear the rebel army, if the rebel leaders should happen to take a notion to try the experiment. The harbor of Alexandria, being the entrepôt for the vast amount of supplies for the Army of the Potomac, requires constant attention to keep it in tolerable passable condition. Never before—no, not even within the memory of the oldest inhabitant himself—has there been such a cold term as the present, and everybody goes about asking everybody if he ever knew the like. . . .

The slippery and icy streets are a great hindrance to locomotion, and the horse railroads are little better than useless, as the one-horse corporation which owns this extensive monopoly has not horses enough to put four horses to each car, as the exigencies of the case require. Consequently the cars run but half the number of times with a double team, and the enormous number of passengers who travel the road are obliged to swarm on the little cars, which look like so many small drops of molasses with a cluster of flies to each. Congress has got after the company to oblige it to fulfill the stipulations of its profitable charter, but when it is known that every member of Congress is a recipient of a free ticket over the road the prospect of any decided action is not especially hopeful.

REBEL PROPERTY

A large tax sale of rebel property is now going on at Alexandria, in charge of the United States commissioners. Generally the property is unimproved real estate or farms of the broad Virginia style, where there is a great deal of land to a very small deal of building material. The most important sale effected yesterday is that of the Arlington estate, formerly the property of the rebel general [Robert] E. Lee, who inherited it from the Custis family by his wife.

It was bought by the government for $26,800 and was valued at $34,400.

Washington, January 18, 1864

GAB

... At this writing the curse of the American Congress is gab—unmitigated, remorseless, and never-ceasing gab. In the House, that benevolent and useful institution, the previous question, cuts off debate and consigns many an embryo speech to unspoken oblivion; but in the Senate the plug-less word-spouts who must talk do talk without let or hindrance. It is gab, gab, gab, and no sense of reverence for the really honest and capable men in the Senate of the United States can induce your candid correspondent to forbear giving that wordy body a righteous kick *en passant*. On Saturday the Senate had a debating society session, the House not being in session, and the Enrollment Act being a special order for the day. They had a nice time and set up all sorts of ridiculous topics to shoot at. Would you believe it, one senator actually proposed to add a new section to the bill authorizing the president to call out 100,000 men to serve ninety days, under special inducements, to go to Richmond forthwith and liberate the Union prisoners there confined. And, what is more, the Senate seriously considered the Quixotic and visionary scheme, as though we had not now a draft impending for 300,000 for the very purpose of liberating our imprisoned men at Richmond and elsewhere, and as though the rebel authorities would keep our fellow fellows at the rebel capital if it was in danger of being taken, and as though we should be able to raise any men for any other purpose if 100,000 men could escape the draft by volunteering for ninety days and thereby secure a great bounty. One senator said that the enthusiasm which would be awakened over the country would have only a parallel in the ancient crusade of Peter the Hermit. Somebody might have said that the new crusade would be equal to that of Peter in another respect than its enthusiasm—its melancholy fizzle....

THE NEW JOAN OF ARC

Perhaps it may not be altogether gallant to place Miss Anna Dickinson in close proximity to the theme of gab, but it is a logical sequence nevertheless, and when I tell you that Miss Dickinson is a nice girl, smart, witty, and possessing in an eminent degree the gift of gab, you will see the point. At the invitation of Vice President [Hannibal] Hamlin, Speaker [Schuyler] Colfax, and a host of other distinguished names, this remarkable young woman addressed our people at the Capitol night before last. The Hall of Representatives was crowded on floor and in galleries, over 2,500 persons being present. The somber seats were made gay with the bright attire of ladies, velvets, flowers, and brilliant hues varying and lighting up the surface of the great crowd. There was a splendid burst of applause when the fair speaker of the evening was led upon the platform by Vice President Hamlin accompanied by Speaker Colfax.

Miss Dickinson was dressed in a black silk dress with a long train and lighted up with red velvet furbelows; her figure is graceful and full, of medium height, and her face is open, sunny, and bright. Her eyes are large and dark; her hair is also dark and cut short, curling slightly.... As she sat on the stage waiting for the hour of beginning, the target of thousands of eyes, her composure was wonderful. We may well suppose that the quick rising and falling of her bosom was a natural throb of triumph that she, an unknown girl of twenty-two, should at last have come to the national capital at the invitation of the President of the Senate and Speaker of the House, to stand up and speak before the President of the United States, members of his cabinet, senators, representatives, and distinguished men and women of the nation.

When she began to speak, every tone of her voice reached the remotest corner of the great hall, and she spoke as easily and smoothly as would any well-bred lady in her parlor. Her manner was impassioned and earnest, and her movements on the platform were graceful as she swept to and fro, slowly pacing the floor. Of course, with her comparatively brief experience in speaking she cannot be faultless, and it was not pleasant to watch a regular falling inflection at the close of each period, monotonous after a time. Miss Dickinson is no genius, and, though Vice President Hamlin likened her to Joan of Arc when he introduced her and the *Morning Chronicle* bestows upon her a column of rhapsodic laudation, but few people have any other estimate of her than that she is a smart, vigorous, young woman with a great deal of courage and self-possession. She has read a good deal and has an apt and telling way of putting things which brings down the house with thunders of applause. She excels in graphic description, and her pictures of the battle of Missionary Ridge and kindred scenes were very admirable. But there were no new or great thoughts in the lecture, the theme of which was "Words for the Hour." The address was a series of random sketches loosely strung together, the whole being a pleasant bit of mosaic, with here and there a patch of very common earthenware dovetailed between the sparkles of wit and hearty good sense. Miss Dickinson has evidently been a close student of the newspapers, and her education speaks well for her training. She will flash out her brief and splendid career and then subside into the destiny of all women and be heard of no more.

Washington, January 27, 1864

A GAY AND FESTIVE SENATOR

Coming up to the Capitol yesterday morning, people stopped and looked and laughed at the apparition of the late Senator McDougall of California, who, tricked out like a circus clown, was "witching the world with noble horsemanship." He sported a fancy South American saddle gay with silver enough to pay a moderate winter's whisky bills, with a dashing fur mantle on the pommel, and a big round affair where the tip of the pommel usually is. He wore a skull crowned Panama hat with an immense flat rim and trimmed with red, white, and green ribbon—as gay and festive as a peacock. Reining up by the curbstone, he lurched heavily to the leeward (time: 10:30 A.M.), chatted with an acquaintance for a moment, then rode majestically off. The big boy shouted, the little dogs barked, and the senatorial sensation disappeared down the Avenue.

A SPECIMEN OF ENGLISH MANNERS

Lord Lyons, the English minister, attends Dr. [Smith] Pyne's (Episcopal) church, St. John's in Lafayette Square, where he has a handsomely furnished pew and all of the accessories of stately worship—such as becomes a lord going to heaven after the luxurious manner of an English diplomatist. Imagine the indignation of Lord Lyons last Sunday upon finding his pew occupied by a lady who had given up her own seat to somebody else. My Lord beckoned to the interloper to come out, which she did, and his lordship seated himself, flanked by an attaché; but the lady followed into the pew again and sat humbly near the door, when the noble lord whispered to his attaché who whispered to the lady that she must go out, whereupon she did, leaving the pattern of English manners and English nobility to go on with his worship of Almighty God untroubled by the sinful proximity of any republican plebeian. When the noble lord gets to other side of Jordan may he find himself in no worse company than the unassuming Sunday school teacher whom he turned out of his pew last Sunday.

THE PRESIDENT'S LEVEES

For some reason not especially apparent the semiweekly levees at the White House are unusually popular this winter, and the crowds which go there are better dressed than heretofore, when some went into the presidential mansion in a garb which no decent man would allow in his family sitting room. The levees are held on Tuesday evenings and Saturday afternoons, the former being "dress" receptions and the Saturday afternoon levees being less formal in character. The President has been present at all of these receptions, and he intends to meet the people always when his duties will permit. Of course, there is a great variety of costume at the evening affair, but most of the visitors go in party dress—the women rigged out in full fig, with laces, feathers, silks, and satins rare, leaving their bonnets in an anteroom; and the gentlemen appear in light kids and cravats got up in great agony by their hairdressers. Mixed in with these are the less airy people who wear somber colors and who dress in more quiet style. At the morning receptions ladies wear their walking dress, and the show is not half so fine as by gaslight when the glittering crowd pours through the drawing rooms into the great East Room, where they circulate in a revolving march to the music of the Marine Band stationed in an adjoining room. The gentlemen deposit their hats and outside peeling in racks, provided with checks, and then join the procession which presses into the Crimson Drawing Room where it is met by the train of ladies which files from a retiring room. Uncle Abraham stands by the door which opens into the Blue Room, flanked by Marshal Lamon and his private secretary who introduce the new arrivals, each giving his name and that of the lady who accompanies him. The President shakes hands, says "How-do," and the visitor is passed on to where Mrs. Lincoln stands, flanked by another private secretary and B[enjamin] B. French, the Commissioner of Public Buildings, who introduce the party. Then all press on to the next room where they admire each other's good clothes, criticize Mrs. Lincoln's new gown, gossip a little, flirt a little, yawn, go home, and say, "What a bore!" Such is our republican court, and the most bored man in it is Old Abe who hates white kid gloves and a crowd.

Washington, January 29, 1864

"FERNANDO WOOD, HE GIN A TREAT"

So said a western member of Congress in conversation this morning, and the topic of current conversation every-

where is the big party last night—who was there, how they
were dressed, who stayed away because they were not invited, and who stayed away because a Copperhead gave
the party.... The party was a very large one, the rooms
being crowded uncomfortably—crinoline, ample and resplendent, crushing the nether integuments of ordinary
mortals and guests bumping each other like boulders in a
tailrace. Servants in livery announced the guests in sono-
rous tones or ushered them upstairs where gilded lackeys
attended them to dressing rooms or to a retreat where
punch and other facilities for taking the oath were in readi-
ness. The Honorable Fernando was resplendent in white
choker and good clothes, while his wife, dressed in the quiet
taste of a lady receiving company, stood by his side at one
end of the parlor where their guests, half of them strangers,
were presented.

How can I describe the women's gear? What with moire
antiques, velvets, satins, laces, diamonds, and gewgaws
innumerable, no man could say much of what was the real
appearance of the ladies. But I could not help noticing
the conspicuous appearance of an enormous matron, the
wife of a Kentucky congressman; she was a huge lady and
wore an ample skirt of some sort of gray silk, and over
her brawny shoulders she wore a three-cornered cape of
white lace, while at the top of her huge, fat arms hung
big white lace bows, and a triangular lace napkin laid on
top of her head; her appearance, looming above the rest
of the crowd, was decidedly "stunning," as the English
say. The predominating wear of the evening was white
satin or silk, though Mrs. Senator [Edwin D.] Morgan
created a sensation in blue satin, white lace, and diamonds.
A young belle from New Jersey was conspicuously beautiful in a cherry colored silk dress looped up over a white
silk skirt by red cords and tassels. Many of the wives and

daughters of foreign ministers were ablaze with diamonds, the wife of the Peruvian minister being especially noticeable for a big rose of diamonds and gold filigree which she wore upon a bracelet. The turnout by the foreign legations was very large, the corps of bewhiskered polyglots being noisy, *distingué,* and voracious.

It had been said that none of the Republican congressmen would be there, but all of the New York representatives and Senators [Edwin D.] Morgan and [Ira] Harris honored the distinguished Copperhead with their presence. Senators [Lazarus W.] Powell [of Kentucky], [Willard] Saulsbury [of Delaware], [Thomas A.] Hendricks [of Indiana], and others of that ilk were present; likewise, Justice [Nathan] Clifford, of the Supreme Court; ex-Governor [George S.] Boutwell, of Massachusetts; Superintendent of Census J[oseph C.] G. Kennedy, and a fair sprinkling of Republicans from the departments and the House of Representatives.

The music was furnished by the famous Marine Band stationed in an alcove decorated with red, white, and blue; and flowers were profusely scattered through the room, one magnificent bouquet bearing a card engraved "with the compliments of Mrs. A. Lincoln to Mrs. F. Wood." The supper was, of course, the event of the evening, at which there was a great rush and crush—a cordon of hungry men being at once formed in front of the tables, making a raid upon the splendid array of good things. It was amusing to see, over the sea of heads, hands convulsively clasping plates of terrapin, oysters, ices, and other goodies. White glasses of champagne, fragments of cake, and empty plates flew to and fro in air like seaweed tossed up from the yeasty ocean which broke in foamy whirls around the loaded tables. There was fat Justice Clifford pressing a little Philadelphia *Inquirer* man against the table while he hacked away at a pyramid of ice cream before him. Yonder were two senators of opposite political faith quarreling over a stray glass of champagne, each endeavoring to outdo the other in denying himself the privilege of drinking it. Under foot were fragments of cut glass, paté de foie gras, fruit, and things. Jammed against the wall by the table were professional party-goers who ate boned turkey, ices, terrapin, jelly, tongue, or charlotte russe, just as they happened indiscriminately to fall upon it. The supper was very superb, however, and I noticed that a great many who came in about eating time reported that they had just come from Postmaster General Blair's party, where they had a great deal of ceremony but not much to eat. They were sensible people and brought up at the Wood party when they got hungry. Consequently the Blairs closed up at midnight—just when the Woodites were in the zenith of their party-giving glory. If the honorable Fernando Wood gave his party for the purpose of showing his splendid plate, china, and fixings, and creating a social sensation, he was successful.

Washington, February 29, 1864

HONORS TO GRANT

After considerable squabbling over particulars, Congress has finally passed the bill to revive the grade of Lieutenant General, and the President has sent into the Senate today the name of General Ulysses S. Grant for confirmation as ex-officio Lieutenant General of the Army of the United States. It is not very probable that Grant will come to Washington as a bureau officer nor that Halleck will lose his place as an office general. It now appears that Grant's powers will be more of an advisory character and that he will dictate from the field the general plan of military campaigns all over the country, leaving the details to be carried out by the respective commanders acting under orders from Washington. Under the new regime we may expect a vigorous administration of our military affairs, which will dispense hereafter with all such unfortunate failures as the last ineffectual "rehabilitation" of Florida, in which we have for a third or fourth time reoccupied Jacksonville and have lost men, means, and munitions of war in a grand fizzle intended to bring back Florida *nolens volens*. It is not supposed that Grant will tolerate this dismal dribbling policy which Halleck has inaugurated and kept up to this time.

This morning a magnificent sword, to be presented to Grant by Jo Daviess County, Illinois, was placed upon exhibition in the office of the Speaker of the House of Representatives. It is a splendid affair costing upwards of $3,000. It was made at the Ames Manufacturing Company at Chicopee, Massachusetts, is of the regulation pattern, and is said to be one of the most beautiful specimens of ornamental work ever made in this country. The scabbard is of gold, richly ornamented with classic designs in scroll work, containing the names of twenty-seven battles and sieges in which the redoubtable Grant has been engaged, beginning with Palo Alto and ending with Lookout Mountain. The grasp is of gold, inlaid with tortoise shell, and the pommel is decorated with fourteen large diamonds. . . .

In one of the committee rooms of the House of Representatives there is now on exhibition a fine oil painting of the hero of twenty-seven successful fights which has just been finished by [John] Antrobus, a well-known artist of Chicago. The painting is a full length portrait of Grant, of life size, and surrounded by the usual accessories of such a character upon canvas. The hero is standing by the wreck

of a dismounted rebel fieldpiece, upon which his right
hand rests lightly, while in his unemployed left hand he
holds a field-glass. His head, firmly set and well-poised, is
slightly turned to the right, his kindly blue eyes being
attracted, apparently, by some battle stir in the distance.
In the distant background, blue and hazy, is Missionary
Ridge over which lines of national troops are moving;
nearer is the general's war horse, held by an orderly, and
various bits of the paraphernalia of war are scattered around,
the accessories being all skillfully subordinated to the general effect and the prominence of the chief figure, about
which the whole interest must center. The painting,
though not a first-class work of art, is highly meritorious,
and is said by those who have known Grant to be an excellent portrait of the General. The composition, or arrangement of the painting, is not original, Stuart's Washington
and one or two other semiequestrian portraits of generals
being almost identical in design. The coloring is pure and
cool but inclined to rawness, while the flesh is too red
and white, lacking the bronze vigor of a working warrior,
as Grant is. But as we have no great artists in historical
painting, this new picture will pass for a fair specimen. It
is proposed to ask Congress to purchase this painting and
place it in the Capitol. There is some trash in the rotunda
which has cost the government much money and is no
better than this.

Washington, March 9, 1864

ENTER THE LIEUTENANT GENERAL

[Congressman Elihu B.] Washburne had the pleasure
of delivering Grant's commission as Lieutenant General
into the hero's own hands; but he might have saved the

journey which he took for that purpose. Grant arrived in this city last evening about dusk. He went very quietly to Willard's, and it was not until he had half-finished his dinner that people knew that he was in town. As soon as it was discovered that he was at the table eating his dinner just like ordinary mortals, there was a shout of welcome from all present, an immense cheer going up from the crowd in the dining room. After dinner the assemblage was introduced to the General by ex-Governor [Congressman James K.] Moorhead of Pennsylvania, and a general and cordial handshaking took place.

General Grant is rather slightly built, has stooping shoulders, mild blue eyes, and light brown hair and whiskers, with a foxy tinge to his mustache. He has a frank, manly bearing, wears an ordinary-looking military suit, and doesn't put on any airs whatever. Last evening he attended the President's levee, where he met the President for the first time in his life, though many letters have passed between these two distinguished men since Grant achieved eminence as a commander. The crowd at the levee was immense, and for once the interest was temporarily transferred from the President to the newcomer. The mass of people thronged about him wherever he moved, everybody being anxious to get at least a glimpse of his face. The women were caught up and whirled into the torrent which swept through the great East Room; laces were torn, crinoline mashed, and things were generally much mixed. People mounted sofas and tables to get out of harm's way or to take observations, and for a time the commotion was almost like a Parisian *émeute*; but the cause of all this disturbance soon withdrew, and the tumult subsided. Of course, everybody is on the *qui vive* to know what will be the character and results of the deliberations upon which Grant has been called here to take part in, but of course nobody knows anything about either one or the other.

Washington, March 18, 1864

THE HOUSE OF REPRESENTATIVES

The scene which is spread out before us as we sit in the gallery of the "third estate" this blustering afternoon is literally and figuratively "checkered." Clouds come and go over the great stained and ground glass skylights of the roof of the House of Representatives, casting their shadows transiently upon the parti-colored scene below. It is half-past two o'clock, and the gallery where we sit has its full complement of reporters busy taking notes or exchanging weighty opinions upon the questions of the day as their relative positions on the different newspapers may demand. [Lewis A.] Gobright, who makes up the dispatches for the Associated Press, and so is responsible for all of the reports which go to the country from this branch of Congress, is busy keeping track of the debate and is writing his longhand sketch from his shorthand notes. He is flanked on either side by the New York *Herald* and *World*, while your special correspondent comes next on the left, being flanked on either hand by two *Tribunes*, one from Chicago and one from New York, with the San Francisco *Journal*, St. Louis *Missouri Democrat*, and other jolly "Jacobins" in the rear. Other reporters are dotted in around us, and many circulate on the floor of the House where they have managed to be smuggled in as committee clerks to the disgustful envy of their less fortunate or less pushing brethren.

But we look down upon the marble dais of the Speaker;

the desks of the clerks of the House are in front of him; the *Globe* phonographers in front of them, the arena next; and beyond rise in rows the carved oaken desks of the members who sit in heavy oak chairs, which are cushioned and lined with dark green leather. These rise in semicircles to the "bar" of the house, which is only a slightly raised space outside the seats, and outside of that is another open space bounded by the square walls of the cloak rooms, above which rise the galleries in which a few hundred silent spectators watch the busy scene below.

The members are variously occupied, some listening to the debate or participating in it; others are reading or writing, one or two are asleep in their comfortable chairs, and on the lounges outside of the desks are many more, who are chatting with their outside friends who have been brought in on various pretexts.... That lawyer-like, pale man with gray hair and whiskers, three seats from the front at the left of the Speaker, is [William] Higby [of California]; he is chatting with [Charles] Upson of Michigan, a sandy-haired, thin-faced man with a pleasant smile; he ... is a good debater and a prominent member of the Committee of Elections. One seat nearer the front is [Cornelius] Cole [of California], a heavy, dark-haired, quiet man; he is reading the *Globe* of today, and on his left, with his feet "cocked up" on his seat is [Thomas B.] Shannon [of California], who is watching the debate and stroking his whiskers comfortably.

Darting about are dozens of pages, impudent young varlets snatched prematurely from their mothers' arms to run messages in the House and to be a hindrance and a nuisance to everybody in general. They are the sons, nephews, cousins' children, or other relatives of the members for the most part. Here and there we discern an unobtrusive porter who comes staggering in under a huge load of enveloped documents which some member proposes to frank and send to his waiting constituents who will value them—for their weight as papermakers' stock unless they are picture books ... and will please children.

The subject before the House is a proposition to buy of the publishers of the *National Intelligencer* one hundred sets of their *Annals of Congress,* a book of seventy-one large volumes giving a history of congressional debates from the First Congress to 1845 inclusive. This is only a small "job," but the price of each set being $355, which would bring the lot at $35,500; that's all. The last Congress authorized the Clerk to buy one hundred copies of the book, although eighty-five copies were already in the possession of the government. Gales & Seaton delivered the books on the very day after the House passed the resolution in 1862, but as there was no money to pay for them the Clerk refused to receive them, and the whole lot was stored in the Capitol, Gales & Seaton retaining the key of the storeroom from that day until this. But before payment could be made the House rescinded its resolution and the books were never received. Now the publishers claim that they performed their part of the contract by a delivery of the books within the walls of the Capitol, and they ask that they may have their money. As might be expected, Kentucky is the champion of the conservative *Intelligencer,* and Green Clay Smith makes a swelling and "high-toned" rejoinder to the remarks of [Ambrose W.] Clark of New York, who speaks about an investigation into the manner in which this "job" was gotten up.

There is a great deal of confusion as to the right to the floor, and the aisles are speedily full of members all wanting to be heard and all claiming that right. Speaker Colfax raps loudly and bawls still more loudly before he can command silence, but [William] Windom of Minnesota gets the floor and reads long extracts from the report of an investigating committee by which it appears that one Coyle, bookkeeper to the *Intelligencer* for twenty-odd years, was instrumental in having a reconsideration made during the last Congress of the vote by which the House rescinded the resolution of purchase; that he urged out-siders to urge members to move a reconsideration; that somebody offered $1,000 or $1,500 for such a job, that Coyle had testified that he never offered money but thought he said he had rather lose $1,000 or $1,500 than lose that resolution, and more to the same effect. Smith of Kentucky wants the floor; so does Washburne, who wants the investigation printed. Dawes of Massachusetts also wants the floor, and so does Mallory of Kentucky; and he interposes a good word for Gales & Seaton who, it appears, got in debt to their bookkeeper, who advanced them money and then undertook the job of getting through this "little bill."

[Rufus P.] Spalding of Ohio, a hard-faced old man, gets the floor and gives a history of the whole affair, during which Coyle, the faithful bookkeeper and bookseller, is observed to quit the floor of the House where he has been all of this time and go up to the gallery where he belongs, being moved thereto by a motion from some of the anti-*Intelligencer* men to the sergeant-at-arms. Spalding having finished, in spite of repeated interruptions which make him very petulant, a dozen members spring up at once, but James C. Allen of Illinois gets the floor and proceeds, in a violent and stridulous speech, to show that the original contract was a good one and should be kept by the House and that the *Intelligencer* ought to have its money.

There are more struggles for speech, but all are choked off by the blessed previous question, which is called upon the motion to lay the whole matter upon the table. The ayes and noes are ordered, and the droning voice of the Clerk goes on with the roll, and amidst considerable excitement—for this affair has stirred up some feeling—the vote is announced as 67 ayes to 50 noes. So the *Intelligencer* has been laid upon the table, apparently; but [Daniel W.] Voorhees [of Indiana], a Copperhead champion of the job, has voted with the majority and moves a reconsideration. More ayes and noes, more motions, more bother, all are needful before the thing is dead and the House adjourns.

Nearly the whole afternoon has been spent in this miserable wrangle which has revealed corruption, bribery, or attempts at them, and has elicited much hard feeling and not a little temper on all sides; but before the House adjourns and the members go hurrying to their five o'clock dinner with a dim consciousness of not having earned it, let me sketch in lightly a few of the more noticeable men who come up from the people to legislate in the popular branch of Congress:

JUSTIN S. MORRILL

We commence with Vermont, which sends the above-named gentleman, among others of lesser note. Morrill is tall, shapely, and very good-looking; is fifty-four years old; a farmer by occupation, and has been in every Congress from the Thirty-Fourth to the present—Thirty-Eighth. He is a prudent, saving man, an excellent financier, and a prominent member of the Ways and Means Committee. He sits beside Thad Stevens, Chairman of the Committee of Ways and Means; of which Morrill is the second member. He is slow of speech and has a hesitating way which a stranger takes for affectation. He is not a fluent debater, but is eminently a sound man.

SAMUEL HOOPER

Stout, white-headed, dignified, quiet, and gentlemanly, Hooper of Massachusetts is the best type of a solid man of Boston. His solid of avoirdupois is well matched by his weight of cash, for he is one of the wealthier men in the House. He is also a prominent member of the Ways and Means Committee and is a good financier. He gives good dinners, always speaks to some purpose, but seldom addresses the House, and is so courteous and gracious that he always commands respect from all parties. He has been a member of the House for the last three terms of Congress.

JOHN B. ALLEY

This mild-mannered gentleman, a little lame, considerably gray, and pale-looking, is the Chairman of the Post Office Committee, and as such is entitled to great respect from Californians, who have a great many axes to grind in that committee. He is, moreover, an agreeable gentleman, belongs in Lynn, Massachusetts, seldom makes a speech, but speaks to the purpose, if at all, and is conservative and diffident in manner and belief.

GEORGE S. BOUTWELL

Of Massachusetts, never in Congress before this term, was formerly Commissioner of Internal Revenue, once Governor of the Old Bay State, as the Yankees fondly term it, and he started life as a village storekeeper. He is a tall, sallow, black-haired, and bewhiskered man. He is able, a good financier, and a good debater. He is a lawyer as well and had peculiar notions upon the subject of reconstruction. He is in the prime of life and achieved much distinction while yet young.

HENRY L. DAWES

Massachusetts has the ablest delegation, as a whole, in the House, and Dawes, as the Chairman of the Committee on Elections, is necessarily a prominent man in many debates. He is youthful-looking, but is forty-eight years old; has been in public life in various ways ever since 1848, having been in his own state legislature, a district attorney, etc. He was a member of Congress from the Thirty-Fifth to the present term, and has been Chairman of the Committee of Elections for two terms. He is a lawyer by profession, able, logical, but of exceedingly poor delivery, having a wasteful, hesitating drawl, which is aggravating to a listener. He can never electrify anybody.

HENRY G. STEBBINS

Represents the Staten Island district of New York. He is a War Democrat, the last member of the Ways and Means Committee, and an able and patriotic man if he does sit among the Copperheads. He is the author of the Gold Bill which he advocated in an excellent, logical, and eloquent speech. He is about fifty years of age and is in the full vigor of florid health.

THE WOODS

Benjamin and Fernando Wood enjoy the bad eminence of being the notorieties who are inquired after by every newcomer in the galleries of the House. Ben Wood is tall, well-shaped, and slightly stooping, has a bad, gray-blue eye, overhanging light, long hair, a doughy face, large, light-colored mustache, and has a vulgar, dishonest look, albeit he wears good clothes. He never speaks and has seldom been in his seat during this session, owing to a prolonged sickness.

Fernando Wood is better looking than his brother. He is tall, dark, polished in appearance, and has a scholarly look. He dresses in gentlemanly black, twirls his eyeglass, is never ruffled in temper; is a good debater, speaking with a great ease and grace, reminding one of descriptions of Talleyrand and Mephistopheles, both at the same time, somehow. He sits in the center of the opposition side of the House and is unquestionably the smartest man among them. He was born in Philadelphia in 1812, consequently he is now fifty-two years old. He commenced life as a cigar maker and was afterward a clerk, merchant, shipowner, and he is rich. He was in Congress from 1841 to 1843 and afterward Mayor of New York....

JAMES BROOKS

Another New York member, is probably the best read man in the House. He is tall, long-headed, has large, dull eyes, a broad forehead, dark hair, and wears eyeglasses, and is forever preaching economy in appropriation, groaning and lamenting every dollar, sighing for the good old times when such things as the Lime Point job were equal to a modern battle with 50,000 killed. Brooks is a Maine man by birth and is fifty-four years old; was originally a clerk, a schoolmaster—climbing up like an ambitious Yankee as he is—was a graduate of Waterville College, and has been a great traveler in his own and foreign countries. He is an accomplished and courteous gentleman, so that I cannot find it in my heart to abuse him even if he be a Copperhead and one of the editors of the New York *Express* which he established in 1835. He has been in public life; was the original "Special Washington Correspondent," having commenced life here when most of the present tribe of scribblers were as yet unbreeched. Brooks was in Congress from 1848 to 1853, and has profited by his experience, being well-posted on public affairs. He does not make much headway but believes that the abolition of slavery is an accomplished fact. He shows his sense.

REUBEN E. FENTON

Of the Cattaraugus district of New York, is one of the oldest members of the House, counting by terms, as he has been in Congress from the Thirty-Third to the present term—more than eight years. He is one of the best-looking men in the House, forty-five years old, tall, shapely, with grayish, wavy hair; polished but quiet in manner; never makes a set speech; is a leading member of the Ways and Means Committee and a useful member of the House.

WILLIAM D. KELLEY

Pennsylvania for so large a state has but a poor show for a delegation in her twenty-four members. A fair average of the lot is the Philadelphia gentleman whose name is given above. He is a tall, slender man with a profusion of auburn hair, blue eyes, and a theatrical manner. His style of oratory is of the flowery, poetic, and conscious order, rolling his eye in fine frenzy and his r's in a truly British manner. One of the best things ever said of him was that by Cox who denominated him in debate as "the Pennsylvania gentleman with the voice." Everybody had to laugh at that; notwithstanding all this, Kelley is an excellent man; useful in debate, and well up on the radical questions of the day.

SYDENHAM E. ANCONA

Looking among the more rabid of the Copperheads you will see this gentleman who represents the Berks County district of Pennsylvania. He is the most forward "peace" man in the House, though he never speaks much. He has been in several terms of Congress. He is small in stature, gray, short-haired, rosy-faced, and has a slight lisp. He votes antiwar and Copperheadism straight.

Washington, March 19, 1864

THE LEADER OF THE HOUSE—THADDEUS STEVENS

... The Ways and Means Committee is the most important one in the House, ... and the Chairman is by virtue of his position the acknowledged leader of the dominant party in the House. ... It will explain to some few persons how Thaddeus Stevens of ... the Lancaster district of Pennsylvania comes by his title. Stevens is also the oldest man in the House, being nearly seventy years old; and first served in Congress during 1849 to 1853 and also in the Thirty-Sixth, Thirty-Seventh, and the Thirty-Eighth Congresses. [President] Buchanan gave a great deal of money to defeat him during the last canvass but did not succeed, the indomitable Thad being returned to serve

his country and be a terror to Copperheads and other evildoers, as usual. Age does not wither nor custom stale his
fund of humor and wit, nor dull the sharpness of his keen
faculties. His forte is in sarcasm and irony. . . . He is a
sound financier and his judgment upon such matters is
viewed with great deference, while upon some other questions his dicta are not so weighty. His heresy upon the
rebel "foreign nation," or recognized belligerent seceders,
has caused his friends considerable annoyance and has
given the Opposition a great many opportunities for ill-
natured criticism of the Republican side of the House.

Stevens, is a bachelor; was born in Vermont; is somewhat grim and crusty though never rude; is stiff and formal
in manner and slow of speech but immovable as Gibraltar
in the midst of the waves of passion which oftentimes surge
around him. In person, he is well-built, has blue, dull eyes,
overhanging brows, a dark brown wig, and is lame, having
a deformed foot. He leads the House as nobody else can,
quiets the perturbed passions of the different factions in
the House with truly paternal impartiality mixed with
grim humor, and is a useful legislator as well as a venerable
relic of the palmy days of the eloquent past.

HENRY WINTER DAVIS

This eloquent and able Marylander disappoints most
people in his personal appearance, as he is small, lightly-
built, and has, from the galleries, a very youthful look. He
is about forty years of age; is light in complexion, with a
round, boyish head, sandy hair, and mustache only; has a
light but clear and ringing voice. He was a member of the
Thirty-Fourth, Thirty-Fifth, and Thirty-Sixth Congresses;
and in the last-named Congress he had the honor of giving
the vote which dissolved the tie and elected [William]

Pennington of New Jersey Speaker of the House over the proslavery candidate. Since that period the record of Henry Winter Davis has been stainless on the great question of human freedom, and he is doubtless as cordially hated by the proslavery secessionists of "My Maryland" as the veriest abolitionist in New England. He is opposed to military governors, has peculiar views on the status of rebel people, and is sharp and smart rather than profound or able. He is a brilliant speaker but not a ready debater; has a compact, direct way of putting things and always commands close attention when he speaks. He is Chairman of the Committee on Foreign Affairs.

ROBERT C. SCHENCK

Represents the district of the Ohio martyr, Vallandigham, who "watches and waits" in vain over the Canadian border for the delivering army of [George E.] Pugh and his pugilistics. It is refreshing to see here a Major General who has distinguished himself in his country's service in the place of the rebel who has left his country for his country's good. General Schenck is fifty-five years old, tall, and well-made. He is sandy and Teutonic as to complexion and sour as to temper, being easily ruffled. He has a maimed hand which may afford some apology for his palpable want of patience, but his red hair never grew on a cool head yet. Schenck is a native of Ohio, a graduate of Miami University, an old legislator, having served in the Ohio legislature and in Congress from 1843 to 1851; was Minister to Brazil in Fillmore's time, a railroad president when the war began, afterwards in command in northern Virginia and at Baltimore, and is an able Chairman of the Committee on Military Affairs. He seldom makes speeches but was, in former days, one of the best debaters in the

House of Representatives. He is the author of the bill to drop from the rolls of the army all officers unemployed or employed in service below their grade, and he took no pains to conceal his chagrin and disgust at the virtual defeat of his favorite measure.

SAMUEL S. COX

Commonly known as "Sunset" Cox, is from the seventh congressional district of Ohio. He is a light, small man; smart and funny in small wit; good at repartee, but sensitive upon "the Abyssianian" he puffed so extravagantly in one of his juvenile books written before western Copperheads were invented. He is ambitious to be the leader of the Opposition in the House, in which desire he is continually thwarted by [George H.] Pendleton and Fernando Wood. In 1855 he was Secretary of Legation at Peru and has been in Congress nearly ever since, this being his fourth term. He is a leading member of the Committe on Foreign Affairs and is a man of good literary acquirements. He is enamored with the sound of his own voice and never lets slip an opportunity to put in a word or crack a joke. Caliber, light; range, limited.

ANOTHER MAJOR GENERAL

Is James A. Garfield, of the nineteenth congressional district of Ohio. He was Chief of Staff to [William S.] Rosecrans; is a gallant soldier and a useful and able legislator; was formerly a clergyman; is about forty years old; stout, good-looking, with a substantial figure; blue eyes, light brown hair; a little heavy, but reliable, courteous, and kind. He is very properly a prominent man on the

Military Committee, and is generally liked by all of the members. He has made no speeches yet of great weight, but he is a pleasant speaker and a good debater.

GEORGE H. PENDLETON

Another Ohio Copperhead, and a rival of Cox, who tries to ride a warhorse as well as a peace donkey, Pendleton is a champion of lightweights, is about forty years old, medium in size, light as to complexion, and querulous as to voice; snarling and meddling. He is a good financier and a member of the Ways and Means Committee. Pendleton has been in the Ohio state senate and in every Congress since the Thirty-Fifth; is a lawyer, smart and sharp.

THE KENTUCKY DELEGATION

Is, on the whole, a very able one. Robert Mallory of the Louisville district is the oldest member as to service, having served in several consecutive congresses. He is a jolly, red-faced man, free and easy, sound on the social and "nigger" questions; says "thar" and "whar" and is unscrupulous. He is a proslavery combatant in Congress and a mild emancipation-unionist at home; was returned to Congress as a radical, which he is—on the proslavery side.

Brutus J. Clay is a tall, shapely gentleman with a silvery head and the true Clay physiogonomy. He is a notable farmer and Chairman of the Committee on Agriculture, but he takes no active part in the business of the House, generally voting right. Green Clay Smith is one of the younger members of the House; is goodlooking, dark-haired, and mustached, of light caliber, a little frothy, and will doubtless improve by age. [Lucian] Anderson and [William H.] Randall are tall, raw-boned Kentuckians of the Lincoln type; useful in their way, and are the most reliable of their delegation when a close party vote is called. They are sound on the main question.

Of the rest nothing special need be said except Aaron Harding, a sour and dyspeptic Copperhead, to use the mildest term. This man, comically enough, was mistaken by telegraph for Senator [Benjamin F.] Harding of Oregon, and a series of bitter, semirebel resolutions which the Kentuckian offered in the House were reported in the Oregon newspapers as having emanated from the senatorial Oregonian. The best part of the joke is that a "Democratic" Club in Salem, Oregon, took up the misrepresented senator when everybody else was abusing him and made the Kentuckian's resolutions their political platform. Kentucky "Democracy" is good enough for the Oregon sort.

DANIEL W. VOORHEES

This eminent Indiana Copperhead is unquestionably one of the most eloquent men in the House; and he can lie—under a mistake—as long as any other man and not acknowledge it, but make it seem far better than the truth. He is tall, well-built, with long reddish hair combed up from his forehead *a la Chinoise*; and has a high, clear voice with a metallic ring like the new national currency. He is graceful in speech, uncompromising, unscrupulous, and vehement in manner. Voorhees has not the smartness of Cox nor the ability of Pendleton, but he is a good lawyer and is sharp and ready in debate, using up many abler men.

THE GREAT OBJECTOR

I wish that I could give as brief a mention of W[illiam] S. Holman, of Indiana, as his single speech deserves. His only speech is "I object." When I have said that, the man is described and the subject exhausted.

SPEAKER COLFAX

In refreshing contrast with the preceding Copperhead Indianans is Schuyler Colfax, the Speaker of the House. As I sit here in the reporters' gallery I can only see the top of his head and notice his small hands as he nervously toys with his pencil, his eyes ever watching keenly the proceedings in the House. Colfax was born in New York City; went to Indiana when young, and has been a printer and editor of the South Bend *Register* ever since he was of age. He is forty-one years old; is a widower; light in complexion, has easy, winning ways, and is courteous and affable to all. He has been in Congress ever since 1854; is a consummate parliamentarian, quick, patient, and well posted. He is ready and fluent, as well as a rapid speaker and hard-working, tireless business man. As Speaker he has fulfilled the highest hopes of his many friends, though he has failed to satisfy everybody in his distribution of places on committees. Californians have nothing to thank him for in the way of committeeships, and straight-out Lincoln men condemn the haste with which he rushed into print to contradict some irresponsible scribbler's statement that he was for Lincoln's renomination. But Schuyler Colfax has a good heart and deserves his wide popularity.

ISAAC N. ARNOLD

Somebody said that the greatest delight of this gentleman is the daily reflection that he is Isaac N. Arnold, of

Illinois. However that may be, he is an intelligent, clearheaded man with sound judgment, an affected speech, and undying faith in Old Abe and the Great Western Ship Canal. He is tall, blue-eyed, bold, small-headed, not fluent, but of great mental culture, and possessing considerable legal acumen. To him belongs the credit of making the first suggestion in this Congress to abolish slavery in the United States by an amendment of the Constitution. He has made two good set speeches during the session.

A BRIGADIER

John F. Farnsworth of the second congressional district of Illinois has achieved some distinction as a Brigadier General in the Army of the Potomac, having passed through the wretched Peninsula campaign of McClellan. He is forty-five years old; has been in the Thirty-Fifth and Thirty-Sixth Congresses and has no special ability. He is a very tall, shapely man with long, straight, dark hair, blue eyes, and is a favorite with the ladies, albeit his manners are rough and repellent. He is the second member of the House Military Committee.

ELIHU B. WASHBURNE

Of the Galena district, of Illinois, is the special custodian of General Grant's fame and fortunes and is suspected of an intention of running him for the presidency—after he is president, if possible, E. B. Washburne is one of the abler men in the House, of indomitable and imperious will; a governing mind, he leads men captive at his will by sheer semibrute force and not by force of logic or sweet persuasion. There is no softness of sentiment about that hard, iron-gray head. . . .

Washburne is forty-eight years old; is a native of Maine, a graduate of Harvard College, and he has been in every Congress from the Thirty-Fifth to the present. He is now Chairman of the Committee on Commerce; is always on the floor of the House. He disputes with Thad Stevens for the leadership and has a finger in everybody's pie. His friends are devotedly attached to him, and his enemies, who are many, hate him like anything that is violently quarrelsome. If Grant is the next president, Washburne will be the premier or burst.

OWEN LOVEJOY

Was an original Illinois abolitionist and swore eternal hatred to slavery over the dead body of his brother, one of the earlier victims of the wanton lust for blood of that autocratic, myriad-handed power. He is now, comparatively speaking, a conservative Republican. He is fifty-three years old; is a native of Maine, a graduate of Bowdoin College, and he was originally a Congregational clergyman. He has served in his own state legislature several terms and has been in Congress from the Thirty-Fifth until the present, making his debut in public life at the capital about the time when the revival of free opinion at the North began to show itself in that revolution which has since driven slavery to the wall. Lovejoy is stout, good-natured, bluff, and full of fun and Scripture quotations. He has not been in his seat much during the present session, being kept housed by a distressing malady which has bleached his iron-gray hair to whiteness and taken off much of his portly look. His state and nation can ill afford to lose his outspoken manliness, genial heartiness, and wholesome faith in the right, from the national councils.

JAMES C. ALLEN

This gentleman is the ablest of the Illinois Copperheads and has the honor of representing the whole state, being the only representative-at-large from any districted state in Congress. He is a full-built man in the vigorous, florid health of the prime of life, being forty-one years old. He is a Kentuckian by birth, and held several public offices in his native state before he emigrated to Illinois where he served in several legislatures. He was a member of the Thirty-Third and Thirty-Fourth Congresses, was the Clerk of the Thirty-Fifth, and he has been re-elected to each succeeding Congress. He is a good debater, but does not speak often, though he speaks with passion and vehemence, if at all, and he has a high, sharp voice which is just suited to startle people with a midnight cry of "Fire!"

FRANK P. BLAIR, JR.

One of the more impracticable men in Congress . . . a Major General, a proslavery, gradual (very gradual) emancipationist, a Kentuckian by birth and a Missourian by accident, he combines in himself more inconsistencies than fall to the lot of most men. His position in the House is equally anomalous, as he claims to be a friend of the administration but sits and votes with its enemies. He is not in sympathy with anybody but "the Blair family," and with them he is trying to smother Lincoln with his doubtful friendship. Blair is tall, well-made, and he has a sour, cynical face, reddish, long hair, and blue eyes. He has an easy delivery and has made one set speech in Congress in which he abused Chase bitterly and villainously. He was a representative to the Thirty-Fifth Congress and was an original champion of emancipation; he always chooses to be in a minority. . . .

THE IOWA DELEGATION

. . . James F. Wilson, the able Chairman of the Judiciary Committee, deserves a "subhead" by himself. Wilson is a sound lawyer, a fair-minded honorable man, a good debater, but slow—a leading mind in the House, and clear, logical, and compact in all of his utterances. He is stout, large-headed, gray, about forty years old, reliable, and eminently useful. Of the rest of the delegation, John A. Kasson, formerly Assistant Postmaster General, is the ablest, being yet young, but a rising man. Like most smart men he talks too much but generally gets the attention of the House, though his manner is slightly affected and finical. He parts his hair high upon his head, uses choice language, and is a good financier. [Josiah B.] Grinnell deserves mention for his frequent utterances on the floor of the House. He is a short, pleasant-faced man, a good farmer, formerly a clergyman. He is a "smoothbore" and is very light in caliber, given to bunkum and futile wit but is an ardent Unionist—as are all of the Iowans in Congress.

Washington, March 23, 1864

AN UNSEASONABLE FREAK

Our Washington climate, true to its own reputation for eccentricity, has been cutting up some strange antics within a day or two. When I last had occasion to allude to the weather it was balmy, mild, and springlike. Flowers were springing through the warm mold, and Nature was buttoning its jacket of grass with golden jonquils, crocuses, and things. All day yesterday it blew and at night it snew, so that this morning eight inches of snow were lying where but yesterday the dust flew in such blinding whirls as only Washington dust can fly. The flowers are hidden by the snow, and the nascent roses and posies are untimely nipped in the bud. Talk about winter lingering in the lap of spring! Why, this is sitting down square in it. . . .

Washington, March 24, 1864

FUTURE MILITARY OPERATIONS

With Lieutenant General Grant at the head of military affairs, our people have renewed hopes for the spring campaign. Of course, while Halleck's powers and duties as Chief of Staff are undefined and indefinable, there will be more or less uneasiness lest he might be able to render nugatory the vigorous counsels of Grant. It is, however, now certain that Grant has assumed the direction and charge of the next movement of the Army of the Potomac. The arrangements as to the command are not yet fully settled.

The Army of the Potomac has been or is being reorganized. Incompetent and semidisloyal men are being continually weeded out, Grant having plenary powers for that purpose. Active preparations for a grand movement are now going on in this army, but it does not appear likely or possible that there will be anything done before the middle of April. It is believed, and it appears most reasonable, that a movement of the armies of the southwest will take place simultaneously with one by the Army of the Potomac. I say that the public expect this, but it will be the first time that the public will have been gratified by seeing the right thing done at the right time. From the highest authority we learn that on April 1 there will be 700,000 active men fit for duty in the armies of the United States. The people demand that these men, the flower of the country, shall be made speedily and effectually useful. I know and believe that before these men return to their homes the administration intends that they shall have finished up all military labors on this continent. Who said anything about Mexico?

Washington, April 5, 1864

A NEW EXECUTIVE MANSION?

The present habitation of the President of the United States is in an unhealthy location, is inadequate and inconvenient for its purpose, and is now crowded into an undesirable portion of the city by the growth of the adjacent neighborhood. It is proposed, therefore, that a new establishment, handsome, spacious and modern in its appurtenances, shall be built in an airy and quiet suburb of the city and that the present mansion shall be transformed into an office for the State Department. The Senate Committee on Public Buildings and Grounds have such a proposition under consideration, but it will depend upon circumstances whether it be reported upon during the present session. The presidential mansion would make a good place for the State Department, which is in a narrow, old-fashioned building now being absorbed into the growing Treasury building.

Washington, April 7, 1864

AN ENGLISH "MEMBER OF PARLIAMENT" IN THE HOUSE OF REPRESENTATIVES

George Thompson, the famous English abolitionist, eight or ten years ago was mobbed in radical, antislavery Massachusetts. I saw him egged in the Boston Tremont Temple. Last night he spoke upon the topics of the times in the hall of the House, being introduced to the audience by John Pierpont, another sufferer at the hands of pro-slavery people. The Vice President of the United States sat upon the platform beside him, and the President, Secretaries, and other notables of our nation were among his auditors. The audience was tremendous, and the vast crowd heaved and surged with enthusiasm at the burning and stirring words of the eloquent speaker. He defined the causes of the war, as understood in England, assured us of the hearty support of the masses of the British people in our struggle for our integrity, and passed upon the President a hearty eulogium which was received with wild applause. Tonight Thompson has a levee at the house of Lewis Clephane, the former associate of the late Dr. [Gamaliel] Bailey in the publication of the *National Era,* the first antislavery newspaper in Washington.

Washington, April 25, 1864

A GRAND MILITARY DISPLAY

... There was a great rush about town to see Burnside's 30,000 as the corps marched into the city on Fourteenth

Street, across Long Bridge to Alexandria, on their way to the front. Both branches of Congress took a recess in order to see the show, and senators, representatives, and governors mingled in the mob which lined the route of the column. The President, attended by General Burnside and his staff, reviewed the troops from a balcony on the Fourteenth Street side of Willard's Hotel as they filed past, banners flying, music swelling on the air, horses prancing, the steady, measured tramp of marching feet, the rolling of the drum, and the harsher music of thundering artillery. All of these conspired to make the scene a memorable one for Washington, which seldom sees so large a force moving at one time through the city. But a stranger sight for this capital, so long slavery-ridden, was the array of 7,000 American citizens of African descent all bravely armed and equipped, their banners flying, and their brawny limbs clad in the uniform of Uncle Sam. These colored troops were greeted with cheers and applause as they passed the crowd along Fourteenth Street, and such shouts as "Remember Fort Pillow!" were flung out to them as they marched by. All of the troops cheered lustily the President and Burnside as they caught sight of them, and Uncle Abraham smiled benevolently down upon them.

There were but few old troops in the Burnside corps, most of the regiments being new ones though composed of re-enlisted veterans. The colored troops extorted universal admiration for their splendid drill, their marching being absolutely perfect, except in the case of one raw regiment whose disorder was truly comical. A full company of Delaware Indians in one of the Michigan regiments attracted great attention—their bearing arms being admirable and their appearance unique. There was a great deal of artillery in the column, most of it being from New

England, and but one cavalry regiment, the Third New Jersey, being in the entire column. This regiment is a new organization—1,500 strong—and gorgeous in a Prussian hussar uniform covered with buttons, braid, and gold lace, and with gay short cloaks of orange and blue fluttering in the wind. There is, of course, a great deal of speculation as to the part which the Burnside corps is to play in the program of the spring campaign, but it appears mostly likely that Burnside's column will cooperate with Meade against Richmond under Grant but not forming a portion of Meade's army.

NEEDLESS PRECAUTION

The War Department, with commendable caution, requested the Washington newspapers not to say anything about the passage of Burnside's column through the city. Consequently all of the evening newspapers are virtuously mum upon the matter; but I happen to know that every New York correspondent sent off by telegraph full accounts of the review and all of the attendant incidents. But a ridiculous aspect is given to this excess of caution when it is known that communication with Richmond from Washington is kept up just as regularly now as before the war, the difference being in the openness and frequency of such communications. Letters, parcels, and passengers are forwarded by underground railway despite the vigilance of military guards. During the rebel invasion of Pennsylvania last summer, while no person could arrive at or depart from Baltimore without a proper pass, it was a matter of common notoriety among the military authorities in that city that a daily mail left Baltimore for Richmond. Of course there was military connivance somewhere, but where no one could find out. The rebels have spies in

Washington whose knowledge is fuller upon most topics than that of most newspapermen.

Washington, May 2, 1864

A UNITED STATES SENATOR WHIPPED

Considerable excitement was occasioned yesterday afternoon by a rencounter in front of the Washington House between a well-known senator and a woman of the town. There appears to have been some former quarrel between the parties, as the woman gave a note to the senator who tore it up insultingly, whereupon the woman knocked off his hat, then grabbed it, and with it for several minutes beat the head and ears of James H. Lane, United States Senator from Kansas.

Washington, May 13, 1864

THE GREAT STRUGGLE—THE WILDERNESS CAMPAIGN

By common consent the struggle now going on upon the campaign ground between the Rapidan and Richmond is considered as that which will determine the fortunes of the Confederacy, although not of the Union. The war cannot end this summer even if we are victorious now, but a successful issue will give us the prestige of ultimate and sure triumph; and this campaign will determine the nearness of the end of the rebellion or hasten foreign interference and so once more give new life to the so-called Confederacy. Accordingly, the most intense attention is fixed upon the progress of the fight; all other topics of news and conversa-

tion are swallowed up and lost sight of in the consideration
of the latest intelligence from the front. The like of it was
never before known here; nothing else appears to be
thought of but what is going forward on the debated territory between the James River and the branches of the
Mattapony, where thousands of brave men are rushing to
victory and immortality each hour.

The city is pervaded with a feeling which can scarcely
be called excitement, it is too intense—it is an absorbing
eagerness which is more fervent than excited. People go
about the streets with their hands full of "extras" from
the newspaper offices, and every messenger from the front
or from any source of news is at once made the center of
a knot of eager questioners. Congress, being made up of
men with feelings of ordinary mortals, shares in the general fervor and cannot take up with calmness any of the
ordinary routine business of the session, especially when
one of Secretary Stanton's admirable war bulletins or General [Rufus] Ingalls's free-and-easy dispatches from the
front are likely to be read from the desk of the presiding
officer of the House or Senate at any time. The Senate
has adjourned for three days at a time—its constitutional
limit—to digest both the news and the House bill to increase the internal revenue. The House has intermitted its
Saturday session for the first-named reason.

Every loyal heart is full of joy at the glorious tidings
which continue to come up from the front; and citizens
everywhere are congratulating each other upon the near
prospect of an end of this wasteful and wicked war. The
"coming man" appears to have come at last, and Grant
is the hero of the war. His name is on every lip in praise,
and his wonderful persistence, his determined courage,
and masterly skill all justify the fondest expectations of
his friends and the hopes of all who love their country

and trust in Grant. It really does seem that God has suffered the hour of our bitter trial and adversity to pass away, and we may hope that we shall yet have occasion to look back with thankfulness upon these passing days, full of mourning and suffering to many thousand hearts but proving a baptism of blood to the better and purer nation which we are yet to be. . . .

Washington, May 17, 1864

PERSISTENCE

Such a continuous holding on by one army attacking another was certainly never known before. Grant fought ten days and still held on the front of Lee, sending back his wounded, burying his dead, and bringing up his supplies and fresh troops. When McClellan had won a victory at Antietam and held the rebels on the north bank of the Potomac, he relaxed his grasp and let them go; when Burnside shattered his columns against the works of Fredericksburg in vain, he executed a retreat which was deemed "masterly;" when Hooker had smitten the rebels to defeat at Chancellorsville, he let them breathe for one day and then let them fall upon Sedgwick, and the Union forces returned the way they came across the Rappahannock; and worst of all, when Meade had pursued the defeated rebels into that elbow of the Potomac at Falling Waters and Williamsport where they lay five days with but four rounds of ammunition in their wagons, Meade sat down to a council of war and decided not to push the enemy, who adroitly slipped across the Potomac, and for the fourth time eluded a great Union army which might have annihilated the rebel horde in one determined onset. All of these facts are a part of history, and it is not surprising that our patient, long-suffering people, who have never expected that the *final result* of this war would be anything but victory, grow proudly enthusiastic over the dogged persistence of Grant, who *will not* let up on his adversary. Judging from the record of all preceding commanders who may be called great in our time, it may truly be said that any one of them would have been back upon Washington before this, with the whole rebel army thundering at his heels. The vastness of Grant's plan is just beginning to be seen, but over all and better than all shines the persistent, indomitable will which might have given us victory with the Army of the Potomac many times in place of the mortifying defeats which we have suffered.

REINFORCEMENTS

People who see the thousands of troops daily passing through this city bound for the front ask wonderingly, "Can Lee stand all this?" Scarcely an hour in the day passes but the sound of martial music betokens the march of some regiment down the Avenue on the way to the scene of battle. The heavy artillery which has been in the forts around Washington is all out to the front, the men being armed and equipped as infantry, and the one-hundred day men from Ohio are replacing them, over 5,000 having already arrived here for that purpose. Furthermore, all of the veteran regiments which had been home on furlough or recruiting service have been ordered back, and many have gone through Washington during the past few days, officers and men eager for the fray. I do not dare to state the extravagant figures which some give as the sum total of the reinforcements which have gone forward, but they are something short of the marvelous; and we only wonder how Lee, hemmed in and with his communications cut off, can hold out as he does against such great odds. The rebel fighting is the splendid daring, courage, and skill of desperate men well aware of the magnitude of the interests at stake.

Washington, May 21, 1864

WASHINGTON AS A HOSPITAL

... All Washington is a great hospital for the wounded in the great battle now going forward in Virginia. Boatloads of unfortunate and maimed men are continually arriving at the wharves and are transported to the various hospitals in and around Washington in ambulances or upon stretchers, some of the more severely wounded being unable to bear the jolting of the ambulances. The sight is a sad one, and it is still sadder to think of the homes made desolate by the multitude of deaths which have been caused upon the battlefield where the greensward is billowy with the new-made graves of thousands of brave men.

There are twenty-one hospitals in this city and vicinity and every one of them is full of the wounded and the dying. Of course, many are but slightly wounded, and a large number are not so severely wounded but they are able to limp about and talk cheerfully of a speedy return to the field, but there are enough painful cases and instances of appalling suffering to grieve the heart of the most indifferent. The Sanitary Commission docs good work among these suffering braves, meeting them upon their arrival with cooling drinks, gentle stimulants, or nourishing food. The greatest amount of difficulty has been experienced in transporting our wounded from the battlefield to Belle Plain on the Potomac, the route being infested by guerrillas and the whole of the transportation via Fredericksburg being by land carriage. The recent heavy rains, however, have served to fill the Rappahannock so that our hospital transports now go directly to Fredericksburg where the wounded are taken on board. Besides this, the Aquia Creek and Falmouth Railroad is now in running order, so that no difficulty will hereafter be experienced in forwarding supplies or bringing up the sick and wounded.

The town is full of strangers from the North who have come in quest of friends and relatives who are in the hospitals or are lying dead upon the battlefield. We recognize these bereaved and anxious people everywhere by their sad and thoughtful faces, their strangeness about the ways of Washington, and by their frequent inquiries for hospitals or the way to Fredericksburg where many thousands of the severely wounded still lie. To help these last-named sufferers, a detail of clerks has been made from the Treasury and Interior departments, the number being readily filled by volunteering. These volunteer nurses or helpers are sent down for fifteen days each and are under military rule and discipline while there. Everything is done that can be done to ameliorate the suffering of our brave fellows, and those who have friends and relatives who have been the luckless victims of rebel arms may be sure that they are well cared for in camp and in hospital.

Washington, May 24, 1864

MILITARY PROSPECTS

After having cheered ourselves hoarse over the successes and prospects of successes by Grant and the Army of the Potomac, we find ourselves pausing to take breath and discovering that our successes are more prospective than immediate, at least so far as the campaign in Virginia is concerned. The smoke and din of the bloody conflict having temporarily subsided, we perceive that our advantages gained are mainly those which will be useful for future operations against Richmond and, of more importance, the rebel army. But just now we have plenty of time for a survey of the ground where the conflict has been raging, for a lull, like that which two blown and half-exhausted combatants would naturally seek, has followed the excitement and rage of the past two weeks. Grant is busy, however, for that indomitable chieftain knows no rest which is useless, and before long another vigorous campaign will be opened. We hope that it will put to the blush the gloomy forebodings of the multitudes of our citizens who see in the present stillness at the front only a confession of our weakness and inability to cope with the foe. 30,000 volunteers of the one-hundred day sort have passed through Washington within a week, all of them destined to fill the forts in and around the District of Columbia. Nearly that number of veteran troops released thereby are being sent to the front. It is true, as it always has been, that we have not men enough yet, but we are fast filling up the great quota called for, and we shall have all that Grant asks for, which ought to be enough.

Washington, May 28, 1864

THE WOUNDED

This lovely weather, perfect in its way, so cool, calm, and clear, would make every heart rejoice, but the air, heavy with summer blooms and fresh with young life, is heavier with woes from the fringed edge of battle. It is inexpressibly sad to see so much pain and waste of life occurring right in the midst of this buoyant and springing season when nature seems her gayest and most vigorous, and only man, dying man, is decaying, perishing, and painfully wasting. Every night, when the glowing hues of evening are gilding the waters of the Potomac and lending a softened splendor to the rich verdure which lines the picturesque banks, boatloads of wounded soldiers arrive at the Washington wharves and discharge their precious freight. Long trains of ambulances are in waiting, and the suffering heroes are tenderly handled and brought out upon stretchers, though with some of them even the lightest touch is torture and pain. These brave men have lain in hospital in the Wilderness, have been carried to Fredericksburg, after having once been in the hands of the rebels for a space, and have been at last, with various kinds of transportation, sent to Washington, the city of hospitals.

There are anguished faces among the avenues of spectators who form the lanes down which the sad processions move from each boat; some are waiting for their own loved ones; others catch a glimpse of a maimed and battle-stained form, once so proud and manly, which they recognize as of their own flesh and blood. Many women and even men weep from sympathy and cannot see the silent suffering of these wounded braves unmoved. Night before last 3,000 severely wounded men were landed at the Sixth Street wharf; and the sight will not soon be forgotten by those who witnessed it. The long, ghastly procession of shattered wrecks; the groups of tearful, sympathetic spectators; the rigid shapes of those who are bulletined as "since dead;" the smoothly flowing river and the solemn hush in foreground and on distant evening shores—all form a picture which must some day perpetuate for the nation the saddest sight of all this war—"The return of the wounded."

Washington, June 1, 1864

THE POLITICAL HORIZON

There are enough men to make a respectable clique in the "Democratic" party who are hoping to be able to nominate Grant at Chicago, trusting to his usual good luck to elect him; and it is true that if Grant were an opponent of Lincoln with the capture of Richmond accomplished, the hero of a thousand fights would press Lincoln very hard. Wise people here say that if the present campaign is successful Grant will be the next president; and if it is not, neither Grant nor Lincoln can be elected—thus leaving a very poor show for Uncle Abraham in either event, you see. The more reasonable hypothesis appears to be that Grant's successes will be very likely to elect Lincoln, and his defeat will elect any man put up by the Chicago convention. Just now, the "Democrats" are very quiet, and little or nothing is said concerning their convention, though it is very evident that it will be inharmonious, as there will be a struggle for the control of the organization between the "peace" and "war" factions. No compromise between such men as Fernando Wood and Sam Cox appears possible, and yet Cox expects to nominate McClellan, and the Woodites are equally determined not to nominate a military or a war man. They have their affections fixed on Governor [Horatio] Seymour [of New York].

The politicians of all schools are gathering at Washington, the preponderance being largely in favor of the Union men who are preparing for the Baltimore convention. George Francis Train, the great North American Bloviator, is here, cheek by jowl with Pendleton, Wood, and Voorhees. Horace Greeley, who says he will support the nominee of the Baltimore convention, is also eagerly buttonholing everybody whom he can find in the Lincoln interest. This morning he was in close conversation for a long time upon one of the sofas on the floor of the House with Fernando Wood and the censured Alexander Long of Ohio. . . .

Baltimore, June 7, 1864

THE NATIONAL UNION CONVENTION

Yesterday saw the beginning of the great assemblage of the representatives of the people who were in the midst of a civil war and in the actual din of battle, to nominate candidates for a president and vice president of the United States. Every train that arrived at Baltimore was crowded with people, and long before the night preceding the opening of the convention the hotels were filled to their utmost capacity with the vast crowds of delegates and seekers after excitement. The day was fearfully hot, and a tremendous shower which came up at sunset did not cool the fever heat or the people, the corridors and passages of the hotels being filled with warm and steamy crowds all anxious for something or another. The various delegations had their headquarters at the principal hotels, banners or signs flung out to the breeze, showing where they were to be found. The delegations from New York and most of the smaller states . . . were at the Eutaw House in the upper part of town. Pennsylvania, Ohio, Illinois, and Indiana held forth at Barnum's City Hotel farther downtown.

Caucusing upon the chairmanship of the convention, the vice presidency, and the platform began forthwith. Everybody was buttonholed by everybody as to the probable indications of any delegation upon a given proposition. Knots of earnest-looking men, all of the better sort, apparently, were canvassing the merits of the different candidates, and mixed up with these were a few of the congressmen (who were not members) who were on hand to see that all was going on right. Three senators—Morrill of Maine, Foot of Vermont, and Lane of Kansas—were delegates, and they were appointed merely as proxies and not original or alternate delegates; but [John] Sherman of Ohio, [Edgar] Cowan of Pennsylvania, and others, were in the crowd last night and today.

At first, everybody was at sea about the chairmanship of the convention, Simon Cameron [of Pennsylvania], [William] Dennison of Ohio, Senator [Solomon] Foot [of Vermont], and ex-Speaker [Galusha A.] Grow [of Pennsylvania] being the most prominent names mentioned. [John] Bidwell of California was also named by those who were anxious to head off Cameron and who thought the Pacific states deserved some such handsome compliment. People generally settled down upon ex-Governor Dennison of Ohio as being the best man for the place, and that was agreed to by a majority of the delegations at their preliminary caucuses this morning. The vice presidency next engaged a great deal of attention, as there were more opinions concerning a candidate for that place than there were states. It being desirable that a War Democrat should be nominated, [Daniel S.] Dickinson of New York was most prominent, but the New Yorkers were anxious to decline that honor, reserving themselves for the contingency of Seward's being again the Premier, which he could not well be if a New York man were vice president. So the Empire State signified its preference for Hamlin. Indiana, Illinois, and California are for Andy Johnson first and Dickinson next. Many who would like to vote for Hamlin say that his renomination would be a renomination of the Republican ticket and that a War Democrat must be nominated. The names of Joseph Holt, Andrew Curtin, [William S.] Rosecrans, and General [Gouverneur K.] Warren are put forth.

I have said nothing about the nomination for the presidency, for it is a foregone conclusion that Abraham Lincoln will be the nominee of the convention. Last night, at a serenade given the New York delegation by the Ohio delegation, speeches were made by [Henry J.] Raymond of New York, [Samuel F.] Cary of Ohio, and Lyman Tremain, a brilliant and personable man who was candidate for lieutenant governor of New York on the [James S.] Wadsworth ticket in 1862. These speakers all admitted that the people had taken this matter into their own hands, had sent their delegates to the convention under the most positive instructions, and that there was, consequently, nothing for the politicians to do but to submit as gracefully as might be to the expressed will of the sovereign people. The same sovereign people cheered like mad whenever the name of Lincoln was incidentally mentioned, and all accounts agree that the voice coming up from the people by these delegates is that Abraham Lincoln is their first and only choice.

In Washington, where a few disappointed placemen and ungratified and over-ambitious congressmen have congregated, less unanimity prevails, and an uninitiated person might be led to suppose that the Union party was widely divided if he believed what these few malcontents say. The California delegation fell into the hands of some of these on their arrival at the national capital and grew shaky over the question of the presidential succession until the unmistakable tone of the convening delegates here straightened them up again. The Frémont letter of acceptance scares nobody, but, on the contrary, disgusts those who see in it a plain bid for the nomination of the Chicago Copperhead convention on the narrow platform of opposition to Lincoln. The crazy Radicals who have gone mad over their anti-Lincolnism threaten direful things, but they are so few that they are not worth consideration, though, like a bumblebee in a bottle, they fancy that the world resounds with the buzzing which they are themselves making. After having all along predicted that the people were against Lincoln's renomination, these same deluded individuals now concede that the people are for him but that he can't be elected. Who will be elected they will not, of course, say. . . .

ORGANIZING THE CONVENTION

At an early hour this morning the Front Street Theater was besieged by crowds of outsiders anxious to get in and obtain seats before the convention assembled. None but members of the press, delegates, and a few privileged outsiders were allowed to go in before eleven o'clock. The building is a large one but quite inadequate to the occasion and very poorly arranged for the purposes of a political convention. The parquet is floored over on a level with the stage and appropriated to the delegates; the alternates sit in the "dress circle;" the family tier is for ladies only, of whom there is a vast crowd on hand, while the "masses" are tenants of that portion of the building known as the "celestial regions" or "nigger heaven." The inside of the theater is profusely decorated with the flag of the Union, and a canopy of flags covers the wings of the stage. In the back of the stage is the chair of the president, and in front of it are the accommodations for the representatives of the press. The different delegations sit by themselves. Pennsylvania and New York occupy the largest space, having fifty-two from the Keystone State and sixty-five from the Empire State. California occupies a corner of the stage, Pennsylvania giving her one back seat for her ten delegates, the New England states and Kansas being the occupants of the opposite side of the stage.

A splendid brass band enlivened the hours of waiting, and precisely at noon ex-Governor [Edwin D.] Morgan of New York, the Chairman of the National Union Committee, called the convention to order in a brief and somewhat weak speech which was received with coolness, except when he mentioned Lincoln's name or alluded to the utter extinction of slavery as one of the articles of faith of the delegates. A tumultuous and long-continued burst of applause shook the theater, showing conclusively where the heart of the people is upon these things. Morgan proposed the Reverend [Robert] J. Breckinridge of Kentucky as the temporary chairman of the convention, and, amidst a great storm of applause, the "Old Warhorse of Kentucky," as his enthusiastic friends call him, was conducted to the chair. Breckinridge, who is the uncle of the fugacious ex-Vice President, is a tall, shapely man, gray and venerable in appearance, with a weak voice but a strong heart and sound brain. On taking the chair he made a clear and logical speech in which he briefly sketched the political character of the contest in which we are engaged, showing the relations which exist between the Union, the Constitution, and the nation, and especially how the life of each was bound up in all. Alluding to the Constitution, however, he said that it should be understood that while we venerate that instrument and will punish with death its enemies, we will, if we, the people, think proper, alter it again as we have altered it before. Slavery, if incompatible with a perfect restoration of the Union, he would have utterly destroyed from the face of the earth, whereat there was tremendous applause. He spoke feelingly of Kentucky and of the position of himself and colleagues who must endure contumely and odium at home for their appearance here, and he besought those who heard him to believe that they were honest in their professions of love for the Union and to believe that if need be they would die like men. The venerable speaker was cheered to the echo, and his peroration was drowned in a whirlwind of most boisterous applause.

But little else was done during the day session but to choose committees on Permanent Organization, Credentials, and Platform, one member being nominated and appointed from each state as the roll was called. Business proceeded slowly; the weak voice and inexperience of the chairman, the poor acoustic qualities of the building, and the great crowd made it difficult to hear what was going on. When the names of states having delegates present were being called great confusion arose from the fact that Missouri had two sets of delegates, Radical and Conservative, and that the territories were present but not called; there were delegates also from some of the states in which a rebellion exists. Missouri had both sets of credentials referred to the committee to be raised; and then [Horace] Maynard of Tennessee made a stirring speech advocating the reception of the credentials of his colleagues and himself, arguing that the state still existed in the Union, though she had no representation in Congress; pointing to the flag of the Union, he said: "Count, I beseech you, those stars, before you decide against us; there is the star of long-suffering, much enduring Tennessee in that bright cluster, and there shall it ever shine, God willing!" Judging from the cheers which followed his remarks, the feeling of the convention was with him. [Lucius H.] Chandler of Virginia, lately an applicant for a seat in the House of Representatives, made an appeal in behalf of "Old Virginny," only asking that her name be called with the other states, leaving all other privileges for the convention to grant or refuse by and by. A long and irrelevant colloquy resulted between Chandler and Thad Stevens on the status of the states in which rebellion still exists, but it was finally agreed that the whole question should be deferred. Then it was agreed that the territories should be called upon for their delegates, only Nevada, Colorado, Nebraska, and Dacotah responding. The roll call showed that 456 delegates were present, omitting the territories and the states in which rebellion exists. . . .

Baltimore, June 8, 1864

THE NATIONAL UNION CONVENTION—
A SHORT EVENING SESSION

. . . At half-past seven o'clock last night Chairman Breckinridge rapped the crowd to order, and, after more delay, the Committee on Permanent Organization reported a list of officers, ex-Governor [William] Dennison of Ohio being the President of the Convention and vice presidents and secretaries from each state.

Ex-Speaker Grow of Pennsylvania and Senator Lane of Kansas were appointed a committee to conduct the president to the chair, which was done amidst great applause. Two immense bouquets were sent up to the stand with the compliments of somebody. Dennison is a tall, good-looking man with a hoarse voice and not much vigor of manner for a presiding officer. He made a short and sensible speech upon taking the chair. He returned thanks for the honor showed him, congratulated the convention upon the fact that it had assembled to discharge one of the sacred duties of American citizens, though a great civil war convulsed the country, and reminded the delegates of the responsibility of the duty before them.

His speech over, a committee on organization of business was appointed. Then matters came to a hitch, the committees appointed in the morning being not half ready to report. Somebody called out that "Parson" [William G.] Brownlow [of Tennessee] was in the house and that a speech from him would be acceptable. Great applause followed this announcement, and the redoubtable parson went up to the stand, opened his ugly mouth, and apologized briefly for not making a speech on the ground that he was sick, sick, sick, and ought to be in bed instead of being here. So, after various ineffectual calls for sundry other speakers, the convention adjourned until this morning, the night being consumed in caucusing for vice president and in speech-making from the principal hotels.

Of course, where so many people from every portion of the Union were present, there would be considerable excitement; but the crowds were all orderly and well-behaved. The only intoxicated person I have seen thus far was a rebellious Baltimorean who wanted Senator Foot of Vermont to discuss abolitionism with him while waiting for the doors of the theater to open. . . .

WHO SHALL VOTE IN THE CONVENTION

This morning . . . Preston King, of New York, . . . made a report on credentials from which it appeared that the following states were represented without contest: Maine,

16 delegates; New Hampshire, 10; Massachusetts, 24; Vermont, 10; Connecticut, 12; Rhode Island, 8; New York, 66; Pennsylvania, 52; New Jersey, 14; Delaware, 6; Maryland, 14; Kentucky, 22; Ohio, 42; Indiana, 26; Illinois, 32; Michigan, 16; Wisconsin, 16; Iowa, 16; Minnesota, 8; California, 10; Oregon, 6; West Virginia, 10; Kansas, 6. Pennsylvania was all right except one district which had sent four delegates where it was entitled to but two. One set was ruled out. When the chairman, in reading a committee report, announced that the delegation known as the Missouri Radicals should be admitted, the burst of applause was tremendous, showing where the feelings of the convention are, hats waving and voices cheering for several minutes before order could be restored. The report went on to say that delegations from Virginia, Florida, Tennessee, Louisiana, and Arkansas should be admitted to the floor of the convention and have the right of debate but not of vote. The territories were placed upon the same footing.

W. E. Stevens of West Virginia made a minority report differing only from that just read in that it was in favor of admitting the last-named states and territories, and still another minority report was made by M[erritt] H. Insley of Kansas in favor of admitting to the privilege of voting Nebraska, Nevada, and Colorado who were about forming, the report averred, state organizations of their own in order to vote for the next presidency. A long discussion arose during which King of New York proposed a compromise that all of the territories be admitted to the right of voting, being limited to two votes only. Pending this the report was adopted so far as the uncontested delegations were concerned, allowing each to vote separately when they could not agree to vote together. [Augustus] Brandegee of Connecticut made a short and sensible speech in favor of admitting the Radicals; and was followed by Breckinridge of Kentucky, who in a conservative speech, deprecated the idea of accepting as facts the testimony of the Radical contestants; and alleging that if this convention was to nominate Lincoln it could not consistently rebuke him or any of his constitutional advisers (Blair) by admitting these radical enemies of his policy.

A call of states was ordered, and, pending this, a dire confusion reigned throughout this most abominably managed, or mismanaged, convention, it being impossible for the chairman to preserve order to guide the business. Fifty men, more or less, were on the floor at once, gesticulating and vainly endeavoring to make themselves heard. Finally, the call began and Missouri was admitted with her twenty-two votes by an almost unanimous vote in her favor, only one vote (Breckinridge's) from Kentucky and three from Pennsylvania being against her, ex-Speaker Grow being one of the conservative three from the last-named state. Immediately upon the result being formally announced a boisterous tumult of enthusiasm broke forth. When it was quelled the vote upon admitting to a vote such states as have no representatives in Congress, rebellion still existing in the borders, was called for.

TENNESSEE KNOCKING AT THE DOOR

After much tribulation, a direct vote was taken upon the proposition to admit Tennessee to a right to vote in the convention. Several amendments and substitutes were put and lost, and the roll call commenced on the main question. . . . When New York and Pennsylvania cast a majority of their heavy vote in favor of admitting Tennessee, a great burst of applause followed, and when Missouri, just admitted to a vote, cast her influence against a like favor for Tennessee, a gust of hisses broke forth. Subsequently, she changed her vote to 19 ayes and 3 noes, which brought out applause. Illinois next changed her entire vote of 32 to the affirmative, which brought the final vote 310 ayes and 161 noes. So the persecuted state of Tennessee was admitted to cast her fifteen votes in the National Union Convention. This was a marked indication of the preference of the convention for Andy Johnson for the vice presidency, and New England, preferring Hamlin, naturally voted against it. . . .

THE PLATFORM

Henry J. Raymond of New York, the Chairman of the Committee on Resolutions, then mounted the stand. . . . The reading of the resolutions was frequently interrupted by boisterous applause, especially at that part in which the extirpation of slavery, as one of the causes of the war, was referred to as an article of faith. Also, when the permanent reward of our soldiers and sailors was alluded to, a great cheer shook the building, and two more loud cheers and a "tiger" for our soldiers and sailors in the fight were added. But when the resolution endorsing Abraham Lincoln was read, the enthusiasm was terrific, the convention breaking out into yells and cheers unbounded as soon as the beloved name of Lincoln was spoken. Order being restored, the resolutions were adopted by acclamation, and the platform, complete, concise, and ringing with patriotic fire, was finished.

CHAOS COMES AGAIN

The next business before the convention was the nomination of candidates for President and Vice President of the United States. [Columbus] Delano of Ohio moved that the convention proceed to that business, pending which Simon Cameron sent up a written resolution which he asked to be considered as a substitute. It asked that Abraham Lincoln of Illinois and Hannibal Hamlin of Maine be renominated by acclamation. The sly old fox had attempted thus to steal a march on the various claimants for the honor of nominating Lincoln. A great gust of applause followed the reading of the resolution, but signs of disapprobation showed themselves. Governor [William M.] Stone of Iowa, being especially irate at the way in which Cameron had got in ahead of all others, moved that the resolution be tabled. Others said that it would not look well for a resolution of that sort to be laid on the table, though the mode of offering it was disapproved of. Lane of Kansas begged Cameron for peace sake to withdraw his resolution, which he did with a very ill grace and immediately moved that Abraham Lincoln be nominated by acclamation.

Stong symptoms of disapprobation again showed themselves, Governor Stone in vain trying to head off Cameron and B[urton] C. Cook of Illinois begging that his own state might make the nomination. Men were popping up all over the convention, each trying to get in his little speech of nomination but in vain, and the confusion was dire and utter until Raymond of New York cut the knot by making a brief, clear speech in which he advocated the nominating by a call of states. He claimed that, as entire unanimity was expected, the moral effect would be better than if a noisy acclamation were made which would give our slanderers an opportunity to say that the nomination was rushed through utterly overwhelming all opposition however small.

These considerations were favorably received, and B[urton] C. Cook mounted a settee and said, "Illinois once more presents to the nation the name of Abraham Lincoln, God bless him." Great applause followed, and Stone of Iowa gained his point by seconding Cook's nomination. It had been partially agreed upon by the Illinois delegation that Thompson Campbell of California should make the nomination, and he was prepared for that honor, but Cameron's cunning movement had upset all calculations. Now, however, Campbell got the floor, but he was instantly interrupted with, "No speeches," "Call the roll," "Order," "Get down," but he kept on speaking in dumb show, wildly gesticulating, not a word of his speech being audible, until forced to subside, when the roll call commenced.

Maine led off with her sixteen votes for Lincoln. New Hampshire tried to ring in a feeble speech with its vote but was choked off with "No speeches," and the call proceeded until Missouri was reached. The chairman of that delegation—[John F.] Hume of the [St. Louis] *Missouri Democrat*—made a brief speech in which he said that his delegation was under positive instructions to cast its twenty-two votes for U. S. Grant, but he and the delegation would support the nominee of the convention, though they must obey orders from home. This caused some sensation, especially as it made the vote fall short of being unanimous. The roll call concluded, the secretary announced the vote: Abraham Lincoln, 507; U. S. Grant, 22. Hume immediately moved that the nomination be declared unanimous, which was done, and straightway the bursting enthusiasm culminated in a scene of the wildest confusion. Men hurrahed, embraced each other, threw up their hats, jumped on the benches, waved flags, yelled, and committed every possible extravagance to demonstrate their exuberance of joy. In the midst of all this the brass band broke out with "Hail Columbia" which added fuel to the flames.

When quiet was half restored and other business was about to be resumed, the band struck up "Yankee Doodle" in its liveliest style, and another flood of enthusiasm prevailed, and it was a long time before the jubilant assemblage could be quieted down and order restored. . . .

VICE PRESIDENT NOMINATING

[Leonard] Swett of Illinois returned thanks for the honor shown her favorite son in a brief speech, during which he was admonished by Jim Lane's "Cut it short". . . . The convention then proceeded to nominate candidates for vice president. The Indiana delegation presented the name of Andy Johnson, and, amidst uproarious applause, Stone of Iowa seconded the motion, and Maynard of Tennessee made a little speech in favor of the same; Simon Cameron of Pennsylvania nominated Hannibal Hamlin without any speech. Kentucky presented General [Lovell H.] Rousseau. Lyman Tremain of New York, on behalf of a portion of the delegation, presented the name of Daniel S. Dickinson with a short but stirring speech. The name was applauded to the echo, and then the balloting began. . . .

Thus of the 520 votes cast, Andrew Johnson had 202; Hannibal Hamlin, 150; Daniel S. Dickinson, 109; Benjamin F. Butler, 28; and 31 were scattering. It being apparent that Johnson was the choice of the convention, Kentucky, having paid her compliments to her favorite general, changed her entire 22 votes to Johnson as soon as the roll call was concluded. Oregon followed suit; Pennsylvania next transferred her 52 votes, with immense applause, to the same candidate, and soon state after state wheeled into line. . . . The nomination was formally declared unanimously carried for Andrew Johnson of Tennessee upon motion of Lyman Tremain and amidst the most boisterous and enthusiastic applause.

WINDING UP

Little now remained to be done, and the delegates at once commenced hurrying up, but amidst the noise and confusion a National Union Committee was formed, each state nominating one member as the roll was called. Then, after some discussion, the territories of New Mexico, Dacotah, and the District of Columbia, South Carolina, Florida, and Virginia were allowed to record their votes for the nominees of the convention. Then the convention at 4:30 P.M. adjourned *sine die* and the members went home to vote and work for Lincoln and Johnson, a goodly number remaining to attend a great ratification meeting which is being held here. . . .

Washington, June 10, 1864

CONGRATULATIONS

People generally have congratulated each other upon the harmonious action of the Union convention and the fruit of its labors. . . . Abraham Lincoln has been the recipient of a multitude of congratulations from all sorts of people, among them being the delegations from several of the states represented in the convention. Among others was the Ohio delegation which serenaded the President last night in fine style, in response to which he spoke as follows:

"Gentlemen: I am very much obliged to you for this

compliment. I have just been saying, and as I have just said it, I will repeat it: the hardest of all speeches which I have to answer is a serenade. I never know what to say on such occasions. I suppose that you have done me this kindness in connection with the action of the Baltimore convention which has recently taken place, and with which, of course, I am very well satisfied. [Laughter and applause.] What we want still more than Baltimore conventions or presidential elections is success under General Grant. [Cries of "Good" and applause.] I propose that you constantly bear in mind that the support you owe to the brave officers and soldiers in the field is of the very first importance, and we should therefore bend all our energies to that point. Now, without detaining you any longer, I propose that you help me to close up what I am now saying with three rousing cheers for General Grant and the officers and soldiers under his command."

The President's request was acceded to, and three rousing cheers were given, the President waving his hat as enthusiastically as anybody else. The National Union League also has sent a large delegation to wait upon the President with their congratulations, all of which were duly attended on yesterday at the White House.

Yesterday afternoon the committee appointed by the convention to wait upon the President and notify him of his nomination was received in the East Room of the White House, a large number of delegates from various states being present, when ex-Governor Dennison of Ohio, president of the Baltimore convention (and a mighty poor presiding officer he was), spoke as follows:

"Mr. President: the National Union Convention, which closed its sittings at Baltimore yesterday, appointed a committee consisting of one from each state with myself as its chairman to inform you of your unanimous nomination

by that convention for election to the office of President
of the United States. That committee, I have the honor
of now informing you, is present. On its behalf I have also
the honor of presenting you with a copy of the resolutions
or platform which were adopted by that convention, as
expressive of its sense and of the sense of the loyal people
of the country which it represented; of the principles and
the policy that should characterize the administration of
the government in the present condition of the country.
I need not say to you, sir, that the convention, in thus
unanimously nominating you for re-election, but gave utterance to the almost universal voice of the loyal people
of the country. To doubt of your triumphant election
would be little short of abandoning the hope of the final
suppression of the rebellion and the restoration of the
authority of the government over the insurgent states.
Neither the convention nor those represented by that body
entertained any doubt as to the final result, under your
administration, sustained by that loyal people, and by our
noble army and gallant navy; neither did the convention,
nor do this committee, doubt the speedy suppression of
this most wicked and unprovoked rebellion. (A copy of
the resolutions were here handed to the President.) I
should add, Mr. President, it would be the pleasure of the
committee to communicate to you, within a few days,
through one of its most accomplished members, George
W. Curtis of New York, by letter, more at length the circumstances under which you have been placed in nomination for the presidency."

The President appeared to be deeply affected, and, with
considerable emotion, he spoke as follows:

"Mr. Chairman and Gentlemen of the committee: I
will neither conceal my gratification nor restrain the expression of my gratitude that the Union people, through

their convention, in the continued effort to save and advance the nation, have deemed me not unworthy to remain in my present position. I know no reason to doubt that I shall accept the nomination tendered; and yet, perhaps, I should not declare definitely before reading and considering what is called the platform. I will say now, however, I approve the declaration in favor of so amending the Constitution as to prohibit slavery throughout the nation. When the people in revolt, with a hundred days of explicit notice that they could within those days resume their allegiance without the overthrow of their institutions, and that they could not resume it afterwards, elected to stand out, such amendment to the Constitution as is now proposed became a fitting and necessary conclusion to the final success of the Union cause. Such alone can meet and cover all cavils. Now, the unconditional Union men, North and South, perceive its importance and embrace it. In the joint names of Liberty and Union let us labor to give it legal form and practical effect."

Washington, June 14, 1864

THE MILITARY PROSPECT

... The struggle in Virginia has been prolonged beyond the popular expectation, and though our people are patient and hopeful beyond all precedent they are bound to be disappointed yet again in the duration of the war in Virginia. The President said the other day: "I wish when you write and speak to the people you would do all you can to correct the impression that the war in Virginia will end right off victoriously. To me the most trying thing in all of this war is that the people are too sanguine; they expect too much at once. I declare to you, sir, that we are today further ahead than I thought one year and a half ago we should be, and yet there are plenty of people who believe that the war is about to be substantially closed. As God is my judge I shall be satisfied if we are over with the fight in Virginia within a year. I hope we shall be 'happily disappointed,' as the saying is, but I am afraid not—I am afraid not." These words of one who is so cool and correct in judgment and who stands at the fountainhead of all knowledge of the workings of the military mechanisms of the country must have great weight with those who hear or read them. For myself, I am free to say that they materially dampened the ardor of my own expectations.

Washington, June 20, 1864

IMPOSING FUNERAL SOLEMNITIES

Yesterday (Sunday) witnessed a remarkable and imposing funeral pageant in Washington, the occasion being the burial of the victims of the late terrible calamity at the Arsenal, when eighteen young women were instantly hurried to death by the explosion of the cartridges upon which they were working. Several of the bodies were taken in charge by the friends of the deceased; but fifteen were buried yesterday from the Arsenal grounds under the charge of the United States government. A pavilion, lined and covered with white and decorated with flags, was erected upon the grounds, and the coffins were ranged upon an altar in the midst of the same. The ceremonies were brief and impressive and admirably adapted to the occasion, a vast concourse listening to them with profound attention.

The funeral cortege, headed by a band playing mournful music, was made up of friends of the deceased, the associates of the victims of the disaster—all clad in white—various benevolent societies, high officials of the government, the employees of the Arsenal, and a very long procession of citizens generally. Among the officials was the President, Secretary of War, Chief of Ordinance, Commandant of the Arsenal, and others. Along the route the vast procession was joined by several other funeral trains, being the private obsequies of other victims, until eighteen hearses were moving to the Congressional Burying Ground where the remains were finally interred. It is estimated that over 25,000 persons were present at this mournful spectacle, the streets being for a space impassable, on account of the great crowd.

It is definitely settled that the disaster was due to culpable carelessness on the part of the pyrotechnist of the Arsenal, who placed some of his work to dry in the sun near the building where the young women were at work in powder. The hot sun ignited the fireworks by heating the iron pans where they were laid. Some sensational stories about rebel emissaries being instrumental in firing the works are in circulation, but no sensible man believes such reports. Gross carelessness, which had been practiced securely for years, was the cause of hurrying to a premature grave this band of young, lovely, and estimable women.

Washington, June 27, 1864

A NATIONAL ELYSIUM

The weather is fearfully and wonderfully hot, the thermometer ranging at ninety-odd daily, and the face of nature is as parched and dry as a desert; great clouds of dust fill the fevered air, choking the lungs and filling the eyes of the unhappy residents of this dirty city; hotels and boardinghouses are afflicted with swarms of flies, and everywhere heat, discomfort, dirt, and languid annoyance reign. Congress is still in session and day by day meets in the Capitol with its thin clothes on and its myriad fans in its myriad hands. Congress is just now a feverish, cross, and impatient monster. Yet there it sits, fanning and fuming, in the oven-like House of Representatives, the small public looking down pityingly from the well-nigh deserted galleries, while doomed reporters, clerks, and doorkeepers watch with anxiety the daily rise of the thermometer and the price of provisions.

Washington is notoriously a dirty and sickly city, but just now it is more dirty and sickly than ever before. There are in the hospitals and in and around the city 20,000 sick and wounded soldiers. Poor fellows! It is too bad to appear to complain of the nuisance which these crowded hospitals must make, but it is nevertheless true that, at its best estate, a hospital is an undesirable adjunct to a crowded and dirty city; but just now we have more than twenty of these institutions in the neighborhood, and to their freight of woe is superadded the filth, offal, refuse, and impurities, which must flow therefrom. The city sanitary regulations are very bad; little or no attempt is made to clean the streets which spend most of their filth in the air; and one section of the city—the Island, upon which the Smithsonian Institution and other buildings stand—is bounded on two sides by a stagnant canal of ooze, open to the sun's hot rays, the receptacle of all of the imperfect system of drainage. So ill-kept, noisome, and stinking is the national capital that one might well believe that the man in the moon would hold his nose in going over it. Yet this penny-wise and pound-foolish Congress spent an hour the other day wrangling over a paltry $6,000 appropriation for clean-ing the streets. The result of all this is that the government will at last have to foot the bills, for the military authori-ties have been obliged to take up the matter. They have given notice that a Sanitary Police will be established for the sake of purifying the city. With every facility for drain-age and the bountiful Potomac flowing past the city, it is a shame and a sin that the capital of the nation should be the ill-favored and dirty place that it is.

Yet the hapless observer in the reporters' gallery experi-ences a grim pleasure as he notes the discomfort of the congressmen who are still detained in this uncomfortable and expensive city by exigencies of the public service, which, if properly attended to before, would have allowed them to go home before this; but dilly-dallying, buncombe, and gab have conspired to protract the session at least six weeks beyond the time it might have ended if the public servants had been more intent upon the public service and less occupied with "making up a record" for the coming fall campaign. They don't enjoy this sort of thing at all, and I am glad of it, but they must do the work now which might have been done long ago.

A PLEASANT INCIDENT

Today, while passing through the circular arched corri-dor leading from the rotunda of the Capitol to the Senate wing, I was attracted by the sound of vocal music and saw that two soldiers, passing through, had discovered the echo there. They were singing a beautiful song called "Drifting Homeward," now very popular with the army. The voices of the singers were well trained, the words very beautiful, and every casual passerby stopped to hear the lovely strains as they rose and fell in perfect harmony through the vaulted chamber. More than one stout-hearted man was touched as the accordant voices of the singers breathed the words:

We dread not the storm that blows us on;
It blows us further home, further home.

It was but a little thing but it showed how much feeling, sentiment, and culture may be found in the ranks of the American army.

Washington, July 1, 1864

THE LATEST NINE DAYS WONDER

Yesterday morning the town was set all agog by the announcement that Secretary Chase had resigned his portfolio of the Treasury department, and that David Tod, late Governor of Ohio, had been named as his successor. There was a general feeling of regret and apprehension among public men and citizens when the rumor of the fact became a certainty and it was positively known that Chase was no longer in the cabinet. The Senate went into executive session at half-past eleven when the name of David Tod was submitted as the successor of the outgoing secretary. The Chase men were nearly frantic, asserting that the movement would cost Lincoln his re-election, that Tod was an idiot, and that Chase had been driven out by the machinations of Blair.

A careful sifting of the facts, however, showed that the disagreement between the President and the Secretary was twofold in character, the first being the refusal of the President to accede to the demand of Chase that Maunsell B. Field, now Assistant Secretary of the Treasury, should be Assistant Treasurer at New York, in place of [John J.]

Cisco, resigned. The second was that the Ways and Means Committee of the House had declined to accede to Chase's request, just made, that Congress should provide, before the adjournment, for $100,000,000 additional to the estimate and appropriations already made, on account of a deficiency in the estimates of the Treasury Department. It is well known that the great moneyed interest of New York has the real control of Secretary Chase's policy, and that circumstances have rendered it possible for the Wall Street magnates to tell him that unless certain things were done, Wall Street would not support him to carry on this system. Chase had designated Field as the successor of Cisco, and the Register of the Treasury, L[ucius] E. Chittenden, was to succeed Field, while [Hanson A.] Risley, a special agent, was to succeed Chittenden. The President insisted upon spoiling his program, and he named [Thomas] Hillhouse, an able financier, for Cisco's place. He also declined sending a special message to Congress asking for a supplemental tax bill to raise the additional $100,000,000 asked by Chase, preferring to postpone all such requests for this session.

Chase resigned, and ex-Governor Tod was nominated but not accepted by the Senate, that body refusing to confirm. The Finance Committee waited on the President, asking him to send in a more acceptable name. While the Senate demurred, Tod had the good sense to telegraph from Columbus his nonacceptance of the dazzling gift offered him. The Chase men were disconsolate—they had hoped that some second-rate man would succeed Chase. If Chase, who is cold-hearted, obstinate, and enormously self-conceited, had desired that a lesser man than he should be shown to be behind him, he could not have named a better man than David Tod—at least so say the Ohioans, who are supposed to know. There were those who said that

Chase had resigned as soon as the report of the Treasury Investigating Committee had been made, for the purpose of embarrassing the administration, and that he had named his own successor for the same purpose. That does not seem probable.

This morning, bright and early, Senator [William P.] Fessenden of Maine, Chairman of the Finance Committee, was named by the President as Secretary of the Treasury, and he was immediately confirmed without the formality of sending his name to the Finance Committee. Everybody was pleased, and the only ones who had aught unpleasant to say were the Chase impracticables, who were bound not to be pleased. They said that gold was up in New York on the report—keeping out of sight that gold had gone up on the report that Hooper of Massachusetts, the author of the Gold Bill, had gone into Chase's place, and also forgetting, apparently, that gold had gone down and government stocks up when Chase's resignation was positively known, the money interest persisting in believing that any change would be for the better or that things could be no worse. But we all suffered a relapse by three o'clock in the afternoon when it was announced that Fessenden had declined the place also, believing his physical ability was unequal to the task. He is one of your narrow-chested, thin men who have not much vitality nor physical endurance, and he did a prudent thing for himself to resign, but he would make a better Secretary than Chase, beyond a doubt. And so at this present writing matters stand *status in quo.* . . .

THE POLITICAL INTRIGUER

It is a matter of regret that a man of so much oratorical ability and legal sharpness as Henry Winter Davis should be so much of a political charlatan as he is; but he is, like the Blairs, insatiate in his hates, mischievous in his schemes, and hollow-hearted and cold-blooded. It is not supposed that he honestly differs in opinion with any member of the present cabinet, except Blair, but he has seized upon every occasion to quarrel with nearly every one of them, and he stands today in an attitude of such intense hostility to Lincoln that he is ready to jeopardize the success of the Union party in the campaign about opening, simply that he may gratify his personal malice toward the President. Revengeful, soreheaded, and proud, Davis, like others of his sort here, appears to forget that the defeat of Lincoln, the nominee of the people and the Union organization, would necessarily be the triumph of a Copperhead minority, under whose rule the status of these individuals would be worse than it now is under an administration which has failed to satisfy their personal demands.

An impending municipal election in Baltimore affords a fine exercise for the peculiar powers of Davis, who has left his seat for the past two weeks and has been busily engaged in fomenting disaffection to the extent that he has succeeded in getting up an independent candidate for mayor in the "Custom House ward"—Davis's ward—Archibald Sterling, Jr., being the bolters' or sorehead candidate in opposition to John Lee Chapman, the regular Union candidate for re-election to the office of mayor. The "Custom House ward" is made up of officials who have been appointed through Davis's influence with Chase, and now in return for the favors the administration thus lavished upon him, the same politician turns himself about and snarls upon the hand that fed him, and he factiously opposes a candidate to whose regular nomination no exception is taken and whose only fault is a warm support of Lincoln for renomination and re-election. Henry Winter Davis is one of the many men in this Congress who expect that local jealousies and petty personal prejudices will have a prior claim in the settlement of national questions.

Washington, July 7, 1864

AFFAIRS AT THE TREASURY DEPARTMENT

Probably no man ever took up the administration of the affairs of our national finance with so much relief and satisfaction on the part of the public as had William Pitt Fessenden, ex-Senator from Maine. Even the bitterest Copperheads have not had a word to say against the purity, honesty, and patriotic purposes of the new Secretary of the Treasury, and everybody admits his great ability, tact, and experience. Probably no man in this nation, not excepting Chase, has so thorough a knowledge of the character and extent of our national sources of wealth, of the best means of getting at them, and of the character and complex interests of the people of the United States. He is a practical financier, which Chase was not when he assumed control of the finances. Chase was always topsy-turvy and behindhand, but Fessenden is cool, methodical, and immovable. Fessenden is democratical and finds himself ill at ease in the palatial splendors of Chase's newly-built quarters at the Treasury building. Chase was inaccessible, dignified beyond all account, and aristocratical. Let me not be understood as attempting to depreciate the great abilities of the ex-Secretary; his services are known to the country, and to the country he will stand or fall by the system of finance which he has himself inaugurated. There are diverse opinions as to the real merit of that system, but it is now too late to make a radical change in it, and it is too early to predict its success.

The faults of Chase above mentioned are minor in

character, and the overweening weakness in his character
was that desire to control everything which finally brought
on his retirement from the cabinet. The only issue of any
moment between Chase and the President was whether
the President or the Secretary should appoint the new
Assistant Treasurer. Chase, who has heretofore controlled
every appointment, from that of the humblest tidewaiter
to a New York collector, made a *sine qua non* of his staying
in the cabinet of the appointment of [Maunsell] B. Field,
a gentleman of ability, perhaps, but against whom some
popular prejudices have become fixed for the reason that
he parts his hair in the middle, wears a white necktie and
lemon colored kids, and has not especially distinguished
himself in the Treasury Department further than to super-
intend the fitting up of Chase's private offices with Ax-
minster carpets, gilded ceilings, velvet furniture, and other
luxurious surroundings which go to hedge about a cabinet
minister with a dignity quite appalling to the unaccustomed outsider. If Chase had been less strong in his pride
of self-opinion he would have been more practicable as a
cabinet minister and would always have harmonized with
the President. . . .

Washington, July 12, 1864

JUBAL EARLY'S RAID ON WASHINGTON

After a week of worry and speculation, we have awaked
to the consciousness that the city of Washington is in a
state of siege. The rebel raid into Maryland has ridden
close up to our gates, and the firing of hostile musketry
has actually been heard in the city, while Union soldiers
have fallen before the foe within the narrow limits of

the District of Columbia. Whatever may be the result of this raid, for we cannot yet call it anything more, the rebels may truthfully boast that they have been in sight of the dome of the national Capitol.

Of course there has been a great panic which has not yet subsided, and more than ever before we realize that Washington is cut off from the rest of the world, for are we not without our New York newspapers? Is not sugar forty cents a pound, beef, eggs, and fresh vegetables unattainable, and the adolescent sheep and jejune oxen sold at thirty-five cents a pound in the markets? These are things which come home to men's stomachs and pockets when the sound of rebel artillery fails to move them. Cut off as we are in every direction, we form a blockaded community of our own, the only communication with civilized society being by the steamers which run semi-occasionally from Georgetown to New York. We have no mail, no telegraphic communication, no railroad travel; and if this state of things shall continue much longer we shall be reduced to the miserable necessity of reading our own one-horse newspapers and making salt provisions our chief diet.

The city is in a ferment; men are marching to and fro; able-bodied citizens are gobbled up and put into the District militia; refugees come flying in from the country, bringing their household goods with them; nobody is permitted to go out on the Maryland roads without a pass, and at every turn an inquiring newspaper correspondent is met by some valiant coward in shoulder straps, pompous and big with importance, in the rear of all danger, with "By what authority are you here, sir?" Last night, while passing by the War Department, I saw an awkward squad of Quartermasters' clerks drilling in the park. Some were short and some were tall; there were slab-sided clergymen who had forsaken the pulpit for the clerkly desk, fast young men in for a frolic; grim, saturnine men buckled into armor and looking destitute of all friends; men in linen coats and men in half-uniform; these all were being put through the manual by an impromptu captain who, not being very well-informed in such matters, was prompted by his orderly sergeant, a messenger in the War Department. These sons of war were to be under the command of Brigadier General Bacon, a worthy grocer who is the militia commander of the District. If they had been drilled each week since the war began, they would have been competent for service by this time, but just now they would be as efficient as a raw hand in a major general's saddle.

The President and his family have been living out at the Soldiers' Home, about four miles only this side of the rebel line of skirmishers; but on Sunday night Secretary Stanton sent out a carriage and a guard and brought in the family, who are again domiciled at the White House. The lonely situation of the President's summer residence would have afforded a tempting chance for a daring squad of rebel cavalry to run some risks for the chance of carrying off the President whom we could ill afford to spare just now. General Halleck still remains at his residence on Georgetown Heights, and the blue-coated "Invalids" continue to mount guard over him. When his buglers nightly blow "peas on a trencher" or "retreat," the peaceful inhabitants of Georgetown go to bed with the blissful consciousness that all is well, for Halleck is yet with us, and the rebels have not yet committed petty larceny upon the United States by carrying him off. Ill-natured people were ready to admit that even war had its compensations when it was reported that the residence of the Blair family at Silver Spring, just on the edge of the skirmish line, had been destroyed by the rebels; such was not the fact, the predatory horde, perhaps being remotely consanguineous to the Blairs, spared the house which they use for a retreat for sharpshooters....

But though Washington is beleagured and we have a small taste of the sweets of a genuine siege, all of the real mischief has been done in Maryland. It does not appear that any considerable force of rebels has crossed the Potomac; and though the wildest estimates have put the rebel invaders up to 40,000 in number, nobody has anywhere at any time seen or known of more than 2,000 men—those being cavalry....

The rebel force... pushed down the road to Rockville, fifteen miles from Washington, reaching that village on the afternoon of Sunday, July 10, scaring the denizens of that region out of all their possessions. On Sunday night Georgetown was crowded with refugees from the vicinity of Rockville and Tennallytown, all laden with their old-fashioned furniture, crockery, and household stuff generally. The throng was further thickened by several regiments of the Invalid Corps going out to the front, wherever that might be. The wildest rumors were afloat; all over Washington and Georgetown people were gathered in excited knots, talking over the news and retailing the latest exaggerations from their outer scouts. People began to talk about what they would do with their "portables,"... when the rebels should come in.

There were not a few domestic rebels who looked on the commotion with great glee. One nest of secessionists was rudely broken into by the provost guard, which discovered a half-made secession flag in the house. The men were marched off to the station house forthwith. This was not the only flag made here to be presented to the rebels when they made their triumphal entry into Washington. On

Monday morning the Sixth Corps of the Army of the Potomac landed at daylight, having come up from the James River in transports. One division (Rickett's) was already in Maryland, and the other two—13,000 men—were commanded by Major General [Horatio G.] Wright in person. About noon a portion of the Nineteenth Corps arrived from the Gulf of Mexico, via Fortress Monroe, and were put in command of Major General [Quincy A.] Gillmore, who had been sent for in haste. So Washington breathed easier forthwith, Major General Alexander Mc-Cook being in command of all of our defensive troops and fortifications.

MANNING THE DEFENSES

The first movement on the part of the military authorities . . . was to get out all of the available men of the Veteran Reserves or the Invalid Corps, of whom six regiments were sent out toward Rockville on Sunday night; and two regiments went north on the Seventh Street road, accompanied by 1,800 men from Camp Convalescent. Monday morning Colonel [Moses N.] Wisewell, Military Governor of the city, got permission to detail all of the able-bodied men in the hospitals; though the Surgeon General had said that there were not thirty such men, before last night 3,200 fighting men from the hospitals were on their way to the front, officered, armed, and provisioned. Contrabands and refugees were pressed into service. Over 900 Quartermasters' employees were armed and sent out, and at twelve o'clock last night there were within the fortifications of Washington 60,000 men, armed and equipped for a fight. . . . Up to the present hour of writing (Tuesday noon, July 12), no active demonstrations have taken place against the enemy.

Washington, July 14, 1864

THE END OF "THE INVASION"

The aim of the rebel invasion of Maryland was to create a diversion of Grant's army from the front of Richmond and to collect such plunder as was most needed by the rebel army at home, cut off from their regular supplies from the south and southwest. The ends sought having been obtained, the foray has ended as suddenly and as mysteriously as it began. While a few hundred troops kept at bay 60,000 effective men within the defenses of Washington, the bulk of the rebel army, however small or large that was, made itself busy in sweeping up all available plunder and taking it across the Potomac, which being done they took themselves across just as our force began to move out on a reconnoissance in force. . . .

A SURVEY OF THE FIELD

It was curious for a peaceful citizen of the national capital to ride out yesterday into the territory just vacated by an invading force; and a party was lucky enough to catch the last glimpse of the clouds of dust which the skedaddling rebel pickets left behind them as they rode off in the direction of Edwards Ferry. We found traces of rebel occupation only five or six miles from Washington; here was a house which had been occupied by the rascals, the family having incontinently fled before the raiders. Horses had been picketed in the orchard; the fences had been used for firewood; the kitchen garden was a waste;

books, letters, and women's wearing apparel were scattered about the grounds "most promiscuous;" within the house disorder reigned supreme, the piano being well banged up, the center tables smashed, crockery broken, and the walls covered with obscene drawings and inscriptions, among which was, "Fifty thousand Virginian homes have been devastated in like manner." All around are fragments of the peculiar dust colored rebel garb, its former wearers having changed clothes from the supplies found on the premises. Several other houses in the vicinity present the same appearance of ruin and despoiliation.

To the left of the Seventh Street road is Fort Stevens in front of which all the fighting on this line occurred. Directly on the road, about seven miles from the city, is the house of [Frank] P. Blair, Senior, known as Silver Spring. This house was used as the rebel headquarters during their brief stay in these parts, and its preservation was due to the authority of the rebel [Major] General [John C.] Breckinridge, the only man of mark among them. Years ago, when a quarrel arose between Francis B. Cutting of New York and John C. Breckinridge, from words spoken in debate, the latter accepted the hospitality of the senior Blair, a fact which the rebel Kentuckian remembers and made the reason for sparing the mansion where he had once been an honored guest. He sent Blair's private papers and plate to the house of a neighbor near our lines, leaving with them a polite note to his ancient friend. One poor old woman, whose premises had been laid waste by the rebels, could not appreciate this chivalrous discrimination against herself, and she said that "nobody knew which side them Blairs were onto, anyhow"—a statement which will find popular approval.

At the Blair mansion there were about seventy wounded rebels in charge of a rebel surgeon and an assistant surgeon, and a ragged, dirty, and forlorn set of fellows they were—footsore and covered with dust, meager, pinched, and haggard. One could not but wonder how they were able to fight at all. Indeed, all of the rebels captured from this raid, numbering about 250, are more miserable in appearance than any we have ever seen before. Scattered along the fields from Blair's westward toward Fort Totten were many dead rebels left unburied by their retreating comrades. Poor fellows, their work is over and they will soon rest in their unknown graves as quietly as if they slept in their own North Carolina. Beyond Fort Totten, northwardly, the house of Postmaster General [Montgomery] Blair stands a mass of ruins, the rebels having fired it on Tuesday night. Nearer the fort are the ruins of three other houses burnt by the shells from our own forts to drive out the rebel sharpshooters. All accounts gathered in this vicinity agreed in stating that the rebels left early yesterday morning, the main body retreating during the night before, and the picket line gradually drawing off during the forenoon. The night before there was a brisk skirmish in front of Fort Stevens in which we lost over 200 men in killed and wounded and inflicted a smaller loss upon the rebels.

Washington, July 21, 1864

ODDS AND ENDS

During the recent rebel raid large numbers of rebel sympathizers showed their colors here and have since been arrested. Twenty-five sympathizers were arrested in the secesh city of Georgetown, but most of them took the oath when threatened with the Old Capitol Prison. Yet I have seen in that city a lady who pops up her head when the

Episcopal prayer for the President is read and pops it down thereafter with a sneer. Her prayers won't do Davis or anybody else any good.

... Passing by the "Circle" yesterday, where there is an indifferent equestrian statue of Washington, I heard one soldier say to the other, "What Brigadier is that? Old Uncle Jake?" "No," replied the other, "that's Washtub a-ridin' on a contract hoss." Soldiers have not a particle of reverence but generally know a "contract hoss" when they see him.

The soldiers of the Army of the Potomac amuse themselves by sending up kites toward the rebel army with amnesty proclamations thereto appended. When the kite is in the right place a slight thread running along the kite string is pulled and the bundle is scattered on the heads of the rebellious fellows below.

Washington, July 23, 1864

A POOR WOMAN'S LETTER TO FATHER ABRAHAM

The following letter which was actually received by the President and sent by him to the proper department of the government is a single illustration of how the worthy Chief Magistrate is made the recipient of all sorts of requests:

"Frederick, June 17, 1864
"tu Abraham linkun President of the U. States at Washington—Deer Sur: I take mi pen in hand to aske yu about the munney cumming to me frum my husband Daniel Spielman who was a solger in the 2d Mariland Ridgment in cumpany C who was kill in a fite with the rebs last fal

near Boonsborrow M.D. I haint got no pay as was cummin toe him and none of his bounty munney and now Mr. President I am a pore widder wumman and have no munny and have borrered all what I lived on last winter and this summer toe—I have one littel gurl who is to smal toe help me—Now Mr. President I can soe and cook and wash and du enny kind of wurk but I cant get none—see if you cant git me a plaice in one of your hospittles and I will goe rite to wurk—but I dont want to leve mi little gurl so I want to git a plaice what I can take her toe—I no yu du what is rite and yu will se tu me a pore widder wumman whose husband fote in your army your younion army Mr. President—So Mr. President I sign myself your servant to command

"Catherine Spielman."

Washington, July 25, 1864

THE EMANCIPATION PROCLAMATION ON CANVAS

[Francis B.] Carpenter's painting of the discussion of the Emancipation Proclamation in the cabinet, previous to its promulgation, is now on exhibition at the White House where it was painted; [it] excites considerable attention. The picture is a measurable success—its chief faults being rawness, lack of finish, and commonplaceness—such as might be expected in the work of a young artist who has grappled with a subject so difficult and yet so interesting now and forever. A group of men, wearing the somber-hued garments of American gentlemen, assembled in a plainly furnished apartment, though earnestly discussing a matter which is now historic, does not furnish a tempting subject for the tricks and bewildering cheats of art, and no amount of accidental lights, warm coloring, and dramatic pose can invest Seward, Blair, and the "Marie Antoinette" of the Navy Department with the supernal glories which gleam on the canvas of painters who had for their subjects kings and emperors in gorgeous robes or renowned knights in "helm or hauberk's twisted mail." The more picturesque costumes of the Signing of the Declaration of Independence make the colors of its modern counterpart and companion seem dim and dull, and the painter has not availed himself of any of the few advantages which the accessories of the signing of the Emancipation Proclamation might have afforded him.

The figures, standing and sitting, are grouped around a table in the executive chamber whose dark green walls, plain furnishings, and somber carpet are all in keeping with the grave personages who make up the picture. The composition is a double pyramid, of which Chase, high-shouldered, ponderous, painty, and purplecoated, forms one apex, and Blair, Quaker-like and somewhat ghastly, tops the other. Smith, formerly Secretary of the Interior, now dead, is on the right of Blair who is standing. On Blair's left, at the extreme right of the painting, is Bates leaning forward on the table with his arms folded. In the immediate front of the picture, between the table and the spectator, forming the base of Blair's "pyramid" and connecting the composition is Seward, a capital likeness, keen, sagacious, polished, and mousy, if I may be allowed the expression. He has his thumb and forefinger pressed on the table argumentatively, and he seems to be saying, "Wait until we have successes in the field before this proclamation is issued." Next, at the end of the table, with his left hand holding his manuscript proclamation is Lincoln, a very fair likeness, but too fresh-looking for the careworn, hard-looking man that he is. He is sitting down, has just read his document, is listening to Seward, and looks slightly bored. Chase, with his folded arms, towers up like a Jupiter Tonans to the top of the picture. He wears a look of uncomfortable consciousness and a short-waisted coat. Stanton sits on the extreme left, observant, sphinx-like and wakeful. His is the best likeness in the group. Secretary Welles, vague and ghostlike, sits in the center of the picture at the further side of the table, over which he is benevolently regarding the cautious Premier. Books, maps, and portfolios, exceedingly well-painted, are scattered about, while a photograph of ex-Secretary Simon Cameron is hanging on the wall, the artist thus paying an ingenious compliment to the man who first broached in a cabinet meeting the proposition which is now under a final discussion.

I have been particular in the description of this picture for the reason that it will soon be popular and familiar with all people through the medium of engravings. The occasion which furnishes the subject of the work is one which will always possess a deep historic interest to our own and to other people, and the artist has anticipated an inevitable demand (and perhaps abler hands) in executing at his own instance and his own cost this picture, which will be engraved in line by one of the first artists of the country. The chief faults which are now noticeable will be remedied in the engraving, and when this large, life-size painting is reduced to a fine, clear engraving of the size of the Signing of the Declaration of Independence there will be furnished a picture which will be prized in every liberty-loving household as a work of art, a group of faithful likenesses of the President and cabinet, and as a perpetual remembrance of the noblest event in American history.

Washington, August 24, 1864

WOOD AND VALLANDIGHAM

Fernando Wood doesn't like Clement L. Vallandigham; per contra, Val doesn't like Fernando—the reason for such mutual lack of affection being, I suppose, that two of a trade can never agree. Just after the return of Vallandigham from expatriation, Wood sought an interview with the President. He said: "We Peace Democrats are the only Democrats; all others are impostors and bastards; there is no such thing as a War Democrat, for that is a contradiction of terms. We don't expect, Mr. President, to elect our candidate this fall; the people of the North are not ready for peace yet; but peace must come sooner or later, and when it does the Democratic party will be the party which will act and assimilate with the dominant party in the South, and so we shall again have our rightful ascendancy. Now, Mr. President, you cannot find fault with that; it is not going to hurt you any."

The President conceded that he was disposed to be generous, and he asked if Vallandigham's reported return was any part of this program. Wood replied that it was not, and added: "You may not believe me, but I assure you that I never knew or expected that he would return, though I acknowledge that I have had a letter from him since he got back. But I tell you frankly, Mr. President, that it will not do to make a martyr of Vallandigham. He has had more notoriety already than he deserves, and I warn you that the true policy is that he be severely let alone." To this the President replied: "I don't believe that Vallandigham has returned; I never can believe it, and I never shall believe it until he forces himself offensively upon the public attention and upon my attention; then we shall have to deal with him. So long as he behaves himself decently he is as effectually in disguise as a slovenly man who went to a masquerade party with a clean face." If anyone wants an explanation of the line of conduct pursued toward Vallandigham since his return, I think they have it above.

Chicago, August 29, 1864

THE CHICAGO COPPERHEAD CONVENTION

There was a great rush Chicago-ward on all the railways leading westward during the week before the convention. On the night of August 25 I found myself weather-bound at Harrisburg on a train burdened with Copperheads, a gale having blown a train of cars off the track ahead of us and obstructed the way we were going. So we failed to connect at Pittsburgh, and waited six and a half hours in that dirty, black, and ill-smelling city for a through train to Chicago, and when we finally got under way we found ourselves on the last of four trains just dispatched for Chicago; whither the unterrified were now going.

Our train was laden with jubilant Copperheads, who, having things all their own way, fancied the whole nation was of their own way of thinking; and they accordingly grew more confident and courageous every hour. One of our fellow passengers was "Tom" Florence of the Washington *Constitutional Union*, chairman of the Breckinridge wing of the Democracy; August Belmont being the chairman of the Douglas wing appointed at Baltimore, in 1860.

Florence is a man of small account but exceedingly gassy withal, and was the Sir Oracle of the small-fry Democrats on board, most of whom were butternuts from the rural districts of Pennsylvania, Maryland, and Ohio. Another notable on the train was [Congressman Benjamin G.] Harris of Maryland, the great censured, who, with Florence, was often called upon by the pastoral inhabitants along the line of travel for a speech. Florence abused Schuyler Colfax to his heart's content whenever he found occasion to speak in the Indianan's district, for which he was well hissed at more than once. Harris very honestly said that he found himself more popular in the West than he was at home, at which all of the butternuts yelled vociferously, like rebels as they were.

The trains ahead of us awoke the people—as well as devoured all of the victuals—and we found great crowds at every station, all eagerly inquiring for McClellan, whom, they supposed, was on the train, and they took it as a personal grievance that he was not to be found; in reparation of which a furloughed colonel on the train was passed off as Little Mac and made a speech to the deluded butternuts at Plymouth, Indiana, with great applause.

THE GREAT CITY OF CHICAGO

Was all alive with flags, banners, processions, music, cheers, and butternuts when we reached there late on the night of August 27. During the day a McClellan side show had been held at which Amos Kendall, the fossilized relic of Andrew Jackson's administration, had presided over his convention of Silver Grays known as the "Union Conservative Association." This virtuous body had recommended McClellan for nomination and has passed a series

of mildly loyal resolutions and was having some nice fireworks in Court House Square as we drove up to the Sherman House. Speechifying was going on at several different
points about the square, the streets being filled and
crowded with an immense concourse of that ilk. George
Francis Train amused the crowd with one of his insane
ravings in which he denounced Lincoln and his cabinet,
made doggerel rhyme, and foamed, ranted, swore, and
tore like a mountebank. Train is for [John A.] Dix [of
New York] and a peace platform, but what his principles
are nobody can tell. He is looked on with disfavor by his
fellow Copperheads, but he has no show to make mischief
as he is only a territorial tadpole, having Nebraska credentials, for which he says that he paid ten dollars in greenbacks.

Inside the Sherman House was another great crowd
of excited people seething and boiling like a veritable witch
cauldron through the immense public hall of this colossal
and palatial hotel. Shouting, debating, and congratulating
were heard on every side—much to the disgust and discomfort of newly arrived and fatigued travelers who fought
their way up to the office to be told that they might possibly have cots on parlor floors for sleeping accommodations but no rooms.

All night long the row and rumpus were kept up, the
people evidently thinking that if they could not get sleeping quarters they could patrol the streets in processions
and compel the more fortunate ones to make speeches
for them. The notorious Isaiah Rynders [of New York] denounced this unholy crusade against our Southern brethren. Fernando Wood implored his Maker, in a blasphemous
prayer, to grant peace to the nation and to the Democratic
party; [Clement L.] Vallandigham asked to be excused
from speaking, and a score of nameless nobodies, rampant

and rabid, rushed gladly forward and made speeches to the tumultuous assembly; and so the night wore on, my last recollections being of a Sunday morning dawning on a vast mob gone mad and yelling for more speeches.

TALK ABOUT CANDIDATES AND PLATFORM

Sunday was no Sunday at all, but as noisy and exciting a day as that preceding, all of the delegations caucusing and canvassing for candidates. It is evident that McClellan has all of the chances in his favor, as his partisans are united and have plenty of money, while his opponents are divided as to their own choice. The peace men are very bitter and very determined, and some of them say they will have a separate convention if their views are not met and satisfied by the convention. The Woods, Pendleton, Vallandigham, and others of like persuasion swear that they will not support McClellan on any account, and they point to his arrest of the Maryland legislature, his advising a draft in 1861, and other damaging features of his record, to show that he is unfit for a Peace Democratic candidate. They say that if a war candidate is to be put forward Lincoln is good enough for them, and that McClellan has never done anything to deserve a nomination, but had promised what he might have done if his military plans had not been interfered with. But the McClellan men are strong, having at command an army of lobbyists imported here by August Belmont, the Hebrew banker, who lavishes money like water in the interest of "Little Mac." [Horatio] Seymour, [James] Guthrie of Kentucky, [Franklin] Pierce, [Millard] Fillmore, and others are favorites with the Peace Democracy, but they are not solidified or combined on any one man, so that the popular current and force of enthusiasm is all in favor of the Gravedigger of the Chickahominy. Here, of course, is the bone of contention in the party—shall we have a peace candidate and a peace platform or a war candidate and a war platform?

Chicago, August 30, 1864

THE CONVENTION—THE SECOND DAY

... At an early hour the reporters' seats were filled; and we amused ourselves by watching the struggling outsiders who rushed up the steps to the floor of the seatless pit of the ampitheater and quickly spread over the vacant space, each man running for dear life to the front and the whole crowd evidently as crazy as bedbugs. The arrival of the notables of the convention was the signal for great applause from the outside sovereigns, who appeared to be the real governors of the convention, the delegates themselves being overawed as they were outnumbered by the surging crowd in the pit and parquet.

Amidst all of this noise and confusion, Bishop [John Henry] Hopkins, a spare, wiggy, and fossilized-looking man, Copperhead Bishop of Vermont, was brought on the stand in full canonicals, read a series of long prayers in which the Lord was addressed on the subject of abolitionism, miscegenation, fraternal strife, and national politics. Most of the members being engaged in reading the New York *World*, distributed gratuitously daily, not much attention was paid to what a New York city delegate denominated "a right good spache for a heritic praste, be gad."

This over, a report from the Committee on Credentials was received but not read, or it if was, the indescribable confusion which followed prevented anybody from hearing it. The crowd of spectators was so great that many had to stand up against the fence separating the outsiders from the select circle within. Consequently, the rest of the crowd was shouting "Down in front," "Sit down," "Order," and a thousand other things. It was impossible for the frantic ushers and policemen to preserve any semblance of decorum. Added to this, the trains on several of the lake shore railroads pass directly by the ampitheater, jarring, whizzing, and screeching, and filling the huge barn of a building with stinking coal smoke....

ENTER SEYMOUR

The appropriate committee now reported a cut-and-dried list of officers of the convention; the name of Horatio Seymour of New York being announced, amidst great applause, as President of the convention.... The distinguished Copperhead governor of New York took the chair and made a short speech. Seymour is tall and fine-looking, being of an imposing figure, has a good face, though colorless, and a bright, black eye, high, bold forehead, dark hair and considerably bald. He has a clear ringing voice with a slight imperfection in the speech, which makes a "w" of an "r." In the main he is a commanding and effective speaker.

Seymour's harangue, calm and cool, was not well received by the crowd who wanted something more fiery and traitorous; accordingly, "Vallandigham!" "Vallandigham!" was the cry—but Val had the discretion to keep still, though I saw his eyes shine with the light of his triumph over his war friends about him. Seymour ruled the agitation of the mob by asking his "friends" to remember that, though they were the sovereign people from various

states, they were not the convention, and had no right
to any voice therein; and that so long as he was in the
chair their presence would depend upon submitting to
the right of the convention to rule out all demonstrations
of assent or dissent, applause or disapproval of men or
sentiments. No sooner was he done speaking than more
yells and calls for Vallandigham broke forth; but were
soon stopped by a call for

A PLATFORM WHICH WAS NOT AT ALL A PLATFORM

The Committee on Resolutions being called, [James]
Guthrie of Kentucky, the Chairman of said committee,
tottered forward to report. Guthrie is about seventy years
of age, is white-haired but florid, speaks clearly, and has
an awkward way of gesticulating with his whole body, as
though he had learned to speak in a boat. He has a high,
bald forehead, and is medium in height, and full-fed. His
report, or rather lack of report, disclosed to the convention
that there was a lack of harmony in the committee. . . . He
hoped that the convention would adjourn until tomorrow
when the committee could report or else ask to be discharged.

There was at once considerable confusion on several
propositions to adjourn, in the midst of which [Samuel] J.
Tilden of New York got on the platform and explained
that a subcommittee had been appointed by the platform
committee, and that it had been at work all night without
coming to an agreement; that Guthrie thought that it
could report by tomorrow; that Vallandigham, one of the
subcommittee, thought even that was not certain, but
that John B. Weller of California, chairman of the subcommittee, thought they could report this afternoon. . . .
Weller said that if the committee was not ready to report

this afternoon, it could certainly report what was the cause of any contrariety of opinion—which everybody knew to be "peace" or "war." After more squabbling, motions and countermotions to adjourn, the convention broke up in great disorder, it being understood that four o'clock in the afternoon was the hour for reassembling. And so, after a session of just an hour and a half, the convention boiled out of the building again, hungering for a platform without which no candidate can be nominated; but that is of slight account so far as the propective candidate is concerned, it being well understood that McClellan will go on any platform which is put up for him.

Four o'clock found the people all ready for further proceedings, but not so the convention. Things lagged somehow and it was long after four when Seymour and Guthrie finally ascended the stage; and Guthrie, tremulous with age, announced that after infinite labor he was able to announce to the convention that a platform which would, he hoped, harmonize all opinions had been formed. A tall, lank young man with a good voice then read a series of resolutions.

The second resolution, for cessation of hostilities, was greeted with most vociferous applause, outsiders and delegates cheering, roaring, and hallooing like mad men for the space of five minutes. "Sunset" Cox looked black and sad, but Wood and Vallandigham rubbed their hands gleefully as though they rejoiced at their work, as well they might. There was also great applause over the resistance clause, but a faint cheer at a grudging mention of our brave soldiers in the field. No mention of the draft, no word concerning the Monroe Doctrine, and no harsh statements for our "erring sisters" of the South; such was the platform, and such as it was, it was all the harmonious Democracy could get.

NOMINATIONS

When [Benjamin G.] Harris of Maryland took the
floor against McClellan, members tried to choke him down,
but in vain. Seymour ruled him to be in order, and he
went on deriding McClellan, quoting from his orders
and scoring him roundly for his arbitrary arrests in Maryland, saying that he had initiated tyranny and oppression
in advance of Lincoln, at which there were more interruptions, but wily Seymour, to whom all this was a pleasant
game of winning for his own chances, held that the merits
of the candidates could be canvassed in convention, and
that the brilliant fame of the proposed nominee could and
should be defended by his friends in like manner. Harris
... proceeded with his vituperation and abuse of McClellan, averring that Lincoln had found an assassin of state
rights in George B. McClellan. Said he, "Will you vote
for such a man? I never will!" Carrigan of Pennsylvania
was on his feet in a moment and made the point that if
Harris was not ready to swear to support the nominee of
the convention, he was not fit to be a member of the
convention, much less make a speech to it. Amidst a
tremendous uproar Seymour finally ruled Harris down, and
that worthy disappeared from the platform, chuckling at
his success in getting up a row. As he went back to his
seat a McClellan delegate struck him across the mouth,
and Harris drew off and knocked the Democratic defender
of free speech over the benches. Immediately there was a
rush and a general uproar with signs of a break-up row,
but the combatant peace men were separated. A Kentucky
conservative, [ex-Senator Joseph R.] Underwood, undertook to pour oil on the troubled water by alluding to
Andrew Jackson; whereupon some Kentuckian outside

howled out, "Why didn't you vote for him?" The old Silver Gray stuttered and stammered and said it was because he had a preference for Henry Clay....

[Alexander] Long [of Ohio] again got the floor and tried to speak, but several members raised points of order against him, calling for a vote by states on the nominations. In the midst of confusion one of the Illinois delegation, [W. W.] O'Brien, got the floor and nominated Horatio Seymour of New York amidst great and enthusiastic cheering. The call of states was begun, but Long insisted on being heard, and after something of a row he got the floor and went on with an excoriation of McClellan and a bitter complaint at the way in which freedom of speech had been denied him in a Democratic convention. He averred that McClellan was the worst and weakest man who could be nominated with the name of Democrat, and he begged that the convention nominate Seymour of New York, Vallandigham [great applause], or anybody but this weak tool of Lincoln. At this point there was a general row, and for a while it seemed probable that the convention would break up in a scrimmage. And so the wrangling and row went on, each faction endeavoring to compass its ends; but darkness put an end to the contest, and about seven o'clock, tired and worried out, the McClellan men gave up trying to get a vote, and by mutual consent the convention dissolved for the day....

Chicago, August 31, 1864

GOSSIP IN THE CONVENTION

This is the last day of the labors of the self-denying patriots who, "in this hour of our country's peril," have rushed to her rescue—not to the front of battle but into the peaceful den of a Copperhead convention. These cow-wards ... talk of resistance and revolution by force of arms against secession. The heart grows sick as we look over the gathering assemblage and mark the plotting conspir-ators who are ready to sell all they have, and all their country has, for a brief hour of riot in the spoils of office.

Yonder pale, sleek-headed man, dapper and smooth, with a "game leg," is August Belmont, an Austrian Jew and agent in America of the Rothschilds; talking earnestly with him is Dean Richmond of New York, his colleague in plotting for McClellan's nomination. Richmond is a tall, pot-bellied, bottle-nosed man, austere and arbitrary, a great manager of conventions, and looming up in his tall white hat and blue-tailed coat, far above little Belmont. Another worthy companion of these New Yorkers is Isaiah Rynders, a very personable man for such a bully; smiling and urbane in face, sedate in garb, black-wigged, and somewhat battered, looking in his face like a withered winter apple with the bloom still lingering on his cheeks. Another notable is Fernando Wood, whom everybody asks to see but seldom sees, as he, like Vallandigham, does not waste his sweetness on the common mob. He is very pale, and his sharp features are sharpened by disappoint-ment, for he has cut no figure in the convention, and it is a foregone conclusion that McClellan, whom he hates, will be the nominee. There is Dr. [Edson Baldwin] Olds, whilom denizen of Fort Lafayette, where he ought now to be; he is a small, wizened man, sharp-faced, gray-whiskered, mousy, and bespectacled. Horatio Seymour, Governor of New York, smooth, oily, dignified, and serene, comes in with a knot of small politicians over whom he towers head and shoulders mentally and physically. The Argus-eyed, Hydra-headed monster public, coiled around the vast ampitheater, recognize him as he comes in and claps its Briarean hands gleefully at the favorite champion of mobs and mob law. . . .

During the night the McClellan men have moved heaven and earth to some purpose, and many of the Peace Democrats have finally weakened under the pressing plea of availability. Thomas H. Seymour, of Connecticut, is the only formiable opponent of Little Mac—the other Seymour being now convinced that all hope for him is useless. The New York delegation is *fornenst* him, having purchased the influence of Pendleton and his friends by a promise of New York's great vote for Pendleton in the final strife for the vice presidency. Even Vallandigham is ready to vote for McClellan, bitter as is the pill, if Thomas H. Seymour cannot be nominated. Vallandigham is a friend of Pendleton. The western men hang on steadily for a peace man and will wheel into line unwillingly. New England is led by New York and Philadelphia and will go as they go—for McClellan with a few lingering regrets for Frank Pierce. . . .

THE BEGINNING OF THE END

The call of states now peacefully proceeded. . . . During the roll call New York said she sacrificed her favorite son on the altar of national honor (availability), whereat Seymour blushed, and the thirty-three votes were given to McClellan; with great applause, which also followed Pennsylvania's vote of twenty-six solid for McClellan. When Illinois was called she gave her sixteen votes for "Little Mac," but one [David] Sheean protested in a rich Irish brogue that though this was done in consonance with their positive instructions to vote as a unit, he thought the convention ought to know that there were ten votes in the delegation for McClellan and six for "Saymour," at which he was hissed down; and the McClellan ring bawled out, "Git out, you Peace Democrat," which was hard on Sheean. Missouri voted four-and-one-half for Horatio Seymour, but the secretary, acting under instructions from the astute governor, gave it to Thomas H. Seymour of Connecticut, at which Missouri protested, but Governor Seymour smilingly said that it was all right and would listen to no explanation. This he did in all similar instances, making Tom Seymour the scapegoat for his few scattering votes....

THE RESULT

... After all changes were made the vote was announced thus: McClellan, 202½; Thomas H. Seymour, 23½. Instantly, the pent up feelings of the mob broke forth in the most rapturous manner; cheers, yells, music, and screams indescribable rent the air, and outside a brace of cannon volleyed a salute to the welkin in honor of the hero of the Chickahominy. The long agony was over, and men split their throats, threw up their caps, and behaved as much like bedlamites as men can....

Vallandigham ... this distinguished and eminently disgusted apostle of peace, now mounted the rostrum and moved that the nomination be made unanimous. He was applauded to the echo as he swallowed this bitter, bitter dose, making himself a real martyr for his party's cause. Having done, he descended again with a very wry face.

NOMINATIONS FOR VICE PRESIDENTIAL CANDIDATE

... Ohio nominated George H. Pendleton; Indiana followed with [Daniel] W. Voorhees; Pennsylvania nominated George W. Cass; Vermont put up James Guthrie; Illinois named John D. Caton, Chief Justice of her state

Supreme Court; Delaware nominated [Lazarus] Powell of Kentucky; Missouri put up John S. Phelps of that state; and Iowa nominated Augustus Caesar Dodge, her favorite Copperhead, once minister to Spain.

THE VOTE

On the first ballot there was no choice. Again the roll call began, and this time all of the contest was between Pendleton and Guthrie, with the odds largely in favor of the Ohioan, the New England states giving a large majority of their votes to him. New York waited wisely until it was perceptible that Pendleton would be the nominee; when she cast her thirty-three votes solid for him. Pennsylvania followed with her twenty-six votes, and in the midst of the roll call all other business was suspended in the wild stampede of states to the winning candidate. The calling of the remaining states was a mere form; they all voted for Pendleton. Of course, there was music, cheers, a salute, and a speech from the smiling Pendleton who was present as a delegate. The work of the convention was done.

FINAL GLEANINGS FROM THE CONVENTION

There is a great deal of dissatisfaction on the part of the border state men. There was no word of comfort for them in the platform, and a resolution inviting them to present a border state candidate for president was quietly squelched; two northern-born men are on the ticket, and they indignantly declare that it is an insult to the "g-r-e-a-t State of Kaintucky." So it is.

The Maryland delegation is a unit against McClellan still, and it swears that he cannot carry the state. . . . One of the Indiana delegates—a peace man—said, excitedly, as the crowd broke up, that the nominee for president was a nobody and the candidate for vice president a putty head. Copperhead would have been nearer the mark, for Pendleton is no putty head but a smart young man. . . .

George Francis Train has not been seen in convention, having been snuffed out at the beginning thereof. From his private parlor at the Sherman House he issued his insane blatherskiting in the shape of funny and sarcastic "manifestoes." Train is crazy beyond a doubt; goes dressed in white always, curls his hair, and froths in his speech.

The McClellanites are in high feather tonight, cheering, brass-banding, processionizing, and firing rockets. The crowd, heretofore well-behaved, is noisy, drunk, and riotous, more cheers being given for Vallandigham than anyone else.

Washington, October 24, 1864

A MAGNIFICENT ELECTION SHOW

. . . We had here last week a splendid torchlight procession gotten up by the Lincoln and Johnson Club of this city. Nothing so fine has ever been seen in this city, and seldom, perhaps, has it been outdone elsewhere. Measuring by the length of the Avenue, the procession was over two miles long. It was resplendent from end to end with banners, torches, fireworks, transparencies, and all of the paraphernalia of such a demonstration. The length of Pennsylvania Avenue, vanishing in the distance, was gemmed with colored lights, flaming with torches, and illuminated with the lurid glare from shooting fires of red, green, and blue Roman candles—the whole procession creeping like a living thing and winding its slow length around the White House where the President looked out upon the spectacle. A marked feature in the line was a detachment of convalescent wounded soldiers from the hospitals whose ambulances bore such mottoes as "Ballots and Bullets," "We can Vote as well as Fight," etc. The Navy Yard men had a miniature monitor named the *Worden* whose revolving turret continually shot fireworks, to the terror of timid spectators. The secesh lined the sidewalks and were very profuse with their insults and abuse, hurrahing for McClellan and groaning for Lincoln and "the Lincoln hirelings" continually. . . .

A TEMPEST IN A TEAPOT

During the passage of the torchlight procession by the McClellan and Pendleton headquarters, a long flag suspended from the building caught fire, as it was hung so low as to sweep on all of the high objects in the procession. A few inches were burned off, and straightway a howl arose. The Copperhead *Union* came out with a big sensation article about the "Abolitionists firing the American flag," etc. The Democracy had a special meeting on Saturday night and passed severe and bitter resolutions, while the Lincoln Club, on the same night, passed the following:

"*Whereas*, During the passage of the Union torchlight procession under the American flag suspended across Pennsylvania Avenue, at the McClellan and Pendleton headquarters, on Friday night, said flag caught fire, accidentally as we believe, from one of the torches borne in the procession; therefore,

"*Resolved*, That though at many points along the line of the procession the McClellan men used exceedingly vile, insulting, and taunting remarks toward those composing the procession, and particularly toward soldiers, even going so far as to hurl stones and other missiles into the line, still, this Club deeply regrets the burning of said flag, and if it resulted from design on the part of any person moving in the procession, we condemn it as an act which no insults can justify, and we believe that every member of this Club would regard such an act in the same light."

Accordingly, "All is quiet on the Potomac." (Vide McClellan's reports any time during 1861–62.)

ODDS AND ENDS

When I had succeeded in showing the President the other day how a California politician had been coerced into telling the truth without knowing it, he said it reminded him of a black barber in Illinois, notorious for lying, who once heard some of his customers admiring the planet Jupiter rising in the evening sky. "Sho! I've seen dat star afore. I seen him way down in Georgy." Said the President, "Like your friend, he told the truth, but he thought he was lying."

Some secesh ladies visiting a hospital at Alexandria the other day thought their instincts showed them a wounded rebel whom they accosted: "Soldier, soldier, what can we do for you?" The jolly Yank rolled over and said "Kiss me for my mother!" Seceshina mizzled.

Washington, November 2, 1864

LIGHT ON A DARK SUBJECT

Last night the colored people of this District held a jubilation in honor of the emancipation of Maryland,

manifesting their intelligent appreciation of the advance
into freedom of Maryland in their own style. One of the
larger of their churches was thrown open, religious exercises were held, and enthusiastic addresses were made by
their head men and preachers. After an hour spent in
this way, they organized themselves into an impromptu
torchlight procession, numbering some few hundred, who
bore aloft the borrowed torches and a few of the transparencies of the late Union torchlight procession, among
which latter were some not specially adapted to the occasion, California figuring as "20,000 for the Union," and
"Indiana gives us a gain of five Congressmen," while
Massachusetts was represented by a picture of Bunker
Hill monument. . . . With these emblems, and a hoarse
band of music, the somewhat irregular procession got up
to the White House, where loud and repeated cheers
brought out the President, who began by saying: "I have
to guess, my friends, the object of this call, which has taken
me quite by surprise this evening." Whereupon a chief
spokesman shouted, "The emancipation of Maryland,
sah"; at which the President proceeded as follows: "It
is not secret that I have wished, and still do wish, mankind everywhere to be free. [Great cheering and cries of
"God bless Abraham Lincoln."] And in the state of Maryland how great an advance has been made in this direction! It is difficult to realize that in that state, where
human slavery has existed for ages, ever since a period long
before any here were born—by the action of her own
citizens—the soil is made forever free! [Loud and long
cheering.] I have no feeling of triumph over those who
were opposed to this measure and who voted against it,
but I do believe that it will result in good to the white
race as well as to those who have been made free by this
act of emancipation, and I hope that the time will soon

come when all will see that the perpetuation of freedom for all in Maryland is best for the interests of all, though some may thereby be made to suffer temporary pecuniary loss. And I hope that you, colored people, who have been emancipated, will use this great boon which has been given you to improve yourselves, both morally and intellectually; and now, good night." Whereupon there was more cheering, and after some boggling about the order of march, the dark torchlighters gathered themselves up, and hurrahing, disappeared in the darkness.

Washington, November 7, 1864

THE ARMY OF THE POTOMAC IN MOTION

Once more the invincible Army of the Potomac is in motion, but this time the movement is not toward the city of Richmond directly but toward the heart of the rebellion by way of the ballot box. The exposures of the various attempts at fraud on the voting privileges of the soldiers by the Copperheads have served to discourage the soldiers from voting, and they are anxious to go home and cast their vote in person. The artful dodge of the framers of the New York voting law, which requires the soldiers' vote to be cast by proxy on the day of election, served to diminish the chances of the vote being received in time; and accordingly, the soldiers from that state have been sent home in vast numbers. Added to these are hosts of men from the hospitals and convalescent wards about Washington, and several Pennsylvania regiments, sent home on furlough; also, the Maryland soldiers, who voted almost as a unit for the new state constitution, have gone home in a body.

These, and thousands of civilians from the various government departments, have swelled the exodus of homeward-bound voters to something a little short of enormous dimensions. The railroad is blocked up with trains going north, and more than once during the past week there were not cars enough to make up the regular trains for Baltimore. Of course, the Copperheads are exceeding wroth at this quadrennial hegira, virtuously forgetting that it has taken place ever since the foundation of the government, the only difference being that the soldiers are now added to the usual number of voters going home; and if the soldiers are all "Democrats," as claimed, why should they not be glad to have them go home to vote? But the fact is, the old, old story of the Democratic proclivities of the soldiers has been about played out in this latitude, and the Copperheads are seldom so barefaced as to make the transparently false assertion that their political creed has many friends in the rank and file of our noble army.

It is true that some of the Army of the Potomac—many, perhaps—will vote for McClellan, but they *do not* vote for Seymour, whom they hate and despise. They go home hurrahing for "Little Mac" in a few instances (which shows, by the way, that no political discrimination is made against soldiers sent home), but they remember that Seymour is opposed to the soldiers voting, and they love him accordingly....

The national village was never duller than now. We unfortunates have no vote for president, and all of the interest is centered in the election which comes off tomorrow outside of the District of Columbia. The stampede of clerks and department heads has suspended the operation of the usual machinery, and scarcely a bureau is in running order today. Washington is deserted, and its dirty dullness is heightened by an unceasing fall of rain which had deluged the streets for the past twenty-four hours. The prospect is not enlivening.

Washington, November 11, 1864

HOW THE PRESIDENT TOOK THE NEWS

... Election day was dull, gloomy, and rainy; and, as if by common consent, the White House was deserted, only two members of the cabinet attending the regular meeting of that body. Stanton was sick abed with chills and fever; Seward, Usher, and Dennison were at home voting like honest citizens; and Fessenden was shut up with New York financiers; so Father Welles and Attorney General Bates were left to "run the machine." The President took no pains to conceal his anxious interest in the result of the election then going on all over the country; but just before the hour for cabinet meeting he said: "I am just enough of a politician to know that there was not much doubt about the result of the Baltimore convention, but about this thing I am far from being certain; I wish I were certain."

The first gun came from Indiana, Indianapolis sending word about half-past six in the evening that a gain of 1,500 in that city had been made for Lincoln. At seven o'clock, accompanied only by a friend, the President went over to the War Department to hear the telegraphic dispatches as they brought in the returns, but it was nearly nine o'clock before anything definite came in, and then Baltimore sent up her splendid majority of 10,000 plus. The President only smiled good-naturedly and said that was a fair beginning. Next, Massachusetts sent word that she was good for 75,000 majority ... and hard upon her came glorious old Pennsylvania, Forney telegraphing that the state was sure for Lincoln. "As goes Pennsylvania, so goes the Union, they say," remarked Father Abraham, and he looked solemn as he seemed to see another term of office looming before him.

There was a long lull, and nothing was heard from New York, the chosen battleground of the Democracy, about which all were so anxious. New Jersey broke the calm by announcing a gain of one congressman for the Union, but with a fair prospect of the state going for McClellan; then the President had to tell a story about the successful New Jersey Union congressman, Dr. [William A.] Newell, a family friend of the Lincolns, but he was interrupted by a dispatch from New York city, claiming the state by 10,000. "I don't believe that," remarked the incredulous Chief Magistrate, and when Greeley telegraphed at midnight that we should have the state by about 4,000, he thought that more reasonable.

So the night wore on, and by midnight we were sure of Pennsylvania, the New England states, Maryland, Ohio, Indiana, Michigan, Wisconsin, and it then appeared that we should have Delaware. Still no word came from Illinois, Iowa, or any of the trans-Mississippi states; and the President was especially concerned to hear from his own state, which sent a dispatch from Chicago about one o'clock in the morning, claiming the state for Lincoln by 20,000 and Chicago by 2,500 majority. The wires worked badly on account of the storm, which increased, and nothing more was heard from the West until last night, November 10, when the President received two days' dispatches from Springfield claiming the state by 17,000 and the capital by 20 majority, Springfield having been heretofore Democratic.

By midnight the few gentlemen in the office had had

the pleasure of congratulating the President on his re-election. He took it very calmly—said that he was free to confess that he felt relieved of suspense and was glad that the verdict of the people was so likely to be clear, full, and unmistakable, for it then appeared that his majority in the electoral college would be immense. About two o'clock in the morning a messenger came over from the White House with the intelligence that a crowd of Pennsylvanians were serenading his empty chamber, whereupon he went home, and in answer to repeated calls came forward and made one of the happiest and noblest little speeches of his life. . . .

With the new term of office will come upon the President a renewal of the crushing responsibilities of the past four years; and I ought to say for the encouragement of loyal, Christian hearts, who daily remember their careworn Chief Magistrate "and all others in authority," that no man within the length and breadth of this Christian land feels more deeply than he the need of divine support, guidance, and wisdom in these great straits than does Abraham Lincoln. On the day following the election he said, "I should be the veriest shallow and self-conceited blockhead upon the footstool if, in my discharge of the duties which are put upon me in this place, I should hope to get along without the wisdom which comes from God and not from men." In many loyal hearts these simple words of trust will find a responsive thrill. God give him grace!

SERENADES AND SPEECHES

Last night an impromptu procession, gay with banners and resplendent with lanterns and transparencies, marched up to the White House, the vast crowd surging around the great entrance, blocking all of the semicircular avenue thereto as far as the eye could reach. Bands brayed martial music on the air, enthusiastic sovereigns cheered to the echo, and the roar of cannon shook the sky, even to the breaking of the President's windows, greatly to the delight of the crowd and Master "Tad" Lincoln who was flying about from window to window, arranging a small illumination on his own private account. The President had written out his speech, being well aware that the importance of the occasion would give it significance, and he was not willing to run the risk of being betrayed by the excitement of the occasion into saying anything which would make him sorry when he saw it in print. His appearance at the window was the signal for the tremendous yell, and it was some time before the deafening cheers would permit him to proceed. . . .

City Point, Virginia, November 16, 1864

A CALL ON THE LIEUTENANT GENERAL

. . . Grant's headquarters are upon the extreme end of City Point, commanding a view of the broad basin, the James, the mouth of the Appomattox, Bermuda Hundred, and the winding shores. Passing the long flight of steps leading to the foot of the river bank and the lines in the rear guarded by sentries, we enter Grant's tent where a cheerful fire is burning in a rude brick fireplace, and the chieftain sits smoking his now world-famed cigar. The cares of the day were over, and the General received us hospitably and pleasantly, like an honest, simple gentleman.

Seats taken and salutations exchanged, we found ourselves in a small wall tent, the rough floor of which was covered by a venerable carpet; the General's narrow bedstead was also up against one side, and opposite it was a rude pine table covered with maps and papers, near which was an old patchwork-covered rocking chair, a relic of the ske-daddled Virginians, and a few campstools, a military chest, and a box or two made up the furniture of this General who has pitched his tent right in the midst of deserted old mansions and newly built barracks and quarters....

He entered into an easy, offhand talk about politics and the late election. The latter victory he spoke of as being greatly overmastering in importance, and he showed by the way in which he spoke of the votes of certain mem-bers of Congress that he had closely watched the course of political legislation and knew full well all of the ins and outs of wily politicians. He spoke pityingly of McClel-lan's defeat but lightly of his abilities, concluding that the defeated hero could do no better than accept the $10,000 annual salary offered him by the Illinois Central Railroad Company. He alluded with evident pride to his own con-gressional district (Elihu B. Washburne's) in Illinois, which had just given 9,000 majority for the Union ticket. Frank M. Pixley, his stovepipe hat, his seriocomic adven-tures at the front, and his unfailing fund of fun, are all yet held in tender remembrance at Grant's headquarters. The odor of a good cigar recalled the fact that among Grant's numerous presents of cigars none were better than a package from [John Bidwell] the newly elected Repre-sentative from the Third Congressional District of Cali-fornia. The General informed us that his national notori-ety for smoking had induced him to limit himself to four cigars per day—during business hours.

Washington, November 25, 1864

THE NATIONAL THANKSGIVING

The recommendation of the President to observe yesterday as a day of national thanksgiving was very generally responded to in these parts, the stores being closed, all the houses of worship open, and a spirit of merrymaking and hilarity prevalent. Old settlers here say that no Thanksgiving Day has ever been so universally observed in public and in private in this city as the one just past; which fact is accounted for by the infusion of the Yankee element and the more than commonly thankful tone of people everywhere since the election. The hospitals and camps had a bountiful supply of the good things of this life sent from northern cities, and the "national bird" (no allusion to mackerel) smoked on the tables of our brave defenders at the Petersburg and Richmond front as well as at home. The lavish Thanksgiving bounty was not entrusted to the direction of the Sanitary Commission, but was distributed directly to the soldiers themselves, so that we may be sure that this time the gifts were received by the persons for whom they were intended. We have much to be thankful for, and I believe our people were really and truly in a thanksgiving frame of mind on the day.

THE NEW CAPITOL DOME

During the recess of Congress the sound of hammer and saw has been continuous at the Capitol, and Congress will come back to find the building greatly beautified and purified since the adjournment. The passages in the House wing, heretofore of a glaring white stucco, have been covered with a soft neutral tint picked out with white, and mock paneling and fresco cover all of the once bare walls. Committee rooms are newly carpeted, the Senate chamber refurnished, the Senate wing front completed, and from the chaos of paint buckets, carpenter's trash, and whitewash, the noble pile is emerging in pristine beauty. But the chief attraction to newcomers will be the completed interior of the new dome. Above the perpendicular portion of the rotunda, which rises in entablature and colonnade to a height of 125 feet above the floor, springs the dome, paneled in iron, painted white and lilac. It rises 200 feet from the floor below. The "eye of the dome" is the level place at the top and in that will be placed a $40,000 painting by [Constantino] Brumidi. Around the eye runs a balcony whence visitors can gaze down upon the pavement of the rotunda below. The effect of the interior is now very fine and will be much admired when the rubbish is cleared out of the way.

GLEANINGS FROM FORTRESS MONROE

While on my way back to Washington from City Point the other day, I tried to take some observations, but how it rained! It fell in deluges all the time, making a visit to some of the historic places about there impossible; but a survey of the operations of the Freedmen's Department showed how much good is being done by patient and persistent effort to ameliorate the conditions of the homeless and friendless refugees from slavery and to set them on their feet.

The abandoned plantations on the peninsula are taken

possession of by the government, the contrabands are put to work upon them, and from the crop enough is taken to compensate the government for the tools, seeds, and rations furnished the Negroes; destitute and infirm persons are provided with quarters and rations. From the wages of every colored man receiving wages from the government is taken a sufficient percentage to defray the expense of the rations so furnished, accurate debit and credit account being kept. As fast as families or individuals become self-sustaining they are cut off from government aid. They become in turn the helpers of the sick, infirm, and destitute, so that the government is not only relieved from the care and expense of the contraband but is becoming an actual gainer.

Last year the Quartermaster's Department was bringing wood from Baltimore at $10 per cord; this year it is paying $1 per cord cut by contrabands and hauled by government condemned teams which have been turned over to the superintendent. Some of these Negroes have turned over as much as 1,000 bushels of corn each to the government as its share of this year's crop; and other gangs have turned out millions of feet of lumber for public use from the six sawmills put up by the Quartermaster's Department on the peninsula above Fortress Monroe. Everywhere there is an appearance of thrift, comfort, and economy which is marvelous to behold. One cannot but wish that the croaking Copperheads who have always said that the Negro is incapable of taking care of himself could witness the extraordinary progress which these poor people are making toward all of the arts which go to make life pleasant and happy. Under the fostering care of a few wise men there is springing up here a colony of blacks whose intelligence, good behavior, and industry will put to shame the lack-labor and spiritless towns and hamlets of the old aristocracy of Virginia.

The War Department has placed here, with a captain's commission, C. B. Wilder, a well-to-do citizen of Boston who has left his comfortable home and business for the sole purpose of guiding and directing the domestic economy of this colony of blacks just emerging from the horrors and barbarisms of slavery. Some time we may be able to do justice to a Christian heroism so remarkable and a self-sacrificing spirit so useful to his kind as that of the gentleman alluded to, but it will be long before our people know how much of ripe experience, Christian patience, wisdom, firmness, and probity have been brought to bear upon this difficult experiment of making free men out of the escaped victims of brutish, besotting, and degrading American slavery.

Washington, November 29, 1864

REBELS IN WASHINGTON

The city is full of butternut-clothed men who are quasi-deserters from the rebel army; scarcely ever can one pass along the streets without encountering squads of these sad-hued, ragged, and haggard mean whites who slouch along in hangdog style as if they were ashamed to look one in the face. Some of these are attracted into our lines by the famous Special Order No. 126 of Grant; which is kept as "standing matter" conspicuously displayed in all of the newspapers allowed to go into the rebel lines. The order states that rebel deserters will, on taking an oath that they will not again take up arms during the present rebellion, be furnished with free subsistence and transportation to their homes if within our lines or to any point in the North; or, upon taking the oath of allegiance, they will be given employment in the Quartermaster's or other departments of the army at the usual wages. Deserters who bring in mules or horses are paid for them by the Quartermaster of the army. This has stimulated desertion, and hosts of discouraged rebels or escaped conscripts are coming over daily; it has become a grave question if we are not in danger of an organized conspiracy from this formidable element in the midst of our loyal country. But it is evident that the exodus does weaken the rebellion, and it has been decided to keep the rebel refugees under close surveillance, but to permit their ready ingress to our lines, facilitating their migration northward where labor is in demand and wages are good.

VANDALISM AT THE WHITE HOUSE

People who visit the White House usually have a free range over the East Room and one or two of the adjoining parlors; accordingly, relic-hunters ... have acquired the practice of cutting out and carrying off bits of rich carpet, damask hangings, and even large pieces of fringe, cords, tassels, gilt scrollwork, and the covering of damask sofas. A few weeks ago an army officer was caught in company with two ladies who had his penknife and were cutting out a square of red brocade from one of the East Room chairs while he stood guard. The *ladies* were let off and the officer was sent to the Old Capitol Prison. Yesterday, a man in the garb of a private soldier was caught skinning off the damask cover of a sofa. He was sent to the guardhouse. Well might an astonished Dutchman say, "Mine Gott, vat a peoples!"

Washington, December 5, 1864

THE PRESIDENT ON PRACTICAL RELIGION

A good illustration of the practical and common sense view which President Lincoln takes of whatever comes under his observation was afforded the other day in his reply to the application of two Tennessee ladies for the release of their husbands who are confined as prisoners of war on Johnson's Island, Ohio. These ladies had been put off from day to day, and one of them continually reiterated as an argument in favor of her husband that he was a religious man. They were finally successful in their suit, and when the President agreed to the release he said to the lady referred to: "You say your husband is a religious man; tell him, when you see him, that I am not much of a judge of religion, but that, in my opinion, the religion that sets men to rebel and fight against their government because, as they think, that government does not sufficiently help *some* men to eat their bread in the sweat of *other* men's faces, is not the sort of religion upon which people can get to heaven." This is one of the shortest and best "political sermons" ever preached in Washington, I guess.

Washington, December 7, 1864

HOW THE PRESIDENT'S MESSAGE WAS RECEIVED

Precisely at one o'clock yesterday the private secretary of the President appeared at the bar of the House of Representatives with the annual message of the President. The ayes and noes were being called on some tomfool proposition at the time, and it was not immediately read; but in a few minutes Clerk [Edward] McPherson, in a loud and clear voice, took up the document and began with the terse and litany-like exordium: "Again the blessings of health and abundant harvests claim our profoundest gratitude to Almighty God." Simultaneously with the utterance of the words a host of small, agile pages spread themselves all over the hall, laying upon the desks of the members printed copies of the message which were eagerly seized and read.

A complete silence pervaded the vast hall and the breathless, crowded galleries, except when the Clerk rang out clarion-like the words, "Maryland is secure to liberty and Union for all the future. The genius of rebellion will no more claim Maryland. Like another foul spirit, being driven out, it may seek to tear her, but it will woo her no more." These triumphant and poetic words brought forth a loud burst of applause, and when the President's dry hit at the "instinctive knowledge" of the politicians on the Union question was reached, there was a ripple of laughter all over the House, and the sovereigns in the gallery showed their appreciation by a half-stifled rumble of applause, for *they* know that the politicians ought to know that "there is no diversity of opinion among the people on the question of Union or no Union." There were smiling faces and long sighs of satisfaction when the reader reached the President's restatement of his own old position on the amnesty proposition, and when the noble sentences which conclude the message were read there was a long, loud, and continued burst of applause, which the Speaker but feebly tried to still.

The reading over, members dropped their copies of the

message and shook hands kindly and smilingly over the acceptable token of the President's policy to come. Some few had expected that there would be an enunciation of some new principles concerning peace and reconstruction, but such were mistaken and had not known or appreciated the eminent sagacity and tact of Abraham Lincoln. The verdict of all men is that the message is immensely strengthening for the President, and that while it has all of the dignity and polish of a first-rate state paper, it has strong common sense and practical knowledge of details which will commend the document to the minds of "the simple people." Thaddeus Stevens says that the message is the wisest and best the President ever sent to Congress, and leading men generally concur in the opinion of the critically wise Pennsylvanian. . . .

HOW THE MESSAGE WAS WRITTEN

It may be a matter of interest to know that the whole of the compact and able message exists, or did exist, upon slips of pasteboard or boxboard. It is a favorite habit of the President, when writing anything requiring thought to have a number of these slips of board near at hand, and, seated at ease in his armchair, he lays the slip on his knee and writes and rewrites in pencil what is afterward copied in his own hand with new changes and interlineations. Then being "set up" by the printer with big "slugs" in the place of "leads," spaces of half an inch are left between each line in the proof. More corrections and interlineations are made, and from this patchwork the document is finally set up and printed. The complete collection of original scraps of the manuscript message would be a valuable prize for an autograph hunter.

BRIEF ITEMS

The President and R[euben] E. Fenton, Governor-elect of New York, were serenaded last evening. Fenton made a good speech, and the President said that he could never yet get over being embarrassed when he had nothing to say and proposed three cheers for Sherman, which were given with a will.

Chief Justice [Salmon P.] Chase was confirmed without his name being referred to the usual committee—that being the custom in the Senate when the name of a former senator is laid before that body for confirmation.

Washington, December 9, 1864

A GOOD POINT WELL PUT

The Maryland Electoral College paid a visit to the President yesterday, and in the course of their formal interview expressed their gratification at the appointment of Chase to be Chief Justice; to which the President responded that he trusted that the appointment was for the best. The country, he said, needed some assurances in regard to two great questions, and they were assurances that could better be given by the character and well-known opinions of the appointee than by any verbal pledges. In the appointment of Chase, all holders of government securities in America and Europe felt assured that the financial policy of the government would be sustained by its highest judicial tribunal. In sustaining that policy Judge Chase would only be sustaining himself, for he was the author of it. His appointment also met the public desire and expectations regarding the emancipation policy of the government. His views were well-known upon both of these great questions, and while there were other distinguished gentlemen whose names had been suggested for this great trust, whose views he believed were sound upon these important issues, yet they did not hold the same relations to them as did Chase.

Washington, December 13, 1864

SUNDRY ITEMS

With Grant scaring the Richmonders half out of their senses, Sherman within fifteen miles of Savannah, Nashville beleagured, and an advance upon Wilmington at last under way, it does not much look as though we were to have a quiet fireside campaign for the coming winter now howling over the bleak hills of Virginia, freezing the Potomac, and whitening the country all around Richmond and Petersburg.

Henry R. Schoolcraft, the Indian historian, or historian of North American Indians, rather, died on December 10, at his residence in this city. This venerable gentleman has been confined to his chair or couch with paralysis for years past, and one of the features of the congressional lobby was the daily appearance of his wife, an eccentric woman, buttonholing members and senators for their influence in favor of a $10,000 job of completing his works. The funeral, which took place yesterday, was attended by many distinguished men, Senators [Ira] Harris and Reverdy Johnson, Commissioner [William P.] Dole, and Peter Force, the bibliopolist, acting as pallbearers.

The Senate Judiciary Committee held the nomination of James Speed, to be Attorney General, four days—not because they hesitated at confirming him but to convey a mild insinuation to the President that they did not know who James Speed of Kentucky is.

Washington, December 15, 1864

AN EVENT IN THE NEW ERA

It is only once in a lifetime that one has the opportunity of seeing a Chief Justice of the United States sworn into office. If Chase holds his office with as strong tenacity as did the late Roger B. Taney, the lusty youth who gazed curiously at the simple ceremonial today will be tottering down the western slopes of life before he sees another such event in our history. This thought, no doubt, passed through the minds of many of our people and caused them six times to fill the narrow limits of the Supreme Court room, and five times they were disappointed, for the Chief Justice was not ready. Precedent prescribes that the letters-patent of a Justice of the Supreme Court must pass through the hands of the Attorney General of the United States; accordingly, while the Senate was boggling over Speed's confirmation, the new Chief Justice was waiting for his commission, for there was no Attorney General.

But this morning the courtroom was crowded with dignitaries, ladies, and congressmen to witness the ceremony which came off without any postponement. There was a rush, of course, and the rippling tide overflowed into the sacred precincts of the bar, where sat the ponderous Tom Ewing, the white-headed Reverdy Johnson, both distinguished lawyers, Senator Sprague, Mrs. Kate Sprague and sister, gorgeous in millinery, erect N[athaniel] P. Banks, gray Ben Wade, and hosts of others. Beyond, in the rear of the supreme bench, to the right, the elegant form of [Senator Charles] Sumner was leaning against one of the marble columns, his fine features too plainly showing his inward glow of gratification. All around stood many a devoted disciple of freedom, once scourged, but ready to say, "Lord, now lettest thou thy servant depart in peace, for mine eyes have seen thy salvation."

The soft stir of the chamber was broken by the voice of the usher who announced in a loud voice: "The honorable Justices of the Supreme Court of the United States." From a side entrance behind the bench appeared the gowned Justices headed by Justice [James M.] Wayne, the senior member of the bench, and Chief Justice Chase. The Justices advanced to the rear of their several chairs, stepped in front, bowed to the left, bowed to the right, and the bar, remaining standing, bowed in reply. The new Chief Justice then stepped forward to his chair and Justice Wayne handed him a paper containing the oath, which he opened and read with a loud but tremulous voice as follows:

"I, Salmon P. Chase, do solemnly swear that I will, as Chief Justice of the Supreme Court of the United States, administer equal and exact justice to the poor and to the rich, in accordance with the Constitution and the laws of the United States, to the best of my ability."

Then laying down the paper, he lifted his hand and said with deep feeling, "So help me, God." A breathless hush pervaded the chamber, and the Chief Justice of the United States took his seat. Then the clerk read the letters-patent of the Chief Justice with considerable tremor withal, and the ceremony was over and the routine business of the court began.

Washington, January 2, 1865

WASHINGTON TAXPAYERS

... Readers may be interested to see who are some of the rich men of the national metropolis as shown in the list of taxpayers who have just paid their assessments on their incomes. We have no big men, no millionaires like [William B.] Astor or A[lexander] T. Stewart, the heaviest taxpayer being George W. Riggs, former partner in banking business with W[illiam] W. Corcoran. Riggs pays on an annual income of $79,540, and his fugacious rebel partner is mulcted on an amount of $46,438. The next heaviest is P[eter] H. Watson, Assistant Secretary of War, who pays on an income of $40,418; Judge Advocate [Joseph] Holt pays for $6,341 per year; Rear Admiral [John Adolph] Dahlgren pays on $2,533 only, not having any prize money in 1863. It would appear that Rear Admiral [Louis M.] Goldsborough fared not much better, as he pays on an income of $3,874; [Rear Admiral William B.] Shubrick pays for $4,058 per annum. Among the military men, Colonel [Richard] Delafield, the author of *Report on the Art of War in Europe in 1854–56*, fares the best, having an income of $13,521 per year; [Abner] Doubleday has $4,849; [Silas] Casey, of *System of Infantry Tactics* fame, has $5,905, having "married money;" Major General [Christopher C.] Augur has $5,022; Henry D. Cooke, once a newspaper man and now a partner in the banking house of Jay Cooke & Company, pays on $4,500 only; the venerable Amos Kendall pays on an income of $22,296, and [Justice Roger B.] Taney's income was $4,976, deducting in all of these instances, of course, $600 exempted from taxation. Notwithstanding this, however, there is a manifest deal of false swearing in this list now published, and some men are ashamed of their returns now that they are printed.

Washington, January 10, 1865

"UNEASY LIES THE HEAD," ETC.

The saying is just as true of a president as of a king, and even now, I suppose, Father Abraham lies uneasy o' nights as he thinks of the sluice of office hunting which may shortly be opened upon him by the cruel thoughtlessness of his friends, as they call themselves. The President considers that as the people have voted to keep him in another term because the public good could best be served, he ought to make no changes in office which the public good does not demand; but politicians will not see it in that light and will avail themselves of the excuse of a new term to have a new deal. I commenced this paragraph to tell a queer story of a well-known actor, J[ames] H[enry] Hackett —Falstaff Hackett—who pleased the President by playing here his well-known character. Hackett, hearing that Lincoln was pleased, sent him a copy of his book on Shakespeare with a request that it be acknowledged in a letter in which the President would give, also, his opinion of Hackett's Falstaff—all of which our good-natured Chief Magistrate did. The letter . . . was first published in London, and a copy was sent to the President by Hackett who sent word at the same time that he would have the honor, he hoped, of playing before the President when he visited

Washington again. Last winter the President did go to see him, the newspapers, much to his disgust, advertising the play as being "at the request of the President." Well, the upshot of the whole matter is that the intercourse between the flattered actor and the President is that the actor wants an office, and what do you suppose it is? Why nothing less than the mission to the Court of St. James! That's a fact, incredible as it may seem. It goes to show how careful a man who has office to give must be in taking any notice of anybody as he is sure to have somebody grinding an ax on his friendship before he is aware of it.

Washington, January 11, 1865

SEWARD IN COURT

Quite a distinguished pleader appeared before the United States Supreme Court this morning, the counsel being no less than the Secretary of State. The case is the celebrated "Troy bridge case," [Coleman v. Hudson River Bridge Company] which has been carried up from court to court until it has at last reached the highest tribunal of the land. The question is simply whether the state of New York has a right to license a bridge across the Hudson River. The plaintiffs in the case appeal on the ground that the United States has jurisdiction in the premises, the erection of such a bridge being an obstruction to the navigation of the rivers under the protection of the national government, which must defend its licensed craft. The question of national and state jurisdiction becomes an interesting one in the case, it will be perceived. W[illiam] H. Seward and J[ohn] V. L. Pruyn appear for the state of

New York and Reverdy Johnson and J. M. Carlisle appear for the appellants. Seward's manner at the bar is somewhat colloquial and yet dignified. He speaks unevenly and not always distinctly. He uses snuff freely and flourishes an old-fashioned colored silk handkerchief of the bandanna species. Among the auditors within the bar of the court were General [Nathaniel P.] Banks, Senators [Henry] Wilson, [Lazarus W.] Powell, Garrett Davis, [Willard] Saulsbury, and [James R.] Doolittle and a great many representatives.

Washington, January 13, 1865

"OLD SALAMANDER"

Vice Admiral [David G.] Farragut was received in the Senate yesterday, that dignified body taking a recess of ten minutes for that purpose. He afterward was the center of a large knot of gentlemen who paid their respects to him on the floor of the House of Representatives. The naval hero is under the medium height and size, apparently about fifty years old, spare in figure and rugged in face, with sharp nose, bright gray eyes, and weather-beaten in appearance, looking like a working man, as he is.

Washington, January 21, 1865

ARBITRARY ARRESTS

Now that there is some prospect of the speedy return of peace and the Union party is firmly re-established, there has commenced a short reckoning with some of the officers of the government who have availed themselves of the docility of our people to trample upon every right and to exercise their arbitrary powers to the fullest extent. The House passed the other day the following resolution:

"*Resolved,* That the Committee on Military Affairs be, and the same is, directed to inquire and report to the House what legislation or action, if any, is necessary to secure to persons arrested and imprisoned by military authority a prompt examination into the cause of their arrest, and their discharge if there be no adequate cause for their detention, and a speedy trial where there is such cause."

[Thaddeus] Stevens of Pennsylvania sought to reconsider the vote by which the resolution was adopted, but the House refused to reconsider by a vote of 136 to 5, the only members voting for a reconsideration being [Amassa] Cobb [of Wisconsin], [Ephraim R.] Eckley [of Ohio], [John R.] McBride [of Oregon], [Rufus P.] Spalding [of Ohio], and [Thaddeus] Stevens [of Pennsylvania]. [Henry] Winter Davis [of Maryland], [James] Garfield [of Ohio], and [John A.] Kasson [of Iowa] made sharp speeches in favor of the resolution. They made some extraordinary statements concerning the imprisonment of men who had had no trial and no notice of the charges preferred against them; the warrants for their arrest and long continued imprisonment being issued on the authority of some insignificant creature of the War Department, the notorious L[afayette] C. Baker, colonel and detective, having a sway which is almost autocratic. It often happens that men claim that they have had no charges preferred against them, but they well enough know that embezzlements and fraud, not proven, perhaps, can be laid at their door. Still, it is a notorious fact that men are and have been confined for months and let out again without a shadow of complaint or trial. If they were guilty, they should not have been let off, and if they were innocent, they should have an honorable exculpation and clearance. The facts should be known, and there is now an opportunity for Congress to settle the matter, once for all.

Washington, February 2, 1865

A MEMORABLE DAY

The last day of January, in the year of grace 1865, will ever be held in grateful remembrance as that upon which the Thirty-Eighth Congress finally desired that the people, through their state legislatures, should vote upon a proposition to amend the organic law of the United States so that involuntary servitude, except for crime, shall be forever prohibited. No man who witnessed the extraordinary spectacle of the passage of the joint resolution will ever forget the sight which greeted the eyes, and many a noble and tired soldier in the old army of freedom was ready to say, "Mine eyes have seen the glory of the coming of the Lord!"

... The Senate had passed the joint resolution at the first session of the present Congress, but the House, on June 15, 1864, refused its passage by a vote of 95 ayes to 66 noes, a two-thirds vote being necessary. At that time, [James M.] Ashley of Ohio threw himself into the breach and voted against the amendment for the purpose of moving a reconsideration which he did early during the present session. The debate from time to time has been of no special interest and has only served to kill time, while individual labor has effected conversions from the opposition.

On Tuesday, January 31, the question came up as a special order, and the hall of the House of Representatives became at once a central point of attraction, it being understood that the previous question would be called at three o'clock. The galleries, corridors, and lobbies were early crowded with an expectant assemblage. The reporters' gallery was invaded by a crowd of fair outsiders, and even the sacred precincts of the floor of the House were swarming with anxious magnates and semiofficials. There was the Chief Justice with his associates, [Noah H.] Swayne, [Samuel F.] Miller, [Samuel] Nelson, and [Stephen J.] Field, Secretary Fessenden, Postmaster General Dennison, senators by the dozen, the electoral messengers of Oregon, Nevada, and California, Montgomery Blair, and hosts of other notable men. Sharp anxiety and expectation sat on every countenance, though on the floor of the House, where the members felt pretty certain of a victory, there was less of doubt than in the upper galleries.

The opening gun came from Archibald McAllister of Pennsylvania, a Copperhead, who sent up to the Clerk's desk the following note, which was read amid a rustle of applause:

"When this subject was before the House on a former occasion I voted against the measure. I have been in favor of exhausting all means of conciliation to restore the Union as our fathers made it. I am for the Union, the whole Union, and utterly opposed to secession or dissolution in any way or shape.

"The result of all the peace missions, and especially that of Blair, has satisfied me that nothing short of the recognition of their independence will satisfy the Southern Confederacy.

"It must therefore be destroyed; and in voting for the present measure I cast my vote against the cornerstone of the Southern Confederacy, and declare eternal war against the enemies of my country."

A[lexander] H. Coffroth of Pennsylvania, of the same stripe, then read in a mechanical manner, hands in pockets, a speech, which nobody heard, but everybody knew was a public recantation of his heresy on the question. Next, [William H.] Miller, a colleague of the above-named gentlemen, interjected his protest against the sentiments just uttered, avowing his intention to die like a consistent Democrat, fighting for slavery and its perpetuation. Anson Herrick, a New York War Democrat, followed in a sensible speech, explaining his change of heart and his intention to vote for the amendment. [James S.] Brown of Wisconsin, a Copperhead of short range and smooth bore, followed in a curious essay which only showed that he was "for the law, but agin its execution." [Aaron] Harding of Kentucky, a solidified lump of selfish sourness, made a bitter, biting, querulous speech in which he branded as renegades such border men as [Green Clay] Smith, [George H.] Yeaman, and [Lucian] Anderson of Kentucky. Then [Martin] Kalbfleisch of New York delivered a long, written harangue which severely tried the patience of everybody and pushed the hour for taking the vote still further on.

This "calves' flesh" having ceasing its plaintive bleat, Ashley moved the previous question of the reconsideration. The ayes and noes were called, and at once all attention was riveted upon the result, which was 112 to 57, a motion to lay the vote to reconsider on the table having failed. It was evident that there must be a gain or the requisite two-thirds would not be obtained. Still the members were serenely satisfied, but the faces in the galleries grew sharper with anxiety.

Now red-faced [Robert] Mallory, lingering among his

Kentucky fleshpots of slavery, rises to a question of order which is that a constitutional majority of two-thirds is necessary to reconsider the vote. Of course, so absurd a point is overruled, the Speaker stating the case in his clear and sharp manner. Mallory next pleads for delay, protesting that it is not fair to force the vote today, though he well knows that such has been the understanding for two weeks. The supreme moment arrives, and the original question is before the House, Colfax's ringing voice demanding "Shall the joint resolution pass?" The roll call proceeded, and as the dull droning of the Clerk's voice went slowly down the list, knots of members gathered around their fellows who were keeping tally. A group of Copperheads hung around Pendleton, gloomy, black, and sour. When the name of John Janson, a New York Copperhead, gave back an echo of "Aye," much to the surprise of all, there was burst of applause, for the rubicon was passed and the resolution was safe. A like burst also greeted the "Aye" of [Charles A.] Eldridge of Wisconsin, heretofore a troublesome demagogue in the opposition ranks. . . .

When the roll call was concluded the Speaker exercised his prerogative and asked the Clerk to call his name, and a rumble of applause followed his clear "Aye." Then the record being made up, the Speaker announced: "On the passage of the joint resolution to amend the Constitution of the United States, the ayes are 119, the noes 56. The constitutional majority of two-thirds having voted in the affirmative, the joint resolution has passed." Instantly there was a pause of utter silence, then a burst, a storm of cheers, the like of which no Congress of the United States ever saw. Strong men embraced each other with tears. The galleries and spaces stood bristling with cheering crowds; the air was stirred with a cloud of women's handkerchiefs waving and floating. Hands were shaken, and cheer after cheer, burst after burst followed, and full five minutes elapsed before enough silence returned to enable [Ebon Clark] Ingersoll [of Illinois] to move an adjournment in honor of the day, upon which [Benjamin G.] Harris of Maryland, white with rage, demanded the ayes and noes. The roll call was begun, and members answered to their names and passed out—Cox, Pendleton, and the rest of the defeated Copperheads taking up their hats and blackly stealing away.

The final blow at the crime of slavery has been struck, but a few more events will follow in natural sequence, when we may truly say that no rood of soil beneath our flag holds a slave. Thank God, the day has passed when freedom is in the minority and oppression dominant in the United States....

A PRACTICAL REVERSAL OF THE DRED SCOTT DECISION

Yesterday morning, upon the opening of the Supreme Court, Charles Sumner of Massachusetts made a motion that John S. Rock, a member of the bar of the Supreme Court of the state of Massachusetts, be admitted to practice at the bar of the United States Supreme Court. The Chief Justice replied, "Let the gentleman nominated be admitted;" whereupon a well-dressed, respectable-looking colored man stepped forward to the desk of the Clerk, a secesh, pro-slavery protégé of the defunct Taney, took the oath of allegiance and of office, paid his fee like a white man, and was forthwith a member of the bar, despite the ill-concealed disgust of the Clerk, who looked as though he could bite off the learned Rock's head with a good appetite. Coming right on the heels of the passage of the constitutional amendment, as this event does, it is apparent to every thinking mind that the ancient palladium of our liberties is destroyed, our constitutional rights invaded, and the Constitution itself on a straight road to the dogs.

BURNING OF THE SMITHSONIAN INSTITUTION

On Tuesday, January 24, a profound sensation was created by the intelligence that the noble edifice dedicated to science and art, the Smithsonian Institution, was on fire. The imposing pile was wrapped in a dense cloud of smoke, and soon the fire burst from all of the upper portions of the towers, forming a striking spectacle, the millions of fiery tongues running rapidly up the tall, windowed, and castellated towers, roaring like the blasts of a great furnace. In broad daylight that splendid edifice, containing a rich store of records and valuable paintings, was permitted to burn almost to the ground, the miserably inefficient fire department of the national capital being unusually conspicuous for its valuelessness. A fireproof floor saved the museum hall on the lower floor housing the chief collections of [Charles] Wilkes, [Elisha Kent] Kane, and other explorers. In one of the upper halls was a fine gallery of paintings of Indians and Indian life, the works of John Mix Stanley, the artist and traveler. These were all destroyed, and the work of a lifetime was thus swept away immediately. Another loss was that of a fine library belonging to the town of Beaufort, South Carolina, sent here for safekeeping by the military authorities when the town was taken from the rebels. The library of the Institution and many valuable records were saved, but the loss of philosophical apparatus and journals was complete and calamitous. The walls of the building stand intact, a sad sight to the lover of science and art. The fire caught in the lofts, from a defective flue, and was not discovered until the chief clerk, W[illiam] J[ones] Rhee, heard the torrents of flames crackling and pouring down from the attics to the floor below.

Washington, February 22, 1865

THE PRESIDENT'S LATEST STORY

President Lincoln likes to relate any good story concerning any of his cabinet officers, and if their dignity has been taken down a trifle he relishes it all the better. He related with great unction how, when Stanton was at Port Royal last month he went up Broad River in a tug with General [John G.] Foster on a reconnoisance. They were hailed by a picket on the bank who inquired who was on board. The reply was, with dignity, "The Secretary of War and Major General Foster." The picket roared back: "We've got major generals enough up here—why don't you bring us up some hardtack?" Stanton's dignity collapsed and Foster conceded that his pickets did not have very large veneration, phrenologically speaking.

A SENATORIAL FUNERAL

Thomas H. Hicks, United States Senator from Maryland, died on February 13, of paralysis. His health had been impaired for a long time owing to a severe attack of erysipelas which supervened just after he met with a slight accident bruising his leg against a carriage step. Amputation was performed, and for the past year and a half the Senator has been in and out of the Senate, assisted by a servant, such was his condition. He had concluded to resign his seat and was to have been collector of Baltimore after March 4; but disease and death intervened; and on February 15 the two houses of Congress assembled in the Senate chamber to pay their last offices of respect, as is the custom when a senator dies during a session of Congress. Eulogies were pronounced in either house by the colleagues of the deceased, and at one o'clock the House of Representatives, headed by the Speaker, Clerk, Sergeant-at-Arms, and Doorkeeper, wearing long white scarfs, entered the Senate chamber, the senators rising to receive them; soon after, the Supreme Court, attired in judicial robes, entered in procession and took seats on the right of the President of the Senate; then the President of the United States and several members of his cabinet quietly stole in by a side door and sat in the center of the chamber. The legislature and governor and council of the state of Maryland then came in, and the mayor and common council of Baltimore and other officials took places within the chamber.

Though the weather was rainy and windy, a large audience filled the galleries and outside corridors. The mournful notes of a military band, resounding through the vast building, announced the arrival of the corpse which was brought in by a guard of honor of Knights Templar in full regalia and preceded by six senators as pallbearers and the senatorial committee. They with the family and colleagues of the deceased occupied seats near the coffin, and the exercises went on. The usual forms of service adopted by the Knights Templar, of which the deceased was a member, were first gone through with, and then the pastor of the Methodist Church, of which Senator Hicks was an attendant, preached a sermon. It was more eulogistic of the successful public man who rose from humble life to be United States Senator than consoling to the bereaved family or admonitory to the late associates of the deceased. The services being over, the procession formed in the great rotunda and accompanied the body to the Congressional Burying Ground where it was placed in temporary burial. The ceremonies, deeply impressive, were the first held in the present Senate chamber, the last senatorial funeral being that of J. Pinckney Henderson of Texas who was buried from the old Senate chamber June 5, 1858, Senators [William H.] Seward and [James M.] Mason being among the pallbearers on that occasion.

Washington, March 12, 1865

EXIT THE THIRTY-EIGHTH CONGRESS

... The night of March 3 was an exciting one at the Capitol, not that there was anything especially exciting in the legislation going forward, but the air was full of the rush and hurry of the occasion; and every point of observation about the halls of Congress was covered with the crowds of sight-seers who had thronged into the city to witness the close of the session and the beginning of a new term of presidential administration. The galleries of the House of Representatives were overflowing with people; and it was almost impossible to pass from the Senate to the House wing, the passages and halls were so full of strangers and citizens promenading, loitering, and humming with curiosity. The great rotunda was a sight to behold, the flood of gaslights from its airy heights pouring down upon a vast throng of well-dressed people slowly circulating around the pictured walls, many, no doubt, thus taking their first glimpse of the national capitol. The lobbies of the House were full of people who were unable to obtain seats in the galleries and were trying to dodge in upon the floor.

About nine o'clock, [George H.] Pendleton offered a resolution that the wives and families of members be admitted to the floor of the House. This was agreed to, and it was the signal for the irruption of a crowd of the fair outsiders, so that soon the floor of the House exhibited the extraordinary spectacle of hosts of nicely dressed ladies cosily seated in among the members, as at an opera, their gay attire and blandishing looks gleaming strangely among the old oaken desks and chairs of the members, who could not pay so rigid attention to the pressing business of the waning hours as was demanded of them. It was eminently fit, however, that the last few hours of the Congress should be distinguished by the same reckless disregard for all of the sterner duties of legislation which has characterized its course from the beginning.

The confusion was excessive, and about nine o'clock the uproar was only something short of Babel. The ayes and noes were called many times when the members did not hear the Clerk, nor could the Clerk, hoarse with bawling the roll, hear the members; the Speaker rapped for order; pages flew about with messages, errands, and various jobs; the members of the Committee on the Enrolled Bills were seated in out-of-the-way corners trying to read over and compare great sheets of parchment bearing what were soon to be the laws of the land rushed through in this indecent manner. Outside of the bar of the House were anxious lobbyists, newspaper men, curious lookers-on, a cabinet officer or two, and seated among the parti-colored throng at the desks were grave senators watching the progress of events and waiting for the passage of some favorite measure from their own branch.

Over all [Speaker] Colfax, patient, watchful, good-tempered, laborious, and impartial, kept watch and ward, bringing order out of chaos, disentangling the disordered web of legislation, ruling the storm, and calming the troubled waters which surged about his seat on high. Later in the night he gave way to E[lihu] B. Washburne who soon bellowed himself hoarse in his imperious efforts to preserve order.

And so the night wore on; bills, which were reckoned as dead, were somehow galvanized into life and lived as laws, while many a healthy child of legislation was nipped untimely and died for want of breath. A moment sufficed to tell the tale, and, sooner than I could write it, a bill was an act or "a dead thing" by the action of the House. In the Senate much the same order or want of order was manifest, though more gravity and decorum, of course, was observed among the "potent, grave, and reverend Seigniors" there assembled. The galleries were crowded with ladies most beautiful to behold. Upon the floor were many of the heads of the departments, prominent public men, and officials. Ever and anon the hardworking and popular Clerk of the House, [Edward] McPherson, appeared at the door of the chamber with his hands full of bills passed by the House but generally strangled by the Senate. In the diplomatic gallery was Mrs. Lincoln, her presidential better half being in the President's Room signing bills with might and main. Mrs. Sprague and Miss Chase, gay and festive in silk attire, were also conspicuous in the ladies' gallery, and other feminine notables were there to see. . . .

At midnight the galleries began to thin out, and the noise diminished; the fair interlopers put on their loves of bonnets and vanished; enrolling clerks flew around with bills seeking the signature of the Speaker or the inspection of the Enrolling Committee; pages improved the departing hours to get the signatures of members in autograph albums or to the parchment duplicates of the constitutional amendment, nearly every member seeking to have one of these interesting momentoes signed by those who voted for the joint resolution. The pages, by the way, do a thriving business in procuring the autographs of members and senators, autograph albums selling well at all the bookstores. [James S.] Brown of Wisconsin tried hard to wind up the House at midnight, quoting Tom Benton to prove that March 3 expired at twelve o'clock midnight, but the Speaker overruled the point, stating that law and usage sanctioned the continuation of the session through the night up to twelve o'clock, March 4, at noon; and so the night wore away, the rush gradually subsiding, the members also subsiding into a series of brief naps, the wakeful ones running the machine, and a quorum being always present.

At daylight a terrible storm broke over the Capitol, and for a moment it seemed as though a tornado had overwhelmed the building; the wind roared and shrieked among the columns; the glass roof thundered with a rattling storm of hail, and the growing daylight was extinguished in a black pall of cloud which covered the angry sky. Members ran, panic-stricken, into the lobbies, and for a moment the confusion was dire, but quiet was soon restored. Shortly after, the House took a recess until nine o'clock in the forenoon, and the hall was still.

INAUGURATION DAY

The weather was dark and drizzly.... Crowds of people kneaded the mud in the streets of Washington and, heedless of tearful skies, stood heroically on guard in front of the Capitol long before ten o'clock in the morning of the momentous 4th. As the hour of noon arrived, flocks of women streamed around the Capitol in most wretched, wretched plight; crinoline was smashed, skirts bedaubed, and moire antique, velvet, laces, and such dry goods were streaked with mud from end to end. Such another dirty crowd probably was never seen, and I must do the fair sex the justice of testifying to their unfailing good nature and the philosophy with which they bore the spoiling of their goods. No greater test of feminine heroism than this could be exacted.

The only entrance to the Senate wing, where the preliminary ceremonies were to be held, was by the main or eastern portico, and the vast flight of marble steps was guarded halfway up by a cordon of soldiers, whose commanding officer harangued the crowd below, ever and anon counseling patience while the rain was falling on the bonnets and velvets of the seething, struggling crowd below. God bless the women! Whatever of harshness has ever mingled in my criticism of them is repented of, when their hearty good nature and patience under great provocation at the Inauguration is held in memory. The epauletted popinjay who acted as Cerberus having received orders to admit the crowd, a small opening in the line was made, and a strong current of ladies, notables, and newspaper men ripped through the gap, surged up the steps, and rushed in the doorway, and diffused itself in all the corridors.

Seated in the reporters' gallery, we found the senators all on one side of their chamber killing time until the hour of noon should come. Soon the doors of the galleries were opened and a crowd of women outside filled the seats like a cloud, presenting a really beautiful sight, every gallery being filled with ladies exclusively. Such a parterre of color and loveliness few ever saw before. All were in full dress—

diamonds flashed, feathers nodded (damply), and bright faces gleamed everywhere. But the noise of feminine tongues was something wonderful to hear. It was like a swarm of bees in summertime hovering over a blossoming apple tree, or a troop of zephyrs chattering among the reeds by the riverside. In vain, Senator Foot, who was in the chair rapped for order; he might as well have talked to the bees or the zephyrs aforesaid; the fair creatures *would not* stop; Senators struggled on in vain with their dry speeches, but they were muted before that rippling storm of small talk in the galleries, and the women actually had not one particle of notion that there was the least impropriety in their permitting their long pent feelings to find vent in words.

Gradually the clamor subsided as the invited notables began to arrive. There was [General] Hooker, handsome, rosy, and gotten up regardless of expense. Then "the dear old Admiral," as the women call Farragut, came stealing in by a side door and subsided into an obscure seat under the burly shadow of Senator [Ira] Harris of New York. Mrs. Lincoln, attended by Senator [Henry B.] Anthony [of Rhode Island], took a seat in the Diplomatic Gallery. Many of the ladies and attachés of foreign embassies were greatly discomposed by one of the ministers of a seven-by-nine European kingdom, whose legs got mixed up in his toggery so that he fell ignominiously downstairs. All of the spectators jumped up and looked disappointed because his ambassadorial head did not break off on the railing and fall into the senatorial pit below.

There was a buzz when the justices of the Supreme Court came in wearing their black robes of office, Chief Justice Chase looking very young, wearing a stovepipe hat, and a long, black silk nightgown (so to speak).... A few stray governors came in and took back seats; then filed in the diplomatic corps, gay birds every one, dressed in gold lace, feathers, and unseasonable white pantaloons. One ambassador was so stiff with gold lace that he could not sit down except with great difficulty and had to unbutton before he could get his feet on the floor. They occupied the seats on the right of the chair, the Supreme Court being in front, and behind were the members of the House who came in procession at noon. Next came the cabinet members who occupied seats in the area on the left of the chair, Seward leading off, followed by Stanton, Welles, Speed, and Dennison. Usher did not come, and Fessenden was in his old seat again. The hour of twelve having arrived, Vice President Hamlin appeared at the main entrance arm-in-arm with Andrew Johnson, the Vice President-elect, who sat at the right of the chair. Hamlin then made the following sensible little speech:

"Senators: Amid these exciting scenes that mark the constitutional termination of this Congress, I ask briefly your indulgence. I assumed the duties of this chair at a period of time unequaled in importance in the history of our country. War of a magnitude unknown in ancient or modern times has devastated the land; measures of deep and vital interest, affecting the very life of the Republic, demanded your investigation; and if amid these stirring scenes, in the chair, by any act of omission or commission, I have wounded the feelings of a single Senator, I take this occasion to ask your indulgent consideration. I know how deeply I am indebted to the Senate. Kindness, and courtesy, and co-operation I have received on all occasions. Whatever of success may have attended my efforts in the discharge of my official duties, I know how deeply I am indebted to the Senate for kindness and co-operation. Permit me to tender to you my undissembled, heartfelt thanks for all your kindness. I shall bear with me in after life a cherished recollection of the associations that have been here formed, and the kindness that has been here bestowed, and I can wish my friend and worthy successor no higher success than that the same relations shall subsist, as I think they will, between him and yourselves.

"Again I thank you for your kindly aid, and for the resolution commendatory of the manner in which the duties of the chair have been discharged; and I tender you my sincere wishes for a safe return to your families and your homes, and for your future welfare and prosperity in life, with the hope that the sun of peace now dawning upon us will soon shed its rays upon a united, a happy, and free people."

Andrew Johnson, Vice President-elect, then stepped in front of the retiring Vice President and began his inaugural address; and I wish that the ungrateful task of an impartial recorder of current events might be given to another, for it must be said that upon that momentous and solemn occasion, where were assembled the good, the brave, the beautiful, the noble of our land, and the representatives of many foreign lands, Andrew Johnson, called to be Vice President of the United States, was in a state of manifest intoxication. I write these words in humiliation of spirit, for what honest American citizen does not feel his cheek tingle with shame at such a recital of the facts? But it cannot be denied, and thousands of outraged witnesses will ever attest the shameful truth.

By the choice of the people, he said, he had been made presiding officer of this body, and might not think it out of place to say right here what a striking thing the Constitution was, as he was presenting himself here in obedience to the behests of the Constitution. It was the Constitution of the people of the country, and here today, before this august assembly, he was proud that he was an American citizen. It was a proud illustration that men could rise from the ranks, under the Constitution, to the proud position of the second place in the gift of the people and of the American government. Those who had labored all their lives for the establishment of free government, as he had, could appreciate its blessings. He would say to senators that they got their power from the people. Then turning to the Supreme Court and addressing himself to Chase, he said: "You, too got your power from the people, whose creature you are." Then he turned upon the cabinet officers, and addressing them as Mr. Stanton, Mr. Seward, etc., he told them the same. Forgetting Welles's name, he said: "And you, too, Mr. ——." Leaning over a person near him he said, "What's the name of the Secretary of the Navy?" and continued as though nothing had happened. He then addressed the foreign ministers and told them that the element of our great strength as a nation was the proximity of the government to the people. "I am going to tell you God's truth," said he. "I am a plebeian; I sprang from the loins of the people, and I thank God for it; and it is strange enough that a plebeian like me should be raised up here to tell you such things as these."

But it is hard to follow the incoherences of this maudlin speech. For twenty minutes he ran on about Tennessee, adjuring senators to do their duty when she sent two senators here, urging that she never was out of the Union, etc. In vain did Hamlin nudge him from behind, audibly reminding him that the hour for the inauguration ceremony had passed. He kept on, though the President of the United States sat before him patiently waiting for his tirade to be over. The study of the faces below was a curiosity; Seward was as bland and serene as summer; Stanton looked like a petrified man; Welles never has any expression; Speed sat with his eyes shut; Dennison was red and white by turns. Among senators, Wilson was as red as a turkey cock, Sumner was smiling, and the rest turned and twisted in long drawn agony. Of the supreme bench [Justice Samuel] Nelson of New York was only moved, apparently, his lower jaw being dropped clean down in blank horror; Chase was marble, adamant, and granite in immobility, until Johnson turned his back to take the oath, when he exchanged glances with Nelson who closed up his mouth.

When Johnson had repeated inaudibly the oath of office, his hand upon the Book, he took it in his hand and facing the audience said loudly, "I kiss this Book in the face of my nation of the United States," which he did with a theatrical gesture. He then repeated, as well as he was able, the long oath of allegiance repeated to him by the ex-Vice President, interpolating such words as "I can say that with perfect propriety" after some of the solemn asseverations of the oath. He then spoke about five minutes upon the nature of the oath which he had just taken, took his seat, and called the Senate to order. Secretary John W. Forney read the proclamation of the President calling an extra session of the Senate, read the names of the senators-elect, and those present came forward and took the usual oath which was administered by Secretary Forney, the Vice President not being in a condition to do it. . . .

The ceremony of swearing in the senators being over, the procession, after some haggling, was formed and proceeded to the temporary platform in front of the Capitol, facing east. . . . The procession from the White House was like the play of *Hamlet* with Hamlet left out (excuse the threadbare illustration), the President having gone up to the Capitol at early morning to sign bills, work which few presidents-elect ever have to do. But as Mrs. Lincoln's carriage headed the procession it was just as well, and the cheering crowd thought that the President was within the vehicle. The procession was long and gay despite the mud, and when it filed into the open space before the Capitol there was no room left for the crowd, which had been kept back until the procession came. When the cortege of the President filed out upon the platform from the rotunda it was followed by a host of spectators from the Senate and passages. Instantly the bases of the columns, the statuary groups, and every coign of vantage swarmed with people. The crash of crinolines was terrific, but vast crowds saw the sight to a good advantage from the great steps of the Capitol, which rose behind the platform and from the wings on either side. Before was a literal sea of heads, tossing and surging, as far as the eye could reach. Cheer upon cheer arose, bands blatted upon the air, and flags waved over all the scene.

The Sergeant-at-Arms of the Senate arose and bowed with his shiny black hat in dumb show before the crowd, which thereupon became still. Abraham Lincoln, rising, tall and gaunt, over the crowd about him stepped forward to read his Inaugural Address printed in two broad columns upon a half-sheet of foolscap. As he rose a great burst of applause shook the air and died far away on the outer fringes of the crowd like a sweeping wave upon the shore. Just then the sun, which had been obscured all day, burst forth in its unclouded meridian splendor and flooded the spectacle with glory and light. Every heart beat quicker at the unexpected omen, and not a few mentally prayed that so might the darkness which has obscured the past four years be now dissipated by the sun of prosperity—

> Till danger's troubled night depart
> And the star of peace return.

The inaugural was well received and well pronounced, every word apparently being audible as the clear, light tones of the President rang out over that vast throng. There was applause at the words: "Both parties deprecated war, but one of them would *make* war rather than let the nation survive, and the other would *accept* war rather than let it perish," and the cheer was injected long enough to make a pause before he said, "And the war came." There was applause at other points, and a long burst when the crowd, with moist eyes, had listened to these noble words which might be printed in letters of gold:

"With malice toward none, with charity for all, with firmness in the right as God gives us to see the right, let us strive on to finish the work we are in, to bind up the nation's wounds, to care for him who shall have borne the battle and for his widow and his orphan, to do all which may achieve and cherish a just and lasting peace among ourselves and with all nations."

Silence restored, the President turned toward Chief Justice Chase, who held up his right hand and his left upon the Book, held up by the Clerk of the Supreme Court, and administered the oath of office, the President laying his right hand upon the open page. Then, solemnly repeating "So help me God!" he bent forward and reverently kissed the Book and rose inaugurated President of the United States for four years from March 4, 1865. A salvo of artillery boomed upon the air, cheer upon cheer arose below, and, after bowing to the assembled host, the President retired within, resumed his carriage, and the procession escorted him back to the White House.

CLOSING SCENES OF THE INAUGURATION

... The last levee of the season at the presidential mansion was the greatest jam ever known in the history of that establishment.... Thousands upon thousands flocked in crowds to see and speak to their beloved Chief Magistrate, and the hard-worked old man, just from the platform of the inauguration, went through the ordeal like a kind-hearted hero, as he is.... Space will not permit me to tell all about the Inauguration Ball. Such a display of laces, jewelry, silks, feathers, gold lace, and things was never seen, no, not since the war began. The President was there, also Mrs. Lincoln, the cabinet, Joe Hooker, Farragut, and such a mob of hungry people that I am ashamed to say that when supper was announced and the bigwigs had fed and gone, they rushed in, pushed the tables from their places, snatched off whole turkeys, loaves of cakes and things, smashed crockery and glassware, spilled oyster and terrapin on each other's heads, ruined costly dresses, tore lace furbelows, made the floor sticky with food, and behaved in the almost invariably shameful manner of a ball-going crowd at supper. The ball was held in the great unoccupied Hall of Patents, Interior Building, and three similar halls were thrown open, making a complete quadrangle of four lighted and decorated halls—a fine sight but all spoiled by the disgusting greediness of this great American people.

Washington, March 22, 1865

WHOLESALE DESERTION

... Every day, about 4 o'clock P.M., soon after the arrival of "the deserters' transport," one meets on the streets squads of brown-faced, long-haired, dirty, moldly-looking men, sometimes numbering forty, fifty, one hundred, or one hundred and fifty deserters from the rebel army; who have taken the oath of allegiance and, "tired of fighting for rich men's niggers," as they phrase it; are sent off up

North to labor in such agricultural districts as chiefly need more laborers. These men are cheerful and appear to be happy enough to get where there is something to eat and a fair chance of earning an honest penny. They are not overintelligent, and their information is not generally worth much to us, but such as it is, it is given honestly and without any dissimulation. Said one of them to me the other day: "You folks needn't have a fight with Old Bob Lee. Just hold on and worry him, as you are doing now, and he ain't going to have anything to fight with." This man was in a North Carolina regiment and was put out on picket with a Virginia regiment set behind to watch them, as is the custom now, the watchword being in rebellion, "Put none but Virginians on guard." But it so happened that the rebel who was sent to watch a rebel was a brother of the sentry on duty, though in a regiment from another state. They came over to our lines together.

Our men fraternize with these deserters from the sinking Confederacy most heartily and one of the most striking commentaries on the oft-repeated statement that men who have fought so bitterly can never be reconciled is afforded by the cordial treatment of these men, lately arrayed in deadly hostility against each other. A Union soldier just out of hospital, hobbling along on crutches, with one leg lost by a rebel bullet at the Petersburg mine, fell into conversation with a rebel deserter near my window the other day, when they mutually discovered that they had both shared in that fight. "What!" exclaimed the Johnny, "was you thar? Well, now, wasn't that just nighly hell? We uns did surelie think that the heavins and yearth was a-comin' together." "You was pretty scared, I guess," retorted Yankee, "but you fought like devils when you got over it." "Well, we did." And the Union boy, whose lost

leg might possibly be charged to the account of "Johnny,"
divided "a chaw of tobaker" with his ancient foe and
hobbled on.

LAME DUCKS

The President says he don't see why, because a man has
been defeated for renomination or re-election for Congress,
he should be returned on his hands, like a lame duck, to
be nursed into something else. But he has managed to take
care of several such, one being John P. Hale [of New-
Hampshire] who, after eighteen years' service in the Senate, packed up his things and got ready to go to Spain
where he has $12,000 per annum. Everybody was sorry
for Hale, not that he was defeated, but that there should
be any good reason—as there was—for his defeat. It was a
great pity that a man who was faithful and true to the
principles of freedom when it cost something to be a disciple should go down under a cloud. Another "lame duck"
is [Morton S.] Wilkinson, late Senator from Minnesota,
whose friends are urging him for the Commissionership
of Indian Affairs. Another is Freeman Clarke of the
Twenty-Eighth (Rochester) District of New York, who
was made Controller of the Currency, *vice* Hugh McCulloch, Secretary of the Treasury. Similar provision had been
made for Ambrose W. Clark of the Twentieth (Water-
town) District of New York, who is appointed consul to
Valparaiso. The few changes which have been made in
foreign appointments have chiefly been made for the benefit of the "lame ducks," though not in that category comes
John Bigelow, made Minister to France, who is an able
diplomatist, a gentleman, and a newspaper man withal,
being formerly editor of the New York *Evening Post*. He

is succeeded in the consulship to Paris by J[ohn] G. Nicolay, formerly private secretary of the President. The new consul does not go out until about June 1.

VARIOUS, DIVERS, AND SUNDRY

The President's health has been worn down by the constant pressure of office seekers and legitimate business, so that for a few days he was obliged to deny himself to all comers. He now rigidly adheres to the rule of closing the doors at three o'clock in the afternoon, receiving only those whom he prefers during the hours of evening. He is considerably better in health now.

Senator [Benjamin F.] Wade and a party of congressmen and their wives have gone on a pleasure trip to Charleston and Wilmington in a government steamer. The economical record in Congress of such men would be worth more if their votes and actions were consistent. The trip will cost the government about $30,000.

Washington, April 6, 1865

THE DOWNFALL OF RICHMOND

... The great news spread like wildfire through the city, the doubted intelligence being speedily made positive by the circulation of thousands of newspaper extras containing the news in the official telegrams. In almost a moment of time the city was ablaze with an excitement the like of which was never seen before. Everybody who had a square of bunting spread it to the breeze, and from one end of Pennsylvania Avenue to the other the air seemed to burn with the bright hues of the flag we love, now made dearer than ever by its bloody baptism and its avenged insults. The sky was shaken with a grand salute of 800 guns, fired by order of the War Department—300 for Petersburg and 500 for Richmond.

Almost by magic the streets were crowded with hosts of people, talking, laughing, hurrahing, and shouting in the fullness of their joy. Men embraced each other, treated each other, made up old quarrels, marched along the streets arm-in-arm, singing or chatting in that happy sort of abandon which characterizes people when they don't care whether school keeps or not. The departments of the government and many stores and private offices closed up for the day, so that hosts of hard-worked clerks had their full share in the unlooked-for holiday. Bands of music paraded the street and boomed and blazed from every public place until the air was resonant with musical expression of the popular joy in all of the national airs. Speechmaking, of course, being a national institution, took a conspicuous place in this impromptu national holiday, and at the hotels and department buildings everybody was called out who could make a speech; and a great many who couldn't make a speech found themselves thrust upon a crowd of enthusiastic sovereigns. One of the best of these offhand speeches extorted by the enthusiastic exigencies of the occasion was that made by Secretary Stanton who was called upon at the War Department by an eager crowd clamorous for more details and a speech. The Secretary, with dignity and unaffected emotion, spoke as follows:

"Friends and fellow citizens: In this great hour of triumph my heart as well as yours is penetrated with gratitude to Almighty God for His deliverance of the nation. [Tremendous and prolonged cheering.] Our thanks are due to the President [cheers]—to the army and navy [cheers]—to the great commanders of sea and land [cheers]—to the gallant officers and men who have periled their lives upon the battlefield and drenched the soil with their blood. [Great cheers.] Henceforth our commiseration and aid should be given to the wounded, the maimed, and the suffering, who bear the marks of their great suffering in the mighty struggle. Let us humbly offer up our thanks to Divine Providence for His care over us and beseech Him to guide and govern us in our duties hereafter—as He has carried us forward to victory, to teach us how to be humble in the midst of triumph; how to be just in our hour of victory, and to help us secure the foundations of this republic, soaked as they have been in blood, so that it shall live forever and ever. [Enthusiastic cheers.] Let us also not forget the laboring millions in other lands, who, in this struggle, have given us their sympathies, their aid, and their prayers; and let us bid them rejoice with us in our great triumph. Then, having done this, let us trust the future to Him, who will guide us, as heretofore, according to His own good will. [Loud cheers.]"

The Secretary then read Grant's dispatch announcing the capture of Richmond and the fact that the city was on fire; upon which the Secretary asked the crowd what they would reply to Grant; some of the crowd cried, "Let her burn!" "Burn it! burn it!" though some said, "Hold Richmond for the Northern mudsills," which sally was received with considerable fun and laughter. Stanton introduced to the crowd Willie Kettles, a bright little Vermont boy about fourteen years of age, an operator in the telegraph room of the War Office and the lucky recipient of the important dispatch announcing the capture of Richmond. Of course, the crowd wanted a speech from the youngster, who only bowed and held his discreet tongue.

Secretary Seward, who was at the War Department to hear the news, was called out, and made a pleasant little

speech in which he said that he had always been in favor
of the change in the cabinet, particularly in the War Department, and that recent events proved that he was right.
"Why," said he, "I started to go to the front, the other
day, and when I got to City Point they told me it was
out to Hatcher's Run, and when I got out there, I am
told it wasn't there, but somewhere else; and when I got
back I am told by the Secretary that it is at Petersburg,
but before I can realize that, I am told again that it is at
Richmond and west of that. Now I leave you to judge what
I ought to think of such a Secretary of War as that.". . .

Senators [James W.] Nye of Nevada, Preston King of
New York, and several others, made speeches from a
building near the War Department and at Willard's
Hotel. Green Clay Smith of Kentucky and General [Ben-
jamin F.] Butler made some good speeches, while Vice
President Johnson made a spirited and dignified address
which measurably eradicated the unfavorable impressions
which his unfortunate inaugural had left in the popular
mind.

The day of jubilee did not end with the nightfall, but
far into the night the rejoicings and merrymakings were
prolonged; many illuminated their houses, bands were still
playing, and five or six regiments of the Veteran Reserve
Corps, which had been parading through the streets all
day, were out in squads, accompanied by their regimental
bands, serenading leading men and public officials. There
are always hosts of people who drown their joys ineffectu-
ally in the flowing bowl, as Richard Swiveller hath it, and
Washington was full of such on April 3. Thousands besieged
the drinking saloons; champagne popped everywhere.
Spirits were up, and a more liquorish crowd was never
seen in Washington; certainly I never saw so many "gay
and festive" men in the whole course of a somewhat

checkered experience. Far into the night and the gray of the early morning, songs, shouts, and yells, the poor expressions of the inward glow, rent the air and afflicted the wakeful ear, while the aching heads and disordered stomachs in Washington next day must have been something wonderful in point of numbers.

THE ILLUMINATION

The recommendation of the Secretary of State that the public buildings be illuminated on the night of April 4 was the signal for a very general lighting up of public and private edifices in Washington. The city was all alight with rockets, fireworks, and illuminations of every description, the streets being one blaze of glory. The War Department, as was fit, was most gorgeously decorated, being a mass of flags and fireworks, the windows filled with lights, and a huge transparency with patriotic devices crowning the portico. The Navy Department, Halleck's office, and the adjacent public offices were appropriately decorated and illuminated; over one portico of the State Department was the motto: "At home Union is Order and Union is Peace; abroad Union is Strength and Strength is Peace." Over another portico was "Peace and Good Will to all Nations, but no entangling alliances and no Foreign Intervention."

The Treasury people had over the Avenue entrance of their building a huge transparency which, in defiance of the law against counterfeiting, was a tolerable imitation of a ten-dollar interest bearing note with a mammoth facsimile of Treasurer [Francis E.] Spinner's signature in all of its unique ugliness. The motto of the design was "U. S. Greenbacks and U. S. Grant—Grant gives the Greenback a metallic ring." Jay Cooke & Company, the famous bankers, had out a big set of transparencies bearing "7–30" and "5–20" in huge characters, with the legend: "The bravery of our Army, the valor of our Navy, sustained by our Treasury upon the faith and subsistence of a patriotic people."

The illumination was very general, especially when one considers how many people in Washington would have gladly lighted their windows at a triumphal entry of "the other fellow," as the President sometimes playfully calls the rebel crew. At the Interior building there was a great mass meeting, the speakers addressing the multitude from the outside steps, a brilliant illumination being all about. Speeches were made by Secretary Usher, Senator [George H.] Williams of Oregon, [Richard] Yates of Illinois, Vice President Johnson, Judge [David Kellogg] Carter of the District Supreme Court, and others, the theme of the evening being chiefly gratitude for our approaching deliverance from a wasting war and our re-establishment as a united nation. But time and patience would fail ere one-half of what was done and said in Washington could be told. Throughout the nation we may presume that the same wave of joy was sweeping—from the bleak shores of Maine to the peaceful sea of the farthest west, save only where the sunny South yet sits in the ashes of desolation, the hour of her humiliation having come.

VARIOUS ITEMS

Secretary Seward was seriously injured yesterday by being thrown from his carriage, breaking his right arm and his jaw. His wounds were promptly dressed, and he is likely to recover as soon as might be expected. . . .

Washington, April 12, 1865

LEE'S SURRENDER—
HOW THE GOOD NEWS CAME TO WASHINGTON

Most people were sleeping soundly in their beds when, at daylight on the rainy morning of April 9, a great boom startled the misty air of Washington, shaking the earth and breaking the windows of the houses about Lafayette Square, compelling the inhabitants once more to say that they would be glad when Union victories were done with or celebrated somewhere else. But boom, boom, boom went the guns until 500 of them were fired. A few people got up and raced around in the mud to see what the news was, and some got up a procession of flags and things, wet as it was. Their ardor was not to be dampened. Others placidly laid abed, well knowing that only one thing yet could raise all this bother, and so comfortaby turned over, breathed a prayer or two, and went to sleep again to dream of guns and drums and men being surrendered to Grant by Robert E. Lee. They awoke betimes to read it in full in the *Morning Chronicle,* for that was Secretary Stanton's way of telling the people at daylight that the great rebel army had laid down its arms and had surrendered to the invincible prowess of the Union legions. . . .

The streets, horribly muddy, were all alive with people, cheering and singing, carrying flags and saluting everybody, hungering and thirsting for speeches. [General] Butler was called out and made a little speech in which he expressed sentiments of toleration towards the rebels. He said he was in favor of disenfranchising the leaders of the rebellion

but believed that the masses of the people should receive
the rights of citizenship as soon as they showed their will-
ingness to submit willingly to federal rule, and acknowledge
unqualified allegiance thereto.

The departments gave another holiday to their employees,
as did many of the stores, and the clerks soon swarmed
in the streets. The Treasury clerks assembled in the great
corridor of the building and sang *Old Hundred* with fine
effect. Then they serenaded the President while at breakfast with *The Star Spangled Banner* and crowded about
the War Department with other songs. The Secretary
declined to make a speech, as he was not well, but he
"detailed" General Halleck for that duty. Halleck said
that he aways obeyed the orders of his superior officer—
except when it came to making stump speeches, which he
was not equal to.

Other speeches were made by distinguished gentlemen,
the crowd, delirious with joy, visiting every cabinet officer
and every man known to be capable of speechmaking.
Later in the forenoon an impromptu procession came up
from the Navy Yard, dragging six boat howitzers which
were fired through the streets as they rolled on; this crowd
soon swelled to a formidable size and filled the whole area
in front of the President's house, where they patiently
waited for a speech, guns firing and bands playing meanwhile. The young hopeful of the house of Lincoln—"Tad"
—made his appearance at the well-known window from
whence the President always speaks. He was received with
a great shout of applause; encouraged, he waved a captured
rebel flag, wherat he was lugged back by the slack of his
trousers by some discreet domestic, amidst the uproarious
cheers of the sovereign people below.

The President soon after made his appearance, and for
a moment the scene was of the wildest confusion; men

fairly yelled with delight, tossed up their hats and screamed like mad. Seen from the windows, the surface of the crowd looked like an agitated sea of hats, faces, and men's arms. Quiet restored, the President briefly congratulated the people on the occasion which had called out such unrestrained enthusiasm and said that as arrangements were being made for a more formal celebration, he would defer his remarks until then, for, said he, "I shall have nothing to say then if it is all dribbled out of me now," whereat the crowd good-humoredly laughed. He alluded to the presence of the band, and said that our adversary had always claimed one good tune—Dixie—but that he held that on April 8 we had fairly captured it—in fact, he said, he had submitted the question to the Attorney General, who had decided that the tune was our lawful property; and he then asked that the band play Dixie, which it did with a will, following with Yankee Doodle. The President then proposed three cheers for General Grant and the officers and men under him, then three for the navy, all of which were heartily given, and the crowd dispersed. . . .

MORE CONGRATULATIONS

After the first ebullitions of joy, the city settled down into comparative quiet, and no demonstration was made until last night, April 11, when the departments were all again illuminated, and the public, more generally than ever before, followed the example. The night was misty, and the exhibition was a very splendid one, the reflection on the moist air of the illuminated dome of the Capitol being especially fine, showing for miles around we have become used to great illuminations here, and there was nothing especially new, the same rush of people, crash and din of bands, and glare of rockets bursting in air, and unending gleam of lighted windows—all these were as before, "only more so."

The notable feature of the evening was the President's speech, delivered to an immense throng of people, who, with bands, banners, and loud huzzas, poured around the familiar avenue in front of the mansion. After repeated calls, loud and enthusiastic, the President appeared at the window, the signal for a great outburst. There was something terrible about the enthusiasm with which the beloved Chief Magistrate was received—cheers upon cheers, wave after wave of applause rolled up, the President modestly standing quiet until it was over. The speech was longer and of a different character from what most people had expected, but it was well received, and it showed that the President had shared in and had considered the same anxieties which the people have had as this struggle drew to a close.

Washington, April 14, 1865

ANOTHER ILLUMINATION

The national capital has certainly had a surfeit of illuminations. We have had—beginning with the fall of Wilmington—no less than five demonstrations of that sort in the city. Good news has come so thick and fast that people have no sooner gotten over one jollification than the occasion for another arrives; the Washingtonians having now become fully equipped with all the needed machinery for the work, the trouble and expense of illumination is comparatively easy and inexpensive, so that this method of celebrating appears to be in a fair way of becoming a chronic disorder.

The illumination of April 11 was a governmental affair, originating with the State Department and spreading to all the national bureaus here and largely participated in by citizens; but the affair last night was initiated by the semi-secesh city government anxious to vindicate the reputation of the municipality whose lukewarmness in such matters had been noted by the city newspapers.

The show was certainly a great success, far eclipsing everything of the sort ever attempted in this country, it is said by those who ought to know. The public buildings were all splendidly illuminated, and there were but few of the stores and dwellings which were not also decorated and in some way made to share in the general exhibition of joy. The whole effect, as witnessed from Arlington Heights, across the river, was very grand, the city being one blaze of light, while fountains of fire were continually spurting up into the cloud of light which seemed to hang over the capital. From that point no object was more remarkable than the Capitol, gemmed with thousands of lights, and the dome, apparently floating in air, outlined by the diminishing curves of the rows of lights which pierced the rounded sides. Arlington House, once the home of General Lee, was decorated and glowed with Union fires, while the people who were once his slaves sang a Song of Jubelo on the lawn, the strains stirring the peaceful shades where the soldiers of the Union, slain by rebel arms, lie tranquilly sleeping near by. We live in strange times.

The War Department was gay and gorgeous with bunting, lamps, transparencies, and calcium lights. So was the Navy Department and the President's house; the former had, among others, these mottoes: "Our iron-clads are a terror to the nations," "Our binnacle lights radiate glory," "U. S. Army, U. S. Navy, U. S. Grant." The latter was the favorite device all over the city. A very unique display was made around the equestrian statue of Jackson on Lafayette Square. A large circle of Bengal lights and colored portfires were set off about the statue, showing off the semicolossal figure in all of its bronze grimness and producing a most beautiful effect as seen through the fresh green foliage of the park. The Treasury building was lighted up as usual and had a big transparency—with an eye to business—of a $50 seven-thirty bond with coupons regularly attached. The Post Office Department had a transparency depicting a pony express rider, with the legend, "Behold I bring you good tidings of great joy.". . . Jay Cooke and Company's marble banking building was magnificently decorated and illuminated and bore immense transparencies in the arched doorways with the following legends: "Response of the loyal people to the cry of traitors—Let us a loan," "Glory to God, who hath to US Grant'd the victory," and "The busy bees—Ballots, Balls, Bonds." All of which were voted good hits.

All of the city buildings were illuminated, even the schoolhouses; and the City Hall, with mammoth mottoes in gas jets, was one of the finer sights in the city. Everywhere the names of Grant, Sherman, Thomas, Sheridan, Farragut, and other heroes of this war were seen in great letters, but it was noted that no name of any commander of the Army of the Potomac was to be seen. "Peace," "Union," and "Victory" were the favorite watchwords everywhere, and if all the people who lighted up such mottoes are sincerely loyal, Washington has been dreadfully slandered. I am very sure that there were not a few illuminated houses and stores the owners of which would have cheerfully eaten every candle that they lighted up if they could have thereby prevented the victory they have celebrated. But we will not cavil at their coerced loyalty; I guess they are glad the war is over, anyhow.

Washington, April 16, 1865

THE GREAT CALAMITY

No living man ever dreamed that it was possible that the intense joy of the nation over the recent happy deliverance from war could be or would be so soon turned to grief more intense and bitter than the nation ever before had known. Just when the national capital was in its brightest garb of joy and while the nation was all pervaded with a generous exaltation, a heavy woe, filling every heart with horror and stiffening once more the relaxing grasp of justice, swept over the land, and all the people stood aghast at the damnable deed which, in our hour of triumph, took away the beloved and revered Chief Magistrate, Abraham Lincoln.

It is hard to realize that he is gone, that we shall no more see his commanding form, hear his kind voice, or touch his pure and honest hand with its well-remembered earnestness. It is hard to take in the dreadful thought that the speaking eye is closed in death, and that the kindly, genial soul has fled, and that the head of the nation has perished by the hand of an assassin; but so it is, and we have only not to reconcile ourselves as a people to the new order of things, gather up the personal recollections of the martyr, commit his mortal remains to the earth, and perpetuate his blessed memory to all coming time.

"THE DEEP DAMNATION OF HIS TAKING-OFF"

At the risk of repeating some things which you have read already, I will present the facts connected with the great crime as gathered from personal observation and from conversation with members of the party who were present at the time the deed was committed. On Friday, April 14, General Grant being in town, the President and the famous General were invited to attend the performance of Laura Keene in *Our American Cousin* at Ford's Theater. The General did not remain in town that night but went on to Philadelphia with his wife, and the President, hearing that the party had been advertised to be at the theater, consented to go rather than that people should be disappointed.

The President was unusually cheerful that evening and never was more hopeful and buoyant concerning the condition of the country. Speaker Colfax and your correspondent were at the house just before he went out for the last time alive, and in his conversation he was full of fun and anecdotes, feeling especially jubilant at the prospect before us. The last words he said as he came out of the carriage were: "Grant thinks that we can reduce the cost of the army establishment at least a half million a day, which, with the reduction of expenditures of the Navy, will soon bring down our national debt to something like decent proportions, and bring our national paper up to a par, or nearly so, with gold; at least so they think." Mrs. Lincoln's carriage was at the door, seated in it being Miss Clara Harris, daughter of Senator [Ira] Harris of New York, and Major [Henry Reed] Rathbone, her stepbrother. The President and wife entered and drove off without any guard or escort.

Ford's Theater is situated on Tenth Street in the central portion of the city, having an alley in the rear which opens upon F Street at right angles with Tenth and on Ninth Street, next above Tenth. On this alley is the stage entrance by which the murderer afterward escaped. The performance had begun when the President and party entered, and their reception caused a suspension of the play, the enthusiasm being unusually great. They took seats in a double box on the right of the stage, as you face the performers, and the door was closed, [John F.] Parker, one of the attendants, first seating the party and then going into the audience, contrary to the custom heretofore; another of the attendants being in the dress circle, where he sat. The box occupied by the President is in the dress circle, having smaller boxes below it and being some fifteen feet above the stage. On the left, as one enters the box from the back, sat Miss Harris, nearest the stage; Mrs. Lincoln sat next on that side, and the President next—those three in a slight curve from the front, the President being almost in the center; opposite, on the right, was a sofa where Major Rathbone sat.

Miss Harris says that when they had been sitting there an hour or more, she saw the door open and a man look in, take a rapid glance at the position of the occupants of the box and go away again, closing the door. This attracted her attention only as being rude, and she thought it some curious person who wanted to look at the President. John Wilkes Booth, a "condemned" actor, had been loitering about the building behind the scenes, and this man was he. Having ascertained that the coast was clear, he went out of the theater by the stage door, which he left open, went around to the front of the theater, ascended to the dress circle, and entered the box. It was now about ten o'clock, two women only were on the stage, and the second scene

of the third act was just begun, when the theater, so often
the scene of a mock tragedy, was made the scene of a real
one of which the world has never seen a parallel since
Caesar was murdered in the Roman Senate.

Miss Harris, hearing the door open a second time, looked
up and saw Booth enter deliberately but rapidly, walk up
behind the President, whose face was turned toward the
audience, and, applying a little pistol exactly under the
left ear, fire. Oh, God! where was Thy providence at that
dreadful instant of time? It was but an instant, and, dropping his pistol, the murderer flashed out a knife, slashed
at Rathbone, and sprang over the edge of the box in front.
The audience had heard the report of the pistol but did not
notice it, as it was very likely to be supposed a part of the
stage business. But a sudden movement caused them to
look up, and there was a marble face, a pair of glittering
black eyes, and a flashing knife as Booth paused on the
gilded cornice of the proscenium long enough to shout "Sic
semper tyrannis!" Then he dropped on the stage, falling
upon his knees, but, quickly recovering himself, he marched
across the stage to the left with that stagy, stilted stride
peculiar to his class of actors, shouting "Revenge for the
South!" as he went.

Gaining the first stage entrance, left side, Booth pushed
aside Miss Keene who was about to enter, met an attaché
of the theater, whose coat he slashed open with his knife,
dashed out of the door which he had left open, mounted
his horse, which a boy had been holding for him, and clat-
tered out into the night, bearing with him the mark of
Cain which will brand him to the day of his death. All of
this happened in a moment of time, and so completely
paralyzed was every person that it was an easy thing for
the wretch to flee almost unpursued; one man only, a lawyer [J. B. Stewart] in this city, had a dim idea of what had

happened, and leaping on the stage he pursued Booth into the alley, saw him knock down the boy who held the horse, mount, and ride away into the darkness of the streets.

When the audience was roused by the piercing screams of Mrs. Lincoln it rushed upon the stage with shouts of "hang him! hang him!" and for a space all was confusion. Miss Harris first recovered herself, and leaning over the box, asked for water. Miss Keene went up, surgeons were on the spot, and everything was done that could be done to recall the bleeding, dying President to life. Mrs. Lincoln on hearing the report had turned, when to her horror she saw the head of her husband fall forward on his breast. He was laid on the sofa at once but breathing only with difficulty and rattling in his throat. He never spoke or gave any sign of consciousness. The ball had gone clear through the skull, glancing obliquely across the brain and lodging under the right eye where a great discoloration settled. He was removed to a private house opposite, and instantly mounted couriers were scouring the city; horsemen galloped to and fro; the patrol encircled the city, which was in a state of terror and alarm. Guards kept the people out of the street where the President lay dying, but crowds, anxious, tearful, and enraged, besieged the place all through the night.

ANOTHER HORROR

At the same moment of time when this bloody deed was transpiring at the theater a man rang the doorbell at Secretary Seward's house and said to the servant that he had a prescription from Dr. Verdi, Seward's family physician, which he must deliver in person; the servant said it could not be done, when the man pushed him aside and ran heavily upstairs to the third story where the Secretary lay in bed, suffering under his late injuries. Seizing the poor man with one hand, he stabbed at his throat cutting his neck and jaws in several places; Augustus Seward and three other persons were in the room, and they threw themselves upon the miscreant who stabbed them all, mortally wounding a male nurse who was stabbed through the lungs. Making for the door he was met by Frederick Seward, Acting Secretary of State, who tried to head him off, but the assassin knocked him down with a heavy blow from a "billy" or club, left him senseless, and dashed downstairs, mounted his horse, which was standing at the door, and he too escaped into the night. The Secretary is very weak from loss of blood, but no one of the wounds is in itself mortal. Fred Seward's skull is fractured, and his recovery is doubtful. The nurse cannot get well. . . .

"THE LAST OF EARTH"

Through the dreadful night which followed, the slow and labored breath of the dying President grew feebler and feebler. He lay upon a bed in an upper chamber, surrounded by the members of the cabinet—Seward, only, absent. General Halleck, Quartermaster Meigs, Chief Justice Chase, Senator Sumner, Speaker Colfax, several distinguished physicians, and the Surgeon General being in attendance. In an adjoining room was Mrs. Lincoln, attended by her son, Captain Robert Lincoln, Major Hay (private secretary), Miss Harris, Major Rathbone (who was severely cut in the arm), and one or two intimate friends of the family. Several times during the night Mrs. Lincoln, who was at times calm and composed and at times delirious, visited the chamber where the President lay, but she could gain no satisfaction, as he was past recognizing anybody. The agony of those long, dark hours can never be estimated, and we drop a curtain over the piteous tragedy.

From the first there was no hope, and the pulse which at midnight fluttered at forty-eight, rallied slowly until half-past one o'clock, when it stood at ninety-five; from this time, however, it declined steadily, and at twenty-two minutes past seven o'clock in the morning he was dead. The long labor of life was ended, and the loving, noble heart was forever still. The Reverend Dr. [Phineas D.] Gurley of the New York Avenue Presbyterian Church had prayed by the bedside of the dying man, and he now prayed in the death chamber, surrounded by strong men who wept like children. The same devotions were had in the chamber with the mourning family, and in an hour or two the corpse, covered by the flag and escorted by a guard of honor and followed by the officers present, was carried back to the White House.

THE POPULAR FEELING

No pen can accurately describe the mingled feeling of sorrow, wrath, horror, and indignation which seized upon the people as soon as the doleful tidings spread through the city. From lip to lip the tale of horror flew; men and women went weeping about the streets; no loud voice was anywhere heard; even children's prattle was hushed; gloom, sadness, and mourning sat on every countenance. To adopt the eloquent language of one of the morning journals: "If tears had audible language, a shriek would go up from these States which would startle the world from its propriety. Strong men use the impressive language of women— tears. Women bow their heads in the dust. Children sleep troubledly. Words are weak and vain."

Flags were raised at half-mast everywhere. The bells tolled solemnly, and, with wonderful swiftness, the whole city went into deep and universal mourning. All stores, government departments, and offices were closed. The hum of driving wheels and busy engines ceased. Everywhere, on proud residences and on humble hovels, waved the black badges of mourning. Nature seemed to sympathize in the general grief, and tears of rain fell from the moist, dark sky, while the wind sighed mournfully through the streets, crowded with sad-faced people and broad folds of black flapped heavily in the wind over the decorations of yesterday's rejoicings. Far and wide flashed the sore tidings, carrying real grief to millions of American homes; and from sea to sea a smitten nation wept in agony over the announcement that God had taken away from earth forever Abraham Lincoln.

THE NEW PRESIDENT

... President Lincoln died shortly after seven in the morning.... At about nine o'clock, Attorney General Speed waited upon Vice President Johnson at the Kirkwood House and gave him an official announcement of the fact, signed by all of the members of the cabinet, and asking him to name the time when he could assume the duties of the office which, under the Constitution, now devolved upon him. He replied that he was ready as soon as it was deemed expedient. At eleven o'clock the cabinet assembled at Johnson's room. The oath of office was administered by Chief Justice Chase, and Andrew Johnson spoke a few solemn words as his brief inaugural as President of the United States. May God give him grace and wisdom to discharge rightly the duties of the office laid upon him at a time and in a manner whose solemn circumstances are without a parallel in the history of the world.

The chief fault of our lamented Lincoln was alleged to be his leniency toward criminals in treason. That can never be true of Andrew Johnson, and rebels everywhere will find to their cost that the cowardly assassination of Lincoln has nerved the people to a demand that his successor shall do a great deal of hanging to expiate the great crime which they have committed. The favorite resort of bullying "Southern chivalry," dark and cowardly assassination, has brought upon that hated gang of fearful retribution. We cannot tell where it will begin or end, but the people, blind with rage, demand a bloody sacrifice and will have it.

A SORROWFUL SUNDAY

This has been a gloomy day in Washington, and it has been remarked that the churches were never as full as on this day, when all hearts were naturally softened by this great national grief and turned toward the Head of Nations over us all with His inscrutable providences. At the New York Avenue Presbyterian Church, where the President was a regular attendant, the services were peculiarly impressive. The church was draped in mourning, and the well-known pew of the Lincoln family, vacant and robed in sable crepe, spoke mutely to the great congregation of him that was gone. The dirge-like music, the earnest prayer, and the solemn lesson inculcated by the preacher all made the service one which will be long remembered by those who heard it. In all of the churches some reference was made to the afflictive event, and everywhere one could see that the sadness of the people was something more than that of a passing hour.

SOME PERSONAL REMINISCENCES

While your correspondent would not obtrude my private grief upon the public attention, I cannot help saying here that I knew and loved Abraham Lincoln well. It was my good fortune to make his acquaintance years ago, during the early days of Republicanism in Illinois, and since my sojourn in Washington that early acquaintance has ripened into intimacy near and confiding. This enables me to testify to his unspotted integrity, his thoughtful kindness for everybody, his unselfish modesty, his genial heartiness, his sagacity, shrewdness, and his knowledge of human nature. Often when I would ask favor for some pool soldier or friendless, deserving youth, he would give his whole attention to the matter, as though that were his most important business on hand, and he would laughingly say: "It seems to me you have a knack for picking up just such cases that nobody else thinks of." Then, with all his geniality, which sometimes broadened into joviality, he was pervaded with a solemn sense of his obligations as a Christian magistrate, which never forsook him. He was a praying man and daily sought from God that aid which he had long since learned man could not give him. With great natural shrewdness and sagacity, he had a transparent simplicity which endeared him to all who met him. It is notable that those who knew him best loved him best, and those who had at a distance been hostile to him were disarmed when they came to know the man.

I could fill columns reciting the peculiarities and the virtues of this most extraordinary man raised by God for this special work, which being accomplished, he has gone to his everlasting reward. It seems cruel that so good and so kind a man should fall in such a dreadful way, but some wise purpose was overall, and it is some comfort at least to know that he passed away without a pang of mental or bodily anguish. He left behind him a smitten household, a knot of weeping friends, and a bowed and mourning nation, but he

> ... Passed through Glory's morning-gate,
> And walked in Paradise.

A martyr to the national cause, his monument will be a nation saved, a race delivered, and his memory shall be cherished wherever Liberty hath a home, "To the last syllable of recorded time."

Washington, April 20, 1865

LYING IN STATE

On the night of April 17 the remains were laid in the coffin prepared for their reception and taken from the guest chamber where they had lain to the East Room, famous as the great public drawing room where so many brilliant receptions and levees have been given and where Harrison, Taylor, and Ellsworth were laid in state. The room was on the occasion draped in deepest mourning, the chandeliers and lusters covered with crepe, the mirrors and paintings hanging with black barège, and the columns and pilasters with black cloth, supported by four pillars and lined with fluted white silk. From the edges of the canopy heavy curtains of black fine cloth were draped, being looped back at the corners and adding a gloom to the dear face lying within. The richly ornamented coffin was about five feet from the floor and was reached by two dais-like steps which formed the base of the structure. The whole was covered with fine black broadcloth and was relieved only by the green and white masses of flowers— the loving tribute of many friends.

A cross of white camelias, a gift from a Roman Catholic college, lay at the head, and an anchor of white roses, sent from New York, attracted attention. Upon the upper face of the coffin a bouquet of myrtle with a single camelia was laid by the California delegation. From the time the body was ready for sepulture it has been watched night and day by a guard of one major general, one brigadier, two field officers, four line officers, and four naval officers. On the morning of the day of lying in state, before the public was admitted, the scene was most solemn and impressive. Oppressive silence pervaded the mansion, and there, within the room where every sojourner at the national capital has seen so much of youth, brilliancy, life, and pride of life, all that remained of one of the great ones of the earth lay rigid within the somber shades of his funeral canopy. The voice of music and mirth had fled. Even the cheerful light of day was excluded. The eyes were oppressed with the great cloud of blackness which pervaded the temporary habitation of death. At the head, foot, and either side of their dead chief stood the motionless figures of the armed warriors who had risked life on so many a hard fought battlefield and were now to stand guard over the coffin of one who had been slain by a secret foe in the midst of his years, his enjoyments, and his friends. How apt the closing words now of a poem which was the President's greatest favorite and which he had committed to memory:

'Tis the wink of an eye, 'tis the draught of a breath
From the blossom of health to the paleness of death,
From the gilded saloon to the bier and the shroud—
O why should the spirit of mortal be proud?

The gates were opened to the public at eleven o'clock in the forenoon, but long before that hour a vast crowd assembled outside, and a long train, five or six deep, extended from the gates to the Potomac front of the Treasury Department, being the distance of two sides of an entire block. The pressure was excessive and continued until five o'clock when the gates were closed and thousands were deprived of the sad satisfaction of looking once more upon the features of him who had in life so won the affections of the people that in death he was more sincerely lamented than any public man of these times or of this nation. The demeanor of those who visited the corpse was remarkable for the deep solemnity and sorrow which sat on every countenance. Many—men and women—involuntarily burst into tears when they suddenly looked upon the familiar features of their beloved Chief Magistrate, lying so calmly and yet so naturally pleasant within his coffin, and those who went away, sobbing, will never forget that placid brow, the smiling mouth, and the murder-scarred eyes of him whom a nation delighted to honor and whom a nation mourns.

THE OBSEQUIES

Yesterday, April 19, always a memorable day in our history, the funeral took place, the services being in the East Room. . . . The floor had been transformed into an ampitheater by the erection of an inclined platform broken into steps and filling all but the entrance side of the room and the area about the catafalque. This platform was covered with black cloth, and upon it stood the various persons designated as participants in the ceremonies. . . .

On the east side of the coffin, which lay north and south,

opposite the grand entrance, stood Andrew Johnson, President of the United States, looking five years older than when he came to Washington on March 3. His faithful friend, [Senator] Preston King, stood to one side and ex-Vice President Hamlin on the other. Just behind was Chief Justice Chase and one or two associate justices, and near them were the members of the cabinet and their wives, all of whom were in deep mourning. On the right of the cabinet was the only relief to all the somber monotony of the room, being the diplomatic corps whose gay costumes gleamed in strange contrast with all of the black robes and drapery about them.

Next came the House of Representatives and Senate, many members of which were present, all of whom were within reach of coming back to assist the ceremony. The rest of the room was occupied by the clergy, delegations of various city authorities, and delegations from several states. At the foot of the catafalque was a semicircle of chairs for the family and friends, but Robert Lincoln, son of the President, was the only one of the family present, Mrs. Lincoln being unable to leave her room on account of nervous prostration superadded to a slight fever. General Grant sat at the head of the coffin and was often moved very deeply by the solemn services....

THE FUNERAL PAGEANT

Long before the services were over the streets were blocked by crowds of people thronging to see the procession which moved precisely at two o'clock amidst the tolling of bells and the boom of minute guns from three batteries in the city and from all the forts around Washington. The sight will probably never be forgotten by any who saw it. The solemn grandeur of the occasion, the beauty of the cloudless sky, and the marvelous length of the pageant made it a spectacle unequaled. It was estimated to be nearly four miles long, and when you imagine this distance filled by regiments of cavalry, infantry, and artillery, mourners, associations, and societies, waving with draped banners and accompanied in their slow march by mournful dirges by innumerable bands, you can form some idea of the procession.

The Ninth and Tenth Regiments of Veteran Reserves headed the column; next came a battalion of marines in splendid uniform; then the Sixteenth New York and Eighth Illinois Cavalry Regiments; and then the Eighth United States Artillery (regular) in all the pomp and panoply peculiar to that branch of the regular service; next were several generals, mounted and accompanied by their staffs; then came naval officers on foot by the hundreds, army officers in like numbers, and more mounted officers; the pallbearers rode in carriages behind the funeral car, a large structure canopied and covered with black cloth but rather cheap and paltry in effect. The coffin was laid on a high platform eight or ten feet above the ground, and as it passed in view many shed tears and all heads were uncovered. The car was drawn by six gray horses led by grooms and was guarded by the First Virginia Artillery, on foot, and the President's body guard (cavalry), also on foot. Next came the carriages of the family, and then both the houses of Congress, preceded by the President, cabinet, and diplomatic corps. The procession was filled up by associations, delegations, fire companies, aid societies, military bands, clerks, and citizens beyond computation.

Such a sight was probably never before witnessed upon the continent, and all were gratified that the best beloved of the American people should be so honored in his burial. Living, he disliked and avoided display, but his people had their wish in the pomp and circumstance of the obsequies of Abraham Lincoln, the simple-hearted and simple-mannered President. A noticeable feature of the procession was the appearance of the colored societies which brought up the rear, humbly as is their wont. These colored people were out in great numbers as Masons, Odd Fellows, Sons of Temperance, and mutual benefit societies, and a general remark was made upon their respectful and respectable appearance. Well-dressed and sober in their deportment, one could not help feeling for them a respect which was enhanced by the reflection that they at least were sincere mourners of him whom they were carrying to the grave with all this long parade and pageantry of death. It was fitting that these emancipated men should be conspicuous in the obsequies of the great Emancipator.

The coffin was taken from the funeral car and placed within the rotunda of the Capitol which had been darkened and draped in mourning and a catafalque erected for the reception of the remains. Then the procession disbanded and the vast assemblages gradually dispersed. Today the coffin is open, and a great crowd has been passing through the rotunda, looking upon the face of the President as he lies in his coffin.

THE FAMILY OF THE DECEASED PRESIDENT

Mrs. Lincoln and her two sons remain at the White House at present, Mrs. Lincoln's health not permitting her to leave just yet. The President will occupy the office part of the mansion, but has kindly informed the present occupant that she can retain use of the family portion all summer if she chooses, as his own family arrangements are uncertain, and he is alone here now. Mrs. Johnson's health is broken, and it is supposed that the lady at the head of the household will be a married daughter of the new President, Mrs. [Mary] Stover, a widow whose husband was killed in battle last summer. Mrs. Lincoln has been invited by several members of the cabinet to make her home with them while she chooses to remain here, but she will go west as soon as she is able and will live hereafter in Chicago. President Lincoln left his family in anything but easy circumstances, as he had but little more than a modest homestead when he was elected, and the great expenses of the White House have absorbed nearly all of his official salary which has not been increased with the increased cost of living. . . .

THE SEWARD FAMILY

All of the wounded in the Seward mansion are slowly recovering—even Fred Seward who was at first thought to be mortally wounded. . . . The vitality of the elder Seward, who is now quite old, is amazing, reduced as he was by low diet and loss of blood; he was stabbed no less than seven times in the neck, face, and shoulders and yet lives. It is thought that the excitement and violence of that dreadful night had the effect to bring on a reaction of the system which the surgeon had in vain endeavored to produce. He promises to live and be of use for years to come.

It was a singular and touching manner in which Seward came to know of the President's death. He had been kept in ignorance of the attack on the President, his physicians fearing that the shock would be too great for him to bear, and all the newspapers were rigidly excluded from his room. On the Sunday following the assassination, the Secretary had his bed wheeled around so that he could see the tops of the trees in the park opposite, just putting on their spring foliage, when his eye caught the stars and stripes at halfmast on the War Department, on which he gazed awhile, then, turning to his attendant, he said: "The President is dead." The attendant stammered and changed color as he tried to say nay, but the sagacious old man said: "If he had been alive he would have been the first to call on me; but he has not been here, nor has he sent to know how I am, and there's the flag at halfmast." The old statesman's inductive reasoning had told the truth, and he lay in silence, the great tears coursing down his gashed cheeks, and the dreadful truth sinking into his mind.

Washington, April 24, 1865

PRESIDENT JOHNSON

Has been overwhelmed with deputations and delegations who have waited upon him to tender him their support and to make and receive speeches. This has continued until it has come to be very like a bore, and people are weary of the speeches if Johnson is not. But on the whole, the new President grows in popular favor, and he shows an earnest desire to do his whole duty by the people, without fear or favor. No man appears to be likely to "run" Johnson any more than they did Lincoln, who was probably the most independent man in the presidential office since the days of Jackson. Preston King of New York took Andrew Johnson under his wing immediately after his unfortunate inaugural in March and has never left him since, day or night. Wherever you see the President now you will always see the rotund form of King, who is a sagacious, coolheaded, and upright man whose influence over Andrew Johnson, whatever it is, will be for good.

For the present the President has his quarters at the Treasury building, occupying the fine, nearby house of Samuel Hooper of Massachusetts, that gentleman having given the use of it as long as he likes. He walks to and from his office, attended only by King and a single military officer, two armed soldiers walking a few steps in the rear. Every loyal heart will pray that God may spare Andrew Johnson's life and give him the wisdom and the strength which he needs in his high office. The lapse of March 4 is now understood to have been only a temporary and single departure. The disgrace will not be repeated.

Washington, April 27, 1865

A RADICAL PRESIDENT

It is an interesting study to watch the Radicals, who appear to think there is some probability that they have drawn an elephant in their Radical President. When the late President was alive they omitted no opportunity for criticism and no chance which promised success to an attack was neglected. Lincoln was accused of slowness, conservatism, desire to retrace his steps, and "lack of blood;" and industrious opposition in the ranks of his own party, small but virulent, was endeavoring to create a wider division than ever before, bringing up Negro suffrage and reconstruction as the issues upon which the Union Party must be divided. All this is changed; the blow which plunged the nation in grief, by removing him whose unbounded hold on the people baffled the politicians, placed at the head of the nation a man whose utterances and supposed views had been applauded to the echo and quoted admiringly to Radicals when he was as far from being President, seemingly, as he ever was. In a single day Abraham Lincoln, the man whom they feared and disliked, was removed beyond the reach of their political designs, and Andrew Johnson, a citizen of a border state, an anti-Conservative, and a disciple of Negro suffrage, reigns in his stead.

Now that the Radicals have their President, however, they are not altogether satisfied. Lincoln used to say that the responsibilities of office had the effect to make men conservative, and Johnson's friends begin to fear that such will be the result upon him. There are now several little cliques of the ultra men who are attempting to get control of the President, just as some such men tried to get control of Lincoln when he came into office. It remains to be seen into whose hands Johnson will fall, or whether he will, like Lincoln, offend and anger those who are thereby to be made his opponents by refusing to be controlled by any. Certain it is, however, that the men who are near the new President and who have any designs upon him at all are those whom we are wont to call Radical; they will at least nominally have the control of the administration. It will afford us, who have stood by the former President against captious criticism and ill-natured attacks, some sort of satisfaction to see how they will manage matters with their former champion, who is radical if nothing else.

Many think that if Seward should recover and stay in the cabinet, he will virtually control Johnson. Seward is sagacious and sound, but Preston King would like his place and is at work to secure it. It should not be understood that any new feud is likely to arise from the sudden change in the presidency. On the contrary, Johnson, a Radical, a Southerner, an old-time Democrat, an outspoken friend of the people, and an ardent friend of popular right, will, it is thought, so administer the government that there will be no chance for a new party to be formed out of the Union organization, unless it may be that Negro suffrage shall be prematurely precipitated on the people. We must come to that but not at once or without some popular education therefor.

"AS JOHNNY COMES MARCHING HOME"

Quite a sensation was created on the streets yesterday by the appearance of the Ninth Corps, formerly Burnside's but now commanded by [Major General John G.] Parke, which passed through the city to the outskirts of George-town, where the warworn veterans went into camp preparatory to being mustered out of the service. It is now nearly a year since this same corps marched through Washington from Annapolis, then about 20,000 strong, and soon after formed a contingent of the Army of the Potomac. . . .

Brown, dusty, warworn, the veterans looked the personification of fighting men come home from the wars. There were flagstaffs preserved from rebel desecration, the shreds of ancient flags, as loved as life, still fluttering in the wind, trophies of victory and signs of hard conflict. No honest heart could behold them without the old tender feeling of respect which we must always have for the soldier who has risked his life upon the field of battle for the things which we are daily thankful for—union, safety, and peace. Yet the boys do not seem to be at all cast down or sobered by their hardships or by the reflection that their ranks are greatly thinned by the loss of those whose graves ridge many a field between the Potomac and Richmond. They trudged along quietly enough but ready to break out into a joke upon occasion. A spruce-looking veteran reserve man driving in a buggy with a young lady was hailed with, "Say, Towney, how's yer gal?" or "How are you, dead beat?" a term of reproach cast upon the invalids by the active soldiers. The rear of the column was brought up by the baggage wagons. In some I saw old-fashioned bureaus, chests, etc., the booty of Petersburg or another rebel town. One soldier had a savage bull terrier chained to his belt. In a knot of men on a wagon of forage was a sheep tranquilly reposing among his friends and blinking at the unusual spectacle of Washington streets.

Washington, May 17, 1865

THE NEW ADMINISTRATION

... Whatever may have been the apprehensions of the people who knew the circumstances attending Johnson's inauguration as Vice President, all now seem to be convinced that no ground for such apprehensions exists any longer. The President looks bright, fresh, and clear and gives great satisfaction in his prompt discharge of business. From a member of his cabinet I learn that he disposes of business about fifteen times more rapidly than did our late President whose ways were such that he had to consume a great deal of time in every interview he had. President Johnson has his secretary take down the opinion of every member of his cabinet upon every question submitted, and each member has to give his opinion when a regular sitting is held. It is not likely that Stanton will remain in the cabinet until the next session of Congress begins.

THE LINCOLN FAMILY

Yet remains in Washington but will leave for the west early next week. Mrs. Lincoln's health has been comparatively restored, and nearly all of the preparations for departure have been made. No President ever received so many tokens of good will from the people as did our late lamented Lincoln; and these gifts, packed for transportation, comprise more than two carloads of bulky boxes—a single set of dinnerware being large enough to require three hogsheads in packing. This was a gift from a Philadelphia gentleman who had the ware made to order, the Lincoln initials being beautifully emblazoned thereon in a monogram. There are gifts of paintings, photographs, statuary, and other works of art and virtue, some of them very beautiful and so numerous that Mrs. Lincoln intends to have a sort of museum attached to her future residence, so that all persons may see these gifts under proper restrictions and regulations.

The private papers of the late President have been sealed up by Robert Lincoln, the oldest son of the President, and he intends to publish them after a considerable lapse of time shall have passed—not before three or four years. Then he will merely spread before the world the letters of his father, arranged in some order, with brief annotations, leaving the material to future historians or biographers to arrange at their own convenience. The correspondence which the President kept in his own hands was not large, comparatively speaking, the whole accumulation of four years being in a set of pigeonholes and locked up in his room in a case about three-by-five feet in dimension. The pigeonholes were lettered in his own hand, alphabetically, different compartments being allotted to a few such prominent men as McClellan, Grant, "Father Blair," Horace Greeley, and Halleck. One pigeonhole was lettered "Weed and Wood," being for Thurlow and Fernando of that name. Lincoln's name will never suffer from the publication of these letters and answers filed away together. But the friends of a few men who now fill a large space in public esteem will have occasion to blush when they know some things concerning their favorites.

The surviving children of Abraham Lincoln are Robert and Thomas, the first of whom is about twenty-three years old, a graduate of Harvard College and a young man of modest and agreeable manners, quiet and with a very good share of his father's sagacity and kindness. The youngest son is a little more than eleven years old and was nicknamed "Tad" by his father when a small boy. The nickname was an abbreviation of "tadpole," the youngster reminding his father of that creature in his short, dumpy shape. The President was passionately attached to his boys and seldom went anywhere without "Tad," of whom he told me an amusing anecdote on the last election day. About a year before a live turkey had been brought home for the Christmas dinner, but "Tad" interceded in behalf of its life and carried the case up to the executive chamber, securing a stay of proceedings until his father could be heard from. The argument was that the turkey had as good a right to live as anybody else. His plea was admitted and the turkey's life spared. The soldiers on duty about the house made a pet of the bird, and on last election day the boy came tearfully into his father's room to call his attention to the fact that the soldiers were voting. Noticing the

turkey among them, the President asked "Tad" if the
turkey was voting, too. The boy promptly responded, "Oh,
no. He isn't of age yet!" The indulgent father thought
that reply was a great deal better than many of the so-called
Lincoln stories.

Washington, May 22, 1865

A GLIMPSE AT THE CONSPIRATORS

One of the most interesting places of resort in Washington at this time is the courtroom of the eight conspirators
arraigned for being concerned in the plot against the lives
of the heads of government. . . . For the sake of looking
at the proceedings and describing the villains on trial, I
went down to the court the other day and found my way
past sentries posted all along the street leading from the
main avenue of the city to the penitentiary where the trial
is held. The penitentiary building is attached to the great
United States arsenal establishment on the banks of the
Potomac in the suburbs of the city.

Entering an old-fashioned brick building, we were shown
into a plain room where sat a couple of staff officers receiving the cards or credentials of persons applying for
admission and sending the same up to the court where
an officer inspected them and returned them with the
requisite pass. Being under the convoy of a United States
senator, our party had no difficulty in procuring admission,
and we soon passed up a narrow flight of stairs to a small
chamber in the second story where a knot of orderlies were
lounging about. Our pass being inspected, we went up
another flight of stairs and entered the courtroom, which
is in the third story.

Here was a room about twenty-five feet wide and thirty
feet long, the entrance being at the end. Looking up the
room, we saw that it was divided lengthwise into two parts,
the right being occupied by the court, sitting around a
long, green-covered table, [Major] General [David] Hunter
sitting at the hither end and Judge Advocate [Joseph] Holt
on the farther extremity with his assistants close by. The
left side of the room was taken up with seats for reporters,
of whom about twenty-five were in attendance, and the
spectators generally, who were crowded confusedly about
and against the bare white walls of the room. At the farther
end of the apartment was a wooden railing, behind which,
on a narrow, raised platform sat the accused men, all in a
solemn row, with an armed soldier sitting between every
two prisoners. At the left corner, behind the rail, was a
heavy, iron-studded door opening into the corridor along
which are the cells of these manacled prisoners. Each man
has his feet chained by manacles connected by a chain
about a foot long, and his hands are in similar iron cuffs
kept apart by a stiff iron bar about ten inches long. Thus
securely fettered, they sit grimly against the wall, facing
the court and witnesses, the witness stand being a raised
box in the center of the room.

. . . Inside the railing on the left sits Mrs. [Mary G.]
Surratt, deeply veiled, with her face to the wall, slowly
fanning herself and never raising her head except when
commanded to show her face for the purpose of identifi-
cation. She is dark-looking, fleshy, placid, and about forty-
five years old. She is accused of being privy to the whole
plot, assisting Booth before and after the assassination.
[David E.] Herold is a small, dark man about twenty
years of age, with a low forehead, scanty black hair on his
face, stooping figure, and a sottish expression generally,
only his small, deep-set black eyes serving to light up his

vulgar face. He sits doubled up, never taking his eyes off the court, and wears a painfully anxious and watchful expression. Herold was Booth's man Friday in all his movements, leaving him only when he was burnt out, like a rat, from the barn.

Next is [Lewis] Payne, the assassin detailed for the murder of Secretary Seward. He sits bolt upright against the wall, looming up like a young giant above the others. Payne has a face in which good and bad are mixed. Determination and courage are evident, and if his coarse, black hair were well brushed off his broad, low forehead, he might pass for a good-looking young man. His eyes are large, dark, and piercing; his hair hangs across his right temple, and he sits with his firm-set mouth never changing expression at any time. His chest is brawny and muscular, and as he has nothing on the upper part of his body but a dark, close fitting undershirt, his appearance is striking. Payne is apparently not much over twenty-four, and his face, figure, and bearing bespeak him the powerful, resolute villain that he proved himself to be. It was curious to see the little gleam of intelligence which involuntarily shot from his eyes when the knife with which he did the bloody work was brought in and identified by the Negro who found it in the street near Seward's house in the gray dawn of the morning after that dreadful night. The knife is a heavy, horn-handled affair with a double edge at the point and a blade about ten inches long and thick at the back. Payne evidently recognized his tool.

The low, cunning man who sits next is [George A.] Atzerodt, detailed to murder the Vice President, but whose heart failed him when the time came to strike. This fellow has the meanest face of the whole crowd. He is small but sinewy, has long, dark brown hair, dark blue, unsteady eyes, a receding narrow chin, under which is a little light hair, and he wears a lightish, curling mustache. This villain has wickedness and meanness written all over his face. He will be the man to confess, if confession will avail him aught, and he will lie, if lying will swear away the life of his fellows and save him his own. He keeps an anxious face on all the proceedings and never smiles when any ludicrous incident disturbs the court, as do the others as if they make haste to show their unconcern.

[Michael] O'Laughlin, supposed to have been set apart for the murder of Stanton or Grant, sits next. He wears all the aspect of the traditional stage villain made up for the occasion. He has a high, broad forehead, a mass of black, tangled hair, a heavy black mustache and tuft on his chin, and his face is blackened by a rough, unshaven beard. His large eyes, black and wild, are never still but take in everything within the room, scanning the people who come in, watching the witnesses, and occasionally resting on the green trees and sunny sky to be seen through the grated window on the right. He moves his feet, his manacles clank, and, recalled to his place, he looks down at his feet and then back and forth at the scene within the court. A California vigilance committee in olden times would have hanged him on general principles. He is known to have been in league with Booth, Surratt, and Herold, and he was seen at Stanton's house on the night of the murder, asking for Grant who dined there.

A man about forty years old, heavy-built, sandy, slovenly in appearance, looking like a mechanic, but cunning hidden in his mask-like face, sits next; this is [Edward] Spangler, the stage carpenter and scene shifter. This man Spangler fixed the scenes at the theater so that Booth had an easy exit when his work was done. He held the assassin's horse, kept the way from the rear of the theater clear, and was a sort of lackey to his superior ruffian at all times.

Spangler has a rough face, reddish hair, and unshaven beard. He wears a deprecating look as though he had wiped his lips and said, "I have done no wrong." When lawyer [J. B.] Stewart, who pursued the assassin out of the theater, testified to the deportment of a man who, when all others were excited, stood calmly in the passage where Booth had just fled, Spangler's hands were nervously feeling along his knees, and when Stewart was asked to look among the prisoners for a man who looked like that man of nerve, Spangler's nerves broke down, and he was white about the gills, and his hands traveled over his knees like spiders, and he sat with eyes fixed on the witness.

The only intellectual face in this gang of big ruffians is that of Dr. [Samuel A.] Mudd, who sits next to the stage carpenter, the customary guard being between. Mudd has a mild blue eye, good broad forehead, red face, hair scanty and thin, and a high head thinly shingled with fine, sandy hair. He sits in his shirt sleeves, a white handkerchief knotted loosely about his neck, and he attentively regards the proceedings around him. Mudd was a companion and associate of Booth, held private consultations in Washington with Booth, Surratt, and O'Laughlin, received the fleeing assassins into his house on the night of the murder, and set Booth's fractured limb, though he afterward swore that he did not know the man for whom he performed the operation. Mudd is about thirty-five years old.

Last in the row, looking out of the window upon the pleasant scene without, lounging about, leaning his head on the rail, inattentive wholly to all that passes, and as uneasy as a caged whelp, is [Samuel] Arnold. He is about twenty-four or twenty-five, has clear blue eyes, brown hair, and a pleasant face. He backed out of the conspiracy and was caught at Fortress Monroe where he had gone to get out of the way until suspicion was well over. It now appears that he figured only in the original plan of abducting the President and was to have caught him on the stage when the rest of the villains had thrown him over from the box. He does not appear to be at all incriminated in the deed which was committed, though he may have known that the assassinations were actually contemplated.

The appearance and demeanor of the court is not very solemn or impressive, the members of the commission sitting about in various attitudes and a general appearance of disorder being evident. Many ladies were present, and their irrepressible whispering was a continual nuisance. The witnesses are first examined by the judge advocate, the members of the court putting in a question now and then, and the counsel for the prisoner taking up the cross-examination, each counsel only attending to the witness whose testimony affects his own client—the witness being brought on without regard to any particular criminal, all being tried at once. Sometimes a counsel for one prisoner develops the witness under examination in such a manner as to injure the cause of another prisoner. Then a pretty quarrel between different counsel ensues. So far the evidence has been all one way, no witnesses for the defense being yet introduced, but the verdict of the people will be, apparently, that the prisoners are guilty and, but for the looks of the thing, might as well be hanged forthwith.

Washington, May 23, 1865

THE GRAND REVIEW—FIRST DAY

This has been a great day, a day of days in Washington, for today the grand armies of the republic, their labors done and their victories complete, have commenced their grand farewell march through the national capital, to be welcomed and applauded in the national metropolis, and many of them will see for the first time that city for whose defenses they have fought so bravely and so well and for which so many noble lives have been laid down upon the field of battle. The sight and the occasion are forever memorable, and it will always be a proud thing to say that we were among those who saw the victorious hosts, and a prouder boast will it be for those who can say that they were among those who fought bravely and returned in triumph to march through the capital of the nation.

The weather was absolutely perfect, and nothing occurred to mar the enjoyment of the scene. Two or three days of rain had cooled the air and laid the dust, so that the streets, scraped and washed, were perfectly clean. The air was cool, calm, bright, and invigorating, and a day made to order for the grand parade could not have been better. All along the route of the pageant stands were erected by private individuals, with gainful or other motives, but the main point of attraction was on Pennsylvania Avenue, opposite the White House. Here were built covered stands capable of seating, comfortably, ten or fifteen thousand people, the central stand on the south side being designed for the use of the President, cabinet, heads of departments, military dignitaries, and diplomatic corps. Opposite was a similar affair for the use of Congress, the judiciary, press, and various other estates, and a commodious stand was also built at the expense of a wealthy and public-spirited Bostonian, John Murray Forbes, for the use of the crippled and convalescent soldiers. I am glad to say that it was well filled, and the cheers of the passing troops were oftener bestowed upon these scarred veterans than elsewhere.

The crowd in the city was tremendous; the trains for

the past few days have been arriving with thousands of visitors from abroad, and all the country about is pouring into the city. The hotels were filled up as at inauguration times, and thousands were obliged to "bunk down" on parlor floors or, worse still, walk the streets all night with the comforting assurance that they would have a good start in the morning exercises. People here say that on no previous occasion has the city been so full of strangers as now.

The public schools, like all the rest of the public institutions, gave a double holiday, and the pupils, in holiday attire, were ranged on the steps of the northern end of the Capitol, crowding the whole of the great porticoes and approaches, forming a beautiful sight and saluting the soldiers with patriotic songs which the men heartily cheered.

At the grandstand the ball was opened by the arrival of the head of the column at half-past nine in the morning, Major General [George G.] Meade with his great staff of officers then appearing on the grounds. Singularly enough but a few of the notables had arrived, and the central compartment was nearly vacant. Soon, however, Grant and staff walked in, greeted with a burst of applause. Then Sherman appeared, saluted in the same way. Next, President Johnson, Secretary Stanton, and one or two cabinet officers came on, and the major part of the notables were there. After Meade passed, Major General [Wesley] Merritt, commanding the cavalry corps, rode in, attended by a brilliant staff. Merritt has a fresh, boyish face, full of determination and force but very youthful in appearance. Many were disappointed at not seeing [Philip H.] Sheridan, who is on his way to Texas, Merritt commanding in his absence.

All at once, in a lull of the passage of staffs, a splendid

blooded charger, covered with foam, plunging madly, and galloping like a wild creature, came rushing by. On his back was a young major general, vainly trying to curb his beast, his feet out of the stirrups, his empty scabbard flying, and his long yellow curls and red scarf flying in the wind. It was the dashing [George A.] Custer whose horse had run away with him. He dashed past the stand but saluted his superior officers as he flew, his presence of mind and grace creating a burst of applause as "Custer! Custer!" flew from lip to lip. Recovering his seat, he curbed his horse and rode back, taking his proper place at the head. . . .

Governor [John A.] Andrew of Massachusetts, boiling over with enthusiasm, was rushing about the stand where I sat, proposing three cheers for diverse New England regiments, and they were given with a will. Governor [Reuben E.] Fenton of New York was also there, and several other governors of states. One dapper little man, with his scanty gray hair parted behind, wearing a major general's straps, a hat looped up at the side, a red nose and white whiskers, with a general air of consequentiality, attracted a great deal of interest, and everybody asked who he was, and everybody laughed at the fitness of his appearance when told that it was Major General [Edward Sewall] Sanford of New York. He looked much like the "milish" general that he is beside our warworn heroes.

It was noticeable that very few of our men commanding corps or divisions are elderly. Almost all of the general officers are young, [George G.] Meade, [Henry W.] Benham, and [Andrew A.] Humphreys being the only exceptions, while [Winfield S.] Hancock, [Charles] Griffin, [John G.] Parke, and almost all of the division commanders are young men. Another notable feature was the great scarcity of field officers. Companies are commanded by lieutenants, who take the places of captains commanding regiments, while colonels lead brigades. The mortality has been great among colonels.

Many inquired why no colored troops were in the lines. That was explained by the fact that all the colored troops are massed at City Point, preparatory to being sent to Texas. They would have had a welcoming cheer from the brilliant assembly today, no doubt, for they have deserved and have earned the plaudits of a generous people. Those near the grandstand noticed that Secretary Stanton and General Sherman kept apart, never speaking with each other, though the President greeted Sherman cordially. This is owing to the bitter quarrel which has sprung up between the two on account of Sherman's anger at Stanton's sharp review of his armistice with General Johnston. There are many mischievous men who seize upon this occasion to incite a new war upon Stanton, and some even are hoping that Sherman's men may make some demonstration of disrespect when they pass Stanton's stand tomorrow.

And so they move on, bristling with bayonets, sabers flashing, banners waving, music crashing on the air—men who have fought at Port Hudson, Cane river, Charleston, Virginia, and men from every loyal state—heroes every one. God bless them, they have come home at last. Everywhere there is yet a tinge of melancholy. Many think of comrades buried on the field of battle. On every pennon, banner, banneret, guidon, and corps flag floats a streamer of mourning for Abraham Lincoln, beloved by the soldiers with a passionate devotion. He who loved the soldier and longed to see this day sleeps in his grave far away, but he, like the gallant men who now march by for their last review, has done his work well.

Washington, May 24, 1865

THE GRAND REVIEW—SECOND DAY

Yesterday we saw the Army of the Potomac pass in review, numbering about 100,000 men in twenty-nine regiments of cavalry, thirty-three batteries of artillery, and one hundred and eighty regiments of infantry—to say nothing of escorts, guards at camps, disarmed and dismounted men. Today we saw the Army of the Tennessee with ninety-four regiments of infantry, and the Army of Georgia with eighty-six regiments—both making one hundred and eighty regiments of infantry, with a full complement of artillery but a smaller cavalry contingent. Each parade occupied about five and a half hours, but the display of the western armies undoubtedly showed more men, as the men marched rapidly and compactly, and there was less room taken up in line by cavalry horses and ammunition wagons.

The day was perfect and beautifully cool, the heavens smiling propitiously upon the great farewell review of the gallant armies of the Union. The crowd was larger, and every spare foot of ground was occupied by dense masses of people perched upon every vantage, clinging in perilous places, and risking life and limb to see the show. The enthusiasm was also greatly increased, whether by the increased number of people or because the novel sight of Sherman's army actually being in Washington I cannot say, but more cheering and more boisterous applause greeted the gallant heroes of Georgia and Tennessee than we ever knew before in this military-sated metropolis.

The arrangements were the same as on the day before,

many officers of the Army of the Potomac being on the grandstand, and many distinguished civilians also being there. Among them were Thomas Ewing, John Sherman, "Prince" John Van Buren, George Bancroft, and others of less note. Precisely at nine o'clock Major General [William T.] Sherman appeared, accompanied by Major General O[liver] O. Howard, their large staffs following behind. Sherman is a fine rider, but his magnificent charger gave him all that he could do to keep himself in his saddle. He doffed his cap, as did the gallant Howard, who guided his horse by the stump of his amputated right arm. The arrival of these men, famous and great, was the signal for cheers, prolonged and loud. Handkerchiefs waved, flags flashed, and wreaths and bouquets fell all around. Passing the stand, where the assembled dignitaries saluted by standing, Sherman dismounted and, followed by Howard, entered the reviewing stand where they remained during the parade which followed.

Sherman is not handsome, and his published portraits, which are generally like him, flatter him exceedingly. He has a high, narrow head, sandy hair and whiskers, a stiff, bristling, reddish mustache, blue eyes, and a forbidding countenance. He is very tall, walks with an immense stride, talks rapidly and nervously, and has an anxious and harassed look, his general appearance not at all improved by an ugly scratch which disfigures his forehead just now. But Sherman looks the man that he is—of imperious, iron will, quick in purpose, rapid and ready in execution, bold and original. The dullest observer would pick him out of any crowd as a man of mark towering far above all comrades in intellect as in physical height. . . .

There was, of course, a great deal of curiosity to see the famous western men who have marched all the way from Chattanooga to the sea and through the Carolinas and

Virginia to Washington. Everybody welcomed these noble
men, veterans in war, with heartfelt enthusiasm. Their
complete drill, soldierly appearance, and truly martial bearing brought forth plaudits on every hand. The western
troops wear a more free-and-easy uniform, generally adopt-
ing the blue blouse and sugar-loaf felt hat, rather than the
close fitting coat and French kepi of the eastern soldiers.
But nothing could be more perfect than their marching
order, each rank stepping out as one man. They are generally much larger than the soldiers whom we saw yesterday, being, for the most part, tall and muscular and of the
same stature. As each brigade reached the stands, its
drum corps and band swung around opposite the reviewing officer and played until the rear came up, then fell in,
giving place to the next brigade band. This kept fine
marching music at the reviewing stand all the while and
greatly assisted the troops in their march.

The Fifteenth Corps is composed exclusively of Ohio,
Indiana, Illinois, Minnesota, Missouri, and Iowa troops,
and the Seventeenth Corps, which followed immediately
after, is composed of troops from the same states, including one Indian regiment raised among the civilized tribes
of Kansas. One noticeable feature in these two corps was
an assemblage, at the end of each brigade, of jacks and
mules laden with camp equipage, attended by darkies and
carrying sometimes chickens, roosters, young racoons, and
all sorts of pets, one being a large white goat. These are
the paraphernalia of "Sherman's Bummers" or foragers.
The livestock was all swept up from southern plantations,
while the contrabands mixed in were once the property
of southern secesh—now free. The plantation of Jeff Davis
had been laid under requisition, and two small white jack-
asses of a fancy breed, led by grinning darkies, were trophies from the rebel "President's" domain.

The Seventeenth Corps is commanded by Major General Frank P. Blair, Jr., who has grown stout since he was last in Congress, and, I must say, looked a great deal better than he did when trying to bring his own quarrels and pro-slavery Republicanism into the House of Representatives. Still, whatever may be said of Blair's politics, none can gainsay or dispute his military abilities and services, which will wipe out all of his past vagaries from the minds of honest men. The Seventeenth is largely composed of Wisconsin men, splendid specimens of humanity—tall and well-made, with the long, free stride and regular, cadent step which no Army of the Potomac man ever got. It comes only from great practice, long legs, and long marches such as Sherman's men have had.

Between the armies and, to some extent, between the corps were small gaps of distance during which the crowd ran in upon the lines to "gawp" at the notables on the reviewing stand. A great mass would collect and call out the President, Grant, Sherman, Howard, and others in sight, making each man get up and bow. Then the guards would ungratefully repay the homage of the people by driving them back at the point of the bayonet. Dresses were torn, crinoline crashed, bonnets smashed, and men, women, and children, soldiers and civilians, become mixed up in a most admired disorder. A squadron of cavalry would sweep through, and the crowd would scatter like a flock of sheep, mysteriously disappearing somewhere or another, and the advancing columns, compact, massive, and soldierly, would fill the space.

The Army of Georgia is commanded by Major General [Henry W.] Slocum, who commanded the Twelfth Corps of the Army of the Potomac under Hooker and who now has many of his old troops from New York, Pennsylvania, and New England under him. His army is made up of the

Twentieth Corps, Major General J[oseph] A. Mower, and the Fourteenth Corps, Major General Jeff C. Davis. Brevet Major General John W. Geary, well-known in California as well as Kansas, commands the Second Division of the Twentieth Corps, and he made a fine appearance on horseback today. The Fourteenth Corps looked more worn and rusty than any on parade, their uniforms being well faded and their equipment not very bright. In all of the armies it is noticeable that while western troops show more fighting trim, the eastern regiments are brighter, cleaner, and more like what we think European armies are.

Like the Army of the Potomac, Sherman's army has gradually adopted distinctive badges. That of the Fifteenth Corps is a cartridge box on a red diamond with the legend "Forty Rounds." The Seventeenth has an arrow, the number of each division being marked by the number of arrows on its flag. The badge of the Twentieth is a star, and that of the Fourteenth is an acorn. Looking upon these novel badges, novel, at least, in these parts, one realizes how foreign to us our brethren from the West are. These brave fellows have fought their way from Tennessee to Washington, and on their banners they bear the magic names of "Atlanta," "Lookout Mountain," "Pea Ridge," "Chickamauga," and the hosts of signal victories which have immortalized their arms. One dreams, looking at them, of the valleys of Tennessee, the precipitous heights which they scaled, and the fertile fields where they foraged in Georgia. Yet, here they are today in the national metropolis.

No wonder that the heart swells with emotion and the eyes grow moist as we look upon these brave and hardy regiments, still full, not skeletons, marching by in conscious power and vigor. Thank God, peace has come and has come to stay—not a traitorous, dishonorable peace, but such a peace as will make rebellion hereafter a terror to rebels; peace such as has been conquered by these blue-coated men to whom the nation owes the only debt it can never pay—its gratitude. We have made no compromise with traitors in arms. The South has been "subjugated" after all, and now, God bless him! "Johnny comes marching home." May joy go with him!

DATE DUE

HIGHSMITH 45-227